The Aurelian Wall and the Refashioning of Imperial Rome, AD 271–855

This book explores the relationship between the city of Rome and the Aurelian Wall during the six centuries following its construction in the 270s AD, a period when the city changed and contracted almost beyond recognition, as it evolved from imperial capital into the spiritual center of Western Christendom. The Wall became the single most prominent feature in the urban landscape, a dominating presence which came bodily to incarnate the political, legal, administrative and religious boundaries of *urbs Roma*, even as it reshaped both the physical contours of the city as a whole and the mental geographies of "Rome" that prevailed at home and throughout the known world. With the passage of time, the circuit took on a life of its own as the embodiment of Rome's past greatness, a cultural and architectural legacy that dwarfed the quotidian realities of the post-imperial city as much as it shaped them.

HENDRIK W. DEY is Assistant Professor in the Department of Art at Hunter College in the City University of New York. He is co-editor with E. Fentress of *Western Monasticism* ante litteram: *The Spaces of Monastic Observance in Late Antiquity and the Early Middle Ages* (2011).

The Aurelian Wall and the Refashioning of Imperial Rome, AD 271–855

HENDRIK W. DEY

CAMBRIDGE
UNIVERSITY PRESS

CAMBRIDGE
UNIVERSITY PRESS

University Printing House, Cambridge CB2 8BS, United Kingdom

Cambridge University Press is part of the University of Cambridge.

It furthers the University's mission by disseminating knowledge in the pursuit of education, learning and research at the highest international levels of excellence.

www.cambridge.org
Information on this title: www.cambridge.org/9781107526532

© Hendrik W. Dey 2011

First published 2011
First paperback edition 2015

A catalogue record for this publication is available from the British Library

Library of Congress Cataloguing in Publication data

Dey, Hendrik W., 1976–
The Aurelian Wall and the refashioning of imperial Rome, AD 271–855 / Hendrik W. Dey.
    p.   cm.
  Includes bibliographical references.
  ISBN 978-0-521-76365-3 (Hardback)
    1. Rome (Italy)–Antiquities, Roman.   2. Walls–Italy–Rome–History.   3. Rome (Italy)–
Buildings, structures, etc.   4. Urban landscape architecture–Italy–Rome–History.
5. Architecture–Social aspects–Italy–Rome–History.   6. Rome (Italy)–Geography.   7. Rome
(Italy)–Social life and customs.   8. City and town life–Italy–Rome–History.   9. Social change–
Italy–Rome–History.   I. Title.
  DG67.D49 2011
  937´.6306–dc22

                                                                                  2010030002

ISBN 978-0-521-76365-3 Hardback
ISBN 978-1-107-52653-2 Paperback

Contents

Abbreviations

Acta IRN	*Acta ad Archaeologiam et Artium Historiam Pertinentia* (Institutum Romanum Norvegiae)
AE	*Année Épigraphique*
AJA	*American Journal of Archaeology*
AnalRom	*Analecta Romana Instituti Danici*
AnTard	*Antiquité Tardive*
ASRSP	*Archivio della Società Romana di Storia Patria*
BEFAR	*Bibliothèque des Écoles françaises d'Athènes et de Rome*
BullCom	*Bullettino della Commissione Archeologica Communale di Roma*
CAH	*The Cambridge Ancient History* (2nd edn.)
CBCR	*Corpus Basilicarum Christianarum Romae* (Krautheimer *et al.* eds.)
CC	*Codex Carolinus* (W. Gundlach ed.)
CCSL	*Corpus Christianorum. Series Latina*
CIC	*Corpus Iuris Civilis* (Mommsen, Krueger, *et al.* eds.)
CJ	*Codex Justinianus*
Dig.	*Digestum*
Inst.	*Institutiones*
Nov.	*Novellae*
CIL	*Corpus Inscriptionum Latinarum*
CSEL	*Corpus Scriptorum Ecclesiasticorum Latinarum*
CTh.	*Codex Theodosianus* (Mommsen *et al.* eds.)
Nov.	*Novellae*
Dura Reports	*The Excavations at Dura Europos* (M. I. Rostovtzeff *et al.* eds.)
EAA	*Enciclopedia dell'Arte Antica Classica e Orientale*
EFR	École française de Rome
EpigAnat	*Epigraphica Anatolica*
Fontes	*Fontes ad topographiam veteris urbis Romae pertinentes,* I (G. Lugli ed.)
FUR	*Forma Urbis Romae* (R. Lanciani)
GR	*Gregorii I. Papae Registrum epistolarum* (Ewald and Hartmann eds.)

HA	*Scriptores historiae Augustae* (E. Pohl ed.)
ICUR	*Inscriptiones Christianae Urbis Romae* (G. B. De Rossi ed.)
ICUR, n.s.	*Inscriptiones Christianae Urbis Romae, nova series* (A. Ferrua and A. Silvagni eds.)
IGR	*Inscriptiones Graecae ad Res Romanas Pertinentes*
ILCV	*Inscriptiones Latinae Christianae Veteres*
ILS	*Inscriptiones Latinae Selectae*
JRA	*The Journal of Roman Archaeology*
JRS	*The Journal of Roman Studies*
Le piante	*Le piante di Roma* (P. Frutaz ed.)
LP	*Liber Pontificalis* (L. Duchesne ed.)
LTUR	*Lexicon Topographicum Urbis Romae* (M. Steinby ed.)
MAAR	*Memoirs of the American Academy in Rome*
MEFR	*Mélanges d'Archeologie e d'Histoire* (École française de Rome; 1881–1970)
MEFRA	*Mélanges de l'École française de Rome. Antiquité* (1971–)
MEFRM	*Mélanges de l'École française de Rome. Moyen Âge* (1971–)
MemAcLinc	*Atti della Accademia Nazionale dei Lincei. Memorie*
MGH	*Monumenta Germaniae Historiae*
AA	*Auctores Antiquissimi*
EP	*Epistulae*
SRG	*Scriptores Rerum Germanicarum*
SRL	*Scriptores Rerum Langobardicarum*
SRM	*Scriptores Rerum Merovingicarum*
Notizie	*Notizie degli Scavi di Antichità*
Pan. Lat.	*Panegyrici Latini* (Nixon and Rodgers eds.)
PBSR	*Papers of the British School at Rome*
P. Ital.	*Die nichtliterarischen lateinischen Papyri Italiens aus der Zeit 445–700* (O. Tjäder ed.)
PL	Migne, *Patrologia Latina*
PLRE	*The Prosopography of the Later Roman Empire* (A. H. M. Jones *et al.*)
Procopius	*BG: Bellum Gothicum*
	BP: Bellum Persicum
	BV: Bellum Vandalicum
RAC	*Rivista di Archeologia Cristiana*
RE	*Paulys Realencyclopädie der classischen Altertumswissenschaft*
RendAcLinc	*Atti della Accademia Nazionale dei Lincei. Rendiconti*
RendPontAc	*Atti della Pontificia Accademia Romana di Archeologia* (Serie III). *Rendiconti*

RIB	*The Roman Inscriptions of Britain*, vol. I (R. G. Collingwood and R. P. Wright eds.)
Röm. Mitth.	*Mittheilungen des kaiserlich deutschen archaeologischen institutes. Römische Abteilung*
RömQSchr.	*Römische Quartalschrift für christliche Altertumskunde und Kunstgeschichte*
SC	*Sources Chrétiennes*
Settimane del CISAM	*Settimane di studio del Centro Italiano di Studi sull'Alto Medioevo*
SRIT	*Società Romana e Impero Tardoantico* (A. Giardina ed.)
VZ	*Codice topografico della città di Roma* (R. Valentini and G. Zucchetti eds.)
Walzing, *Étude*	*Étude historique sur les corporations professionnelles chez les Romains depuis les origines jusqu'à la chute de l'Empire de l'Occident* (J. P. Waltzing)

Figures

Acknowledgements

This book is the end result of a minor epiphany I had in the fall of 2002, which consisted of a series of thoughts along the lines of the following. The Aurelian Wall is the single largest and most influential structure ever erected in Rome. During the seventeen centuries that have passed since its construction, it has exercised a profound effect on the infrastructure and topography of the city as a whole, on the daily lives of Romans, and, at least until the later nineteenth century, on the political, administrative, and ideological horizons of its rulers. Yet incredibly (particularly in light of the oceans of ink spilled on undoubtedly fascinating but ultimately – in the larger scheme of things – insignificant structures in the city and its environs), the Wall has occupied the attentions of a minuscule cadre of scholars, who moreover have concentrated almost exclusively on its architectural features and the chronology of its building phases. No serious attempt has ever been made to consider the Wall as a dynamic and often decisive presence in the history of Rome over the *longue durée*. It is a story well worth telling.

My epiphany was almost immediately followed by a remarkable string of luck that carried me to Rome for most of the following five years, during the course of which I wrote this book and incurred more debts of gratitude than I can possibly acknowledge here, much less repay.

The Horace H. Rackham graduate school at the University of Michigan generously funded the first two of my years in Rome, when most of the research and writing for the doctoral-thesis-version of this project occurred. The thesis was finished and most of the revisions necessary to transform the manuscript into a book undertaken between 2005 and 2007, when I had the surely undeserved good fortune to receive a two-year Rome Prize Fellowship at the American Academy in Rome. Final tweaking occurred during the 2008–9 academic year when, thanks to the Department of Classical Archaeology at the University of Aarhus, I enjoyed a year of research time, free from any teaching responsibilities.

Among the countless people whose kindness and generosity allowed me to bring the project to conclusion, a few stand out. Paolo Squatriti read and commented on multiple drafts of the manuscript at various stages of its gestation, providing a constant and probing voice of reason that among other things helped to ensure that I maintained some touch with reality – historical and otherwise – in my self-imposed exile. He also gave me the run of a stunning house in the Umbrian countryside for the better part of a year, where only occasional olive-picking duties intruded on my thoughts about the Aurelian Wall. Robert Coates-Stephens was kind enough to welcome an importunate and wholly anonymous graduate student newly arrived in Rome, passing along wise counsel first over the course of coffee and later (and more frequently) over beers, and eventually reading the entirety of the manuscript, saving me from countless errors of fact and omission on a topic he knows as well as anyone in the world. Thelma Thomas, David Potter, and Patrick Geary also read and commented on early drafts of the book, bringing their prodigious and extremely varied expertise to bear on my blithe forays into topics, disciplines, and periods which they know far better than I. Carmela Vircillo Franklin, the director of the American Academy in Rome, did more than she can possibly know to make my two years at that institution memorable.

Among the others who sustained me at various times over the past years with their hospitality, their good cheer, their erudition, and/or their sincere interest in "my wall," or in my efforts to say something useful about the thing, particular thanks are due to Lisa Fentress, Massimiliano "la Lazzie" Ghilardi, Sabine MacCormack, Federico Marazzi, Lisa Marie Mignone, and Riccardo Santangeli Valenzani. Dave Schragger turned the plan of Rome kindly given me by Riccardo Santangeli Valenzani into something better suited for a book on the Aurelian Wall, and for very little reward to boot. Further thanks are due to Michael Sharp and his editorial team at Cambridge University Press, as well as to the two anonymous readers he enlisted, one of whose detailed comments were extremely useful. Nonetheless, due to factors beyond my control, the project has taken rather longer to come to fruition than I might have hoped in 2007, when the manuscript was already in essentially its final form. Hence, while I have made some effort to include noteworthy bibliographical citations for the years 2007–10, the additions are largely cosmetic; in its essence, this book is a product of the years 2003–6.

It is dedicated to the memory of my father, who would have feigned interest in the Aurelian Wall for my sake, and been genuinely pleased that I managed to see a lengthy and challenging project through to completion; and to my mother, without whom none of it would have been possible.

Introduction

What's in a wall? From 1961 until 1989, an ugly and otherwise unprepossessing ribbon of reinforced concrete was the embodiment of a divided planet; an "Iron Curtain" dividing two halves of a city that had once been whole, making two countries out of one, and two worlds where previously there had been many; a manmade terminator between two hemispheres that soon became known simply as "East" and "West." Another wall remains the only artificial feature ever claimed to be visible from the Moon, an assertion whose utter mythicality only increases its suggestiveness: the "Great Wall of China" is neither a single wall, nor is any of it visible to the unaided human eye from the Moon, yet its legend continues to grow in a technological age inclined more frequently to the systematic evisceration of myth and legend than to their proliferation.[1] In North America, proposals to build a continuous wall between Mexico and the United States to impede the passage of illegal immigrants into the latter have repeatedly driven the Mexican government to the brink of apoplexy.

At the beginning of the third millennium, another wall has come to make world headlines. A squat and utilitarian thing assembled from various prefabricated materials (concrete, chain-link fencing, barbed wire, and so on), this barrier has been erected on the initiative of the Israeli government for the stated purpose of curtailing the movements of militants living and operating within predominantly Palestinian areas of settlement, around and through which its several sections make their unsubtle way. It is a testament to the complex and often brutal dynamics of power relations, a model and a microcosm of the processes whereby racial, ethnic, religious, and national identities are defined, asserted, protected, and ultimately polarized, for nothing makes insiders and outsiders quite like a wall. Building one means choosing sides. It requires picking teams, or rather one team. Everyone not selected is left to compose the opposition, whether they want to play or not. And like many of its predecessors, this new wall has come to symbolize the political and ideological conflicts that literally

---

[1] Cf. Waldron 1990, 1–10 and *passim*.

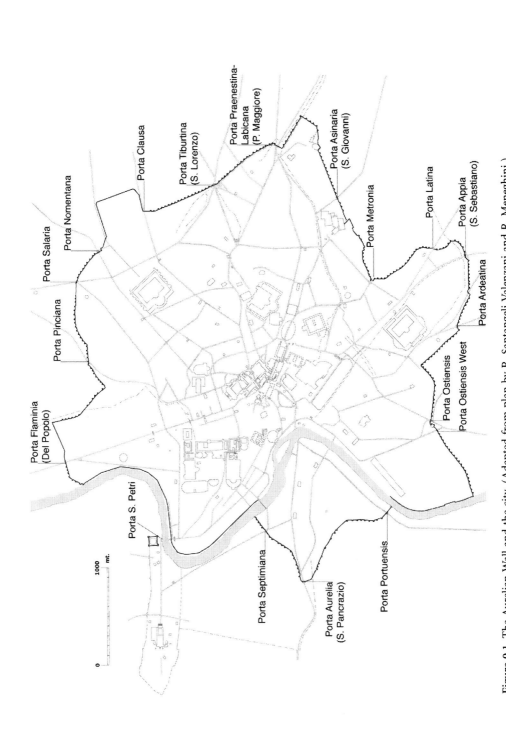

Figure 0.1 The Aurelian Wall and the city. (Adapted from plan by R. Santangeli Valenzani and R. Meneghini.)

Porta Clausa

Porta Praenestina-Labicana (P. Maggiore)

Porta Tiburtina (S. Lorenzo)

Porta Asinaria (S. Giovanni)

Porta Nomentana

Porta Salaria

Porta Metronia

Porta Latina

Porta Appia (S. Sebastiano)

Porta Pinciana

Porta Ardeatina

Porta Flaminia (Del Popolo)

Porta Ostiensis

Porta Ostiensis West

Porta S. Petri

Porta Septimiana

Porta Aurelia (S. Pancrazio)

Porta Portuensis

1000 mt.

0

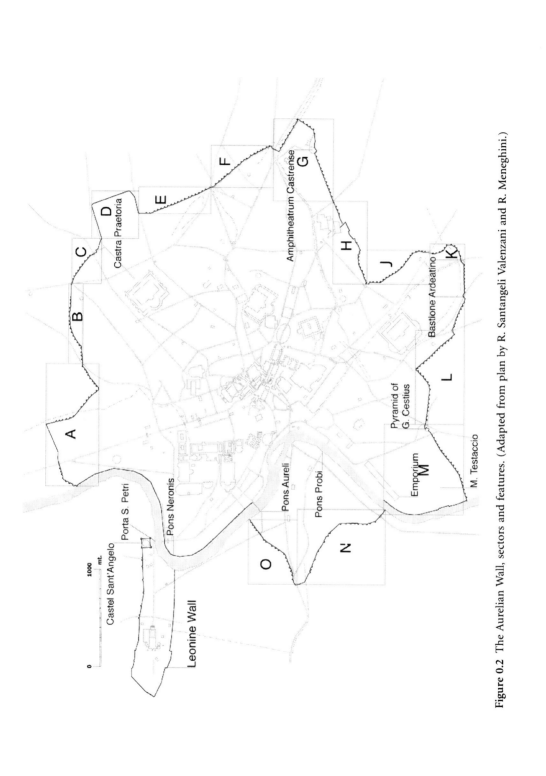

Figure 0.2 The Aurelian Wall, sectors and features. (Adapted from plan by R. Santangeli Valenzani and R. Meneghini.)

surround it, and to embody the pathos and the often profound suffering of the people whose lives it bisects. Hence, its impact routinely transcends its immediate surroundings. As the anxious and often charged debate simmering around the globe demonstrates, its divisive power reaches many thousands of miles beyond its physical confines.

Walls, in other words, tend to "speak" with a degree of power and immediacy which few other buildings can rival. They can be simultaneously eminently pragmatic and symbolically polyvalent, a complex blend of practicality and bluster, an ostentatious demonstration of might, and an acknowledgement of debility. It is hence peculiarly appropriate that the city of Rome came to have, from the age of the emperor Aurelian (AD 270–5), the monumental enceinte which it has largely retained up to the present (Figures 0.1–0.2). Ancient Rome was itself a potent blend of legend and reality, a physical presence and a concept, a place and a culture, as we still implicitly suggest when using "Rome" to recall a Mediterranean-wide empire as readily as its eponymous founding city. It was both a living city and an enduring figment of the popular consciousness of the West, a creation of a collective cultural imagination that continued to evolve and ramify long after the place had changed and contracted, along with its territorial dominions, almost beyond recognition.[2]

Like a high-profile wall, that is, Rome has long been greater than the sum of its parts, which makes it particularly fitting that its own high-profile wall was distilled over the centuries into the essence of the city. Indeed, from the third century into the Middle Ages, no other topographical feature mirrored the fortunes of the city so closely, nor influenced them so immediately, as the Aurelian Wall. At the same time, the vast defensive circuit came to represent the city to all – friends and foes, locals and foreigners alike – who cared to look, and to reify the idea and the ideal of Rome in an age when its aura of invincibility was no longer assured by the exploits of legions spread throughout the Mediterranean world, as the city metamorphosed from imperial powerhouse into Christian capital, from *caput mundi* into *sedes Petri*. At some point, the Aurelian Wall became a symbol of a symbol, in addition to being the bricks and mortar that framed and increasingly shaped the physical reality of Rome for many centuries. How and why this came to be so is one of the central preoccupations of what follows.

---

[2] Recent additions to a large and venerable body of relevant literature include: Edwards and Woolf 2003, esp. Chapter 1, "Cosmopolis: Rome as World City"; Giardina and Vauchez 2000. Dated but still powerful is Graf 1882–3, esp. vol. 1, 1–43.

Like so many others, it is a question long overdue in the asking for, given the physical prominence of the Wall and the quantity of its extant remains, it has received remarkably little scholarly attention. The modern scholarly tradition on the Wall was born in 1820 with the publication of *Le Mura di Roma*, written by the Italian archaeologist Antonio Nibby and illustrated by the British engraver Sir William Gell. After several chapters on the earlier walls of the city (among which he included the one attributed to Aurelian by the ancient sources), and a chapter of historical background on the extant circuit (which he thought the work of Honorius), Nibby closed his account with a detailed description of the Wall as it looked in his day, describing a clockwise circuit beginning from the vicinity of the Piazza del Popolo. While erroneous in some of its most fundamental premises, Nibby's study was the first to attempt an identification of all construction phases of the Wall, including the post-classical interventions, and the first to plumb the literary and epigraphic tradition in depth.

Though the intervening century was not devoid of important contributions,[3] the next great leap forward came in 1930 with the appearance of Ian Richmond's *The City Wall of Imperial Rome*, an authoritative critical

---

[3] Several figures may be singled out for mention. The British archaeologist John Henry Parker produced an enormous collection of photographs which includes many views of the Aurelian Wall and its gates, the most valuable among them documenting excavations since covered over, and parts of the Wall sacrificed in the course of Rome's post-unification urban expansion. A number of important examples are included among the plates illustrating the first volume of his *The Archaeology of Rome* (Parker 1874, vol. 1, Part 2). The German topographer Heinrich Jordan included a careful discussion of the Wall's standing remains in the first volume of his great topographical survey, which he prefaced with a brief history of its construction – correctly attributed to Aurelian – and subsequent restorations; see Jordan 1878, 340–92. In many respects, Jordan's work represents the culmination of the scholarly tradition as it stood until Richmond (who indeed felt that Jordan's work "must…form the basis of any critical study of the Wall"; Richmond 1930, 3). The general study of Léon Homo on the reign of Aurelian contains a lengthy section on the Wall that seems to me still useful, though it was never much cited, even when less dated than it appears today (Homo 1904, 214–306). Finally, Rodolfo Lanciani stands out for the volume and quality of his archaeological and topographical observations on the Wall. In addition to his rendering of the Wall in the *Forma Urbis Romae*, which remains the standard more than a century after its appearance, he made notes on sections of the circuit that, in the process of demolition, rather ironically provided unique insights into their structural composition, and published in addition several important articles on the Wall and various subsections thereof. Lanciani's large and scattered corpus of notes, sketches, and archaeological observations on the Wall has been rendered vastly more accessible with the publication of the five volumes of the *Appunti di topografia romana nei codici Lanciani della Biblioteca Apostolica Vaticana* (Lanciani 1997); a section devoted to the Wall appears at vol. 4, 31–60. The publication of his prodigious research on the history of archaeological excavations in Rome (from the year 1000 to 1878) has also reached completion, with the appearance of the seventh and final volume of the *Storia degli scavi di Roma* (Lanciani 1989–2002); the bulk of the indications relevant to the Wall appear in accounts of excavations conducted in the mid

study that immediately superseded all previous accounts, and remains the *sine qua non* for continuing study of the "ancient" phases of the Wall. Richmond integrated copious literary, documentary, and artistic sources with the archaeological evidence available at the time, and with the records of his own extensive autopsy of the Wall's extant sections. The result was, as Richmond put it in the subtitle of his book, "an account of its architectural development from Aurelian to Narses." The "account" itself chiefly seeks to identify and date the major building phases of the Wall, and then to associate the various phases with individuals and notable historical events: to summarize, that is, who put what where in the Wall, when they did so, and why.

More recently, there has been a minor surge of interest in the fortifications of Rome in general, and the Aurelian Wall in particular.[4] Starting in the 1980s, Lucos Cozza began producing a series of articles devoted to various segments of the Wall, which he has followed in a clockwise circuit beginning on the right bank of the Tiber in southern Trastevere.[5] At present, approximately half of the standing remains of the Wall have been covered. Cozza has primarily served to update and expand on Richmond, with the benefit of several decades' worth of new archaeological data, as well as a more refined typological framework for the study of late-antique and medieval masonry.[6] In essence, his remains an architectural history concerned principally with the chronology and the physical characteristics of the various parts of the Wall, which unlike Richmond he covers over the full seventeen centuries of its existence.

eighteenth century (vol. 4, 129–140). His historical and architectural observations on the Wall are most cogently outlined in Lanciani 1892, 87–111.

[4] This is not to say that the middle years of the twentieth century were entirely devoid of Wall-related scholarship. Lugli's summary of the Wall is useful, though it rarely improves on Richmond: see Lugli 1930–8, vol. II, 139–261. A. M. Colini deserves special mention, particularly for being the first to (correctly) place the post-Aurelianic heightening of the Wall in the reign of the emperor Honorius, *contra* Richmond, who thought it occurred under Maxentius; see Colini 1944, 107ff.; Richmond 1930, esp. 251ff. Relatively recent books on Rome's fortifications, all (naturally) prominently featuring the Aurelianic circuit, include Cassanelli, Delfini and Fonti 1974; Todd 1978; Quercioli 1993; and Cardilli *et al.* 1995. None of these, however, improve significantly on Richmond's treatment of the ancient phases of the Wall, though all of them, save Todd, do extend their lower chronological limit well past Richmond's sixth-century terminus.

[5] The most recent in the series is Cozza 2008; his previous contributions all appear below, in the bibliography.

[6] Much of the credit for recent advances in knowledge of post-classical masonry belongs to Theodora Heres, whose monograph on late-antique structures at Rome and Ostia (Heres 1982) has since helped to inspire a new generation of studies, e.g. Cecchelli 2001.

Two other current scholars deserve special mention. Robert Coates-Stephens has made a number of important observations over the past decade, among which the identification of the Wall's previously unrecognized early-medieval phases is perhaps the greatest material contribution.[7] Finally, the appearance of Rossana Mancini's historical "atlas" of the Aurelian Wall (in 2001) should mark something of a watershed. An architect by trade, Mancini has produced color-coded diagrams of the entirety of the circuit, indicating to the best of her ability, in light of the current state of knowledge, the absolute chronology of all its visible sections. While by no means the final word on the standing stratigraphy of the Wall, the "atlas" is already a valuable resource in its current form; it should, moreover, provide a literally graphic stepping-off point for further work, if only by indicating how much presently remains to be known.[8]

On the whole, then, past analyses of the Wall have been mostly confined to architectural histories, focused primarily on the physical fabric of the structure and the chronology of its various building (and rebuilding) phases.

Remarkably, nobody has yet been much inclined to consider how the Aurelian Wall fits in with its surroundings, or to see it as an integrated and integral component of a larger whole encompassing all of Rome and its geographical and conceptual hinterlands.[9] Hence, it is my intent to explore Rome's relationship with its Wall (and vice versa) during the centuries between its construction in the 270s and its lengthy "abandonment" following the pontificate of Leo IV (847–55). While such a study will inevitably incorporate analyses of specific points of architecture, topography, and archaeology, the overall scope of the project is considerably broader. The appearance of the Wall had an immediate and lasting impact on the infrastructure of the city and the rhythms of its daily life; and its subsequent history has profound implications for any understanding of the ways in which the image and the reality of Rome were defined, propagated, and redefined, at home and throughout western Christendom and beyond, before, and after the dissolution of the western empire.

On the subject of Rome in its international context, I will further contend that the Wall became a milestone in the long process whereby circuit-walls developed into the defining topographical constituent of the

---

[7] See Coates-Stephens 2001; 1999; 1998; 1995; Coates-Stephens and Parisi 1999.
[8] Mancini 2001. Also useful are the summary descriptions of the Wall and its gates at *LTUR* 3, 290ff.
[9] A void recently noted by Coates-Stephens (2001, 232).

late-antique city; and that its appearance partially inspired both the construction and the ideological posture of other walls, particularly those around cities with pretensions to political and/or religious pre-eminence. In this sense, the present work takes its place generally within an exponentially proliferating corpus of studies on urbanism in late antiquity and the early Middle Ages. Since the 1980s, the combination of new archaeological evidence with new historical and interpretive paradigms has revolutionized approaches to the late- and post-Roman city, and substantially modified – without universally overturning – the picture of "Dark Age" urban collapse that previously dominated scholarly and popular perspectives, particularly for the western Mediterranean.[10] Change is often now recognized as a better model than unmitigated catastrophe and disintegration; and one of the most dramatic changes to the cityscapes of late antiquity was unquestionably the new visibility and ubiquity of circuit-walls, features that often represented permanence and continued vitality more than collapse, as they continued to do for centuries.[11]

But although the Aurelian Wall is inevitably linked to wider discussions about walls and urbanism in late antiquity and the early Middle Ages, I will repeatedly stress the extent to which Rome is exceptional, an extraordinary place where the effort to build an enceinte of unparalleled size, and then to maintain and even privilege it after the city imploded, is best explained by a range of local factors related to the unique position Rome occupied in the political, cultural, and religious matrix of the Latin West. In topographical terms alone, Rome's exalted status tended to render monumental architecture unusually independent of demographic realities, this in an age broadly characterized by declining urban populations: People disappeared at Rome, too, but important or representative buildings were kept up to fill – or in the case of the Wall to

---

[10] Noteworthy contributions to the study of urban transformation in late antiquity and the early Middle Ages include: Henning 2007; Saradi 2006; Krause and Witschel 2006; Augenti 2006; Ghilardi, Goddard and Porena (eds.) 2006; Christie 2006; Wickham 2005, 591–692; Kulikowski 2004; La Rocca 2003; Gelichi 2002; Lavan 2001; Speiser 2001; Liebeschuetz 2001; Brogiolo, Christie and Gauthier 2000; Brogiolo and Ward-Perkins 1999; Ward-Perkins 1998; 1997; 1984; Bauer 1996; Lepelley 1996; Loseby 1996; Rich 1992. Late-antique urban transformations are assessed in more detail below in Section 3.3; for the literature directly pertinent to Rome, see esp. Chapter 5.

[11] On circuit-walls and their transformative impact on late-antique cities, see Section 3.3, below. Key studies include Christie 2006, esp. 281–399; 2001; Fernández-Ochoa and Morillo 2005; Bachrach 2000; Pani-Ermini 1993–4; older but still useful syntheses include Foss and Winfield 1986; Hobley and Maloney 1983; Johnson 1983a.

surround – the void they left behind. Beginning in the fifth century, the Wall grew so vastly – and anomalously – out of scale with remaining settlement that its use as a case-study for the influence of walls on the configuration of urban life more generally is frequently problematic. Hence, while I have introduced comparative evidence where possible to help contextualize the Wall and situate it with respect to wider currents in the study of late-antique urbanism, I have mostly concentrated on Rome, leaving it for specialists in other areas to tease out additional implications of the Roman exemplar for the places they know best. For this to be done effectively, however, much ground must first be covered in Rome itself.

As I believe that the Aurelian Wall both shaped and reflected the priorities, perceptions, and activities of those living within it, and of those located (often far) without, I think there remain multiple histories of the Wall to be written, which jointly have much to reveal about the city of Rome during the tumultuous centuries spanning the end of antiquity and the beginning of the Middle Ages. In addition to more traditional archi-tectural studies, there is the history of responses to the Wall, the story of how people more or less actively engaged with both its contemporary reality and its ever-growing legacy in ways that informed thoughts and actions alike. There is also the history of the Wall as agent: as an imposing presence that came to mould its surroundings in increasingly pronounced ways, and as an instrument used to further the political, military, and ideological agendas of the city's ruling elite. The amalgam of these several histories should point the way to a new appreciation of the crucial role the Wall came to play in the evolution of the city around and within it.

It has seemed best to approach these issues within a conceptual scaf-folding divided into two principal parts. The first deals with the Wall as what I would call a cultural artifact or "object," a thing acted upon and shaped by human forces. Under this rubric I include first architectural history (who put what where, and when...); then administration and logistics; and finally political history, by which I intend the use of the Wall as an instrument of policy on the part of the leaders of the late-Roman state who brought it into existence. The second part treats the Wall as "subject," a thing with a bodily presence akin to that of a geographical feature, which informed the parameters of the human activ-ity that unfolded around it. Beginning with its impact on urban infra-structure and the evolving mechanisms of trade, communications, and settlement reflected therein, I proceed to its role in the delineation of the legal, administrative, and (especially) religious frontiers of the urban center, before finally turning back to political history at a later moment, when Rome's newly empowered papal authorities were confronted with the unavoidable fact of the Wall, a legacy of their imperial forebears that could be neither ignored nor fully controlled.

Though the Wall assuredly functioned in diverse ways and meant many different things to different people at different points during its history, if there is a unifying narrative thread running through the centuries of my purview, it is that the Wall increased in prominence, physical and mental, in inverse proportion to Rome's contracting topographical, economic, and imperial horizons. I have concluded my account in the ninth century because it seems to have been only then that the trend was arrested. For nearly three centuries, from the later ninth to the middle of the twelfth, the Wall largely disappeared from both the popular memory of the Romans and the civic agendas of their rulers. The popes, long responsible for its maintenance, either stopped spending money on its restoration, or otherwise ceased to advertise their expenditures, while the Roman people considered it less frequently in their reckoning of local geography and topography.[12] Only following the *renovatio senatus* of the 1140s does the Wall again regularly appear in the calculations of the powerful and the collective consciousness of the rest.[13] Its subsequent history is a worthy subject for another study entirely.

I close with a hedge against an anticipated critique. I view the Aurelian Wall as a leading protagonist on the Roman stage between the third and ninth centuries, an approach perhaps susceptible to objections about putting – forgive me – the Wall before the horse. Biographers everywhere face a temptation to overestimate the importance of their subjects, as have I in attempting what amounts to a biography of the Aurelian Wall.[14] Have I overstated the role of "my" Wall? Perhaps, though naturally I think not. I can say only that the more I learn from the ensemble of

---

[12] The relative absence of the Wall in the surviving property documents of the tenth and eleventh centuries, and its subsequent resurgence in the twelfth, has been masterfully demonstrated by Étienne Hubert (Hubert 1990, 64ff.)

[13] An inscription of 1157, placed at the rear of the Porta Metronia, commemorates a restoration of the Wall undertaken by the senate of Rome, the first such recorded intervention since the pontificate of Leo IV (847–55; see *LP* 2, 115). On the *renovatio senatus* and the twelfth-century and later restorations of the Wall, see Mancini 2001, 59ff.; cf. Nibby 1820, 278–9.

[14] I use the term biography – in retrospect – to describe what I seem to have done with the Aurelian Wall, though the project in its formative stages was never consciously envisioned as a cultural biography of a "thing"; my results might nonetheless be usefully viewed in light of, or in comparison with, the premises outlined in Kopytoff 1986, esp. 66–8.

written and archaeological sources known to me, the more convinced I become that the Wall has been a truly elemental force, like dark matter or plate tectonics, just waiting to be discovered to shed light on much in Roman history that was previously obscure.[15] In any case, it is high time for scholars to approach the Aurelian Wall as something more than a large, rather skillfully assembled, pile of bricks and concrete. Among the many possible avenues for further research, the majority will be most effectively exploited when Rome is perceived as a walled precinct, and the ramifications of its enclosure accounted for.

---

[15] For more fully elaborated theoretical perspectives on the potential of objects as agents, a topic currently in the scholarly spotlight, see (e.g.) Gell 1998; Gosden 2005.

1 Toward an architectural history of the Aurelian Wall, from its beginnings through the ninth century

1.1 The basics: an overview

Though the process of identifying and dating the various phases of the Wall has consumed the large majority of the scholarly ink spilled since the time of Nibby at the beginning of the nineteenth century, the picture in its entirety really began to come into focus only with Richmond's study of 1930. Further significant advances have been made since his time, and still a number of vexed issues remain. The labor of identifying various bits of the Wall's fabric and ordering them in historically plausible sequences potentially spanning more than seventeen centuries is exceptionally challenging. Even relative chronologies can be difficult to establish in places, and the search for absolute dates is harder still. The process is often not unlike looking at a massively complex puzzle, mostly complete, and then trying to determine the order in which various bits were inserted. It is a work in progress: I have attempted to discuss the pieces already relatively securely fitted, by now the majority of the whole, and where possible to propose modifications and additions. For every advance that permits new linkages between the Wall's various construction phases and the temporal circumstances of their realization, it becomes more feasible to transcend these very architectural particulars, and to begin replacing the Wall in its historical context.

Hence, while the bulk of this study will in fact aim to replace the Wall in the grand narrative of Roman history, it will first be necessary to propose a chapter of detailed description and analysis of the structure, particularly because a reliable and up-to-date overview of its construction history and architectural particulars is currently lacking, above all in Anglophone circles, where reliance on Richmond and his later epitomator Todd remains nearly total. The salient points of the more detailed discussion that occupies the remainder of this chapter may be summarized as follows.[1]

[1] For the relevant bibliography on all of the following points, see below.

Nearly six centuries after the erection of the so-called Servian Wall, the last significant set of urban defenses seen in Rome, and two centuries and more after the effective eclipse of these older fortifications beneath the urban sprawl of the expanding imperial city, the emperor Aurelian set in motion a new project to refortify the ancient imperial capital. The new Wall, begun in AD 271 and completed within ten years, traced a rough circle nearly 19km long around the urban center. It was approximately 8m high, 3.5m thick, and was constructed entirely in brick-faced concrete. It had square towers spaced at intervals of 100 Roman feet (29.6m), and featured some 16 gates spanning major roads leading out of the city, and a similar number of smaller posterns (*posterulae*) over secondary routes.

For the period of the ensuing six centuries, at least four more principal phases of additions and/or repairs to the original structure are identifiable in the standing remains of the Wall. Further indications for the date and historical context of these various phases can be deduced from a limited but by no means negligible corpus of textual and epigraphic sources. The combination of physical and textual data attests to an initial sequence of (re)construction in the fourth century, when some sections of the Wall were heightened by 1–2 m, repairs undertaken on its curtains and towers, and an effort allegedly made to dig a protective ditch (*vallum*) in front of the Wall proper. While many of these additions likely fall within the short but architecturally prolific six-year reign of the emperor Maxentius, it is likely that others occurred over the remainder of the fourth century. The third distinct phase in the architectural development of the Wall, and the most substantial after Aurelian's initial construction, can be dated quite closely to the years 401–3, during the reign of the emperor Honorius. At this time (and not a century earlier under Maxentius, as Richmond thought) the Wall was nearly doubled in height; new upper stories were added to its towers; substantial modifications occurred at many of the principal gates; and a number of smaller posterns were permanently blocked. With the Honorian building campaign, the Wall reached the peak of its size and architectural elaboration, taking on the basic contours it would preserve throughout the Middle Ages and beyond. A fourth phase of occasional additions, best identified at the Porta Appia (S. Sebastiano) and Porta Flaminia (del Popolo), and limited repairs should then be placed roughly in the fifth and sixth centuries. Thereafter, a relative lull in construction between the later sixth and early eighth centuries seems to have preceded the fifth and final phase in the architectural history of the Wall for the period in question. This phase consists of sizeable repairs to damaged curtains and towers, executed in a combination of rough *opus quadratum* masonry and irregular brickwork fully consonant with prevailing Roman construction techniques of the later eighth and ninth centuries; it must in fact date to the same period, and not to the era of the Gothic Wars in the mid sixth century, as prevailing opinion maintained until Coates-Stephens' reconsideration of the question in the 1990s.

My own contributions and modifications to the sequence outlined above consist chiefly of the following points. First, the fourth-century repairs and additions previously ascribed *en masse* to Maxentius more likely reflect multiple interventions on the Wall executed over the course of the 125 years that elapsed between its completion in the 270s and its reconfiguration under Honorius. Second, the final construction phase of the largest and architecturally most complex gates in the Wall, the Portae Appia and Flaminia, should date between the second quarter of the fifth century and the third quarter of the sixth, with some preference for the latter date. In the admitted absence of definitive proof, I would attribute a substantial portion of the work to the period of Byzantine reconquest in the mid sixth century, and specifically to the initiatives of Justinian's generals Belisarius and Narses. In this case, there would be some physical evidence to associate with an epoch otherwise denuded of identifiable remains in the wake of Coates-Stephens' re-dating of the eighth- and ninth-century repairs. Third, there is the real possibility of continuing work on the Wall even in the particularly "dark" period of the seventh century: The general paucity of material and textual remains from seventh-century Rome does not prove a corresponding dearth of interest in the Wall, and there are in fact circumstantial hints that limited repairs continued to occur. Fourth and finally, I stress the importance of the substantial eighth- and ninth-century restorations, which between them represent a sizeable portion of the extant traces of public building in early medieval Rome. As such, they have much to reveal about the strategy elaborated by an increasingly assertive and politically autonomous line of popes anxious to manifest their claims to temporal hegemony over the city of Rome and its environs.

The identification of this early medieval building phase also provides an excellent illustration of the value of the methodical visual and comparative analysis upon which the re-dating is based, and points as well to the broader relevance of such putatively arcane detail for historians operating well outside the purview of the dedicated masonry buff. The mechanics of papal government and administration in the early Middle Ages, the formation of a "Republic of St. Peter," and the elaborate nexus between

Roman topography and the social, political, and even theological aspirations of the papacy, for instance, should never again be considered without at least tacit reference to the Aurelian Wall, or better to the scope and technical standard of the repairs that consumed such a significant portion of the material resources available to several of the most dynamic and active popes of the early Middle Ages, notably Hadrian I (772–95) and Leo IV (847–55). Similarly in the case of the Honorian heightening of the Wall in 401–3, it was only careful observation and description on the part of A. M. Colini and (later) L. Cozza that demonstrated the implausibility of an early-fourth-century date, and succeeded in placing this massive project in its proper historical context. In both instances, moreover, the details of the construction are intimately related to the historical circumstances of their creation, and have much to reveal about both the methods and motives of their instigators. The occasional Latin crosses traced in the brickwork of the Honorian heightening, for example, mean something entirely different in the early fifth century than they would have in the early fourth; and the lowering of the date of the rather rudimentary masonry characteristic of the early-medieval restorations by more than two centuries has serious implications for current discussions about the apparent decline of social complexity in post-imperial Rome, to name but two examples.

Thus the social (and economic, and political, and religious…) history of the Aurelian Wall begins very literally with its bricks and stones and mortar, a fact to be borne in mind when approaching the sections of architectural description and interpretation that constitute the remainder of this chapter. The majority of the following information derives from extended empirical observation of the standing sections of the Wall, and is often best conveyed in a specialized language of masonry analysis which may not be immediately familiar to the non-specialist. Among the visual cues and technical features most useful for dating and distinguishing the Wall's component parts, the following items will recur frequently. "Standing stratigraphy," an archaeological term extended into the realm of architectural analysis, refers to the relative sequences that can usually be established between contiguous sections or phases of a building (one section either covers, abuts, or is covered by another, and so on). These individual sections or phases of a building are themselves best individuated by reference to the materials and techniques used in their construction, which nearly always differ to some extent over the course of time. In the case of the brick and mortar facing employed for the great majority of the Wall, the shape, color, thickness, and homogeneity of the bricks employed tends to vary noticeably from one of the five principal construction phases outlined above to the next. The same is true for the mortar, which differs considerably in quality, between friable (crumbly) and tenacious (hard and compact), as well as in texture and color, depending on the size and color of the particles of sand or stone (inclusions) mixed with the lime bonding agent. Another standard diagnostic feature of coursed masonry is its module, the vertical measure of five courses of brick and five beds of mortar. The third-century sections of the Wall generally have a module under 30cm, while the module of its Honorian components usually exceeds 30cm. Other distinguishing features include bonding courses, single files of large bricks spaced at regular intervals that are only common in the Aurelianic sections; and putlog holes, the apertures which housed the horizontal supports for the scaffolding used by construction crews as they worked: They are nonexistent in the Aurelianic sections, square and regularly spaced in Honorian work, and smaller, rounder, and more erratically positioned in the early Middle Ages. Together, such indicators underpin the detailed architectural history of the Wall that is the *sine qua non* for any investigation of its relationship with the city of Rome and its inhabitants, and thus by definition for the remaining chapters of this volume.

With all of these preliminaries in mind, we may turn to a more detailed analysis and description of the Aurelian Wall in its entirety. For the sake of clarity, subsequent references to particular locations around the circuit will follow the alphanumeric system devised by Richmond, which has now become standard.[2] The Wall is subdivided into sectors, usually bounded by principal gates, which proceed in alphabetical sequence in a clockwise direction, beginning from the Porta Flaminia in the extreme north of the circuit.[3] Individual towers in each sector are numbered in ascending order, again in a clockwise progression, and surviving gate-towers are included in the sequence. Thus, the first tower in sector K (K1) is the south tower of the Porta Latina, and the last (K13) is the north tower of the Porta Appia.

---

[2] See Richmond 1930, Appendix II (pp. 269–70). The system has been adopted by *inter alia* Cozza, Coates-Stephens and Mancini.

[3] The sectors are as follows: A: Porta Flaminia – Pinciana; B: Pinciana – Salaria; C: Salaria – Nomentana; D: Nomentana – Viale dell'Università (including the *castra praetoria*); E: Viale dell'Università – Porta Tiburtina; F: Tiburtina – Praenestina-Labicana (Maggiore); G: Praenestina-Labicana – Asinaria (S. Giovanni); H: Asinaria – Metronia; J: Metronia – Latina; K: Latina – Appia (S. Sebastiano); L: Appia – Ostiensis (S. Paolo); M: Ostiensis – Tiber River (including the southern river wall); N: southern Trastevere; O: Porta Aurelia (S. Pancrazio) – Porta Settimiana; P: Porta Settimiana – Tiber – Porta Flaminia (including the nonexistent northern river wall).

Sections of curtain wall are labeled with the numbers of their two flanking towers, such that curtain J4–5 lies between the fourth and fifth towers south of the Porta Metronia, counting from the first surviving tower south of the Gate, which is itself without towers. Unless otherwise indicated, my alphanumeric designations are identical to those in Mancini 2001, whose diagrams are recommended for those seeking to individuate precise locations at a glance, with a degree of exactitude that the necessarily smaller-scale plans in the present volume cannot always provide.

1.2   Aurelian's Wall

We begin with a detailed physical description of the monument as it appeared in its original phase, which there is overwhelming evidence for assigning to the reigns of Aurelian and his successor Probus, beginning in 271 and finishing no later than the latter's death in 282. The ancient sources are unanimous in attributing the project to Aurelian, and while Zosimus is the sole author to mention Probus in connection with its completion, his testimony is plausible if only for the magnitude of the undertaking, which likely did require some years to complete.[4]

The literary record is consistently, if circumstantially, supported by archaeological data, all of which point to a date somewhere in the second half of the third century. While comparative evidence, masonry typologies and the like, is of very limited utility, since almost nothing survives in Rome that can be dated with confidence to the reign of Aurelian, excavation has provided more convincing testimony. On the left side of the Tiber, the main circuit cut through rooms of the *Domus Lateranorum* and the Sessorian Palace which were clearly in use until well into the third

---

[4] For the most closely contemporary sources, see Aurelius Victor, *De Caes.* 35, 7: *His tot tantisque prospere gestis fanum Romae Soli magnificum constituit donariis ornans opulentis, ac ne unquam, quae per Gallienum evenerant, acciderent, muris urbem quam validissimis laxiore ambitu circumsaepsit; Epit. de Caes.* 35, 6: *Hic muris validioribus et laxioribus urbem saepsit; Chron. anno 354* (VZ 1, 278): *Hic muro urbem cinxit, templum Solis et castra in campo Agrippae dedicavit; HA Aur.* 21, 9: *cum videret posse fieri, ut aliquid tale iterum, quale sub Gallieno evenerat, proveniret, adhibito consilio senatus muros urbis Romae dilatavit. Nec tamen pomerio addidit eo tempore sed postea;* 39, 2: *Muros urbis Romae sic ampliavit, ut quinquaginta prope milia murorum eius ambitus teneant.* In the final passage, the figure of 50 miles must be a corruption, as Rome never had a circuit anywhere near this size. It has been suggested that "Vopiscus" copied a Greek source, from which he mistakenly translated *murorum* (*techeion*) in place of the actual cubits (*pecheion*): see Richmond 1930, 27, n. 2. In this case, the original source would have given 50,000 cubits, or a bit less than 23 km a total much closer to the actual length of 18,837 m.

century, as the presence of stamped lead pipes installed during the first half of the century demonstrates.[5] A *terminus post quem* around AD 250 thus results. On the right bank of the river in Trastevere, the Wall bisected the *cellae vinariae nova et arruntiana*, a double portico erected at the beginning of the second century AD. The remains on the inside of the Wall were flattened and covered with new houses at the end of the third century AD, while the section lying outside was apparently never again inhabited.[6] The presence of the Wall and the apparent advantages of living within its bounds present themselves as much the likeliest explanation for this phenomenon, which would then yield a *terminus ante quem* shortly before the year 300. On the likely assumption that the sections of the Wall on both sides of the river were built at approximately the same time (or at least that Trastevere was not walled much before the heart of the city), these indications place the erection of the whole circuit quite close to the period indicated in the texts.

Given that the attribution to Aurelian is nowhere in contention, it is as well to turn to the particulars of his Wall. The length of the entire circuit, according to Lanciani's calculations, reached 18,837 m, or a bit more than 12 miles.[7] From the Porta Flaminia (Porta del Popolo) in the north, it described a meandering arc around the city center, arriving finally at the Porta Ostiensis (Porta S. Paolo) in the south, past which it encountered the Tiber south of Monte Testaccio. Turning sharply to the right, it followed the left bank of the river for nearly 800 m before crossing it 500 m south of the modern Porta Portese. It thence described a pointed salient, with its apex on the Janiculum at the Porta Aurelia (Porta S. Pancrazio), which encompassed much of modern Trastevere and the summit of the Janiculum. From the Porta Aurelia, the Wall descended again toward the Tiber, which it re-crossed on the site of the modern Ponte Sisto, whence it proceeded northward along the left bank, past the mausoleum of Hadrian and the Pons Aelius (Ponte Sant'Angelo), and continuing upstream as far as the Porta Flaminia, which it rejoined shortly after turning away from the river. Its shape was roughly that of a seven-pointed star, with one point separated from the rest by the Tiber. As the particulars of its course and the

---

[5] The evidence is more fully discussed in Richmond 1930, 15ff. On the topography of the former, see now Liverani 2003, esp. 156; 1998, 6–16. While it appears that the traditional identification of the complex as an imperial palace *per se* (as Richmond assumed) may need reconsideration, the large private baths, living areas, etc. on the site were certainly imperial property well before the time of Aurelian. On the latter, see Colini 1948, 137–77.

[6] See Lanciani in *Notitizie* 1880, 127ff.; Richmond 1930, 17–18, with Chapter 4.3, below.

[7] Lanciani 1892, 88.

factors that determined it are discussed at greater length in Chapter 2, suffice it to say at present that the circuit was chosen with an eye to enclosing as much of the populated city center as possible with a topographically viable defensive perimeter, while minimizing the expenditures of time and money necessary for the completion of the task.

The end product was a solid wall approximately 7 m high and 3.5 thick, rising from a foundation between 3.5 and 4 m wide that was sunk down to densely packed subsoil, or to bedrock where possible.[8] The Wall proper was generally set back from its slightly thicker foundations, which often project between 20 and 40 cm beyond the springing of the brick-faced curtains.[9] It was reinforced at intervals of 100 Roman feet (29.6m) with projecting square towers, and surmounted by an open rampart-walk fronted by a low parapet, topped with merlons that varied in size and spacing. The presence of the merlons, in places incorporated in the fabric of a later heightening, proved essential for Richmond's seminal work in distinguishing the first phase of the Wall from its successive elaborations.[10] Their positioning indicates that the total height of Aurelian's Wall generally approached 8 m, from ground level to the top of the parapet (Figure 1.1).

The structure was faced with curtains of brick and mortar, which fronted a concrete core made of mortar and rough fragments of tufa packed in ascending courses into the void left between the brick facings as they were built progressively higher. The foundations were laid by dumping a similar concrete aggregate between wooden forms, which left characteristic imprints in the hardened concrete. They were unfaced except in the case of small sections left exposed above ground level, where courses of squared tufa blocks are occasionally still visible.[11] A string

[8] As the foundations of the Wall have never been examined by systematic excavation, it is impossible at present to be more precise about their depth in most places, nor to estimate how successful the Wall's builders were in reaching bedrock throughout the extent of the circuit. Good sense alone suggests that this was done wherever possible, as Vitruvius recommended (*De arch.* 1, 5, 1): ...*tunc turrium murorumque fundamenta sic sunt facienda uti fodiantur, si queat inveniri, ad solidum et in solido, quantum ex amplitudine operis pro ratione videaur, crassitudine ampliore quam parietum qui supra terram sunt futuri, et ea impleantur quam solidissima structura.* My measurements of the Wall appear in Appendix A.

[9] A relatively wide 30 centimeter setback, topped with a course of tiles from which the brick curtain springs, appears at the rear of sector B19–21 (Pinciana-Salaria); cf. Cozza 1993, 120. A rather narrower setback is visible e.g. by the Modern Viale Cristoforo Colombo, on the outer facing south of tower L13; cf. Vitruvius, *De arch.* 1, 5, 1, cited in the preceding note.

[10] Richmond 1930, 58.

[11] Tufa facings occur, for example, on the outside of the Wall between tower L13 and the Bastione Ardeatino, and on its interior between towers L21 and 22, by the Via Guerrieri.

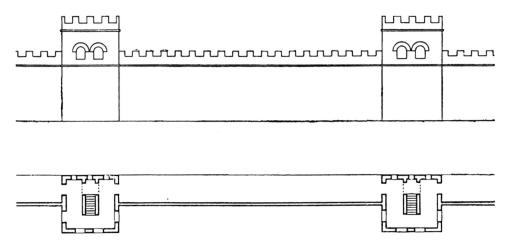

Figure 1.1 The Aurelian Wall, first phase. (After Colini 1944, 111.)

course that projected slightly from the facing of both curtains and towers at the level of the rampart-walk was the lone decorative element in the original scheme. This was made up of two to four courses of large tiles, some, with one rounded or beveled edge placed facing outward, apparently made to order. In the areas where it is extant, the string course, like the battlements, provides a useful indicator of the division between the original elevation and later additions (Figure 1.2).[12]

While the Wall had a solid core for its full height over the large majority of the nineteen-kilometer circuit, significant variations on this arrangement did occur. The most distinctive saw the occasional use of curtains outfitted with an internal covered walkway rising from a solid foundation, open at the rear and roofed with an arched gallery. In these segments, the original height of the curtains seems to have been greater than the norm, perhaps approaching ten meters.[13] This configuration occurred at the Porta Asinaria, and probably also for some distance to the east, where it would have heightened the sector spanning the low ground between the gateway and the Amphitheatrum Castrense. Other such galleried curtains were probably used east of the Porta Pinciana, and on each side of the Porta Metronia, where they may have continued for some distance to the east, throughout much of Sector H.[14]

---

[12] Bits of the string course appear at points all around the circuit, though surviving traces are concentrated in the south, in sectors L and M.

[13] On the height of these curtains, cf. Cardilli *et al.* 1995, 68; Colini 1944, 130.

[14] At the Porta Metronia, and in part of the Porta Pinciana-Salaria sector, as Richmond sagely noted, the Honorian covered gallery springs from a solid base much too low to have been the

Figure 1.2 Curtain M7–8, projecting string course.

Clear traces of this constructional variant remain visible at the Porta Asinaria, where the outer facing of the curtain contains two now-plugged archers' slits, or *feritoie*, on each side of the gateway-arch, at a level well within the original elevation of the Wall, here clearly signaled by immured merlons (Figure 1.3). These apertures evidently perforated the thin front curtain of an original galleried arcade, one bay of which remains visible at the rear of the gate, neatly framing one of the *feritoie*.[15] In the adjacent valley toward the Amphitheatrum Castrense stand two unique curtains, composed of two superimposed galleries, the lower of which stands at or near the ground level of the original wall (Figure 1.4). Although the

top of a standard Aurelianic curtain; and the bays of the later gallery are disproportionately tall and narrow (Richmond 1930, 66; on the Porta Metronia, cf. Colini 1944, 129–32). In Sector H, the floor of the Honorian gallery is some six meters below present ground level: as it is hardly likely that the foundation of the original Wall lies 6–7 m lower still, the logical conclusion is that here, too, the Honorian gallery does not spring from solid Aurelianic curtains built to their usual height. This phenomenon is probably best explained by an extension of the piers of a lower, pre-existing gallery, heightened as much as possible without the expenditure of time and materials that the replacement of the Aurelianic gallery with a solid wall would have required.

[15] Cf. Colini 1944, 122–4; Richmond 1930, 146ff., 1927a, 64.

Figure 1.3 Porta Asinaria: archer's slit beneath level of Honorian heightening (note immured merlons above).

Figure 1.4 Curtain G20–1, interior facing.

technical characteristics of both galleries and the homogeneity of the brickwork between them indicate that they were probably erected at the same time during the Honorian building campaign of the early fifth century, the absence of Aurelianic masonry is telling.[16] Had the first wall been built with its usual solid core, it is almost certain that the second gallery would have risen directly from it, as it did elsewhere. That Honorius' builders were constrained to raise these curtains from the ground up suggests that something flimsier was replaced in the process, and hence that the first-period gallery of the neighboring Porta Asinaria extended at least to this point.

Other significant constructional variations occurred in the sectors where the Wall fronted the Aqua Claudia-Anio Novus, on both sides of the Porta Praenestina-Labicana (Porta Maggiore), and a short stretch of the Aqua Marcia-Tepula-Iulia, to the east of the Porta Tiburtina. In these spots, the Wall was built just outside the arches of the aqueducts, to which its core was bonded, leaving on the inside only the interstices between the existing pillars to be faced in brick, and resulting in a combined width approaching six meters for the composite structure. A narrow space remained above where the rampart walk ran between the parapet and the front of the pre-existing structures, except in the curtains on both sides of the Porta Praenestina-Labicana, where the aqueduct was incorporated for its entire thickness into the core of the Wall, with its arches filled in and faced in brick.[17] As the Wall did not reach the top of the aqueduct, there resulted the awkward mutual isolation of the fighting platforms in each bay of the aqueduct, which could only have been connected by means of a more or less temporary platform or scaffolding, of which, however, no traces remain.[18]

There was, finally, a third variation, the almost total disappearance of which has left it under-represented in past discussions of the Wall. By the time of Procopius, and very probably from the beginning, river walls ran along the left bank of the Tiber, in the south by Monte Testaccio, and in the north from the Ponte Sisto to the Porta Flaminia, covering all the riverine approaches to the city save in the one section shielded by the Transtiberine walls. Though the architectural particulars of Procopius'

---

[16] Richmond thought the lower gallery here the work of Aurelian (1930, 65), a view long ago disputed by Colini (1944, 120), but which still has its supporters today (e.g. Mancini 2001, 23); my examination of the section in question convinces me that Colini was correct in assigning it to Honorius in its entirety.

[17] On the particulars of the situation at the Porta Maggiore, see now Coates-Stephens 2004, 82ff.

[18] Richmond 1930, 63–4; cf. Colini 1944, 109 and 114ff.

account are brief and garbled, it is clear that the fortifications along the riverbank were already long-established in the 530s.[19]

Much of the southern stretch was visible until its remains were razed almost completely during construction of the Tiber embankments in the 1870s.[20] One tower still stands today, with a bit of wall attached to it on both sides. In the north, nothing is left, nor has there been anything since the later Middle Ages, if the surviving maps and plans are any indication. Still, there were without doubt walls here, too. While Procopius oddly claims the northern stretch of river wall was without towers, the inventory of the Wall in the Einsiedeln Itineraries list 16 between the *pons Sancti Petri* (Ponte Sant'Angelo) and the Porta Flaminia, which cannot all have been located in the short stretch between the Porta Flaminia and the Tiber, but must have belonged in part to walls along the river. For several centuries after the Einsiedeln Itineraries, there are continued references to gates leading from the Campus Martius to the Tiber, which obviously perforated these walls.[21] Nor should the fact of their disappearance come as a great surprise, given first that these must have been the sections most vulnerable to the periodic, catastrophic floods of the Tiber; and second, that the walls along the river were indeed, as Procopius says, smaller and flimsier than the rest, as will be shown shortly.

The one surviving section near Monte Testaccio is a precious bit of evidence that has been too frequently overlooked, a strange oversight given that it permits several important points to be made.[22] As it has never

[19] According to Procopius, the walls along the river were built by the "ancient Romans," albeit "carelessly, low, and entirely without towers"; see *BG* 2, 9, 16: καί, ἦν γάρ τις αὐτῷ ἐπιμαχωτάτη μάλιστα μοῖρα, ᾗ τοῦ Τιβέριδος ἡ ὄχθη ἐστίν, ἐπεὶ ταύτῃ οἱ πάλαι Ῥωμαῖοι θαρσοῦντες τοῦ ὕδατος τῷ ὀχυρώματι τὸ τεῖχος ἀπημελημένως ἐδείμαντο, βραχύ τε αὐτὸ καὶ πύργων ἔρημον παντάπασι ποιησάμενοι...; cf. *BG* 1, 22, 16; 1, 22, 25.

[20] Beginning with e.g. Bufalini and Dupérac in the sixteenth century, and continuing through the more scientifically redacted plans of Nolli, the *Direzione Generale del Censo* of 1829, and others as late as *c.* 1870, the southern river wall is a regular feature; see A. P. Frutaz, *Le piante di Roma* (3 vols., Rome, 1962), tavv. 396ff. (Nolli *ibid.*); 489ff. (Direzione Generale *ibid.*); 534 (Marré, *c.* 1870 *ibid.*). A picture of this stretch of the riverbank taken in 1861 shows at least two additional towers upstream of the remaining one, amply corroborating the plans; see Mocchegiani Carpano 1985, fig. 25 on p. 49. Father Luigi Bruzza observed sections of the river wall during his excavations of 1868–70, shortly before its demolition; his manuscript, published and annotated by G. Gatti (Gatti 1936), is the best available description of the remains. Bruzza noted curtains with arched galleries (apparently similar to those by the one surviving tower, described below), later extensively repaired in massive reused tufa blocks, a technique that can now be dated securely to the eighth/ninth centuries; see Gatti, 67ff.

[21] On these *posterulae*, see below, n. 34.

[22] Richmond appears to have been totally unaware of its existence. Brief mention is made in Mocchegiani Carpano 1985, 49ff., with fig. 30. Mancini includes it in her plans of the Wall,

previously been analyzed in detail, a brief description is warranted. The tower is two stories high, with an upper floor apparently accessible only from the top of the wall (Figure 1.5). It has two arched windows at front and back, and doorways on both sides, now blocked, which led to the rampart-walk. The lower chamber is covered with a solid vault; and there are no traces of an internal stairway. It is approximately and irregularly square, measuring 4.5m at its outer face, 4.3 at the rear, and projecting between 1.10 and 1.16m from the plane of the wall at both front and back. While the very top is a modern restoration, it is preserved to nearly its original height, which will have been in the vicinity of 9 m, significantly less than the towers of the land walls. To the north of the tower, the adjacent stretch of wall is backed by two arched bays, with two small *feritoie* in the thin front curtain of the northernmost (Figure 1.6). To the south, the wall is solid, with neither arches nor slits. While it becomes increasingly ruinous, its foundations continue for some 75 m, fronting the very top of the sloping embankment with a solid tufa and mortar core that looks much like that of the land walls. It was approximately 2 m thick, and appears not to have exceeded 5–6 m in height, judging by the elevation of the door that once opened onto the rampart-walk from the tower, though the steep slope of the embankment in front would have increased its effective elevation.

The remains thus confirm Procopius' statement that the walls along the river were lower and less imposing than the rest, though they of course support the Einsiedeln Itineraries in the matter of the towers. Moreover, they corroborate the proposition that a river wall existed well before Procopius, as the technique of the surviving remains is almost certainly earlier than the sixth century. The module of the brickwork ranges consistently between 30 and 34cm, thus closely approximating the norms for Honorian work elsewhere on the Wall, though it does not fall beyond the outer fringe of the Aurelianic parameters. The four regular courses of square putlog holes visible in the upper section of the tower likewise suggest an Honorian provenance, as they do not occur in the masonry of the 270s. If the standing remains are indeed Honorian, they perhaps represent a rebuilding undertaken after three disastrous floods in the late fourth century, which also seem to have put a large warehouse just inside the river wall in this sector out of commission.[23]

---

without commenting further, save to date it between the time of Aurelian and Honorius (2001, tav. 30e).

[23] See R. Meneghini, in *BullCom* 1986, esp. 594; cf. Le Gall 1953, 29.

Figure 1.5 Tower of river wall (M15), interior facing.

Figure 1.6 Interior of river wall, just north of tower M15.

Although I am not prepared to date the extant structures to the 270s, I have included them in my discussion of the Wall's initial phase on the premise that some sort of river defenses will have been built along with the rest of the circuit, for all that the standing section may be a later repair or addition.[24] The military utility of Rome's enormous new enceinte, on which so much time and labor had been spent, would have been significantly compromised had the riverbank been left unprotected; and as the additional effort required to fortify it was practically negligible relative to that already expended, it seems most logical to assume that a wall existed here from the beginning. The evidence of approximately contemporary urban enceintes elsewhere suggests the same conclusion: cities on rivers throughout the empire were fortified on their riverward sides, albeit often, precisely as at Rome, with smaller walls and fewer towers.[25] Similar conclusions follow from a passing reference in Claudian, which implies that walls with towers rose along the banks of the Tiber already by the end of the fourth century.[26]

Thus concluding the discussion of the curtains of the Wall in its original phase, we return to the land walls, and specifically to the towers. These quadrangular structures are generally between 7.5 and 7.75 m wide, and project 3.5–3.75 m beyond the curtains, while at the back they are flush with the internal face of the Wall.[27] The most common type was fashioned with a solid concrete base to the level of the rampart-walk, and a single chamber above, roofed with three barrel-vaults, the central one pierced by a flight of stairs giving access to an open rooftop parapet. The walls of the upper story were two Roman feet (60 cm) thick, precisely and not coincidentally matching the width of the

---

[24] A premise shared by e.g. Corvisieri 1878, esp. 85; Richmond 1930, 19–20; Le Gall 1953, 288ff.; Cozza 1986, 107.

[25] To cite a very few examples: the circuits at Andernach on the Rhine and Coblenz on the Moselle, built *c.* 300, both had lower and thinner walls on their riverward sides. The river wall at Andernach was without towers (unlike the rest of the circuit), while at Coblenz, the one tower attested in the river wall is considerably smaller than the rest: see Butler 1959, 36–7. At the opposite end of the empire, the river wall of Zenobia, on the Euphrates, was considerably less imposing than the rest of the circuit, and defended by fewer, smaller towers: see Foss and Winfield 1986, 8, with fig. 15 on p. 219.

[26] *De Probino et Olybrio coss.*, 226–9 (anno 395): *est in Romuleo procumbens insula Thybri,/qua medius geminas interfluit alveus urbes,/discretas subeunte freto, pariterque minantes/ardua turrigerae surgunt in culmina ripae.* It is just possible that a passage in Ammianus Marcellinus on the destructive flood of 374 is also to be taken in reference to the river walls; see 27, 6, 17: *Tiberis, qui media intersecans moenia....*

[27] Specifications calling for towers 26 Roman feet wide (7.70m), projecting by 12 feet (3.55m), would account well for the average of the measurements recorded in Appendix A.

bipedalis, the largest brick used in their construction.[28] Arched entrances on each side of the towers gave access to the rampart-walk, which passed unimpeded through the chambers themselves. Most often, the chamber was provided with five windows, two at the front, one on each side, and one at the rear. These were large enough to permit the effective use of the defensive artillery, primarily the crossbow-like *ballista*, that figured prominently in the design of later Roman fortifications throughout the empire.[29]

As with the curtains, however, numerous variations on the standard schema occur, some apparently prompted by practical exigencies, while others more likely resulted from the independent initiatives of their various builders. The towers flanking the more important gates of the Wall were semicircular in form, with hollow bases housing the stairs that led to their upper chamber. A number of otherwise standard square towers flanking smaller gates and posterns likewise featured internal stairs, which ascended along the inner face of the three exterior walls.[30] A similar configuration occurred in the galleried stretches of the Wall, where several towers were provided with an internal stair, again ascending along three walls to the upper chamber.[31] These hollow towers were the only means of reaching the open walkway atop the Wall, which was otherwise inaccessible from the base of the curtains, a provision apparently made to keep those not directly involved in its defense out of the way.

Practical explanations for other peculiarities are more difficult to come by. Enough of the original fabric of tower K2 survives to demonstrate that it was round from the beginning, as it remains, though it was rebuilt almost completely in the Middle Ages.[32] In some towers, no provision seems to have been made for rooftop access, for instead of the usual three

---

[28] Cf. Richmond 1930, 78.

[29] As used by late-antique writers, *ballista* referred to a machine resembling an overgrown crossbow, capable of shooting heavy darts with enormous range and penetrating power: see Ammianus 23, 4, 2; Vegetius, *De re militari* 4, 1, 30; Anon. *De rebus bellicis* 18, 2; Procop. *BG* 1, 21, 14. Generally on *ballistae* and other types of Roman artillery, a subject of growing scholarly concern in recent decades, see Southern 2006, 213–17; Landels 2000, 99–132; Chevedden 1995 (the implausible claim that torsion artillery disappeared by the sixth century aside); Feugère 1993, 215–25; Marsden 1971, esp. 234–65, 1969.

[30] The north tower of the Porta Nomentana is a good example of the semicircular type. It contains an original stair composed of six flights joined at 90-degree angles; see Cozza 1994, 87; Richmond 1930, 93ff.

[31] This is the case, for example, at towers G15 and G17 (near the Amphitheatrum Castrense), where the now bricked-in stairway entrances remain visible in the clearly Aurelian work at their base: see fig. 1.18.

[32] Perhaps the proximity of the immediately adjacent Porta Latina, with its rounded towers, has some (unexplained) bearing on the decision to build a third tower to similar specifications.

barrel vaults with a central staircase, they were covered completely with two wider vaults, supported by a wall running through the middle of the chamber.[33] The number, spacing, and size of tower windows also varied in practice, a phenomenon probably best attributed to the diverse inclinations of the many different work-crews that must have been employed in a project of this size.

The Wall was initially perforated by thirteen gates on the left bank of the Tiber and three in Trastevere, in addition to a number of secondary posterns, or *posterulae*.[34] The main gates were constructed in three primary orders of magnitude – though individual variations existed from the beginning – that seem generally to have corresponded with the importance of the roads they spanned. And though all the gates have been extensively remodeled since the third century, most dramatically under Honorius at the beginning of the fifth, some general observations about their original appearance are possible. The four largest and most important were the Portae Flaminia, Appia, Ostiensis, and Portuensis, all of which almost certainly had two travertine arches, one each for inbound and outbound traffic, flanked by semicircular brick towers (Figure 1.7).[35] The curtain above the arch rose to the full height of the towers, and

---

[33] For example, at tower B17 of the Pinciana-Salaria sector: see Cozza 1993, 116–17.

[34] There is another small gate just west of the Porta Ostiensis, called by Richmond the Porta Ostiensis West, that on the basis of its extant remains seems to me better classified amongst the *posterulae* (see Richmond 1930, 219–20). Strangely, while Richmond concurred in calling it a *posterula*, he included it among his count of the major gates of the Wall; this explains why I count one gate less on the left bank of the Tiber than did he. There was, finally, a gate in the river wall leading to the Pons Aelius and Hadrian's mausoleum across the river, known by the sixth century as the Porta Sancti Petri, and mentioned by Procopius, who called it the Porta Aurelia (*BG* 1, 19, 4). Given the importance of this river crossing (see below, Chapter 4.3), I would guess it was more imposing than a common postern from the beginning.

[35] While the façades of the gates were later reworked, remains of travertine curtains most likely belonging to the first phase have been identified at both surviving ones, the Portae Ostiensis and Appia: see Richmond 1930, 112–13 and 122–4. Clear evidence for a double archway remains at the rear curtain of the Porta Appia, which preserves traces of a second travertine arch blocked up when the single arch extant today was installed (Figure 1.19). At the Porta Ostiensis, the walled enclosure, or *controporta*, at the rear of the gate retains its two arches, which must originally have corresponded with two apertures in the main façade, traces of which were revealed in excavations of 1920 (see Richmond 1930, 112; cf. 134–5). Seventeenth-century drawings of the since-destroyed Porta Portuensis show that it preserved its twin arches to the very end: see Cozza 1987–8, 145ff.; Richmond 1930, 200ff. The Porta Flaminia, razed in the 1870s, closely approximated the other three in its dimensions; based on this evidence and the great importance of the Via Flaminia, Richmond plausibly suggested that it too was similarly configured, though there is nothing to prove this absolutely, with the physical evidence long gone (1930, 198–9); cf. Cozza 1992, 100ff. The demolition of the gate and the various finds uncovered in the process are documented by C. Visconti and V. Vespignani, *BullCom* 1877, 210ff., and 1880, 169ff.; cf. *Notizie* 1880, 468.

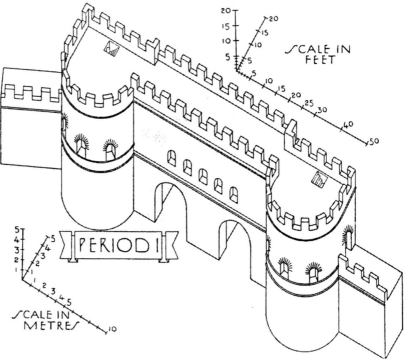

Figure 1.7 Porta Appia, first phase. (After Richmond 1930, p. 140.)

enclosed a narrow covered chamber from which a portcullis could be raised and lowered. Gates of the second magnitude, among them the Portae Nomentana and Latina, had a single archway again abutted by semicircular towers, and topped by a covered passageway.[36] Gates of the third rank consisted of simple brick arches placed midway between standard square towers spaced at the usual hundred-foot interval. The Porta Asinaria and the Porta Metronia were originally so configured, though the Asinaria later received more imposing semicircular towers. It is likely not coincidental that these least imposing gates are located in the few places where the Aurelianic galleried curtains stood: here, the provision for a second rank of defenders below those on the open walkway above was perhaps intended to compensate to some degree for the lack of a fortified gateway proper.

[36] Other examples include the Portae Salaria and Tiburtina; a variant arrangement appeared at the smaller Porta Pinciana, which was initially flanked by only one round tower, though a second was subsequently added; see Cozza 1992, 127ff.; Richmond 1930, 159ff.

Figure 1.8 Aurelianic postern in curtain F7–8.

The *posterulae* were built in various sizes and degrees of elaboration. Medieval literary sources indicate that there were five or six in the northern stretch of the river wall, between the Ponte Sisto and the Porta Flaminia, of which nothing remains today.[37] In the land walls, traces of at least eight are still visible, all of which were filled in from an early date, perhaps at the beginning of the fifth century.[38] The most imposing were provided with travertine sills, jambs, and lintels, with two brick relieving arches immediately above; the two largest are in curtains D2–3, east of Porta Nomentana, and F7–8, south of Porta Tiburtina (Figure 1.8). Another, similar but smaller, occurs a bit farther east of Porta Nomentana,

[37] The Einsiedeln List mentions five, while later medieval sources indicate the presence of at least one more, though this may have been a later addition; on the river gates in general, see De Caprariis 1999, 220ff.; Hubert 1990, 99–101; Le Gall 1953, 288–90; Richmond 1930, 236–9. For Lanciani's reconstruction of the course of the river walls, and the location of the *posterulae*, see *FUR*, tavv. 8–9. These studies are all indebted to the fundamental work of Corvisieri 1878, 79–121; 137–71.

[38] The original number must have been higher, on the assumption that others were present among the many ancient tracts of Wall no longer extant. One certain example between the Portae Salaria and Nomentana was destroyed during the taking of Rome in 1870 (it was located in curtain C4–5, where there now stands a memorial to the fallen); see Cozza 1994, 82.

near the junction with the north wall of the Castra Praetoria; a sill and the lower part of a jamb in travertine indicate the presence of a fourth just north of the cut made for the railroad tracks (curtain F12–13). The fifth and final postern with stone elements pierces the Wall just north of the modern arches spanning the Viale Cristoforo Colombo (in the Appia-Ostiensis sector). Like the one near the Porta Nomentana, it was placed in a protected angle where the Wall zigzags outward. Now open, it was previously blocked like all the rest, as photos from the beginning of the twentieth century demonstrate.[39] Three other still smaller gates (Richmond called the two he noted "wickets") remain visible, constructed entirely in brick with one or two arches of *bipedales*. One is just around the corner from the second postern east of Porta Nomentana (Figure 1.9), another is south of the Viale Cristoforo Colombo, again close to a larger postern, and the third, almost totally buried, was observed by Richmond and others south of Porta Asinaria, beneath the Lateran.[40]

1.3   Honorius' Wall

While the first phase of the Wall has been well documented and under-stood since Richmond, the dating of the later phases of construction, which constitute nearly the upper half of the structure in its entirety, remains a work in progress. As Richmond first recognized, most of the original fabric of the upper sections of the Wall belongs to a single building campaign that is distinct from the Aurelianic phase below.[41] Following a description of its architecture, we will outline the reasons for assigning this massive addition – *contra* Richmond – to Honorius in 401–3, instead of Maxentius in 306–12. In part because the redating has

---

[39] In this case, the archway and the immediately surrounding masonry belonged to a pre-existing monumental arch incorporated into the Wall; see Homo 1904, 254–5, with fig. 1, showing the gate still blocked with masonry; cf. Quilici 1987.

[40] Richmond did not mention the first of these three, of which only two concentric relieving arches in *bipedales* are now visible at the front of the Wall, the rest being covered by a later restoration. As it occurs above the foundations of an earlier structure, he perhaps thought the arch part of the pre-existing building, blocked when the Wall was built. The surrounding brickwork looks very much like it belongs to Aurelian's Wall itself, however, which suggests that the relieving arches were designed to span a passageway through the Wall. Its inclusion in my reckoning of *posterulae*, in addition to that of the partially preserved feature in curtain F12–13, explains the discrepancy between my total figure of eight, and the six listed by Richmond (1930, 229–35); with the addition of the "Porta Ostiensis West," the number rises to nine (above n. 34).

[41] Richmond 1930, 57 and 67ff.

Figure 1.9 Small postern between tower D4 and the *castra praetoria*, partially covered by sloping reinforcement, probably of the sixteenth century.

yet to receive the general recognition it undoubtedly deserves, scholars have also been slow to investigate its profound historical implications. The convincing arguments in favor of the new, later date should hence be restated in full, both to make the case once and for all, and to provide the requisite background for the interpretation of its consequences that will feature prominently in subsequent chapters of this study.

Around the full periphery of the circuit, a brick curtain extends upward some seven meters from the level of the original rampart-walk, often incorporating in its exterior the Aurelianic parapet, in places with its merlons intact (Figure 1.10). It was topped by another open wall-walk with a crenellated parapet, now almost everywhere disappeared, at the base of which projected a second string course.[42] For the majority of the circuit, the new second level was enclosed at the rear with an arcaded gallery similar to the galleried sections of the first Wall, with six arched bays between towers, each usually provided with a *feritoia* centered in an apsidal niche built into the thickness of the front curtain (Figure 1.11). The finished curtains rose to the commanding height of 15 m, and the newly heightened towers (see below) to as much as 23.[43]

In other sections of considerable length, the vaulted gallery was omitted in favor of a simple curtain wall about half as thick (*c.* 1.8 m, or six Roman feet) as the original beneath, which rose to the usual height and was topped with a much narrower rampart-walk. The rear half of the Aurelianic wall-walk was left open to the sky, and one or sometimes two arched recesses with *feritoie* were built into the new curtain for the use of defenders on this level. Such sections comprise a significant chunk of the entire circuit: they appear between the Portae Flaminia and Pinciana, between the Nomentana and Tiburtina, and for the entirety of the Tiburtina – Praenestina-Labicana and Bastione Ardeatino – Ostiensis sectors (Figure 1.12).

A second variant occurred in the tracts abutting the Aqua Claudia-Anio Novus and the Marcia-Tepula-Julia. At the former, a solid wall rose from the Aurelianic parapet, fronting the open arches of the aqueduct that had overtopped the original circuit. The space between the front of the curtains and the aqueduct was filled in totally to the level of the water-channel, or *specus*, in front of which an open wall-walk was built. This walkway was reached from the pre-existing Aurelianic platforms inside the arches of the aqueduct, which gave onto stairs located inside the towers, leading to their

---

[42] Two Honorian merlons remain just north of Porta Tiburtina (E14–15), immured in a modern restoration; others are visible in the north wall of the Castra Praetoria, likewise immured in later brickwork.

[43] Cf. Coates-Stephens 2004, 89–90.

Figure 1.10 Curtain L14–15: Aurelianic merlons immured in heightened Honorian curtain.

Figure 1.11 Curtain G14–15, interior facing: arcaded gallery rising from original solid curtain.

Figure 1.12 Heightened curtain without covered arcade, between tower L13 and the Bastione Ardeatino.

newly added upper chambers, and thence to the rampart-walk. The heightened Wall also reached to the full height of the Aqua Marcia-Tepula-Julia, though the configuration of the upper wall-walk is harder to determine, as all traces of it vanished with the construction of the sixteenth-century Acqua Felice, which here runs along the top of the Wall.

Concurrently with the elevation of the curtains, the towers of the Wall were heightened by a full story, and its various gates embellished and enlarged. The standard square towers had a second chamber placed above the first, the walls of which were first doubled in thickness to support the additional weight.[44] The second story was connected with the room below by an internal stair, and to the rampart-walk atop the heightened curtains via arched apertures on each side, which left an unimpeded route for the movement of personnel and equipment, as in the older walkway beneath. A small vaulted vestibule protected the entrances to the upper chambers, and provided cover for the latrines, or *necessaria*, which projected out from the parapet of the curtains in the lee of the towers, each resting on two stone corbels that still appear today in a number of places

---

[44] For further description of the new towers, see esp. Cozza 1987, 29ff.; cf. Richmond 1930, 81ff.

Figure 1.13 Corbelled supports for a latrine (*necessarium*), curtain J13–14.

(Figure 1.13).[45] Where the elevation of the Wall changed from one curtain to the next, the vestibules also contained the stairs required to connect the disparate levels of the wall-walk. In the non-galleried sections, these vestibules were built up in two stories from the Aurelianic walkway, whereby they served to buttress the new towers as well as to cover their approaches.[46] Where the tops of the towers rose clear of the Wall, the covered entrances seem to have been integrated into the fabric of this upper chamber (Figure 1.14), a detail with implications for the construction sequence of the Wall's heightening: As the new tower tops had lateral extensions supported only by the elevated curtains, the latter must have been constructed before the heightening of the towers.

---

[45] Seven curtains between towers J3 and J16 today contain traces of these corbels, a testament to the preservation of this tract to nearly its original height, and the apparent ubiquity of the *necessaria* when the Wall was whole. While Richmond counted only twenty remaining sets of corbels, many more *necessaria* once existed: the Einsiedeln Itinerary, compiled when the Wall was substantially better preserved, lists 116 for the whole circuit, for an average of one every two to three curtains. Richmond and Cozza both imagine that when the Wall was whole, it contained one *necessarium* for nearly all of its approximately 280 towers (Cozza 1987, 39; Richmond 1930, 84ff.). Other examples appear at B5–6, G17–18, etc.

[46] See Cozza 1994, 76–7 and 103ff.; cf. Colini 1944, 112. The lower vestibule was commonly built separately from the towers themselves, being rather integrated in the new curtains up to the level of the upper walkway, and abutting the towers in the same way that the galleried curtains did elsewhere.

Figure 1.14 Tower P3 in Trastevere, showing the bond between the wall of the covered entranceway, now shorn off, and the core of the Honorian top chamber.

The new "fighting top" had eight windows, three at front and back, and one on each side, again making ample provision for the use of projectile weapons, which at their new and more commanding elevation would have been substantially more formidable.[47] The windows of the Aurelianic towers were either walled in completely or turned into archers' slits. In one common layout, an arch built around a single slit in the front wall of the tower supported a new stairway giving onto the upper chamber (Figure 1.15).[48] As usual, however, variation is the rule, and the arrangements made by Honorius' builders defy generalization.[49] Further, few of

[47] Richmond (1930, 81) claims that the majority of the new towers had only two windows in the back, and cites as an example tower B15, which in fact has three (original) rear windows, as do the majority of the extant examples; Cozza (1987, 29) and Mancini (2001, 28) both give eight as the standard figure. As always, there are variants, and a number of the heightened towers were provided with two rear windows, as in the case of the adjacent towers G15, 16, and 17 in the Castrense-Asinaria sector. Another permutation occurs at tower H15, just north of the Porta Metronia, which was (re)built with one central window and a second much smaller one to its left (or north).

[48] This arrangement is easy to spot in several towers now lacking their rear walls, e.g. B8 and B18 (Pinciana-Salaria), and J3 (Metronia-Latina).

[49] One variant, in which no internal connection existed, as at B17, has been previously mentioned; another occurs at G23, which has an ascending stair running along the back wall of the bottom chamber instead of the front. Richmond (1930, 81), in fact, believed that many of the Aurelianic towers were not heightened at all, though their generally ruinous state

Figure 1.15 Tower J3 (interior): stairway to top of heightened tower at right, with blocked Aurelianic window in arch at center. The arch at far right leads to the covered gallery.

the heightened towers are preserved to anything like their full elevation, leaving scarce testimonia to the configuration of their summits. The best-preserved example is in the Pinciana-Salaria sector; dubbed by Lanciani the *turris omnium perfectissima*, it constitutes the best surviving evidence for the contours of the new towers in their pristine form (Figure 1.16).[50] Here, a hipped roof springing from an ornamental cornice of thin, marble corbels was substituted for the flat, crenellated top of the Aurelianic towers. The inside of the chamber was covered by an octagonal cement dome resting on soffits that sprang from the wall-tops of the square enclosure beneath.[51] The remains of other well-preserved towers suggest that this configuration was standard.[52]

---

leaves it nowhere certain that this was the case. There are certainly no towers that preserve their Aurelianic contours intact without traces of subsequent additions, nor has anyone since Richmond claimed to identify an un-heightened tower.

[50] See *FUR*, tav. 3; cf. Cozza 1993, 111–12.   [51] V. Cozza 1987, esp. figs. 40 and 43.

[52] The plans of Dupérac of 1577 (Frutaz 1962, XXII) and Maggi of 1625 (*ibid.*, CXLIII), for example, depict many more towers with roofs similar to the ones described here. Numerous towers had their crumbling tops removed in the course of demolitions undertaken to

Figure 1.16 Tower B15, the *turris omnium perfectissima*.

"stabilize" the Wall, many in the eighteenth century, when indeed several towers in the immediate vicinity of the *turris omnium perfectissima* lost their upper stories: see Cozza 1993, 94ff. For other surviving examples of the type in Trastevere, see Cozza 1986, esp. 112ff.

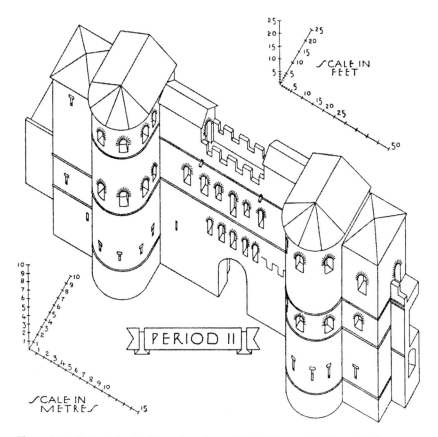

PORTA ASINARIA
(WITH · SUBSEQUENT · ADDITIONS)
ISOMETRIC · RESTORATION

PERIOD II

SCALE IN FEET

SCALE IN METRES

Figure 1.17 Porta Asinaria, Honorian phase. (After Richmond 1930, p. 157.)

The gate-towers also grew by a story during the elevation of the Wall, and several of the smaller gates of the first period were more substantially re-edified. At the Porta Asinaria, large new semicircular towers resembling those at the Portae Appia and Ostiensis were added; and the east tower of the Porta Pinciana, which had previously been flanked by only one tower, was erected from the ground up (Figure 1.17).[53] It was probably also at this

---

[53] On the Porta Asinaria, see Richmond 1930, 150ff.; on the Pinciana, 162ff. Richmond's treatment of all the gates remains fundamental, with the important caveat that his second and third phases should nearly always be jointly attributed to a single Honorian phase (more on this below), as Cozza has said in his update of Richmond's remarks on the Porta Pinciana (Cozza 1992, 127–31).

period that walled enclosures were added at the back of the Portae Pinciana, Salaria, Nomentana, Tiburtina, Praenestina-Labicana, Asinaria, Latina, Appia, Ostiensis, and Flaminia, perhaps for reasons of security, perhaps to house officials engaged in the collection of customs dues, or both.[54] Finally, the front and rear curtains of many gates were redone in large and generally well-cut blocks of travertine, most or all of them reused.[55] Three of the restored gates, the Portae Praenestina-Labicana, Tiburtina, and Portuensis, bore the dedicatory inscriptions to Honorius commemorating the reconstruction of the Wall discussed further below.

Broadly speaking, the masonry of the upper sections of the Wall differs noticeably from its Aurelianic antecedents, though the technical charac-teristics of the two phases are similar enough, and their internal variants sufficiently diverse, to make them occasionally indistinguishable.[56] Aur-elianic brickwork is usually regular and skillfully laid, with well-leveled courses bonded with a tenacious, off-white mortar speckled with small, reddish *pozzolana* inclusions, and a module ranging commonly between 25 and 30cm, though it occasionally reaches as high as 34cm.[57] While there are significant variations between sectors, the bricks in individual curtains are quite uniform in thickness, and must either have been chosen with care if recycled, or made new.[58] Bonding courses, single files of large *bipedalis* bricks sunk deep into the cement core, their faces flush with the

---

[54] Richmond discussed all of these *controporte* save the one at the razed Porta Flaminia, the existence of which Cozza suggested on the basis of a Renaissance drawing by Heemskerck (Cozza 1993, 101), and the one today visible behind Porta Asinaria, which came to light when the rear of the gate was excavated in 1951; see Scarpa 1953, 87–8. Richmond thought these enclosures primarily connected with the collection of customs-duties, while Cozza has emphasized their potential military utility (Richmond 1930, 138; Cozza 1998, 101–2).

[55] Reused stones bearing fragmentary inscriptions appear, for example, in the Portae Pinciana, Tiburtina, and Appia. During the demolition of the Porta Flaminia, the majority of the blocks used in its facing were found to come from tombs of the early empire; see *BullCom* 1880, 169ff. and plates 12–13.

[56] As Richmond put it, "…although it is possible to detect a deterioration in the standard of the best (in the sense that the best work of the first period outclasses the best of the second), it is equally true that the best work of the second period is often superior to that of the first" (1930, 69).

[57] For general descriptions of the Aurelianic brickwork, in addition to the previously cited works of Richmond, Colini, Cozza, and Mancini, cf. also Heres 1982, 92ff.; Lugli 1957, 615. The modules cited are my own measurements, which seemed necessary in light of the significant discrepancies evident in past "descriptions" of the Wall's masonry. The numerical data are presented in Appendix A.

[58] The debate over the relative quantities of new and used bricks employed in the Wall is long-running and by no means yet resolved; it is discussed in more detail in Chapter 2. The state of the question is lucidly summarized in Coates-Stephens and Parisi 1999, 89 and n. 7.

surface of the Wall, occur at irregular intervals between one and two meters apart. In the subsequent heightening, the bricks used were less homogeneous, frequently thinner, and separated by thicker beds of a mortar whiter and coarser than the earlier stuff. The module tends to exceed 30cm, and bonding courses are almost nonexistent. Putlog holes, small, quadrangular apertures that housed supports for the scaffolding used by the construction crews, occur regularly for the first time (their absence in the Wall's initial phase is not terribly surprising when its relatively low maximum height is considered: Evidently, scaffoldings anchored in the ground were sufficient for the task). While these general-izations are neither so precise nor so universally applicable that appear-ance alone should play a deciding role in the resolution of debatable attributions, they hold sufficiently to permit a reasonably trained eye to distinguish at a glance, more often than not, where the first type ends and the second begins (Figure 1.18).

Such are the physical contours of the Wall, as they developed from its inception to the point where it reached the pinnacle of its physical development. The challenge for all since Richmond has been successfully to date the post-Aurelianic phases and to connect them with known historical circumstances and especially with people, chief among them Maxentius and Honorius, the only two emperors mentioned in the sources. The lone reference to a Maxentian intervention in the Codex-Calendar of 354, which properly speaking does not credit Maxentius with the laying of a single brick, but rather with the digging of an unfinished ditch around its outer perimeter, prompted Richmond to assign the great heightening to him, and to suggest that the Honorian building campaign described in the epigraphic and literary sources was mostly limited to work on the gates.[59] Yet even on their own merits alone, the texts give

---

[59] Chiefly to the installation of the travertine curtains; see Richmond 1930, 251ff. The *Chronographus* describes Maxentius' intervention thus (VZ 1, 281): *Fossatum aperuit, sed non perfecit.* Two additional texts require mention. The first is Lactantius' description of Maxentius' political maneuvers in 307 (*De Mortibus Persecutorum*, 27): (Maxentius)...*urbe munita et rebus omnibus diligenter instructa proficiscitur in Galliam, ut Constantinum partibus suis conciliaret suae minoris filiae nuptiis.* While the phrase *urbe munita* need not refer specifically to the Wall or the *fossatum*, it may well do. Less plausible is Coarelli's reinterpretation of an inscription found near the Sessorian Palace (*CIL* 6, 37118, dating approximately to the reign of Maxentius), which seeks to connect it with Maxentian work on the Wall. The inscription is a fragmentary list of donors of senatorial rank, all of whom contributed the substantial sum of 400,000 *sesterces* for an unspecified cause. Gatti originally suggested very cautiously that the money was destined for a bath complex, while Coarelli has proposed that it was to be used in the (putative) Maxentian restoration of the Wall itself, basing his argument on a dizzying sequence of conjectures (see G. Gatti, in

Figure 1.18 Tower G15: the Honorian masonry, with thinner bricks and wider mortar beds, begins in line with the two putlog holes.

better *prima facie* cause for assigning the primary reconstruction to Honorius, as he alone is credited with apparently extensive construction on the curtains, gates, and towers of the Wall, an undertaking commemorated in three dedicatory inscriptions as well as in a passage from Claudian's panegyric of 404 in honor of the sixth consulship of Honorius.[60]

Of greater importance for the dating argument is the standing stratigraphy of the Wall, which contains important clues, overlooked by Richmond, that together provide the key to the construction sequence already hinted at in the textual sources. In 1944, Antonio Colini made the crucial observation that in several sections of the Wall, there is a clear intermediate stratum between the Aurelianic brickwork and the fabric of the heightening, composed of alternating courses of brick and small,

BullCom 25 (1907), 115–21; Coarelli 1986, 29–31, esp. n. 143; cf. *LTUR* 3, 290–91). He first connected this inscription with another from the Forum, a dedication to Atteius Insteius Tertullus, prefect of the city in 307–8 (*PLRE* 1, 883, see under Tertullus 6), who also bears the (fragmentary) title *praefectus fabri*[... (*CIL* 6, 1696). Coarelli filled the lacuna by creating the otherwise totally unattested position of *praefectus fabri*[*cae muri et portarum*], whence he proposed that Tertullus, apparently serving simultaneously as *praefectus fabri*[*cae muri...*] and *praefectus urbi*, was responsible for the restoration of the Wall allegedly commemorated in the inscription from the Sessorian palace, which in fact mentions neither the Wall nor Tertullus. These would be dubious assumptions even if a large-scale Maxentian restoration were certainly attested (as Coarelli, following Richmond, believed). The further use of the inscription as "evidence" for work undertaken by Maxentius is untenable (as occurs in Cardilli *et al.* 1995, 45, a book co-written by Coarelli himself: here, the brackets have vanished from the utterly hypothetical *praefectus fabricae muri et portarum*, and the two unrelated inscriptions are conflated into one (!), given as *CIL* 6, 37118, which is said to refer to a restoration of the Wall carried out by Tertullus). Even assuming that Maxentius did work on the Wall, his reign is noteworthy for the number of costly buildings erected, a number of which could have been the object of the money in question.

[60] Claudian, *De sexto consulatu Honorii*, 529–36: *sic oculis placitura tuis insignior auctis/collibus et nota maior se Roma videndam/obtulit. addebant pulchrum nova moenia vultum/audito perfecta recens rumore Getarum,/profecitque opifex decori timor, et, vice mira,/quam pax intulerat, bello discussa senectus/erexit subitas turres cinctosque* [or *cunctosque*] *coegit/septem continuo colles iuvenescere muro.* Nibby was sufficiently impressed by these lines to base upon them in part his mistaken claim that Honorius built the existing circuit in its entirety (1820, 223–4). Of the texts of the three inscriptions (*CIL* 6, 1188, 1189, 1190), I give the text of 1189, still preserved beside the modern Porta Maggiore, as the most complete and best preserved: *S. P. Q. R./Imp(eratoribus) Caes(aribus) d(ominis) n(ostris duobus) principib(us) Arcadio et Honorio victorib(us) ac triumphatorib(us) semper Aug(ustis)/ob instauratos urbi aeternae muros, portas ac turres, egestis immensis ruderib(us), ex suggestione v(iri) c(larissimi)/et inlustris, com(itis) et magi(stri) utriusq(ue) militiae Stilichonis, ad perpetuitatem nominis eorum/ simulacra constituit,/curante Fl(avio) Macrobio Longiniano v(iro) c(larissimo), praef(ecto) urb (is), d(evoto) n(uminibus) m(aiestatibus)q(ue) eorum.* Given that the heightening of the Wall occurred under Honorius, the nature of the work described on the *muros, portas ac turres* is quite clear.

rectangular tufa blocks (*opus vittatum* or *listatum*).[61] Noting the striking technical similarities between this work and that of the securely attributed structures at the Villa of Maxentius on the Via Appia, Colini proposed that the major heightening of the curtains, gates, and towers was in fact carried out under Honorius in 401–3, and that the *opus vittatum* segments represented Maxentian repairs to the original circuit.[62] While decades passed before the value of Colini's remarks was fully appreciated, his hypothesis was broadly vindicated and at last incorporated into the mainstream scholarly tradition on the Wall in the 1980s, with the work of Theodora Heres and Lucos Cozza. Both concurred that the circuit contains numerous and often quite expansive *opus vittatum* repairs between the Aurelianic brickwork and that of the heightening; and that the technique of these sections often resembles that of securely Maxentian structures, while that of the heightening finds its closest analogues in the fifth century.[63]

The significance of this intermediate stratum increases greatly in light of another observation made by Colini that has since fallen on fallow ground: Even sections of facing that clearly date between the Aurelianic brickwork and that of the principal elevation above are occasionally neither homogeneous nor contemporary, and there is clear evidence at one point for at least two discrete interventions. This comes from a curtain near the Porta Maggiore, which contains traces of two superimposed parapets, both in brick and with their merlons intact, the second of which is in turn surmounted by a layer in *opus vittatum* from which the brickwork of the heightened curtain springs (Figure 1.19).[64] As it is

---

[61] Generally on *opus vittatum/listatum*, see Righini 2005.

[62] Colini 1944, 110 and n. 7. The period of the Honorian restorations is fixed by the prosopography of the three dedicatory inscriptions and the details of Claudian's poem (of 404), all discussed in detail by Richmond (1930, 30–6); cf. Cozza 1998, 99. On the putatively Maxentian sections, see Appendix B.

[63] For decades, Colini's thesis received scant attention. While L. Cassanelli *et al.* readily accepted his views in their 1974 book on Rome's fortifications (42–3), and G. Somella Beda concurred on the date of the heightening, though without mention of Colini, he could still be ignored totally as recently as 1995, when Cardilli *et al.* were content to accept Richmond's attribution to Maxentius without even a mention of the alternative dating: see Cardilli *et al.* 1995, 68–9; Somella Beda 1972, 9. Works in English resolutely championed Richmond for decades, and to this day, a full explanation of the reattribution to Honorius and the reasons for preferring it has yet to appear. For generally uncritical regurgitations of Richmond, see Johnson 1948, 261–5; and M. Todd, who in 1978 still felt it "beyond question" that the main heightening predated Honorius (Todd 1978, 47ff.); cf. also Johnson 1983a, 118–19. Hence, much recent Anglophone scholarship on the period continues to labor under this misconception: see e.g. Watson 1999, 151; Christie 2006, 321; Lenski 2008, 205. The seminal works in Colini's resuscitation are Heres 1982, esp. 103–5; and Cozza 1987, 25ff.

[64] See Colini 1944, 111, with an arresting photo of the same curtain shown in Figure 1.19.

Figure 1.19 Two superimposed sets of brick merlons topped by a third intervention in *opus vittatum*, between the Porta Praenestina-Labicana and tower G1.

difficult to imagine that two new parapets would have been constructed in the three decades separating Aurelian from Maxentius, the elevated curtain which springs from the uppermost of these parapets must date after the reign of the latter.

Cozza has further strengthened the case for a fifth-century heightening with his examination of the decorative motifs incorporated into the brickwork of several of the Wall's elevated curtains. Among them are several clearly "Christian" crosses that unquestionably formed part of the original fabric of the heightening, which are much more likely to belong to the beginning of the fifth century than the beginning of the fourth (Figures 1.20–1.22).[65] As Cozza also noted, these decorations are closely paralleled in the walls of Terracina, which are best dated to the second quarter of the fifth century.[66] In Rome itself, the church of S. Giovanni e Paolo on the Caelian, which is almost exactly contemporary with the inscriptions on the gates of the Wall, makes for the most compelling comparison.[67] Here, the technique of the brickwork – its module, the color and thickness of the bricks, and the composition of the mortar – closely echoes that of the heightened sections of the Wall. Additionally, there is a well-preserved brick cross in the facing of the apse that strongly resembles the ones in the Wall. The nearby church of S. Stefano, built later in the fifth century, also contains similar brickwork and decorative motifs, as do a number of other roughly contemporary buildings in and around Rome.[68]

All told, then, the upper sections of the circuit were executed in a style much more characteristic of the fifth century than the early fourth. Coupled with the unmistakable signs of an earlier phase (or phases) of limited heightening and repair, this observation makes it difficult not to connect the principal elevation of the Wall with the literary and epigraphic record of Honorius' building campaign of 401–3.

1.4 The fifth and sixth centuries

The beginning of the fifth century marks something of a watershed in the history of the Wall, for at this point, "primary" construction – significant

---

[65] Other crosses, inscribed and in relief, appear on many of the new travertine gateway arches, as at the Portae Pinciana, Latina, Appia, Asinaria, and Ostiensis.

[66] See Christie and Rushworth 1988, esp. 86; Ortolani 1988, 76ff.; cf. Cozza 1987, 28–9.

[67] For additional comparisons and further technical analysis, see Heres 1982, 126ff.

[68] On S. Stefano, cf. Cozza 1987, figs. 28a–d; and more generally Heres 1982, 138ff. The basilica of S. Sabina on the Aventine, built about thirty years after the Wall, is another particularly good comparison.

Figure 1.20 Curtain M25–6, detail of cross in Honorian brickwork.

Figure 1.21 Cross in Honorian brickwork, interior facing of curtain L39–40.

Figure 1.22 Porta Ostiensis, east tower, Honorian brickwork with cross.

new work as opposed to maintenance and restoration of what already existed – came almost completely to an end. The following two centuries present something of a puzzle, which recent scholarly advances have in some respects only complicated. On the one hand, the literary record for the period, which is on the whole more expansive and detailed than ever before, suggests that often substantial interventions in the fabric of the Wall occurred with some regularity. On the other, extant traces of these repairs are proving difficult to identify and date with any degree of precision, whence there is a relative scarcity of material evidence that has recently increased dramatically with the redating of the vast majority of the masonry once attributed to this period to the eighth and ninth centuries. Yet the explicit testimony to the upkeep of Rome's defenses in sources as varied as the *Novellae* of Valentinian III, the *Variae* of Cassiodorus, and best of all Procopius' account of the Gothic Wars cannot be dismissed as pure fantasy.[69] Indeed, such references jointly foster the impression that the rulers of Rome consistently attended to the defenses of the city, in an era when assiduous maintenance is *a priori* likely to have been required to counteract a long series of potentially destructive occurrences: in the generations that followed the heightening of its enceinte under Honorius, Rome was sacked three times, by Alaric in 410, Genseric in 455, and Ricimer in 472, and experienced in addition its share of

[69] On the historical credibility of Procopius, who for all his occasional distortions was in the thick of many of the events he describes in the *Wars*, see Rance 2005; cf. also Cameron 1985.

natural disasters, among them destructive earthquakes in 443 and 502.[70] The subsequent events of the Gothic Wars in the middle of the sixth century were probably more damaging still. The challenge is therefore to fill in as many of the architectural lacunae as possible, and then to combine the resulting data with the vague but tantalizing implications of the written sources, the better to establish how the Wall was treated by those responsible for guiding Rome through one of the most tumultuous periods in its history.

If Valentinian III's *Novella* of 440 is any indication, provisions were already being made for the repair of damaged sections of the circuit scant decades after Honorius.[71] Thereafter, serious work was evidently performed at the beginning of the sixth century, when the Ostrogothic ruler of Italy Theoderic is recorded as having shown particular concern for the upkeep of Rome's public buildings and its enceinte, though the sources are insufficiently precise to locate his repairs to the Wall.[72] Fortunately, the material record furnishes more revealing information in the form of stamped bricks bearing the name of Theoderic himself. Four variant types are known, all found in small, localized groups. These stamps are important insofar as they theoretically allow the tracts of brickwork where they occur to be attributed

---

[70] For the quake of 443, see *Fasti Vindobonenses Priores* (*anno* 443, *MGH AA* 9, 301); on that of 502, *Victoris episcopi tonnensis chronica* (*anno* 502; *MGH AA* 11, p. 193); cf. Guidoboni and Molin 1989, 199–202.

[71] *Nov. Val.* 3, 5: *Ex illa sana parte totam sollicitudinem omnemque fortitudinem vestris animis censuimus auferendam, ut huius edicti serie cognoscat universitas, nullum de Romanis civibus, nullum de corporatis, ad militiam esse cogendum, sed tantum ad murorum portarumque custodiam, quoties usus exegerit, inlustris viri praefecti urbis dispositionibus ab omnibus obsequendum. Cuius ordinatio etiam in muris, turribus et portis, quae sunt labefacta, restituet, ita ut a reparatione murorum vel omnium, quae supra dicta sunt, nullus penitus excusetur.*

[72] See *Anon. Vales.* (*MGH AA* 9, p. 324; *anno* 500): *Per tricennalem triumphans (Theodericus) populo ingressus palatium, exhibens Romanis ludos circensium. Donavit populo Romano et pauperibus annonas singulis annis centum viginti milia modios et ad restaurationem palatii, seu ad recuperationem moeniae civitatis, singulis annis libras ducentas de arca vinaria dari praecepit;* and Cassiodorus, *Chronica* (*MGH AA* 11, p. 160; *anno* 500): *Hoc anno (Patricio et Hypatio Conss.) dn. rex Theodericus Romam cunctorum votis expetitus advenit et senatum suum mira affabilitate tractans Romanae plebi donavit annonas, atque admirandis moeniis deputata per singulos annos maxima pecuniae quantitate subvenit.* The likely conclusion that the term *moenia*, which by this time had long had a generic sense of "public buildings" (as already in e.g. Victor, *de Caes.* 39 and 45), was meant to include the Wall is backed by a later reference in Isidore of Seville, who states unambiguously that Theoderic attended to the walls (*muri*) of the city (*Historia Gothorum, MGH AA* 11, p. 283; *anno* 513): *Inde Italiam repetens (Theodericus) aliquamdiu omni cum prosperitate regnavit per quem etiam urbis Romae dignitas non parva est restituta: muros namque eius iste redintegravit, cuius rei gratia a senatu inauratam statuam meruit.* On the broadening connotations of *moenia* in late antiquity, see Della Valle 1959, 167–76; cf. Richmond 1930, 37.

quite precisely to the years of Theoderic's reign (493–527). While it is certainly possible that some of these bricks were recycled from other structures and reused long after Theoderic, Richmond was probably right in thinking it "hardly likely that not a single one of the known groups found belonged to him."[73] As Cassiodorus informs us that large numbers of bricks were produced for the restoration of Rome's *moenia* under Theoderic, it seems all the more probable that at least some of the stamped bricks found in the Wall were inserted at the approximate time of their manufacture.[74] This being the case, the known stamps would serve to identify two areas implicated in Theoderic's restoration. All four types turned up in the rubble of the collapsed curtain G19–20, east of the Porta Asinaria, and one of them surfaced also during the dismantling of the towers of the Porta Flaminia.[75] As neither of these sections of the Wall survive, however, there is little more to be said about the extent or the technique of the repairs.[76]

In the case of the Porta Flaminia, however, the presence of the stamp of Theoderic is nonetheless useful for its potential bearing on the Porta Appia, the largest and architecturally most intricate of all the extant city gates, and the point in the circuit where the most significant, demonstrably post-Honorian construction still in existence occurs (Figure 1.23). The complex phases of its building and repair are described at length by Richmond, whose interpretation of the remains, however, should be modified to restore to Honorius the additions ascribed to Maxentius, and those attributed to Honorius to a still later period.[77] In short, it seems that the Porta Appia was once typical of the larger Honorian gates, with lofty new towers, built over and around those of Aurelian, which looked much like the elevated towers of the Porta Ostiensis, and those newly added to the Porta Asinaria.[78] Richmond was able to observe what he considered clear traces of this phase – though it is almost entirely obscured by later additions – which

---

[73] Richmond 1930, 37.

[74] Cassiod. *Var.* 1, 25, 2 (*anno* 509–10): *Sabiniano V. S. Theodericus rex... Dudum siquidem propter Romanae moenia civitatis, ubi studium nobis semper impendere infatigabilis ambitus erit, portum Licini deputatis reditibus reparari iussio nostra constituit ut xxv. milia tegularum annua illatione praestaret.* [On Cassiodorus' use of the term *moenia*, see above n. 72]

[75] On the *bolli* from the Castrense-Asinaria stretch, all corresponding with types *CIL* 15, 1664, 1665a, 1665b, and 1669, see Armstrong, Pfeiffer, and van Buren 1905, 52 (nos. 214–16), 54 (nos. 217–18), etc.; the example from the Porta Flaminia appears as *CIL* 15, 1665b, 27, where it is said to have been found among the stored rubble from the gate.

[76] On the Porta Flaminia, rudimentarily documented during its demolition in the 1870s, see Appendix C.

[77] For Richmond's full treatment of the gate, see 1930, 121–42; cf. 1927a, 59–63. The full case for the dating of the various post-Honorian phases of the gate is made below in Appendix C.

[78] Cf. Cambedda and Ceccherelli 1990, 47.

Figure 1.23 Porta Appia, exterior view.

he attributed to Maxentius only because he believed him responsible for the reconstruction now confidently ascribed to Honorius; there is no reason to question Richmond's *relative* chronology, however, nor therefore to doubt that all subsequent additions to the gate date *after* Honorius (Figure 1.24).[79]

Chief among these later additions were the monumental square casings added at the foot of the two gate-towers. Built in reused blocks of fine marble, these stone shells enveloped the semicircular bases of the Honorian towers, to which they were firmly bonded by a solid mass of concrete poured into the interstices between the backs of the marble blocks and the existing brick facings. The curtain of the gateway was also refaced, front and back, in the same building campaign. The original two travertine arches were replaced with a single one, faced with the same sort of marble blocks used in the casings, and fitted closely to the projecting flanks of the square towers on both sides (Figure 1.25).[80] Above the marble

[79] Richmond 1930, 124–5.

[80] Cf. Richmond 1930, 125. The older curtain, then, is either that of Honorius, or more probably (as Richmond thought) the original one of Aurelian, left in place by Honorius' builders. It should be noted that it has become something of a *locus communis* to assign the new bastions and gate-curtain to Honorius, perhaps because Richmond's attribution has been followed without adequate attention to his crucial identification of the intermediate phase beneath, which is far more likely to

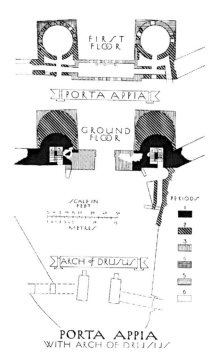

Figure 1.24 Porta Appia, construction phases. (After Richmond 1930, p. 123.)

facings, the angular contours of the casings continue upward in brick, covering the windows of the Honorian towers behind,[81] and rising approximately to the height of the upper wall-walk. The rough joins between the tops of the square casings and the semicircular facings of the older towers were clearly visible prior to the restorations of the 1920s.[82] At some point, the towers were also heightened by an additional story, thus becoming the tallest in the Wall. The brickwork of these top chambers is distinct from the rest, and their walls are set back noticeably

be Honorian: see e.g. Ceccherelli and D'Ippolito 2006 (esp. 88–93), whose careful observation and analysis of the standing stratigraphy of the gate unfortunately begins with the assumption – never critically examined – that the square facings are Honorian; this despite Ceccherelli's earlier acceptance of the intermediate Honorian phase, with all its unavoidable implications for the relative chronology of the overlying additions (Cambedda and Ceccherelli 1990, 47–8).

[81] My observation of the inside of the first-floor chambers convinces me that they belong to the period of the Wall's heightening, as Richmond already believed. The module of the brickwork (well over 30 cm), and the springing of the window arches from a slight setback are both characteristic of fifth-century work in general, and Honorian construction on the Wall in particular; cf. Heres 1982, 104. The square casings that variously obstruct or completely block the windows must be later still.

[82] Richmond 1930, 125.

Figure 1.25 Porta Appia, internal facing. Spoliated blocks of marble blocking one of the original two entranceways.

on their interior facing from the thicker Honorian structures below, which still conserve traces of their original ceiling vaults (Figure 1.26). Perhaps at the same time, judging by its technical characteristics, a second covered walkway between the towers was added above the Honorian portcullis chamber.[83]

While the Honorian heightening of the Wall gives a solid *terminus post quem* for most or all of these modifications, a precise *terminus ante* is more difficult to establish. They are likely not later than the sixth century, however. From the Lombard invasion in 568 until the eighth century, there is no indication that anything beyond the most essential localized repairs to the Wall occurred; and when work on a grander scale recommenced, it no longer belonged to the Roman building tradition to which the latest additions to the Porta Appia still clearly did. Further, the monumental marble façade probably does not date to the period of Rome's involvement in the Gothic Wars, between 536 and 552. It has a distinctly ornamental

---

[83] In any case, a look at the external facing of the two passageways demonstrates that the upper one was added, in considerably less regular masonry, after the lower (cf. Richmond 1930, 137), which does look much like the work of Honorius.

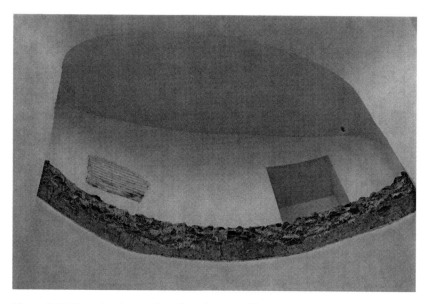

Figure 1.26 Porta Appia, interior of north tower. The remains of Honorian vaulting are visible beneath a later addition.

character that would seem incongruous in the context of the hurried and utilitarian repairs, described at length by Procopius, undertaken by Belisarius and others in defense of the city. Its custom-made cornice in particular is hardly the sort of architectural flourish likely to be included among the preparations for an imminent siege (Figure 1.27).[84] But while the facings cannot date much later than the Wars, it is possible that they were erected in their immediate aftermath, when the Byzantine commander Narses restored various structures in and around Rome.[85] Among his projects was a rebuilding of the Ponte Salario, the

[84] The cornice was carved after the blocks beneath were in place, as it follows their uneven contours exactly. Richmond thought it characteristic of the "late Roman" period, following J. Strzygowski's study of the Porta Aurea in Constantinople, one of the gates in the fifth-century land walls of the city, which does broadly resemble the stone façade of the Porta Appia, and has a similar cornice (though Stryzgowski nowhere mentions the Porta Appia among his comparative examples, of which he has several from Italy); see Richmond 1930, 131, and Stryzgowski 1893, esp. 12–13. It is at least safe to say that the cornice, and thus everything underneath it as well, is best dated no later than the sixth century. On the date of the Porta Aurea, see below n. 87.
[85] The Pragmatic Sanction of 554 stipulates that funds for the repair of Rome's public buildings were again to be drawn from the same sources as previously (*Constitutio pragmatica* 25; see below Chapter 6, n. 1). Cf. Coates-Stephens 1998, 167 and n. 3, listing additional references for unspecified repairs made by Narses.

Figure 1.27 Porta Appia, decorative cornice and join between projecting bastion and façade of gateway arch.

surviving arches of which are realized in well-cut blocks of travertine, employed with technical proficiency comparable to that displayed at the Porta Appia.[86] Further, if the distinct similarity between the Porta Appia and the Porta Aurea at Constantinople, which likewise featured monumental square towers in white marble, is more than casual, it is probably best attributed to an effort at conscious emulation on the part of Rome's Byzantine garrison, acting to shape the greatest gate of the city in the image of the most monumental entrance in their own capital, the "New Rome" on the Bosporus.[87] All things considered, then, the final phases of the gate best fit chronological parameters stretching from the first quarter of the fifth century through the third quarter of the sixth, with some preference for the latter date.

Still less can be said with any certainty about the remainder of the circuit, for which there is presently no scholarly consensus on the individuation – in theory or in practice – of other work of the fifth and

---

[86] The reconstruction is recorded in an extant dedicatory inscription, *CIL* 6, 1199 (*ICUR* 1, 77a + b), dated to the thirty-ninth year of Justinian's reign (AD 565).

[87] On the ongoing debate over the date of the Porta Aurea, see Bardill 1999, who convincingly re-attributes it to Thedosius I (in the context of his triumphal entry into Constantinople in 391 following the defeat of the usurper Magnus Maximus in 388); cf. Mango 2000, 179 with n. 45.

sixth centuries. This is true even for the period of the Gothic Wars, which
witnessed the series of large-scale destructions and repairs described by
Procopius: the recent redating of the sections of the Wall once attributed
to Belisarius to the eighth and ninth centuries has left the best-
documented period in the Wall's history bereft of archaeological corollar-
ies in the monument itself.[88] Yet *a priori*, remains there must be. If any
serious damage from the earthquakes of 443 and 502 had yet to be
repaired in 536, when Belisarius prepared the Wall in anticipation of the
first Gothic siege, it must then have been addressed.[89] Likewise, whatever
the correct interpretation of Procopius' statement that Totila destroyed a
third of the Wall in 547 to render it indefensible, great harm was clearly
done, which Belisarius remedied sufficiently to hold the city against a
renewed assault.[90]

Subsequently, Totila reoccupied the city, which he then attempted to
restore, according to Procopius.[91] Among his projects, Procopius lists a
substantial enlargement of the fortifications of Hadrian's Mausoleum,
which had long been incorporated into the circuit of the Wall as a sort
of monumental fortified bridgehead on the far side of the Pons Aelius.[92]
Totila appears not to have neglected the remainder of the Wall, as it still
presented a difficult obstacle to Narses in his final capture of the city in
552: It is worth mentioning that the Byzantine troops are said in the end to
have gone over it at a poorly guarded section, and nowhere through it.[93]
Finally, there is the distinct possibility of further postwar repairs under
Narses, alluded to previously. Therefore: on the likely assumption that
every brick (or stone) laid in the Wall in these turbulent decades has not
since turned to dust, some of them must remain. As only Procopius'
account is detailed enough to give any sense of what some of the repairs

[88] On the redating, discussed in more detail below, see Coates-Stephens 1999, 210–14; 1998,
167–71; 1995, *passim*; cf. Mancini 2001, 37–53.
[89] See *BG* 1, 14, 14–15; cf. *LP* 1, 290 (*anno* 536): *Ingressus autem Vilisarius patricius in urbem
Romam IIII id. decemb., custodiis et munitionibus vel fabricis murorum aut reparationem fossati
circumdedit civitatem Romanam et munivit.*
[90] For Totila's destruction, see *BG* 3, 22, 6–7. Procopius' "third" (*tritomorion*) has been much
discussed, as enough of the Wall survives to demonstrate that Totila cannot literally have
leveled a third of it. Richmond suggested that Totila perhaps reduced the Wall by a third of its
thickness, removing the exterior facings and leaving the more vulnerable core exposed
(Richmond 1930, 42). On Belisarius' *ad hoc* repairs and his successful defense, see *BG* 3, 24.
The much briefer accounts in the *Auctarium Marcellini* and Jordanes generally match
Procopius' version of events: see *Auct. Marc.*, MGH AA 11, p. 108; Jordanes, *Romana*,
MGH AA 5, p. 50.
[91] *BG* 3, 37, 3.　　[92] *BG* 4, 33, 14–16.　　[93] *BG* 4, 33, 17–21.

may actually have looked like, it is obviously crucial. A brief look at what he says will suffice to assess the relevance of his comments to the existing remains, and to explain how past commentators have been led astray.

The relevant sections of Procopius' history begin with Belisarius' arrival in Rome in December of 536. At this point, the only specified addition to his general repairs of the Wall was the construction of a new type of "L" shaped battlement, realized by adding a spur to the left side of the existing merlons, which projected back onto the rampart-walk behind and served to cover the left side of its defenders, who thus had no need to carry a shield, and had both hands free for the use of their weapons.[94] He is said also to have re-dug the ditch in front of the Wall (the one begun but left unfinished by Maxentius?), but this nowhere remains, nor would it likely be much help in dating repairs to the Wall if it did.[95] As for the battlements, since the Honorian parapet into which they were incorporated is almost everywhere gone, there cannot be many surviving examples. They have been identified with confidence only in one brief tract between the Portae Labicana and Tiburtina.[96]

The next bit of pointed architectural description comes from the winter of 547–8, when Belisarius repaired the "third" of the Wall razed by Totila. This he is said to have accomplished in the remarkably short span of twenty-five days, in the following manner: "Gathering stones which lay close by, he (Belisarius) threw them one on top of the other, regardless of order, without putting anything at all between the stones, since he had neither lime nor anything else of the sort, but caring only that the face of the masonry should be preserved, and he set a great quantity of stakes at the outside."[97] This passage first led Nibby, followed by Richmond and nearly everyone else, to attribute to Belisarius a number of sections of the Wall composed of large, reused blocks of tufa and *peperino* rather roughly fitted together.[98] The difficulty here is that the blocks in these places are set firmly in beds of mortar, into which are also often set bricks and small

[94] *BG* 1, 14, 15.   [95] *Ibid.*

[96] Richmond first noted these probable traces of Belisarius' L-shaped merlons, "where the front of the merlons has gone, while the traverse wall is to be seen in section" (1930, 38); the projecting spurs of these "traverse walls" came clearly to light during the course of the restorations executed in 1965: see Romeo 1965–7, 177–8, with fig. 52. Precisely such battlements topped the early fifth-century enceinte at Saint-Bertrand-de-Comminges, where recent studies have revealed remarkably well-preserved traces of the original parapet: see Wood 2002, with references to similar features documented elsewhere, e.g. Trier.

[97] *BG* 3, 24, 4. The translation is that of H. B. Dewing in the *Loeb* edition of Procopius (vol. 4).

[98] See Nibby 1820, 254–5; Richmond 1930, 42; cf. Cassanelli *et al.* 1974, 42–3, with plate 60.

stones, without which many of the larger blocks would lack the support
necessary to remain in place (Figures 1.28–1.29).[99] The mortar and small
insertions, that is, are integral components of the existing structures,
which thus do not fit Procopius' description nearly as well as a casual
glance might suggest. Further, this construction technique finds far closer
parallels, in Rome and beyond, in securely dated work of the eighth and
ninth centuries than it does in the sixth.

These observations, in conjunction with the passages in the *Liber
Pontificalis* that assign repairs of some magnitude to a number of eighth-
and ninth-century popes, combine to make a convincing argument for
assigning the tracts in question to the later period. In this case, no evident
traces of the earlier repairs would remain, a conclusion not terribly
surprising given the decidedly *ad hoc* and impermanent nature of their
execution.[100] It is nonetheless possible that the patched sections were
those undermined by Totila, subsequently restored in more permanent
form, perhaps using some of the stones employed in the original
hasty repairs.[101] Certainly the fact that no piles of unbonded stones
remain demonstrates that at some subsequent stage, the parts of the
Wall which they faced were reconstructed; this leaves the early medieval
tufa facings as a promising locator for the demolitions orchestrated
by Totila.

The final addition to Rome's fortifications mentioned by Procopius is
Totila's expansion of the defenses of Hadrian's mausoleum, where he is
said to have attached an additional circuit of walls shortly before Narses'
final capture of the city in 552.[102] As the entire complex has since been

---

[99] See Coates-Stephens 1995, 515; cf. Mancini 2001, 35. Richmond explained the presence of the
mortar as an addition of Narses to the face of the unmortared blocks, which he thought
remained *in situ* (Richmond 1930, 42); the particulars of their construction, however, do not
support this interpretation.

[100] Interestingly, at the time when Gell prepared his engravings for Nibby's book in the early
nineteenth century, a pile of large stone blocks, obviously unbonded and hence much more
closely resembling the sort of work described by Procopius, was visible at the base of a tower
west of the Porta Asinaria, beneath S. Giovanni in Laterano (see Nibby 1820, tav. XX; cf.
Coates-Stephens 1998, 171; 1999, 213–14).

[101] Cf. Coates-Stephens 1999, 213.

[102] *BG* 4, 33, 14: ἐν ὑστάτῳ δὲ λογισάμενος [Totila], ὡς ἐς ὀλίγους ἀποκεκριμένοι οὐχ οἷοί
τέ εἰσι τὸ λοιπόν Γότθοι ἅπαντα τὸν περίβολον Ῥώμης διαφυλάξαι, τειχίσματι βραχεῖ
ὀλίγην τινὰ τῆς πόλεως μοῖραν ἀμφὶ τὸν Ἀδριανοῦ Περιβαλὼν τάφον καὶ αὐτὸ τῷ
προτέρῳ τείχει ἐνάψας φρουρίου κατεστήσατο σχῆμα. ("He ultimately reasoned that,
since the Goths had been reduced to a few, they were not able to guard all the rest of the wall
of Rome; and surrounding a small part of the city with a short wall around the tomb of
Hadrian, and attaching it to the earlier wall, he made a sort of stronghold").

Figure 1.28 Curtain L15–16: early medieval restoration.

Figure 1.29 Tower M10 (interior facing): detail of early medieval restoration.

drastically refashioned, however, no plausible traces of sixth-century for-tifications remain.[103]

---

[103] D'Onofrio suggested that a part of the Leonine Wall constructed in *opus quadratum* essentially identical to the tufa restorations of the Aurelian Wall originally belonged to Totila's fortifications (D'Onofrio 1971, 63), but it far more likely belongs to the ninth century,

Taken as a whole, Procopius' narrative is remarkable for its unusually keen sense of the strategic and tactical potential of walls writ large. For Procopius, at least in the personae of his characters, battles and entire wars can hang on the fate of a wall. Rome's enceinte is a protagonist in his reckoning of events to an extent that makes it difficult to believe that it was not seen as such by other leading political and military minds of the day, who cannot then have been oblivious to the importance of keeping it in good repair. Yet for all Procopius' value in this and other respects, his account is of minimal utility for individuating and dating standing tracts of the Wall, none of which appear to correspond with the limited technical indicators he gives. The remaining fifth- and sixth-century sources are still less informative. Hence, if additional traces from the period between Honorius and the later sixth century are to be identified, only careful analysis of the standing remains will serve, coupled where possible with comparative references to roughly contemporary structures in Rome and beyond.[104]

The same should indeed be said for the seventh century, a period which the sparseness of the literary record has conspired to erase from the architectural history of the Wall, as has the traditional conception of the era as a sort of black hole in the narrative fabric of Roman history. Yet it is entirely possible that repairs continued to occur: as it turns out, all indications from a crucial series of recent excavations suggest that Rome's socio-economic landscape in the seventh century far more closely resembled that of the century before than the one following; and that, as in so many other respects, construction techniques of the period maintained a broad continuity with the "classical" past that was definitively ruptured only in the eighth century.[105] The seventh-century churches of S. Agnese and S. Pancrazio were built in a

with the rest of the Wall, as Ward-Perkins and Gibson realized (1979, 50–1; 1983, 226). Of course, the blocks in this particular section may again be material recycled from earlier fortifications, perhaps even Totila's. Alternately, they could have been among the more than 12,000 tufa blocks said to have been taken from the embankments of the Tiber for the reconstruction of the covered colonnade to St. Peter's by Pope Hadrian I (*LP* 1, 507).

[104] My preliminary efforts in this direction are reported in Appendix C.

[105] The important recent excavations at the Crypta Balbi and in the vicinity of the imperial fora are considered in more detail in Chapter 4; the results are briefly synthesized, and seventh-century continuity emphasized, in Santangeli Valenzani 2003b, 115–26 (with essential bibliography). On construction techniques, see Santangeli Valenzani 2007, 2003b, 120–4; and esp. 2002, 419–26.

Figure 1.30 S. Agnese, exterior of north wall of apse.

typically late antique *opus vittatum* that is worlds apart from the
spoliated tufa blocks and rudimentary brickwork employed in Roman
churches of the eighth and ninth centuries (Figure 1.30). Other signs
suggest that it would be unwise to assume that the Wall was totally abandoned or ignored. It was certainly in sufficient repair to withstand repeated
Lombard sieges at the end of the sixth century, though its defensive viability
in the seventh is more difficult to gauge.[106] Still, as a *curator* was still being
appointed to maintain the imperial palace near the end of the seventh
century, it is possible that ongoing provision was also made for the upkeep
of the Wall.[107]

[106] Rome was surrounded in 579, for example, when news of Pelagius II's election could not
go to Constantinople for imperial confirmation (*LP* 1, 309). Under Gregory I (590–604),
provisions were made for the defense of the city against Agilulf and the Lombards
that may have involved work on the Wall, though this is nowhere stated. The guarding
of the Wall, however, was apparently an important concern: see *GR* 9, 240 (*anno* 599):
*Romana enim civitas peccatis nostris facientibus diversis est attrita languoribus, ut neque
in murorum custodia idonei persistant*; cf. *GR* 2, 45 and 5, 36, cited below in Chapter 4,
nn. 158–9.

[107] See Chapter 6. The epitaph of Plato, the father of the future pope John VII, proclaims
him the latest in what was presumably a succession of officials charged with the *cura
palatii Urbis Romae* (*ICUR* 2/1, p. 442, 152, *anno* 687 [*LP* I, 386, n. 1]); cf. Augenti
1996, 46ff.

1.5   The early-medieval renaissance of the Aurelian Wall

The final significant building phase of the Wall's first six centuries was also
the last to be recognized in its standing stratigraphy. Though the numerous passages in the *Liber Pontificalis* describing eighth- and ninth-century
papal restorations to the Wall were of course known, the absence of
corresponding physical remains, coupled with the near-complete silence
of the literary – and of course archaeological – record for the century and a
half following the close of Procopius' narrative in 552, resulted until the
very recent past in a general sense that early-medieval attempts to restore
the Wall were negligible at best, and by implication that the *LP* passages
were the whimsical hyperbole of pliant papal chroniclers seeking to paint
the meager achievements of their patrons in the rosiest possible light.
Traditional histories of the Wall hence tended to end in the mid
sixth century, leaving it to fall thereafter into a state of oblivion that
fit comfortably into prevailing narratives of "dark-age" Rome.[108]
Coates-Stephens' "rediscovery" of the later restorations was hence something of a watershed moment that necessitates a new appraisal of the
testimony of the *LP* and the concerted papal interest in the defenses of
the city which it chronicles.

   As it turns out, the reappearance of the Wall in writing at the beginning
of the eighth century marks the beginning of a new tradition of papal
involvement in its upkeep that was to endure, albeit with lapses, through
the nineteenth century. Three popes in the first half of the eighth century
are credited with work on the Wall in the *Liber Pontificalis*, beginning
with Sisinnius I in 708, followed by Gregory II (715–31) and Gregory III
(731–41). Sisinnius is said only to have ordered the preparation of mortar
for repairs to the Wall, which his imminent death prevented him from
realizing.[109] Subsequently, Gregory II began to restore the circuit beginning from the Porta S. Lorenzo (Tiburtina), though the project was
delayed by "adverse circumstances and various tumults," among them
repeated, imperially sanctioned attempts at his deposition and a particularly nasty flood.[110] Hence, the bulk of the work was apparently left to

---

[108] Neither Richmond nor Todd, for example, seriously countenanced the possibility of
    substantial work on the Wall in the centuries following the Byzantine reconquest: see
    Richmond 1930, 267; Todd 1978, 67.
[109] *LP* 1, 388: *Qui et calcarias pro restauratione murorum iussit dequoquere.*
[110] *LP* 1, 396: *Hic exordio pontificatus sui calcarias dequoquere iussit; a portico sancti Laurentii
    inquoans, huius civitatis muros restaurare decreverat; et aliquam partem faciens, emergentibus
    incongruis variisque tumultibus praepeditus est.*

Gregory III, who repaired "the greatest part of the walls of the city."[111] Following these efforts, the Wall preserved its defensive integrity sufficiently to withstand the siege of the Lombard king Aistulf in 756, which lasted three months and involved multiple parts of the circuit.[112] There was evidently no lack of crumbling sections in the years following the siege, as the *LP* credits Hadrian I (772–95) and Leo IV (847–55) with the most extensive restorations of all. Hadrian is said to have spent 100 pounds of gold to put the circuit into working order, rebuilding entire curtains and towers "destroyed to the foundations."[113] The compiler of the life of Leo IV is more specific still. In addition to making general repairs to the circuit, Leo is said to have replaced the wooden gates of the city, and rebuilt fifteen towers "from the ground up," including one on each bank of the Tiber by the Porta Portuensis which are described in detail.[114]

The *LP* thus indicates a series of significant building campaigns between approximately 715 and 850, which have at last been accounted for in the standing stratigraphy of the Wall.[115] In addition to the curtains and towers reconstructed with the roughly leveled tufa blocks discussed previously, further repairs were executed in distinctively undulating brickwork, composed of reused bricks in all shapes and sizes, joined by thin courses of a friable grey mortar liberally

---

[111] *LP* 1, 420: *Huius temporibus plurima pars murorum huius civitatis Romanae restaurata est....*

[112] The siege is described in lugubrious detail in two surviving letters of Stephen II to Pippin, requesting the latter's immediate aid (*CC* 8–9). Aistulf himself is said to have camped at the Porta Salaria, while another part of his army invested all three Transtiberine gates; a contingent of Beneventans meanwhile beset the southern part of the city, at the Portae Asinaria and Ostiensis (called the *Portae beati Iohannis baptiste* and *beati Pauli apostoli*, respectively; see *CC* 8, p. 495); cf. also *LP* 1, 441ff. Siege engines were also used against the Wall, evidently with little success, though they may have contributed to the damage later repaired by Hadrian I: see *CC* 9, p. 499: *...cum diversis machinis et adinventionibus plurimis contra nos ad muros istius Romanae urbis commiserunt;* cf. Mancini 2001, 38; Coates-Stephens 1999, 210–11.

[113] *LP* 1, 501: *Verum etiam et muros atque turres huius Romane urbis quae diruti erant et usque ad fundamenta destructi renovavit atque uiliter omnia in circuitu restauravit; ubi et multa stipendia tribuit, tam in mercedes eorum qui ipsum murum fabricaverunt, quamque in ipsorum alimentis, simulque et in calce atque diversis utilitatibus usque ad centum auri libras expendit.*

[114] *LP* 2, 115. The towers were apparently provided with fixtures that allowed a chain to be stretched across the river, to prevent ships from entering: *Ipsam igitur turrem non solum lapidibus verum etiam ferro munire curavit, quatinus, si necessitas fuerit, per eundem locum nulla valeat navis transire.*

[115] The credit goes primarily to Coates-Stephens, whose individuation of early medieval masonry in the Wall has been taken up in Mancini's "Atlas" (Mancini 2001), and now summarily reprised in Meneghini and Santangeli Valenzani 2004, esp. 57–63.

speckled with bits of reddish *pozzolana* and other roughly sifted inclusions. This brickwork appears often within the interstices between courses of tufa blocks, thus forming an integral and obviously contemporary part of their structure (Figures 1.28–1.29, above). Elsewhere, it is found in close proximity to sections repaired with the tufa blocks, which it often directly adjoins; and at other times, it appears on its own, sometimes in quantity: tower M14, for example, is entirely reconstructed in this technique (Figure 1.31).[116] Here and elsewhere, work of this type is further distinguished by the appearance of small, round putlog holes arranged in meandering files spaced at irregular intervals.

As Coates-Stephens has said, both the tufa and the brickwork without a doubt find their closest parallels in structures dating between the later eighth century and the middle of the ninth.[117] The earliest dated example is the church of S. Angelo in Peschiera, built shortly after the middle of the eighth century, which has foundations in the same sort of reused tufa blocks found in the Wall, laid in similar fashion.[118] Another early example is Hadrian I's reconstruction of S. Maria in Cosmedin, where the exterior walls of the apse feature typically undulating courses of brick.[119] The more numerous ninth-century parallels include S. Giorgio in Velabro, S. Martino ai Monti (Figure 1.32), and SS. Quattro Coronati, to name only a few.[120] The latest *comparandum*, perhaps the most valuable of all, is the circuit of walls around St. Peter's and the Borgo built by Leo IV in the immediate aftermath of the Saracen incursion of 846.[121] The remaining traces of this "Leonine" wall's original facings preserve the same sort of brickwork employed in various restorations to the Aurelian Wall, on which Leo of course intervened (Figure 1.33). Further, one section of

---

[116] Cf. Mancini 2001, 51; Coates-Stephens 1995, 502–6; another example is tower G2, near the Porta Maggiore (Coates-Stephens, 511).

[117] See e.g. Coates-Stephens 1999; 1998; 1995, esp. 514ff.

[118] Useful analyses of early medieval murature at Rome include: Bertelli, Guiglia Guidobaldi and Rovigatti Spagnoletti 1976–7, 95–173; Bertelli and Guiglia 1976, 331–5; and most recently, Santangeli Valenzani 2002; Meneghini and Santangeli Valenzani 2004, 135ff. On S. Angelo in Peschiera, see *CBCR* 1, 64–74; it dates either to 755 or 770 (*ibid.* 65).

[119] *LP* 1, 507; cf. *CBCR* 2, 301–3.

[120] S. Giorgio in Velabro: *LP* 2, 76 (Gregory IV, 827–44); cf. *CBCR* 1, 263–4; S. Martino ai Monti: *LP* 2, 93–96 (Sergius II, 844–7); cf. *CBCR* 3, 108ff. and 124; SS. Quattro Coronati: *LP* 2, 108ff. (Leo IV, 847–55); cf. *CBCR* 4, esp. 29–30 and 34.

[121] The project is described at length at *LP* 2, 123–4. The definitive modern study is Ward-Perkins and Gibson 1979 and 1983; see also Meneghini and Santangeli Valenzani 2004, 63–5; Pani Ermini 1992, 514–18; Giuntella 1985; Bella Barsali 1976, 201–14.

Figure 1.31 Tower M14, early medieval brickwork.

Figure 1.32 S. Martino ai Monti, exterior of north wall of apse.

Figure 1.33 *Civitas Leoniana*, interior of wall, near Vicolo del Campanile.

Leo's new wall near the Castel Sant'Angelo was built entirely in tufa blocks, in a manner again closely resembling the repairs to the urban enceinte previously described (Figure 1.34). The two construction techniques favored in the erection of the ninth century's most important new fortification, that is, are mirrored in repairs to the neighboring Aurelian Wall.

Of course, the dating of the early medieval restorations to the Wall is not an exact science, and it will never be possible positively to connect bricks (or tufa blocks) with individual popes, barring the discovery of evidence as yet undreamed of. Coates-Stephens is inclined to think that most of the visible remains belong to the time of Hadrian I and Leo IV, both because the *LP* seems to give these two the lion's share of the work, and also because the series of comparative structures in Rome only begins from the middle of the eighth century, though he has acknowledged the possibility that any of the tracts in question could also belong to the earlier part of the century.[122] The masons of Gregory II and III are as likely as not to have worked in a style similar to what their successors were using two generations later. There simply are not enough surviving buildings of the time to know for certain.

[122] Coates-Stephens 1999, 213; cf. 1995, 516.

Figure 1.34 *Civitas Leoniana*, interior of wall, near Via della Transpontina.

And that, for present intents and purposes, is that. The principal third- to ninth-century architectural phases of the Aurelian Wall have at last been fixed in a chronological sequence that can be regarded as sufficiently definitive, various matters of detail aside, to eliminate a number of surprisingly persistent misconceptions about its construction history once and for all. The fourth century witnessed *more* than one effort by the emperors of Rome and their agents to intervene in the fabric of the Wall, seemingly because repairs and limited expansion were judged practically expedient or essential, though the possibility of some precocious interest in visibly marking and thus appropriating the most massive and imposing building in the city should not be ruled out. The really significant expansion of the curtains, towers, and gates of the Wall, however, occurred not under Maxentius in 306–12, but rather under Honorius in 401–3, a fact proven beyond reasonable doubt by a critical mass of literary, epigraphic, and architectural evidence. With regard to the ensuing half-millennium, the crucial development is the new recognition that the large segments built in meandering brickwork and recycled tufa blocks once attributed to the period of the Gothic Wars actually belong in the eighth and ninth centuries. In addition to prompting a critical reappraisal of what Procopius' descriptions allow us to deduce about the standing remains of the Wall, this discovery has recreated a forgotten epoch in its history, and opened a new chapter in the history of papal government in the early Middle Ages in the process. All the same, the testimony of Cassiodorus, Procopius *et al.* to substantial bouts of construction around the circuit in the preceding period is not wholly bereft of archaeological corroboration, though more work will be necessary to identify other traces of fifth-, sixth- and seventh-century work to add to the probable examples identified above.

If there is an underlying theme to be deduced from the new, "reformed" architectural chronology of the Wall, it must be the regularity with which Wall-related construction occurred over the course of the 600 years that followed the completion of Aurelian's circuit. The lengthy sequence of early-medieval interventions is only the final, albeit striking piece in a progression that begins with the signs of multiple campaigns of fourth-century construction in the standing stratigraphy of the Wall, and continues on by way of Honorius to the persistent hints of ongoing repairs and additions in the written sources of the fifth and sixth centuries. These recurring signs of vitality combine to situate the Wall neatly within prevailing currents of historical scholarship that have flowed some distance since Richmond's day. Its history emphatically does not end with "ancient" Rome, however this is defined, nor indeed does this "ancient" city now seem so much to have ended as to have changed, blended often quite imperceptibly, into something else.[123] The eighth- and

---

[123] I imagine few would now agree with Richmond that "it is vain to attempt the extraction of historical facts" from parts of the Wall – or nearly anything else in Rome, for that matter – postdating the Gothic Wars, for all that one might still argue that "the subsequent history of the City is therefore not that of an Imperial Capital, but of the small metropolis of a Byzantine exarchate" (1930, 267). Even before the identification of the early medieval tracts of the Wall, L. Pani Ermini (1992, 496) lamented the lack of attention given to its post-classical phases, and stressed the importance of moving beyond the traditional "visione classica."

ninth-century repairs come as yet another timely indication of how ancient monuments were often medieval monuments, too, with as much to reveal about subsequent ages as those of their construction. More to the point, they again demonstrate the extent to which the maintenance of the Wall was a truly diachronic process, a recurring constant in Roman history over the *longue durée.*

2 | Planning, building, rebuilding, and maintenance: the logistical dynamics of a (nearly) interminable project

In past discussions of the Wall's historical context and architectural development, the practical and logistical aspects of its construction have been given conspicuously short shrift. The central question, that of how the Wall was actually built, is deceptive in its simplicity. Its exploration involves a wide range of issues, some of which remain to be elaborated more fully, and others to be raised seriously for the first time. Among them: Who planned the Wall, supervised its construction, and marshaled the personnel and material necessary for the task? Who saw to its funding, and where did the money come from? Further, how were building materials produced or acquired, how were they transported, and where did they come from? Finally, we must ask who physically set their hands to the task, how these people were organized, and how the execution of the work proceeded. These questions are fundamental not only for an understanding of how Aurelian's Wall came to be, but also for their capacity to provide valuable insights into the social, political, and economic dynamics of life in the capital following the chaotic years of the mid third century, in the ill-documented period just prior to the radical reforms of Roman society that began – or that in some cases, perhaps, were rather reified, codified, and transmitted to posterity – upon the accession of Diocletian in 284.[1]

In large part, the direction taken in past scholarship has been dictated by the nature of the evidence directly relevant to the Wall, and particularly that of the literary sources, which are notably reticent with regard to many of the questions posed above. There are, however, other means of approach that remain fully to be exploited. On the one hand, there is the internal evidence of the Wall itself, which contains a number of clues

---

[1] On Aurelian's reign, the venerable studies of E. Groag (Groag 1903) and L. Homo (Homo 1904) are still useful, though they have at last been supplemented by two approximately contemporaneous works apparently undertaken in mutual isolation: see Kotula 1997 and (the only one of the four in English) Watson 1999. For the reforms of the late-third and early-fourth century, see e.g. Corcoran 1996; Barnes 1996; 1982, Williams 1985; Seeck 1910. See also the recent general surveys, all covering the period in question, of Demandt *et al.* 2004; Potter 2004; Witschel 1999; Cosme 1998; Christol 1997; Strobel 1993.

as to how the project unfolded, the priorities of its planners, and the sort of materials used and their provenance. There is also a good deal of comparative information on the construction of defensive walls in late antiquity, a period that witnessed their proliferation on an often unprecedented scale. Finally, something is known of the organization of labor, the management of public works, and the production and reuse of building materials in the imperial period. And while it is generally only isolated vignettes that remain – bits of text, inscriptions, and archaeological remains often separated by vast expanses of time and space – nowhere is the documentation more extensive and internally coherent than it is at Rome. On the basis of such sources, a reasonably cogent case can be made for who was responsible for building, rebuilding, and maintaining the Wall, during the period when traditional Roman civic institutions still existed in recognizable form, and thus until the second half of the sixth century, roughly speaking. Similar questions will be posed for the early-medieval period in a later chapter: they are deferred here on the premise that when large-scale interventions recommenced in the eighth century, both the people directing the work and those actually performing it had little in common with their predecessors, in terms of their civic mandates, their training and experience, and the resources at their disposal.

2.1   The planning and placement of the Wall

To begin, as it were, from the beginning, it is apparent that a good deal of planning was done in the early stages of the project, before the start of construction. In fact, something of a scholarly consensus has developed to the effect that experienced military architects were responsible for the general design of the Wall, and for the course it took. With regard to the former, we are on solid ground, as is clear from testimony regarding construction of several closely contemporary circuits. According to the *HA*, following the Gothic invasions of Thrace in the 260s, the emperor Gallienus ordered the construction of defensive walls around the cities of the province, to be constructed under the auspices of two experienced military architects, Cleodamus and Athenaeus.[2] An inscription from the walls of Adraha in the province of Arabia, built in the same period,

---

[2] *HA Gal.* 13, 6: *quibus compertis Gallienus Cleodamum et Athen<a>eum Byzantios instaurandis urbibus muniendisque praefecit...*; cf. Johnson 1983a, 63.

prominently features the name of the architect in charge of the project.[3] Skilled professionals must likewise have been tasked with planning a circuit as important as that of Rome.[4] The matters left largely or entirely to their discretion will have included the height and thickness of the Wall, the shape and spacing of its towers, the orientation and layout of the gates, and other purely technical matters of the sort enumerated by Vitruvius in the sections of the *De Architectura* devoted to defensive fortifications.[5]

As for decisions about where the Wall was to be built, and what exactly it was to enclose, however, it is likely that leading government officials, including the emperor himself, were intimately involved, as many of the factors that determined the course of the Wall must have exceeded the purview of military architects. By way of addressing these issues, it will be well to consider first how its perimeter was established, one of the first of the many challenges confronting those tasked with erecting nearly nineteen kilometers of wall around, and indeed in the midst of, the biggest city in the world.

Two essential and inter-related considerations faced by the planners of the Wall were construction costs and pre-existing networks of urban topography and proprietorship. All land and buildings expropriated from the private sector naturally had to be paid for, while the property of the imperial patrimony, grown ever larger over the three centuries of the Principate through bequest, inheritance, and confiscation, was wholly at the emperor's disposal.[6] Extending in a rough crescent around the city, there was a "greenbelt" of suburban villas and gardens, largely

---

[3] *IGR* 3, 1287; cf. *ibid.* 1,286 and 1,288; cf. also Johnson 1983a, 65.

[4] Cf. Richmond 1930, 66. The value of trained architects in the fourth century was such that powerful incentives were introduced by law that exempted students and practitioners of the trade from payment of taxes and all responsibility for other burdensome civic *munera*; see *CTh.* 13, 4, 1 (*anno* 334): *Architectis quam plurimis opus est... Quibus ut hoc gratum sit, tam ipsos quam eorum parentes ab his, quae personis iniungi solent, volumus esse immunes ipsisque qui discent salarium competens statui*. Under Theoderic, the *praefectus urbis* (*sic*) was responsible for designating a chief architect for the city of Rome (Cassiodorus, *Var.* 7, 15: *Formula ad praefectum urbis de architecto faciendo in urbe Roma*); the position had evidently been in existence already for some time by the beginning of the sixth century: *ad eum* (architectum) *volumus pertinere quicquid decessores eius constat rationabiliter consecutos* (*ibid.*).

[5] *De Arch.* 1, 5, 1ff. Generally on the role of the "master-builder" in late antiquity, see Zanini 2007; esp. 387–8 on the contribution of the celebrated architects Anthemius of Tralles and Isidore of Miletus to the reconstruction of the walls of Dara in the sixth century.

[6] The dedicatory inscription of the baths of Diocletian, completed some thirty years after the Wall, makes prominent mention of the purchase of the buildings that had previously occupied the construction site: see *CIL* 6, 1,130: *...coemptis aedificiis pro tanti operis magnitudine...* On the subject of compensation paid to owners of property requisitioned for the Wall, cf. Lanciani 1892, 105–6.

under imperial ownership, through which a special effort was seemingly made to direct the Wall.[7] Thus, while it cut through densely populated quarters in some sectors, at times leaving busy neighborhoods outside its circuit, where it crossed land belonging to the emperor, it often ran well beyond the limits of dense habitation.[8] The additional cost of expanding the Wall to run through imperial property and other "rural" estates on the periphery of the city was apparently more than offset by the reduction in real estate costs and indemnities thereby realized. While estimates of the total length of the circuit built on imperial land vary somewhat, depending on the presumed location and extent of various holdings, it was clearly a significant portion of the whole, and thus represented a real saving.[9] Further, the planners of the Wall did not hesitate to truncate or destroy even large and opulent structures belonging to the imperial patrimony: both at the *Domus Lateranorum* and the Sessorian Palace, extensive complexes of rooms scrupulously maintained well into the third century were demolished to make way for the Wall.[10] Again, it appears that the benefits of routing the Wall through imperial property outweighed the negative consequences of the resulting demolitions, which, if nothing else, did not require the further payment of compensation.

Elsewhere, pre-existing structures were not destroyed, but instead incorporated in the fabric of the Wall. The motives governing the treatment of these edifices seem to have been twofold, with tactical expedients and convenience variously predominating. On the one hand, things that could be incorporated whole, with only the necessary additions and modifications necessary to render them defensively viable, in some instances allowed the Wall's builders to conserve time, labor, and materials. This aspect has been emphasized in the past: Lanciani calculated that

---

[7] On the proliferation of these "suburban" villas in the second and third centuries, see Marazzi 1988, 261–2; "greenbelt" is Krautheimer's term (Krautheimer 1980, 16–17). While some portion of these lands may still have been held by private families, the vast majority already belonged to the emperor, as Homo demonstrated in his studies of the imperial domain. His list of the various properties and pre-existing structures traversed by the Wall remains among the most complete accounts available (see Homo 1904, 239ff.; see also Richmond 1930, 11ff.).

[8] Some of the more densely populated areas bisected by the Wall included much of Trastevere, and the quarter between the Porta Nomentana and the Castra Praetoria; on Trastevere, see Chapter 4; for houses near the Castra Praetoria, see Lanciani 1892, 105–6.

[9] Lanciani (1892, 106) suggested 7,100 m of the total 18,837 (the total includes 3,700 m of wall along the banks of the Tiber). Homo (1904, 261–2) put the total higher still, at almost 8 km. Cf. Mancini 2001, 22; Cassanelli *et al.* 1974, 35–6.

[10] See Chapter 1, n. 5.

fully one-sixth of the circuit was composed of pre-existing buildings, the reuse of which he thought of substantial importance for the timely and economical completion of the project.[11]

In several cases, however, the task of immuring older buildings more plausibly involved as much or more effort than the construction *ex novo* of the equivalent length of rampart. Most of the largest and most celebrated structures incorporated into the Wall actually fall into this category. The biggest one of all, the Castra Praetoria, projects well beyond the line taken by the Wall on both sides of it; and its inclusion required the heightening and reinforcement of its three projecting flanks, as well as the construction of wholly new towers spaced at the usual 100-Roman foot intervals. It is thus in a sense misleading to see the 1,050 m of its perimeter built into the Wall as "found work," (as Lanciani, Homo, and Richmond all to some extent did), as Aurelian's builders might have made do with a stretch less than half as long – and thus also easier to defend and maintain – had the camp not been there in the first place.[12] Since, however, the enormous fortified enclosure could neither have been left outside the Wall as a ready-made bulwark for would-be attackers, nor razed entirely (thereby leaving thousands of praetorian guardsmen homeless), the only good option remaining was to bring it up to the defensive standard of the remainder of the circuit.

Motives of convenience are still less adequate to explain the immuring of other pre-existing structures. From the Porta Asinaria, the Wall describes a pointed salient, including in its perimeter the Amphitheatrum Castrense and the Aqua Claudia-Anio Novus. The resulting projection, with its culminating acute angle, was one of the most vulnerable sectors of the Wall (a fact later appreciated by the Goths, who made concentrated attacks there in the sixth century).[13] Further, it required the erection of a stretch of wall nearly twice the length of what would have been needed had a direct path been followed from the Porta Asinaria to the Porta Praenestina-Labicana. The latter course, however, would have left the imposing bulk of the Amphitheatrum Castrense immediately outside the circuit, as an inviting stronghold for prospective attackers. The inclusion of the

[11] See Lanciani 1892, 106; cf. 1897a, 72; and Homo 1904, 261–2, who concurred with Lanciani's figure of one-sixth. The "convenience" hypothesis remains popular today: see e.g. Sommella 2007, 51ff.

[12] See Lanciani 1897, 72; Homo 1904, 266–8; Richmond 1930, 64. For Richmond's important study on the Castra Praetoria and its relationship to the Wall, see Richmond 1927b, 12–22; on the date of the towers, see Appendix C, n. 14.

[13] Procop. *BG* 1, 22, 10–11; 1, 23, 13.

amphitheater, that is, was evidently a tactical priority of sufficient magnitude to outweigh the considerable difficulties involved, as it was with the
amphitheater at Verona, which had been awkwardly and laboriously
immured a few years earlier.[14] Similar considerations probably applied also
to Hadrian's massive mausoleum on the right bank of the Tiber, in the
likely event that it was connected to the circuit from the beginning.[15] While
its inclusion required the construction of additional walls to fortify the
mausoleum adequately and to connect it with the river and the Pons
Aelius, the extra labor was justified by the unappealing prospect of leaving
such a massive bastion in close proximity to the fortifications of the city.[16]

Ease of construction also fails to explain adequately the lengthy sections
of the Wall built fronting the Aqua Claudia-Anio Novus and the Marcia-
Tepula-Julia, which must in fact have presented serious difficulties for
Aurelian's planners and builders, while permitting only minimal savings in
materials.[17] Because the Wall directly fronted the arcades of the Aqua
Claudia-Anio Novus, communication and movement at wall-walk level
was seriously cramped, if not inhibited altogether, by the bulk of the
arches behind. The towers had to be awkwardly grafted onto the outside
of the wall, leaving their bases inaccessible from within: access to the top of
the Wall here could only have been achieved with temporary wooden stairs
or ladders, of which no traces remain. Further, since it was usually only the
rear facing of the new curtains that came into contact with the aqueducts,
they required nearly the same amount of raw materials as elsewhere; and
the technical challenges of integrating them with the existing structures if

---

[14] The parallel is striking. When Verona was refortified in 265, two projecting spurs were built
out at right angles from the line of the earlier republican circuit, connecting with the apexes
of the oval amphitheater. The effort of deviating from the course of the existing circuit and
building an additional 200 m of wall *ex novo* was evidently preferable to leaving such a
massive edifice standing only some 80 m beyond the fortifications. On the extension of the
walls, see Cavaliere Manasse 1993, 636–7; C. La Rocca 1986, 47 and n. 80. The Tetrarchic-
period(?) enceinte of Périgueux also apparently included the amphitheater, a likely
inconvenient necessity sprung from the desire to enclose the highest ground in the city: see
Garmy and Maurin 1996, 149–50 and 190.

[15] For more on the probable (Aurelianic) date of the fortification of the mausoleum, see Chapter 4.

[16] In this case, there was the additional strategic benefit of providing a fortified bridgehead on the
right bank of the Tiber, thereby allowing safe passage to the *Ager Vaticanus*, which otherwise
could have been reached only by the unfortified Pons Neronis, or via the Pons Agrippae,
situated well south within the compass of the Transtiberine walls (see below, Chapter 4);
cf. D'Onofrio 1971, 43–4; Cassanelli *et al.* 1974, 63–4. For a detailed hypothetical
reconstruction of the defenses of the mausoleum, based on the account of Procopius,
see Richmond 1930, 20ff.

[17] Cf. Richmond 1930, 64, *contra* Homo 1904, 245, 249, and 269–70. Richmond therefore revised
the Lanciani's estimate of one-sixth (see above n. 11) to "something like one-tenth or less."

anything probably increased the time necessary for the completion of these sections. This might explain why, over most of the Marcia-Tepula-Julia stretch, the Wall was actually built just in front of the pillars of the aqueduct, from which it was kept completely separate.[18]

Without going too far into the difficult question of why the Wall touched the aqueducts in some places and not others, it can at least be said that a preoccupation with incorporating as many existing structures as possible into the circuit does not adequately explain their mutual proximity. The basic problem was that, in two areas, aqueducts did in fact run roughly parallel to the line that the Wall needed to take. In the case of the Marcia-Tepula-Julia, there may be some merit to the traditional view that the Wall was built beyond the aqueduct to deny its looming profile to besiegers, for whom it could have served as a ready-made shelter and base for offensive operations against defenders on the Wall. Yet this rationale does not work at all for the Claudia-Anio Novus sector, where another aqueduct (the Marcia-Tepula-Julia) was in fact left to stand barely twenty meters outside the defenses (Figure 2.1). It seems an inelegant configuration that I find difficult to explain (is it permitted to speak of "mistakes" in planning?).[19] More generally speaking, the decision to build the Wall immediately next to the aqueducts it paralleled is perhaps best envisioned as a solution designed to require the fewest possible expropriations and demolitions in advance of construction, by taking full advantage of the corridor of open space maintained by law around the aqueducts of Rome.[20]

[18] Since Richmond's day, excavations have made it clear that some three meters separated the Wall from the pillars of the aqueduct, in the places where the remains of the latter have turned up between the Porta Tiburtina and the cut for the railroad. The diverse tracts of the two structures coincided only at the Porta Tiburtina, where the arch carrying the aqueducts over the road became also the gateway of the Wall; see Volpe 1993, 59–64; Caruso and Volpe 1989–90, 76–8.

[19] Coates-Stephens and Parisi (1999, 94) explain this "potentially perilous choice" on economic grounds, suggesting that by following the Claudia instead of the Marcia, the builders avoided having to build two separate gateways for the Viae Praenestina and Labicana, and were able to reuse the existing double arches of the Claudia, which spanned both roads at the point where they diverged, as a single monumental gateway; cf. Coates-Stephens 2004, 81. Yet the line of the Marcia could easily have been followed to the same gate, whereby its defenses would if anything have been enhanced, with minimal additional effort.

[20] In the urban center of Rome, defined as the area covered by "contiguous buildings" (*continentia aedificia*), an unimpeded strip at least five feet wide was to be maintained on each side of aqueducts; beyond city limits, the number rose to fifteen (Frontinus, *de aqua.* 126, 2–127, 1). Repeated injunctions to keep aqueducts clear of impediments appear in the Theodosian Code, at section 15, 2.

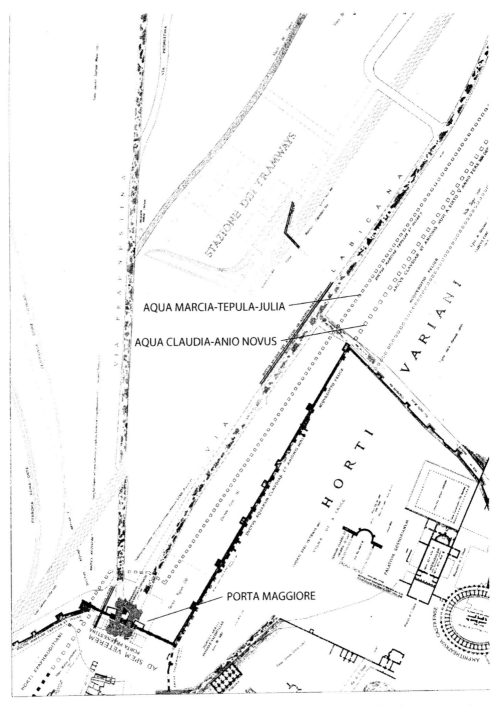

Figure 2.1 The Aqua Claudia-Anio Novus and Marcia-Tepula-Julia and the Wall at the Porta Maggiore. (After Lanciani, *FUR* tav. 32.)

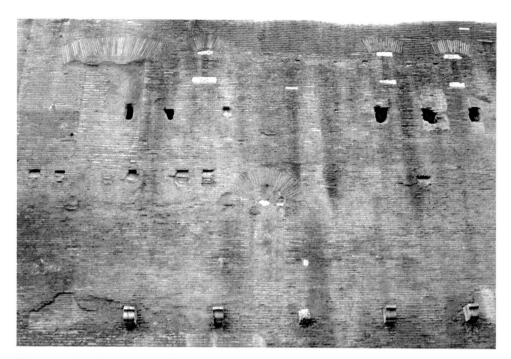

Figure 2.2 Second-century *castellum aquae* in curtain F6–7.

Many of the various smaller structures immured in the Wall can be less ambiguously imagined to have saved its builders time, labor, and materials. The largest number of these are tombs, though the remains of other structures are also visible, the most impressive of which is the so-called *insula* that stands three stories high in curtain F6–7, east of the Porta Tiburtina (Figure 2.2).[21] Some of the better-known tombs built into the circuit include that of the baker M. Vergilius Eurysaces at the Porta Praenestina-Labicana; those of Quintus Haterius at the Porta Nomentana (curtain D1–2) and Sulpicius Maximus in the east tower of the Porta Salaria; and most spectacularly, the monumental pyramidal sepulcher of Gaius Cestius, located just west of the Porta Ostiensis (Figure 2.3).[22] Inevitably, such structures occurred in the path of the Wall when it cut

---

[21] It has recently been noted that the ground floor of this structure was actually a cistern with a capacity of approximately 500,000 liters, connected with the Aqua Marcia-Tepula-Julia (Volpe 1993, 62); hence, in this celebrated example, practical motives for its inclusion may again supersede those of convenience.

[22] As several extensive listings of the houses and tombs built into the Wall already exist, another full summary seems unnecessary. All the examples mentioned above and many more are discussed in Homo 1904, 239ff., and Richmond 1930, 11ff.; cf. also Lanciani 1892, 107ff. For the parts of the circuit they include, Cozza's articles provide still more detailed coverage.

Figure 2.3 Pyramid of Gaius Cestius, with Porta Ostiensis behind.

through populous and architecturally cluttered areas; and in some cases, it will have been easier to build around and over them, trimming off any projecting bits, than to raze them entirely, when they served as well as sections of core built *ex novo.*[23]

While features of this sort do little to illustrate the broad strategic sensibilities of the Wall's planners, given that their individual presence cannot have altered its course dramatically, it is not impossible that various sections of the Wall were moved forward or back by a matter of meters to make more efficient use of pre-existing edifices. Further, their appropriation again poses interesting questions about the organizational hierarchy of the project, and specifically the issue of whether military architects were given *carte blanche* to requisition property in the most strategically expedient way, or whether representatives of the authority

[23] The pyramid of Cestius makes an interesting and somewhat anomalous example. Its inclusion was tactically inadvisable, as it inhibited all communication and movement between its flanking curtains (cf. Richmond 1930, 243). From a practical military standpoint, it should either have been razed and built over, or left inside the circuit; as it was, defensive capability was seemingly compromised in the interest of economy (or display?), as it rarely – if ever – was with other engulfed edifices, both greater and smaller.

legally and economically responsible for the undertaking – those paying the bills, so to speak – were involved even on such a relatively minute scale.

The relationship of the new Wall to several long-established boundaries also bore heavily on the determination of its contours. A great deal has already been written on this subject, and more will be said in a later chapter; here, a few remarks on the nature and location of the previous circuits that most plausibly affected the planning of the new Wall will suffice. These were the customs boundary of the city, where taxes were levied on goods in transit and for sale; the periphery of the city's fourteen administrative districts, or *regiones*; and the line of the *pomerium*, the ancient religious demarcation of the urban center, which reached its largest pre-Aurelianic extent under Vespasian in AD 75.[24] As the dimensions of all three lines are not everywhere known, the full extent of their inter-relations, and likewise of their relationship to the Aurelian Wall, cannot always be determined. Still, from the various tracts plotted with some certainty, it is clear that all three often, though by no means always, corresponded closely with one another and with the course of the Wall.

The lines of the *pomerium* and the customs circuit have been in part revealed by the discovery of a number of *cippi*, or boundary markers, belonging variously to one circuit or the other.[25] On their testimony, it is apparent that the Wall at least approximately followed the customs boundary for much of its northern flank, between the Portae Flaminia and Salaria.[26] In the east, however, the situation is less clear. One *cippus* is attested from the vicinity of the old Servian Walls on the Esquiline, but as it was not found *in situ*, its value is highly questionable.[27] The fourth and final customs *cippus*, from just outside the Porta Asinaria, provides the sole secure point of correspondence between the Wall and the customs

---

[24] All three are discussed in e.g. Richmond 1930, 7–9; Homo 1904, 222ff.; Lanciani 1892, 102ff.; cf. Cardilli *et al.* 1995, 74; Cassnelli *et al.* 1974, 37.

[25] C. Hülson's remarks on the customs circuit remain important, though the subsequent discovery of additional *cippi* has altered its presumed parameters somewhat: see Hülson 1897, 148–60; for more detailed listings of the various extant *cippi* and updated analysis, see G. Gatti in *BullCom* 1913, 67ff.; and P. Romanelli in *Notizie* 1933, 240–4; for a summary account of the relationship between the Wall and the customs circuit, with convenient appendices listing relevant textual and archaeological indicators, see Palmer 1980. For the *pomerium*, Labrousse 1937 is still fundamental, though some of his conclusions about its spatial extent at various times, particularly in the Campus Martius, have since been modified: see Andreussi 1988, 233–4; Coarelli 1977, 822–3.

[26] *Cippi* of Marcus Aurelius and Commodus, dating to *c.* 175, have been found just outside the Portae Flaminia and Salaria (*CIL* 6, 1016c and 1016b, respectively).

[27] *CIL* 6, 1016a.

boundary for the entirety of the stretch between the Porta Salaria in the north and the Tiber in the south.[28]

Hence, the presumed course of the customs boundary between the Portae Salaria and Asinaria is largely a matter of conjecture, as is its relationship to the later Wall. Richmond thought the evidence of the *cippus* from the Esquiline sufficiently compelling to postulate that the Wall significantly expanded on the earlier circuit, which he placed along the line of the Servian Wall, while Chastagnol later preferred to think that the customs circuit was approximately coextensive with the outer limits of the fourteen regions, and thus also with the Aurelian Wall.[29] In the south, the Wall is again generally assumed to have corresponded closely with the customs circuit, most clearly between the Porta Ostiensis and the Tiber. And while it is indeed likely that the large warehouses in this area would not have been left outside thereof, it should be noted that the only boundary stones known from this sector, all found very near the Wall, belong to the *pomerium*. As the *pomerium* was not everywhere coextensive with the customs circuit of Marcus Aurelius and Commodus, there is no proof that it was here, though it seems the likeliest supposition.[30] In any case, it is fair to say that the few known customs *cippi* found *in situ* all correspond closely with the course of the Wall, even more so than those of the *pomerium* in the one case where the latter circuit can be shown to have diverged from the former, in the area of the Porta Flaminia.[31]

---

[28] *CIL* 6, 31227; cf. Lanciani 1892, 94.

[29] See Richmond 1930, 7–8, followed by Palmer 1980, 219–20, and Chastagnol 1960, 336, whose views correspond generally with those earlier expressed by Labrousse (1937, 197–9) and Hülson (1897, 152–3). In the second case, the customs circuit would have been substantially enlarged under Marcus Aurelius and Commodus, since the eastern boundary of the city evidently did not extend to the line of the Aurelian Wall in the first century AD, when according to the elder Pliny it still corresponded with the old Servian Wall: see *Nat. hist.* 3, 5, 66: *clauditur* [Roma] *ab oriente aggere Tarquini Superbi, inter prima opere mirabili.*

[30] Labrousse suggested that until the expansion of the customs circuit in the 170s, it was in fact precisely coextensive with the *pomerium* (Labrousse 1937, 198–9). Given that only pomerial *cippi* are known from the preceding period, it seems the more plausible that these were understood also to mark the limit of customs collection: only when the confines of the latter were separated from the *pomerium* in the 170s – principally in the eastern part of the city, if Chastagnol, Labrousse *et al.* are right – were discrete markers required, *uti finem demonstrarent vectigali foriculari et ansarii promercalium.*

[31] At the Porta Flaminia, a Claudian pomerial *cippus* was found *in situ* 330m beyond the gate itself (*CIL* 6, 40852; Gatti in *BullCom* 41 [1913], 67–70), where the customs circuit ran, as the *cippus* found there shows (see n. 26). Two other Claudian *cippi* were found *in situ* some tens of meters north of the Wall, one outside the Porta Salaria (*Notizie* 1909, 130–1; *CIL* 6, 31537c), and the other outside the Nomentana along the Viale del Policlinico (*CIL* 6, 40853). This fairly minor deviation marks the greatest known projection of the *pomerium* beyond the course of the Aurelian Wall; it is also the one place where it can be demonstrated to have over-reached the customs barrier.

The same is true in the case of the fourteen regions, the broad outlines of which are known thanks to the two fourth-century Regionary Catalogues, the *Notitia* and *Curiosum*, which give detailed lists of the buildings found within each. Their evidence is sufficient to demonstrate that, while the Wall often conformed closely with the outer limits of the peripheral regions, it nonetheless left out large chunks of several. Features mentioned in *Regio V* extended some 300 m beyond the Porta Praenestina-Labicana, and *Regio I* continued well past the Porta Appia, perhaps as far as the banks of the Almo. In Trastevere, less than half of the diffuse *Regio XIV* was enclosed.[32]

Hence, though Lanciani, Richmond, and later Palmer were probably correct to see the customs boundary as the one that most directly affected the course of the Wall, they may have somewhat overstated the case.[33] While a direct parallel can be demonstrated between the Portae Flaminia and Salaria, and again at the Porta Asinaria, it remains true that between the Porta Ostiensis and the Tiber, the *pomerium* alone can be proven to have corresponded with the Wall, as it did again at the Porta Metronia. As more *cippi* belonging to the religious boundary have been found, in various points around the circuit, than those of the customs circuit, and as the *pomerium* was tied to the contours of the new Wall even before it was completed (I will argue subsequently that Aurelian made the two coterminous), it would be unwise to dismiss it summarily from considerations of the Wall's planning.[34]

Yet all the competing and at times conflicting interests that affected its physical parameters notwithstanding, the Wall was intended to fulfill the practical function of keeping enemies out of the city, and its designers never lost sight of the need to make it a tactically effective fortification. Natural topography was thus also taken into account in the planning of its course, to the greatest extent possible within the broad limits imposed by the configuration of the city and the disposition of the various manmade features judged worthy of inclusion within the circuit. Two related preoccupations predominated. Natural eminences were either included within the Wall, or left far enough outside that they did not offer attackers a commanding position with respect to its defenders. In practice, this

---

[32] On the boundaries of the regions, see Lanciani 1890; for their relation to the course of the Wall, see Homo 1904, 231–4; cf. Hülson 1897, 152–3.

[33] See Lanciani 1892, 93ff.; Richmond 1930, 7–9; Palmer 1980, 219; cf. also Watson 1999, 145–6.

[34] Cf. Labrousse 1937, 169–72; for an up-to-date list of all known pomerial *cippi*, see *CIL* 6, p. 4,359. The Porta Asinaria *cippus* is *CIL* 6, 1231b. On Aurelian's expansion of the *pomerium*, see Chapter 5.1.

meant that the Wall was often built just outside of elevated terrain, in such a way that it fronted earthen ramparts carved out of the slopes behind, leaving the ground level on its interior facing considerably above that on its exterior. In these sections, the earth backing served as a natural bulwark, vastly increasing the solidity of the structure, and its effectiveness against rams and mines.[35] The elevation of the ground at the rear of the Wall is pronounced between the Portae Flaminia and Pinciana; Tiburtina and Praenestina-Labicana; and for the entirety of the long stretch between the Viale Cristoforo Colombo (north of the former Porta Ardeatina) and the Porta Appia. It is beyond coincidence that when the Wall was heightened under Honorius, it was in precisely these areas that the inherently less solid, non-galleried upper curtains were employed.[36] Here, the tactical advantages that the galleried arcades provided (increased resistance to projectiles, increased provision for defenders) was evidently judged unnecessary, allowing time and money to be spared without unduly compromising the integrity of Rome's defenses.[37]

While these various considerations suffice for the most part to explain the particulars of the Wall's course, a further element was added to the mix in the early 1970s, when there occurred a minor outbreak of theoretical

[35] Cf. Vitruvius, *De Arch.* 1, 5, 5: *item munitiones muri turriumque aggeribus coniunctae maxime sunt tutiores, quod neque arietes neque suffossiones neque machinae ceterae eis valent nocere;* and Vegetius, *Epit.* 4, 3: *...quia nec murus ullus potest arietibus rumpi, quem terra confirmat....*

[36] It should be said that in other sections where the Wall was backed by high ground, galleried arcades were nonetheless built, as between the Portae Metronia and Appia. Still, it is clear that natural topography bore directly on the type of wall built: nowhere were the thinner curtains erected in the more vulnerable areas where the Wall crossed flat or low-lying ground. It is surely not fortuitous, for example, that the arcaded walls resume in precisely the spot where the terrain behind the Wall drops sharply to the level of the Tiber floodplain (curtain M7–8, beyond the Porta Ostiensis), after well over a kilometer of non-galleried curtains fronting the slope of the Monte d'Oro.

[37] To my mind, Richmond makes too much of the putative inferiority of the non-galleried curtains, which he concludes must have been thus built only because time, money or will failed before the whole circuit could be provided with enclosed galleries (1930, 74–5 and 255; cf. Todd 1978, 50). I see no reason why the simpler curtains could not have been planned from the beginning, with an eye to the natural advantages of the terrain in the sectors where they were used. On the negative side, the defenders at the base of the simpler curtains had fewer loopholes and were more exposed to the elements than the ones in the enclosed arcades, while those on the upper wall-walk had less room for maneuver. Yet these seem to me minor disadvantages better explained as calculated time- and cost-saving measures than as signs of desperate haste or poverty on the part of the Wall's builders. The fifth-century circuit of Ravenna was little thicker at any point (it ranged between 1.9 and 2.4 m) than these curtains; as at Rome, this size was evidently judged sufficient where the use of rams was impracticable, as was the case nearly everywhere at Ravenna, surrounded as it was by marshes and tidal lagoons; see Christie and Gibson 1988, 184.

speculation, verging at times on the mystical, regarding the putative iconographical resonances of Aurelian's circuit, which according to some played an influential role in the determination of its configuration. A first article by M. Fagiolo and M. Madonna appeared in 1972, in which the Wall's perimeter was simultaneously likened to a seven-pointed star and an eagle.[38] According to the authors, both semblances were conscious manifestations of Aurelian's political and religious agenda. The seven points of the "star" allegedly recalled the seven-pointed halo of Sol, Aurelian's patron deity, and the seven (known) bodies of the solar system, as well as the seven hills of Rome, the seven kings, and so on; while the eagle, traditionally associated with Jupiter, had long been a symbol of the emperor and his cult. In the same year, in an article focused principally on the Coliseum's (allegedly) central place in the development of Christian networks of sacred topography, E. Guidoni matter-of-factly remarked that "with Aurelian, who had made public the private cult of Sol, the amphitheater had been used as a center of visual reference for the new walls."[39] These various suggestions, in turn, soon made their way into some more or less mainstream literature on the Wall, where they have continued occasionally to crop up.[40]

Without delving too far into the deficiencies of such undoubtedly original hypotheses, a few things may be said. As far as the Coliseum is concerned, it could not but have lain near the center of any circuit of walls designed to enclose the most important and populous parts of Rome; and if in fact by "center of visual reference" we intend simply that it was visible from parts of the circuit, then certainly it was a focal point of sorts. Any further contention that the course of the Wall was altered in accord with some perceived spatial relationship with the Coliseum would first require a plausible demonstration of how (and why) it could possibly have been configured in such a way that the Coliseum was anything but a central and prominent landmark. Such a feat should not be too anxiously anticipated.

With regard to the seven-pointed star and the eagle, even granted that both of these symbols were of special interest to Aurelian, there remains no good reason to imagine that the new fortifications of the city were

---

[38] Fagiolo and Madonna 1972, 389 and esp. n. 77.

[39] Guidoni 1972, 9: "Con Aureliano, che aveva reso pubblico il culto privato del Sole, l'anfiteatro è stato utilizzato come centro di riferimento ottico per le nuove mura...".

[40] They were enthusiastically embraced in Cassanelli *et al.* 1974, 40–1; the seven-pointed star symbolism continued to receive serious consideration in Cardilli *et al.* 1995, 73–4.

tailored to resemble more closely one or both. It would be difficult to find
an animal that could not, properly viewed, contorted, or accessorized, just
as easily be drawn into the silhouette of the Wall as an eagle; and as for the
seven points of the "star," there are more than sufficient topographical,
economic, and strategic considerations to explain the presence of each
projecting segment, without recourse to overarching iconographical
imperatives. The Castra Praetoria was one of the seven; the rationale for
its inclusion has already been explained on entirely practical grounds. If a
second example is required, that of the two southernmost protrusions will
serve. The more easterly of the two, divided roughly in half by the Via
Appia, closely skirted the marshy edge of the Paludes Decenniae along its
northern flank. The marshes, aside from being impractical ground on
which to lay the foundations of a wall, also provided an effective natural
defense.[41] The southern side of the "point" is defined quite precisely by the
elevated contour of the Monte d'Oro, which the Wall follows as far as the
Porta Ostiensis. Here, it turns slightly to the south, thereby enclosing
the looming bulk of Monte Testaccio, whose commanding heights had
either to be included in the circuit, or left far enough outside that they did
not directly menace the fortifications. Had the latter option been chosen,
however, much of the populous thirteenth region, with its numerous
warehouses and granaries along the Tiber waterfront (long included
within the *pomerium* and, probably, the customs circuit), would have been
left unprotected. As it was, the Wall reached the Tiber south of Testaccio,
whence it turned abruptly to follow the riverbank, thus completing
the outline of the second of the "points." If anything, these examples
highlight the importance of topography, natural and manmade, in deter-
mining the layout of the Wall: its perceived resemblance to any number of
ostensibly significant imperial symbols is therefore best considered purely
coincidental.

Finally, it should be noted that the surviving evidence will never suffice
to explain every particular of the Wall's course. The interests and influence
of powerful landed proprietors, for example, and the presence and precise
locations of important structures that needed either to be preserved whole
within the Wall, or infringed upon by its construction, cannot be known
in all their particulars. Nor, for that matter, will the relative extent to
which such considerations mattered to those designing the Wall,

---

[41] Vegetius (*Epit.* 4, 2) specifically recommends marshes as a valuable natural barrier, to be
utilized whenever possible in siting defensive walls; the efficacy of heavy siege engines in
particular would have been severely impaired by soggy terrain.

particularly given their other concerns with natural topography, earlier boundaries, etc. Still, enough indicators remain to give some idea of the complex dynamics and competing interests that must have come into play, many or all of which could only have been addressed at the highest administrative and executive levels. Questions of whose land it was to be built on; how to treat obstructing private structures, sacred and profane; the incorporation or demolition of public buildings and those belonging to the imperial domain; and the relationship between the new Wall and pre-existing economic, administrative, and religious boundaries were surely too important and potentially controversial to leave totally in the hands of military architects. This brings us back to the organizational and supervisory hierarchy of the project, and to considerations of who was in charge, in theory and in practice.

2.2   Building the Wall

The textual sources are unanimous in attributing the decision to fortify the city to Aurelian himself. There is no reason to doubt that this was so, nor that the project unfolded under his supreme auspices. The emperor and his provincial governors were in fact the only people in the empire with the legal authority to sanction the construction of city walls, as a passage from Ulpian preserved in Justinian's legal code demonstrates.[42] Moreover, no public edifice of such magnitude could have been undertaken in third-century Rome without the emperor's active support in addition to his consent, if for no other reason than that he more or less directly controlled the vast majority of the funds available for the construction of public works.[43] Nor did the emperors let anyone forget the extent of their dependence on the imperial coffers: by the later fourth century, city prefects risked charges of high treason if they failed to mention the emperors on the dedicatory inscriptions of public buildings.[44] And indeed, the most impressive edifices to appear in the city in the third and fourth centuries were without exception undertaken on imperial initiative, among them the massive bath complexes of Caracalla

---

[42] *Dig.* 1, 8, 9: *Muros autem municipales nec reficere licet sine principis vel praesidis auctoritate nec aliquid eis coniungere vel superponere.*

[43] Chastagnol 1960, 335ff.; cf. Anderson 1997, 50–1 and 92; Jones 1964, 709–11.

[44] *CTh.* 15, 1, 31 (*anno* 394): *Si qui iudices perfecto operi suum potius nomen quam nostrae perennitatis scripserint, maiestatis teneantur obnoxii.*

and Diocletian, the Basilica of Maxentius in the forum and his villa on the Via Appia, and the Diocletianic restructuring of the Curia.

The Byzantine chronicler John Malalas further implied that Aurelian played an active role in the planning and administration of the project in its initial phases, stating pointedly that the emperor himself saw to the organization of the labor force.[45] This fits well with the notion that imperial fiat was required also for the siting of the Wall; and it adds another dimension, discussed further below, to the nature of Aurelian's presumed participation. Still, the responsibility for the Wall's completion must soon have devolved upon others, as Aurelian left the city for the east in 271, where he spent the next two years engaged in curbing the imperial pretensions of Queen Zenobia of Palmyra.[46]

With one rather dubious exception, however, no additional governing authorities are cited in connection with the Wall in the sources, which are likewise mute regarding the details of its construction. The lone exception comes in a passing reference to the Senate in the *HA*, where Aurelian is said to have acted in accordance with its counsel.[47] Given the singularity of the remark, however, and the strong senatorial sympathies of the *HA*, however affected they be, it would be unwise to make too much of it.[48] True, the Senate had a traditional supervisory responsibility for public works in the city, and the control of a minor treasury, the *arca publica*, with which to fund building projects; and both for its trappings of authority and its money, therefore, it may have been involved at least nominally in the erection of the Wall, perhaps increasingly so in the

---

[45] *Chronographia* 12, 30; see below n. 85.

[46] *HA Aur.* 22, 1: *Transactis igitur, quae ad saeptiones atque urbis statum et civilia pertinebant, contra Palmyrenos, id est contra Zenobiam, quae filiorum nomine orientale tenebat imperium, iter flexit.*

[47] *HA Aur.* 21, 9: *...adhibito consilio senatus muros urbis Romae dilatavit.*

[48] The *HA* purports to be written by senators and, indeed, the life of Aurelian begins with a particularly elaborate fiction in which the "author," "Flavius Vopiscus," presents himself riding together in a chariot with his old acquaintance, the *praefectus urbi* (*HA Aur.* 1, 1). Though the range of opinions expressed in the secondary scholarship is dizzying, A. Chastagnol's summation may be taken as representative of something like a general consensus on its apparent ideological slant: "D'abord, l'HA est issue d'un milieu social bien défini: l'aristocratie sénatorial de la Ville de Rome, dont elle exprime, sous le couvert des empereurs de jadis et non sans anachronismes, les intérêts politiques, sociaux et économiques..." (Chastagnol 1964, 63). While Syme took issue with the "belief that this man is an aristocrat, writing, or if not that, superintending the composition of the HA in a clear political design," he did so only on the basis of "his erudite and scholiastic predilections" (Syme 1968, 197). Whatever his background, that is, the author is at least affecting senatorial sympathies: hence, the reliability of the phrase *adhibito consilio senatus* must remain suspect, as must the real extent of the senate's role in the decision to build the Wall.

emperor's absence.[49] None of this, however, should be taken to indicate that the project required the consent of the Senate, or that it was carried out under its direct supervision. Aurelian would have had his Wall with or without its "counsel," and as we shall see, the officials in charge reported directly to him, for all that they generally belonged to the senatorial order.

If more is to be said, it must be drawn from what is more generally known, or knowable, about the mechanics of public building in Rome from the third century on.

Since the time of Augustus, officials appointed personally by the emperor had been in charge of municipal services, streets, sewers, public edifices, and so on.[50] This remained the case during the later empire, though the rank, titles, and effective responsibilities of the various functionaries were often changed. As in so many respects, so too in the matter of civic administration, the third century witnessed systemic changes that are singularly poorly documented. While something is known about the management of public works through the Severan period, and again in the fourth and fifth centuries, the precise state of affairs at any point during the intervening decades, during which the Aurelian Wall was built, can be difficult to pinpoint.[51] Still, the ensemble of several centuries of epigraphic, legal, and literary sources gives a good general sense of the personnel in place to accomplish the directives of the emperor, and to act in his stead, in the case of his prolonged absence from the city, which became more the rule than the exception beginning in the third century. Since these individuals were also in practice responsible for the labor, materials, and funding required for a given project, the construction of the Wall is best considered in its ensemble, the better to appreciate the scope and complexity of the undertaking, and the potentially lasting impact of its sweeping social, legal, and economic ramifications. Also, in light of the

---

[49] Homo, evidently struck by *adhibito consilio senatus*, probably exaggerated the role of the senate in both the planning and the construction of the Wall, particularly in his suggestion that Aurelian required its permission to proceed (1904, 221; see also Groag 1903, 1376ff.). He also overestimated the importance of the *arca publica*, which was hardly the crucial source of funding for public works that he imagined; on its relative insignificance, see Chastagnol 1960, 335 and 346. For the senate's continuing importance and prestige in the late empire, particularly as construed by its members, see Humphries 2003.

[50] See e.g. Millar 1977, 313–15; 338–9.

[51] The classic work on Roman civic administration under the later empire is Chastagnol 1960, whose chapter on "finances and public works" informs much of what follows (335–71); cf. Jones 1964, 687ff.; see also Janvier 1969. Our understanding of the administration and logistics of public building under the earlier empire in particular has been greatly enriched by several recent publications, among which J. Delaine's study of the baths of Caracalla is exemplary (Delaine 1997); see also 2000 and 1995; Anderson 1997, 3–179.

fact that the textual and epigraphic evidence is best for the post-Aurelianic phases of the Wall, much of what can be said conjecturally about what went on in the 270s can and will be applied more confidently to the fourth, fifth, and sixth centuries.

Here, then, is a brief outline of what the act of realizing 19 kilometers of Wall around the capital of the Roman empire would have required, and how it might have been accomplished. Under the Principate, and seemingly until well into the fourth century, public buildings in the city were under the care of two officials selected by the emperor, the *curator aedium sacrarum* and *curator operum publicorum*. While the *praefectus urbi* was always the ranking official in Rome, these and other *praefecti* and *curatores* appear to have had independent mandates, and to have answered directly to the emperor, until or shortly after 331, when they were all placed under the jurisdiction of the city prefect.[52] For the preceding period, there is little to indicate how the respective spheres of responsibility of the *curator operum publicorum* and the *praefectus urbi* were defined; and it is possible that the latter official was already involved in some capacity in the management of Rome's infrastructure. A dedicatory inscription found in the forum of Trajan in the name of Flavius Orfitus, *praefectus urbi* in 273–4, may hint at such involvement already under Aurelian.[53] Nonetheless, it looks as though the *curator operum publicorum* was a more influential figure when the Wall was built than his successors were a century later. In 301, the principal building corporation of the city, the *fabri tignuarii*, was still dedicating statues to this official, while from the 340s on, only the *praefectus urbi* was commonly commemorated in connection with important public works.[54] Presumably, then, when the decision to build the Wall was made,

---

[52] Chastagnol 1960, 43–9; see Section 2.3, below, for more on developments in the later fourth century.

[53] See *CIL* 6, 1112, with Chastagnol 1960, 44.

[54] *CIL* 6, 1673. Elsewhere in Italy, there existed officials responsible specifically for urban defenses already in the time of Aurelian: the towns of Fanum Fortunae and Pisaurum, both of which lay between the invading Alemanni and Rome, were refortified under the auspices of the *curator reipublicae* of the two municipalities, C. Julius Priscianus, who, interestingly enough, also took the title *p(rae)p(ositi) mur(is)*: see *CIL* 11, 6308, and esp. 6309, with Homo 1904, 76 and 211. At Rome, however, there is no evidence for the presence of such a functionary, Coarelli's effort to create one aside (see Chapter 1, n. 59). Under the early empire, another imperial servant called the *redemptor operum caesaris*, first attested in an inscription of AD 100 (*CIL* 6, 9034), apparently played a prominent role in public building commissions. This official seems to have functioned as a sort of head contractor, responsible for engaging the men and materials required for new projects (Delaine 2000, 121; Anderson 1997, 88ff.); to my knowledge, however, the position is not attested in the third century or later.

the commission sooner or later reached the *curator operum publicorum*, who then took the necessary initiatives to get the project underway.[55]

The first step would have been to engage the architects charged with the design of the Wall, who would have given estimates of construction costs, and the materials and labor required for the task, once its course and dimensions had been determined.[56] The supervising official would then have reported the estimated costs to the emperor, whose task it was to allot the necessary funds, as occurred in 383–4, when the reigning emperors Valentinian II, Theodosius, and Arcadius responded to the *praefectus urbi* Symmachus about the plans for the new and expanded St. Paul's basilica which he had sent for their approval.[57] A remarkable parallel comes from Constantinople where, in a law of 413, the towers of the new land walls are described as lying on the property of citizens "through whose lands the wall is erected, in accordance with the care and planning (*studio ac provisione*) of Your Eminence, following the counsel (*arbitrio*) of Our Serenity": here again, a ranking prefect (in this case a *praefectus praetorio* instead of a *praefectus urbi*) seems to have been responsible for individuating and expropriating the land required for a new construction, under the (at least nominal) supervision, and the supreme executive authority, of the emperor himself.[58]

Provision then had to be made for obtaining massive quantities of bricks, mortar, and tufa, which had not only to be produced or otherwise acquired, but also transported.

The lime and volcanic sand, or *pozzolana*, used to make mortar were imported from the provinces around the city, often from as far away as

---

[55] Cf. Waltzing, *Étude* 2, 115.

[56] For more on the role of Roman architects, see Zanini 2007; Delaine 2000, 120–1; Anderson 1997, 3–67.

[57] *Collectio Avellana*, 3 (*CSEL* 35), 46–7; cf. Chastagnol 1960, 349–50.

[58] *CTh.* 15, 1, 51 (anno 413): *Turres novi muri, qui ad munitionem splendidissimae urbis extructus est, conpleto opere praecipimus eorum usui deputari, per quorum terras idem murus studio ac provisione tuae magnitudinis ex nostrae serenitatis arbitrio celebratur, eadem lege in perpetuum et condicione servanda, ut annis singulis hi vel ad quorum iura terrulae demigraverint proprio sumptu earum instaurationem sibimet intellegant procurandam, earumque usu publico beneficio potientes curam reparationis ac sollicitudinem ad se non ambigant pertinere. Ita enim et splendor operis et civitatis munitio cum privatorum usu et utilitate servabitur.* This is a document of singular importance in other respects as well. It is, first, essential evidence for the date of the Wall's completion: taking the phrase *conpleto opere* at face value, as seems reasonable on the further assumption that legislation on the proprietorship of the towers was not passed long before their completion, the date of its promulgation (April, 413) is the most precise existing *terminus ante quem* (cf. Speck 1973, 135–43). It has further important implications for the use of civilian labor for the upkeep of the finished structure, which are assessed below.

Tuscia and Campania.[59] This was a *munus* of supreme importance, essential both for the erection of new buildings and the maintenance of existing ones; and elaborate measures were already in place to ensure the ready availability of mortar, though the Wall must still have placed extraordinary demands on the system. The raw materials came from privately owned estates, whose proprietors, by the fourth century if not earlier, were obligated to provide a fixed number of cartloads on a yearly basis, and to bear the lion's share of the cost for the processing and transport of the finished product.[60] They would thus have had to pay the lime-burners (*calcis coctores*) who cooked the mortar and prepared it for use, as well as the carters, *vecturarii* or *vectores*, needed to transport it to the city.[61] In the early sixth century, the mortar supply for the capital was supervised by a dedicated official, the *praepositus calcis*, as it may have been earlier.[62]

The tufa for the core of the Wall was available closer at hand, thanks to the abundance of rich sources in superficial geological strata in the immediate vicinity of the city.[63] Its ready accessibility evidently made reuse unnecessary, as recycled bits were rarely employed in its foundations and core.[64] The freshly mined stone would have been taken from

---

[59] The best source for the production and transport of mortar are the laws in the Theodosian Code (14, 6, 1–4), on which Jones (1964, 708–9) and Chastagnol (1960, 348–9) primarily based their accounts, as will I. On the geographical extent of the territory from which the materials were drawn, see *CTh.* 14, 6, 3, mentioning imports from the province of Tuscia, to the north of Rome, and the municipality of Terracina, well to the south; from *CTh.* 14, 6, 1, we learn that carters of mortar were employed in four regions of Italy, presumably those immediately contiguous with the city: Campania, Samnium, Picenum, and Tuscia (as Chastagnol likewise assumed, 348). On the composition and fabrication of mortar, see Anderson 1997, 145ff.; Adam 1984, 69–84.

[60] *CTh.* 14, 6, 1: *Ex omnibus praediis, quae iam dudum praestationi calcis coeperunt obnoxia adtineri, coctoribus calcis per ternas vehes singulae amphorae vini praebeantur, vecturariis vero amphora per bina milia et nungenta pondo calcis. Quin etiam volumus non personas, sed ipsos fundos titulo huius praestationis adstringi;* cf. 14, 6, 2; 14, 6, 3. In the fifth century, the mortar and labor for the upkeep of Rome's aqueducts were still drawn from dedicated estates, held exempt from the payment of additional taxes and the provision of recruits for the army; such holdings likely provided for the maintenance of the Wall as well: see *Nov. Val.* 5, 4 (of 440): *cespes formensis, arensis, calcarius et vecturarius habeatur immunis...;* cf. Coates-Stephens 2003c, 426–7.

[61] *CTh.* 14, 6, 3 (*anno 365*): *Statum urbis aeternae reformare cupientes ac providere publicorum moenium dignitati iubemus, ut calcis coctoribus vectoribusque per singulas vehes singuli solidi praebeantur, ex quibus tres partes inferant possessores, quarta ex eius vini pretio sumatur, quod consuevit ex arca vinaria ministrari.*

[62] Cassiodorus, *Var.* 7, 17: *Formula de praeposito calcis.*

[63] See Jackson and Marra 2006; Bertelli 2001, 151–3; Anderson 1997, 139–45; Delaine 1995, 556–7.

[64] Cf. Mancini 2001, 24; Richmond 1930, 57–8.

the source to the construction site by the *vectores*, where only the minimal effort of breaking it into pieces of the requisite size was necessary before use.

The final and most labor-intensive material required was the fired bricks with which the entirety of the Wall is faced, inside and out. The question of the provenance of these bricks has been considered by nearly all past commentators on the Wall, and the range of opinions is so diverse that it is at times difficult to believe that various scholars were looking at the same structure. Lanciani thought the bricks were mostly new, citing specifically the *bipedales* used in relieving arches and bonding courses, but referring also more generally to the bricks employed in the Wall's facings.[65] While Richmond likewise assumed that some bricks were made new, he seems to have thought the majority of them recycled, as Heres later did.[66] Lugli felt that a high percentage of new bricks was used, and Cardilli stated unequivocally that the Wall was built with bricks made expressly for the task, which he proceeded to describe.[67] Most recently, Mancini blandly, and without further ado (or references), remarked that the bricks in the Wall were reused.[68] Following their brief summary of the debate, Coates-Stephens and Parisi took the most judicious line, acknowledging that the physical evidence does not permit an unequivocal resolution of the question, and speaking instead in terms of broad probabilities.[69]

Several things can be said for certain. Recycled bricks were definitely used in various parts of the circuit, as is proven by the discovery of

---

[65] Lanciani 1892, 90–1.

[66] Heres 1982, 92; Richmond 1930, 58 (new bricks mentioned at 244). Richmond, strangely, thought that the Wall was faced primarily with old roof tiles, which Vitruvius (*De arch.* 2, 8, 18–19) recommended for use in protecting the upper portions of mud-brick walls from moisture (followed by Watson 1999, 146). This is false: the overwhelming majority of the bricks in the curtains of the Wall were precisely that – flat squares of fired clay, meant to be broken into roughly triangular pieces and inserted into the facing of walls. Part of the confusion perhaps arose from a matter of terminology. In Vitruvius' time, *opus latericium* specifically designated structures made from unfired mud bricks, while the less common technique of inserting pieces of tile into a mortar backing was properly called *opus testaceum* (*De arch.* 2, 8, 9; cf. 2, 8, 16ff.). From the later first century AD on, however, when fired brick became the material of choice for the construction of load-bearing walls in Rome, *opus latericium* came generically to refer to structures built in this manner. Like the great public baths, aqueducts, palaces, etc. built in Rome from the later Julio-Claudian period on, the Wall was faced not with roof tiles, but with bricks; cf. generally Heres 1982, 25ff.; Lugli 1957, 529–33 and 541–2. To my knowledge, Richmond's error has only once been noted, in a footnote buried in Bloch's fundamental study of the Roman brick industry: see Bloch 1947, 313, n. 234.

[67] Lugli 1957, 614–15; Cardilli *et al.* 1995, 67, referring to "light-red bricks 3.5 cm. thick."

[68] Mancini 2001, 24.   [69] Coates-Stephens and Parisi 1999, 88–9.

many pre-Aurelianic stamps, most from the second century AD, and none from later than the beginning of the third. It is also true that not a single identifiable stamp of the age of Aurelian has turned up anywhere in the Wall.[70] The arguments of those who assert the preponderance of recycled materials rest heavily on these observations, which however are neither conclusive nor as convincing as they might seem at first sight.

First of all, the lack of Aurelianic stamps is by no means proof that no production occurred in his time, given that fewer bricks in general were stamped from the Severan period on, and further that the scarce stamps referable to the third century on the basis of their architectural context are almost all anepigraphic, and hence lacking the detailed (and datable) references to consuls, emperors, brick-producers, production sites, etc. that appear in various combinations on stamps of the first and second centuries, and to a lesser extent also on those of the age of the tetrarchs and Constantine.[71] The proposition that the Wall is composed primarily of recycled bricks further implies that these were available in sufficient quantity to face nineteen kilometers of wall, inside and out, and indeed that such excesses were ready to hand that only the most homogeneous among them were selected.[72] On the assumption that the building of the Wall, much of which ran through undeveloped land, did not occasion the demolition of enough buildings to provide the requisite quantities of bricks, it is difficult to imagine where they would all have come from. Moreover, I am not convinced that the act of dismantling buildings with sufficient care to recover bricks whole, removing them individually from beds of mortar and cleaning them would have been any less labor-intensive than the production of bricks from scratch, particularly if the recycled bricks had to be transported some distance, instead of being transposed directly from their original site in the path of the Wall to the Wall itself.

---

[70] Cf. Chapter 1.

[71] In addition to the pioneering work of Bloch, the essential studies are those of M. Steinby: on the late empire, see Steinby 1986 and 2001. More generally, see 1974–5 and 1978; see also Helen 1975.

[72] Cf. Coates-Stephens and Parisi 1999, 89. Even where recycled bricks were clearly in the majority, as in the collapsed curtain near the Porta Asinaria (see Armstrong *et al.* 1905), they are remarkably similar in thickness, and generally less fragmented and heterogeneous than the recycled bricks of subsequent ages. Standing sections elsewhere faced with bricks of the same dimensions and color are at least as likely to indicate fresh production as the recycling of homogeneous bricks from a common source; several good examples are noted in Cozza 1993, 110; 114; 120, etc.

Further, as more attention is devoted to the question of brick-production under the later empire, the conviction grows that manufacture never ceased entirely during the third century. The enormous baths of Caracalla were only finished perhaps in the 220s, when new bricks were apparently still being produced in quantity.[73] In the 290s, in turn, when the equally gargantuan baths of Diocletian were built, brick manufacture was clearly again in full swing.[74] This implies either that the industry was functioning before Diocletian's time, and that the sudden surge in production was possible because the system did not have to be reconstituted from scratch; or otherwise that large-scale production could be resumed *ex novo* in very little time.[75] In either case, it is apparent that new bricks could have been provided for the Wall in relatively short order, in the (probable) event that they were needed. In the case of imperial commissions, it would have been particularly easy to boost supply to meet sudden demand: the emperors, by the turn of the third century, enjoyed a *de facto* monopoly on brick production, since all the principal known *figlinae*, the clay-rich estates where bricks were produced, had in one way or another made their way into the imperial domain during the first two centuries AD, where they remained still in the fourth.[76] Hence, the emperors of the third century had raw materials in abundance, surely no shortage of slave labor, and thus the rudiments of a production system that would never have been more pressingly needed than under Aurelian, whose building projects in addition to the Wall included the massive temple of Sol, and repairs to the Baths of Caracalla.[77]

The exceptional nature of Aurelian's requirements could even explain the lack of stamps, particularly of the epigraphic sort. As the Wall was an obviously extraordinary project of a one-time nature, undertaken after decades of limited building activity, an *ad hoc* spike in production might neither have prompted the resuscitation of the stable production apparatus adumbrated by the administrative titles and legal formulae contained in earlier and later *bolli*, nor indeed have occasioned much concern about who was making the bricks, or precisely

---

[73] Bloch 1947, 301–3; cf. Steinby 1986, 108; and on the chronology of the structure, Delaine 1997, 15–16.

[74] See esp. Bloch 1947, 303ff.; also Steinby 1986, 111ff.

[75] Janet Delaine estimates that only some 300 to 400 brickmakers were needed to supply the needs of the city of Rome during the Severan period, even during the years when the baths of Caracalla were being constructed (Delaine 1997, 202; cf. 1995, 261). If this figure is remotely accurate, the task of reinstituting brick production for the Aurelian Wall, from scratch if need be, will have presented a relatively minor logistical hurdle.

[76] Steinby 1986, 103; Bloch 1947, 313–14.

[77] Steinby, too, is convinced that the volume of Aurelian's projects required the production of new bricks, despite her contention that the Wall itself was faced chiefly with bricks from buildings razed in anticipation of its construction (1986, 108–11; cf. Steinby 1978, 1515; also Bloch 1947, 313).

where they came from. It was left to Diocletian to overhaul the system, and provide for the long-term manufacture in quantity that would have been necessary for the rebuilding of the city after the catastrophic fire of 283, which had gutted much of its monumental center. Only then, perhaps, was the permanent administrative hierarchy – the network of production sites staffed and managed by career employees – re-established, of which the new series of epigraphic tetrarchic stamps formed part and parcel.[78]

Hence, though the ratio of new to recycled materials in the Wall is impossible to determine, my sense is that a very significant portion of the bricks was made new, in the traditional sites of production, or *figlinae*; and that they would thence have been transported to the city and used almost immediately in diverse points around the rapidly growing circuit. While few if any of the principal *figlinae* have been pinpointed by excavation, many of their locations have been roughly stabilized on the basis of toponyms.[79] The majority seem to have been north of the city, often as far away as the Sabina, and usually located near the Tiber or one of its tributaries, which furnished abundant supplies of the fluvial clay most commonly employed in the fabrication of bricks.[80] Ready access to riverine transport evidently justified locating centers of manufacture quite far from the areas where the finished product was needed, as might be expected when the superior efficiency of transport by water in the ancient world is considered.[81] Thus, assuming bricks were made for the Wall,

---

[78] For Bloch, it was the baths of Diocletian themselves that provided the primary impetus for the resuscitation of the brick industry (1947, 314ff.); the need to reconstruct e.g. much of the Forum Romanum in the wake of the fire seems to me at least as convincing an explanation, particularly as the rebuilding of the city center was likely envisioned as a longer-term effort than the baths.

[79] One probable *figlina*, apparently out of use by the mid second century AD, has been documented not far outside the Porta Salaria, though its size and relative importance are difficult to gauge; see Pavolini *et al.* 2003, 56. The *civitas figlinae*, which several late-antique sources (e.g. *LP* 1, 180) place in the same area, has yet to be archaeologically documented; cf. Pavolini *et al.* 2003, 67–9. Lidia Paroli has recently credited the Tiber Valley Project of the British School at Rome with identifying the remains of the *Portus Licini* on the bank of the Tiber near Bomarzo (Paroli 2004, p. 19 and n. 58; on the *Portus Licini*, see Chapter 1, n. 74). I have yet to find anyone at the British School with knowledge of such a discovery, however.

[80] Steinby 2001, 129–30; 1986, 153–4; Helen 1975, 17–20. The *registrum* of the abbey of Farfa contains a number of place-names in the Sabina which appear to correspond with imperial-era *figlinae*.

[81] Indeed, Roman bricks have been found in quantity as far away as North Africa and Spain, the ease of shipping being such that it was evidently still cheaper to import bricks from factories in Italy than to make them locally: see Helen 1975, 17–20; on findspots of Roman bricks outside of Italy, see also Steinby 1978, 1,493. On transport in the ancient world, and the relative costs and efficiency of shipping goods by land and by water, see Landers 2003, 72–97; Greene 1986, 39–41; and Chevallier 1972, 228–32, with the useful correctives in Laurence 1999, 78–122; see esp. 109–14 on the Tiber as an artery of transport for Rome.

many of them will have reached the city by boat, in a supply operation that the corporation of *caudicarii*, the boatmen traditionally responsible for the transport of enormous quantities of public grain from Ostia and Portus to the city, or Aurelian's new college of *navicularii amnici* would both have been well-qualified to undertake.[82] Other bricks might have come from several *figlinae* located just outside the city center, on the Viae Salaria and Nomentana, and near the baths of Caracalla, all of them thus in close proximity to the circuit of the Wall.[83] Hence, neither the production nor the transport of new bricks for the Wall is likely to have required much more effort, if any, than the recuperation and reuse of older ones; and while it is possible that the previously (semi?) dormant *figlinae* were unable to meet demand, they were very probably required to produce as many new bricks as possible.[84]

Finally, once the course of the Wall had been planned, the property it was to cross vindicated to the public domain, its design established, and provisions made for acquiring the necessary supplies and delivering them where they needed to go, it remained only to build the thing. For this, labor was required, in sufficiently massive quantities to erect the projected length of wall in a handful of years. According to Malalas, writing 300 years after the fact, Aurelian accomplished this by mobilizing the members of the city's professional trade organizations, the *collegia*, to undertake the work.[85] There is good reason to accept the basic truth of this statement,

---

[82] Though, of course, others could also have been employed to float bricks downstream to the city. The introduction of the *navicularii amnici* at any rate shows that Aurelian was willing and able to arrange for the transport of riverborne commodities in quantity: see *HA Aur.* 47; cf. De Robertis 1955, 131.

[83] For *figlinae* on the Viae Salaria and Nomentana, see Steinby 1974, 82 and 100ff.; cf. 1986, 154, with n. 142; on the *figlinae sulpicianae*, probably located on the *vicus sulpicius*, and thus in the general vicinity of the baths of Caracalla, see Steinby 1978, 1,509; *LTUR* 5, 192–4.

[84] This is Bloch's explanation for the need to use recycled bricks in the Wall (1947, 313); whatever the capacity of the *figlinae*, recycled bricks were certainly used wherever readily available.

[85] Malalas, *Chronographia* 12, 30 (Dindorf ed. 300–1): ἣ μόνον δὲ ἐβασίλευσεν, ἤρχατο τὰ τείχη Ῥώμης κτίζειν γενναῖα ἣν γὰρ τῷ χρόνῳ φθαρέντα. αὐτὸς δὲ ἐφέστηκε τῷ ἔργῳ καὶ ἠνάγκαζε τὰ συνέργεια Ῥώμης ὑπουργεῖν τῷ κτίσματι καὶ πληρώσας τὰ τείχη ἐν ὀλίγῳ πάνυ χρόνῳ ἐποίησε θείαν αὐτοῦ κέλευσιν, ἵνα ἐξ ἐκείνου τοῦ χρόνου οἱ τῆς πόλεως πάσης ἐργαστηριακοὶ Αὐρηλιανοὶ χρηματίζουσι, τοῦ βασιλικοῦ ὀνόματος λαβόντες τὴν ἀξίαν ὑπὲρ τιμῆς καὶ κόπων ("As soon as he began ruling, he started to build anew the walls of Rome, for at that time they were ruinous. He set to the work and pressed into service the colleges (*sunergeia*) of Rome to undertake the project, and having completed the walls in very little time, he gave his official proclamation that from that time on the workmen (*ergasteriakoi*) of the whole city should be styled *aurelianoi*, taking the right to the regal name in honor of their labors"). The fundamental work on Roman corporations is still Waltzing 1895–1900; also important are the shorter and more recent works of De Robertis 1955 and 1963.

and past commentators on the Wall have invariably done so, without going much further into the matter.[86]

The technical standard of the Wall is certainly far too high to have been achieved by workers without long experience and specialized expertise. As the bulk of the army was away in Palmyra when the Wall was being built, this leaves the professional civilian builders of the city as the logical candidates; and the number and diversity of the attested specialists suggests that these would indeed have been sufficient for the task, particularly if all qualified personnel were forcibly enlisted. In addition to the principal *collegium* of builders, the *fabri tignuarii*, which alone counted 1,300 members in Hadrian's time, there were also the bronzeworkers, ironworkers, pavers, stonecutters, demolitions experts, and possibly an additional college of builders, the *structores*, all of which would have had their part to play.[87] Moreover, it has been plausibly argued that all or most of the builders wealthy enough to qualify for membership (and pay dues) in the building corporations them- selves employed groups of something like three to ten subordinates, in which case the total number of skilled builders available in the city, even after the building slump of the mid third century, must still have numbered in the thousands.[88] Presumably, then, these are the corporations which Malalas meant to indicate with his blanket reference to *sunergeia*, along with those responsible for transport, discussed previously.[89]

As for the organization of the labor, and the manner in which the Wall was constructed, little can be said for certain. Joins visible in the facing of many curtains demonstrate that it was built in discrete sections, a practice commonly attested for other circuit walls, some of which preserve inscriptions detailing the contributions of particular groups of laborers.[90] It can be further assumed that these sections rose approximately simultaneously in different parts of the

---

[86] Cf. Richmond 1930, 29.

[87] On the *fabri tignuarii*, see Waltzing, *Étude* 2, 117–19; the others are listed on p. 122, with full textual and epigraphic citations. Following the order in which they appear above, they are attested as the *collegium aerariorum fabrum*; *conlegium fabrum ferrarium*; *collegium pavimentariorum*; *conleg. Secto[rum] serrarium*; *co[llegium] subrutor(um)*; *collegium struc [torum]*. For the *structores*, see *CIL* 6, 444; cf. *CJ* 10, 64, 1: *structores, id est aedificatores*.

[88] See Delaine 1997, 195–205, esp. 199; cf. 2000, 132; Anderson 1997, 115–16.

[89] It is, of course, entirely possible that additional practitioners of unrelated trades were employed in supporting roles that did not call for specialized skills.

[90] Two extant inscriptions record that work-gangs from two papal estates (*domuscultae*) each built one tower and length of curtain in the Leonine Wall (see Ward-Perkins and Gibson 1979, 33). Where the joins in the Aurelianic Wall are visible, they come at intervals spaced *c.* 8–15 meters apart. In the Honorian heightening, the vertical spacing between rows of putlog holes indicates that the curtains were elevated in increments of approximately 1.5 meters, corresponding with the reach of a standing mason.

circuit, and that construction did not begin at one point and proceed continuously in a clockwise or counterclockwise direction. As only a limited number of people could physically have been employed on any one stretch of the Wall, the more efficient and expeditious means of employing the thousands of available collegiate laborers would have been to disperse them widely around its perimeter.[91] This solution also best accounts for the numerous localized variations visible around the circuit, such as the single files of bricks arranged around the outer contours of relieving arches, which appear only in a few instances.[92] The subdivision of the labor force is surely also necessary to explain the relatively speedy completion of the Wall in the span of *c.* 5–10 years, an impressive accomplishment that is nonetheless not at all remarkable relative to other ambitious Roman fortification projects. The massive fifth-century land walls at Constantinople were completed within nine years, according to a recently discovered inscription, and Breeze and Dobson have estimated that the entire 120 km of Hadrian's Wall, where the participation of multiple work-gangs is quite certain, were largely completed in three years' time (!) by perhaps 10,000 legionary soldiers, plus some additional support personnel.[93] Hence, we may imagine that the course of the Wall was first surveyed – and presumably marked with paint or (better) ropes and stakes – and that demolitions, the digging of the foundation trench, the pouring of the foundations and, finally, the erection of the Wall proper were undertaken by multiple work-gangs following a common and publicized set of general specifications.[94]

[91] Similar conclusions about the simultaneous use of multiple work-gangs have been reached regarding the construction of enceintes in Gaul, at e.g. Le Mans and Jublains; see Guilleux 2000, 229–36.

[92] E.g. around the windows of tower A23, and the doorway leading to tower G15 (Figure 1.18).

[93] The Theodosian walls of Constantinople are actually a double wall, 5.7 km in length, with a lower *proteichisma* in front of the principal rampart. The inscription (found in 1993 and published in Lebek 1995), which commemorates repairs to the wall following an earthquake in 447, explicitly states that it was first built in nine years (see Chapter 3, n. 156). On Hadrian's Wall, see Breeze and Dobson 1976, esp. 72–4. A new study of the Saxon shore forts in Britain suggests that the eight built in the late third century were jointly accomplished in less than three years, and perhaps in a single building season (Pearson 2003, 106–8). Closer to Rome, more than a kilometer of wall was built at Verona in eight months in 265 (*CIL* 5, 3329; cf. La Rocca 1986, 47 and n. 80).

[94] There is growing evidence for the use of both two-dimensional scaled plans and three-dimensional architectural models in the Roman period; the data are surveyed in Haselberger 1997, esp. 88ff., and Taylor 2003, 27–36. The standardization in the dimensions and spacing of towers, forts, and wall-curtains at Hadrian's Wall likewise strongly suggests that its builders were following a plan drafted in advance: see Breeze and Dobson 1976, 38 and 72. Here, it would seem that the foundations were poured everywhere in advance of the erection of the curtains themselves, some of which were built only after some time (months, if not years) had elapsed (*ibid.* 67–8); my guess is that the same sequence was followed at Rome. On the use of ropes and stakes to mark out the location of future walls, see Taylor 2003, 64–6.

2.3   Subsequent history

On Chastagnol's interpretation, the care of the Wall should have come, by the middle of the fourth century, within the purview of the *praefectus urbi*, along with the rest of the city's infrastructure.[95] A law of 368 describes the new duties of the prefect explicitly: he is to watch over all other officials in the city administration, particularly those in charge of public services (*publicum munus*), "as though looking out from a watchtower."[96] By this time, the gamut of compulsory *munera* over which he presided must have been elaborate indeed, as was the functioning of the system designed to ensure the availability of the supplies and labor necessary to maintain the architectural patrimony of the city.[97] In 365, for example, the *vectores* and *calcis coctores* were required to transport and prepare 3,000 cartloads of mortar, half for the maintenance of the aqueducts, and the rest for other public buildings, all to be accomplished under the *praefectus urbi*'s supervision.[98]

The sparse evidence for the Wall accords well, as far as it goes, with the more general picture. On the inscriptions commemorating the building campaign of 401–3, the *praefectus urbi* appears as the sole official in charge, with no sign of a *curator operum publicorum* or the like.[99] Valentinian III's *Novella* of 440, on the upkeep of the Wall, is likewise directed to the *praefectus urbi*, and states in no uncertain terms that the ultimate responsibility for the task was his.[100]

The labor for the maintenance of the Wall in this period would again have come, at least in large part, from the building *collegia*, now bound by law to government service. Yet by the end of the fourth century, all was not well with the corporations, largely because of the increasingly burdensome nature of the mandatory services required of them. Reams of legislation aimed at recalling fugitive workers testifies to the increasing debility of the corporate system;[101] and it is probably not by chance that the years around

---

[95]   The evidence is exhaustively presented in Chastagnol 1960, 43ff.

[96]   *CTh.* 1, 6, 6 (*anno* 368): *Illustris sinceritas tua quasi in speculis tuebitur, quemadmodum singuli, quibus intra urbem Romam publicum munus iniungimus, credito sibi famulentur officio...*

[97]   Cf. above nn. 59–61.   [98]   *CTh.* 14, 6, 3.

[99]   In the approximately contemporary *Notitia Dignitatum*, the *curator operum maximorum* and *curator operum publicorum* are listed as subordinate officials, appearing in the tenth and eleventh positions on the list of city administrators: see *Notitia, Occ.* 4, entitled *sub dispositione viri illustris praefecti urbis habentur amministrationes infrascriptae;* cf. Jones 1964, 691.

[100]   *CTh Nov. Val.* 5, 2–3; see Chapter 1, n. 71.

[101]   *CTh.* 12, 19, 1 (*anno* 400): *Destitutae ministeriis civitates splendorem, quo pridem nituerant, amiserunt: plurimi siquidem collegiati cultum urbium deserentes agrestem vitam secuti in secreta sese et devia contulerunt. Sed talia ingenia huiusmodi auctoritate destruimus, ut, ubicumque*

400 witnessed the enactment of a series of imperial decrees requiring the participation of the civilian population as a whole in the maintenance of public works, and the repair of walls and roads above all. The earliest such laws relate generally to the provinces of the empire, in the case of city walls, and perhaps to rural populations above all in the case of roads.[102] As the Honorian heightening of the Wall was clearly not the work of amateurs, enough professionals were apparently still available in the city of Rome, or within range of imperial summons, that the general populace was not pressed into service.

Forty years later, however, the *Novella* of Valentinian III makes a point of stating that "absolutely nobody," among both the corporations and the citizenry of Rome as a whole (*Romani cives*), was to be excused from the repair of the Wall.[103] The Roman situation was closely paralleled at Constantinople, where in 413, the towers of the new Theodosian wall were no sooner completed than given over to the free use of the private citizens on whose land they stood, in return for which their individual proprietors were expected to shoulder the expenses and the legal responsibility for keeping them in working military order.[104] In both the old Rome and the new, then, the first half of the fifth century witnessed the widespread institutional sanction of the use of non-specialists in the maintenance of city walls. It is certainly tempting to connect this development with the appearance of the more technically rudimentary repairs to the Aurelian Wall, and to attribute, for example, the most irregular *opus vittatum* to conscript workers brought in, as it were, off the street. Still, in light of the precipitous decline of the urban *collegia* from the early fifth century on, and the progressive depopulation of the city as a whole that culminated with the Gothic Wars in the middle of the sixth, it may be more accurate to imagine simply that the gap between "professionals" or "specialists" and laymen grew less pronounced, to the point where such distinctions become effectively meaningless.[105]

---

terrarum repperti fuerint, ad officia sua sine ullius nisu exceptionis revocentur, cf. 14, 7, 1 (397); 14, 2, 4 (412); 14, 1, 179 (415).

[102] *CTh.* 15, 1, 34 (*anno* 396): *Omnes provinciarum rectores litteris moneantur, ut sciant ordines adque incolas urbium singularum muros vel novos debere facere vel firmius veteres renovare...*; cf. *CTh* 15, 1, 35 (of 397), and *CJ* 9, 11, 7 (of 384). A law of 412, addressed to the *praefectus praetorio* of Illyricum, likewise states that the construction of walls, and the transport of supplies, was to apply to everyone, from the upper classes to the lowest (*CTh.* 15, 1, 49). On roads, *CTh.* 15, 3, 3 (*anno* 387): *a viarum munitione nullus habeatur immunis...*; cf. 15, 3, 4; 15, 3, 6.

[103] *CTh Nov. Val.* 5, 2–3; cited at Chapter 1, n. 71.

[104] See *CTh.* 15, 1, 51, cited above at n. 58.

[105] On the decline and dissolution of the collegiate system, see De Robertis 1955, 230ff.

2.4   The Wall and the refashioning of the urban administration

The Wall has often been made a key piece of evidence in an ongoing
discussion about whether Aurelian "militarized" the *collegia* of the city,
binding their members for life and making the public services they
performed mandatory, a situation that unquestionably prevailed under
Constantine. The *collegia* at Rome had existed since the early days of the
republic, if not before, as free associations between individuals practicing a
common trade or profession. Many had long had a relationship with the
city government, voluntarily performing essential services, among them
the construction of public buildings, in return for immunities from
taxation and other privileges.[106] When the baths of Caracalla were built
early in the third century, the principal college of builders, the *fabri
tignuarii*, was still free to negotiate the terms of its participation as it
pleased.[107] A hundred years later, the *collegia* were subject to the compulsory execution of their public mandates, with their members bound to
them in perpetuity (*obnoxii*), along with their posterity and their lands
and possessions (*patrimonium*).[108]

A dramatic change had thus occurred at some point in between, the
causes and chronology of which have been much discussed. E. Groag long
ago attributed a seminal role in the process to Aurelian, basing his
arguments largely on Malalas' account of the building of the Wall.[109] More
recent scholarship has downplayed Aurelian's importance, as it has

---

[106]   On contracts between corporations and the city government, see De Robertis 1955, 138–56;
Waltzing, *Étude* 2, 121; 393–430. The recruitment of the corporate members likely
devolved upon the *praefecti* and *curatores* responsible for the various sectors in which they
were needed, which included, in addition to construction, firefighting, grain-transport,
maintenance of sewers, streets and waterways, etc.: cf. Waltzing, *Étude* 2, 115ff.

[107]   *CIC Dig.* 50, 6, 6, 12 (Callistratus, writing *c.* 200): *Quibusdam collegiis vel corporibus, quibus ius
coeundi lege permissum est, immunitas tribuitur: scilicet eis collegiis vel corporibus, in quibus
artificii sui causa unusquisque adsumitur, ut fabrorum corpus est et si qua eandem rationem
originis habent, id est idcirco instituta sunt, ut necessariam operam publicis utilitatibus*; cf. De
Robertis 1955, 125 and 149; Waltzing, *Étude* 2, 118). It is noteworthy that the builders (*fabri*)
are singled out as the example *par excellence* of a "publicly useful" corporation.

[108]   A lengthy series of laws in the Theodosian Code, beginning early in the reign of Constantine,
repeatedly affirms the "freezing" of the *collegia*: The *navicularii* were so obligated by 314
(*CTh.* 13, 5, 1); the *pistores*, bakers of the loaves distributed in the grain dole, by the
following year (13, 5, 2); and the *suarii* responsible for the urban pork dole, in 334 (14, 4, 1).
On the individual holdings that comprised the endowment of each *collegium*, which were
also made inalienable, see *CTh.* 14, 3, 1 (319); 13, 6, 1 (326); and 14, 3, 7 (364). On the new status
of the *collegia* in the fourth century, see De Robertis 1955, 157–85; Waltzing, *Étude* 2, 259ff.

[109]   *RE* 5 (1903), 1410.

regarding his role in the transitions of the third century more generally; and as has been noted previously, claims that he redefined the role of the *praefectus urbi,* or radically overhauled the brick industry, have probably been exaggerated. Yet while many have been unwilling to consider the conscription of the builders described by Malalas a permanent measure, or therefore to attribute to Aurelian a sweeping reform of the corporate system, I believe that a number of corporations, the *fabri* among them, were indeed first brought under rigid state control during his reign.[110]

Aurelian is widely credited with a reorganization of the food dole in Rome, whereby the range of commodities to be distributed free or at a reduced price was expanded to include pork and wine, and the grain and oil rations increased.[111] The *HA* says that he augmented the daily ration of bread by an ounce, and introduced the *navicularii amnici,* a new association of Tiber boatmen, to ensure the ready and permanent distribution of the increased supplies.[112] This is apparently explicit testimony that, under Aurelian, at least one college was created from the outset for government service. Even if the specifics of the *HA*'s account are inaccurate, the underlying premise that Aurelian's initiatives required a restructuring of the labor force directly involved in alimentation is unlikely to be wholly false, as most have agreed, some while denying a concomitant reorganization of the building corporations in nearly the same breath.[113]

[110] See e.g. Rostovtzeff, 1957, 462: "I cannot think that this measure, which consisted in a careful registration of all the members of the building corporations and in giving to these the title of *Aureliani* ... was perpetuated, and that it should be considered as the beginning of a new era for all the corporations of the capital." Bloch concurred (1947, 313, n. 235), while De Robertis (1955, 163) felt that it was wasted effort ("fatica sprecata") trying to determine which emperor imposed compulsory service on the corporations, again explicitly *contra* Groag's suggestion of Aurelian. Steinby (1986, 109), on the other hand, is unwilling to discount the possibility that Aurelian did in fact "militarize" the builders of the city.

[111] See Durliat 1990, 42–51; Homo 1904, 176–83. More generally on Aurelian's various alleged economic and administrative initiatives, see now Watson 1999, 125–202; and Kotula 1997, 76–81 and 158–74. With some reason, Coarelli has suggested that some alimentary reforms, including the distribution of bread instead of grain and the introduction of pork, may have begun under Alexander Severus: see Coarelli 1987, esp. 452–53. Still, these would seem to have been tentative beginnings, suspended during the difficult years at mid-century, which remained for Aurelian definitively to realize; see Chapter 4.

[112] *HA Aur.* 47, 2–3: *nihil mihi est magnificentius, quam quod additamento unciae omnem annonarum urbicarum genus iuvi. quod ut esset perpetuum, navicularios Niliacos apud Aegyptum novos et Romae amnicos posui...*; cf. *ibid.* 35, 1–2.

[113] Immediately after voicing his belief that the enrolment of the builders was a temporary measure, Rostovtzeff continued (1957, 462): "On the other hand, it is highly probable that, in connexion with the reorganization of the system of victualling the city of Rome, Aurelian reorganized the associations which were connected with the food trade and the transport of foodstuffs and made them real agents of the state... For the corporations this meant that their

Yet there is reason to suspect that the conscription of the builders for the Wall resulted in changes no less permanent. Both before Aurelian and after, the building *collegia* were frequently featured as paragons of publicly useful corporations. The jurist Callistratus, writing under Septimius Severus, used the *fabri* as the example *par excellence* of a *collegium* upon whose services the state depended.[114] In the fourth century, Symmachus ticked off the corporations most essential to the urban administration, among which the *fabri* are cited in the midst of a list otherwise dominated by *collegia* involved in the provisioning of the city, and thus in precisely the sectors, in addition to public building, where Aurelian is supposed to have intervened.[115] The builders, then, were frequently and specifically included in a relatively confined list of essential "public-service" corporations; and they are no less likely to have been permanently reorganized than any of the rest: just as the forced service of the *navicularii, suarii, pistores* and others was required to realize Aurelian's effort to augment and diversify the dole, so was that of the building corporations for the erection of his enormous Wall, and his other projects besides.

There is in addition the issue of Malalas' rather strange allusion to the conferral of the title "Aureliani" on all those involved in the construction of the Wall. While it was ostensibly an honor, a token of extraordinary

members were now definitely bound to them, and that they themselves might be reinforced by the compulsory enrolment of new members."

[114] *CIC Dig.* 50, 6, 6, 12 (above n. 107). Plenary immunities specifically for artisans, among them a wide range of construction-workers, were confirmed in a law of 337 (*CTh.* 13, 4, 2), promulgated to encourage the teaching and proliferation of their various professions.

[115] During his tenure as city prefect in 384–85, Symmachus wrote to the emperor asking him to reconsider the imposition of a "horse tax" (*conlatio equorum*) on the collegiate members of the city of Rome (traditionally immune from all taxes and duties unrelated to their compulsory service), whom he rhetorically enumerated thus: *Hic laniati pecoris invector est, ille ad victum populi cogit armentum, hos suillae carnis tenet functio, pars urenda lavacris ligna conportat, sunt qui fabriles manus augustis operibus adcommodent, per alios fortuita arcentur incendia. Iam caupones et obsequia pistoria, frugis et olei baiulos multosque id genus patriae servientes enumerare fastidium est* (*Relatio* 14, 3). The public services described, evidently the ones Symmachus thought most noteworthy, correspond remarkably closely with those in which Aurelian is supposed to have interested himself in the *HA*, where it is said that he made distributions of tunics (requiring wool brought by Symmachus' *laniati pecoris invector*), pork (*suillae carnis functio*), and wine (*caupones*); increased the ration of grain and oil (*frugis et olei baiulos*); and initiated the distribution of loaves of bread instead of unmilled grain, for which bakers, precisely those described by Symmachus' *obsequia pistoria*, would have been required (see *HA Aur.* 48; on the change from grain to baked bread, Durliat 1990, 42). The only additional *corporati* to appear in Symmachus' list are the firemen, or *vigiles* (*per alios fortuita arcentur incendia*), those who supplied wood for the heating of the public baths (*pars urenda lavacris ligna conportat*), and the *fabri* themselves (*sunt qui fabriles manus augustis operibus adcommodent*).

service, one may wonder just how honored the conscripts felt, and whether their novel designation might not have euphemistically recalled a harsher reality. Questions of popular sentiment aside, the substance of Malalas' statement appears to be that an unprecedented link was forged between the corporations and the emperor, which earned the *corporati* a lifelong "distinction" perhaps as indicative of their newly permanent ties to the imperial service as it was of their outstanding contributions.

It might, of course, be argued that the Wall was envisioned as a unique undertaking that would not have prompted long-term, systemic changes, and therefore that business as usual resumed upon its completion. Given that mandatory collegiate labor was an established fact from the beginning of Constantine's reign, however, and that builders in the fourth century were an integral component of the system, it is hard to deny that the example of the Wall at least set a precedent that, if not made permanent under Aurelian, became so very soon thereafter. Of course, sweeping changes in the legal status of the urban *collegia* were not fully realized in the five years of Aurelian's reign (nor the alimentary reforms in general, nor probably the Wall itself), and the corporate system continued always to change and evolve. On the current state of the evidence, however, the burden of proof should rest with those who believe the novel initiatives of Aurelian's time only temporary (or nonexistent). In the absence of such proof, I prefer to think that these reforms did not vanish without trace for a decade or two following his death, only to be resuscitated *ex nihilo*, in surprisingly mature form, under the Tetrarchs and then Constantine.

Taking Malalas at his word, then, it seems that the construction of the Wall itself prompted an unprecedented mobilization of compulsory corporate labor, which likely had lasting effects on the way public building in Rome was conducted. Further, there is reason to suspect that the ripple effect of the Wall project affected more than the management of human resources: there may have been additional ramifications especially with respect to the financing of public structures under the later empire, when the private *munificentia* that had underwritten so many of the architectural undertakings of the high empire was in wholesale decline.[116]

As is generally the case, the results of the hypothetically Aurelianic innovation are better attested in the fourth century, by the second half

---

[116] On "the decline of secular munificence," see Ward-Perkins 1984, 3–48; cf. also 1998, 373–82; Liebeschuetz 1992, esp. 3–9.

of which the *arca vinaria*, a public treasury administered by the prefect of the city and the *comes sacrarum largitionum*, was the single most import-ant source of funding for the upkeep of the city's physical infrastructure, as it remained in the sixth.[117] It is thus quite striking to learn that the *arca vinaria* apparently traced its origins to Aurelian's introduction of a state-subsidized wine ration. In the *HA*, we are told that he gave vast tracts of uncultivated land to *possessores*, to be planted with vines and worked by prisoners, to furnish abundant supplies of cheap wine for consumption in the capital. The wine was sold from the steps of Aurelian's new temple of Sol, where the *arca vinaria* itself had its seat.[118] The particulars of the system are confirmed in detail by an inscription, probably carved not long after the time of Aurelian.[119] The *possessores* of the new estates were responsible for delivering the wine to the city, where the wooden barrels (*cupae*) in which it was shipped were unloaded on the banks of the Tiber in the Campus Martius, *ad ciconias*, and thence transported to the temple of Sol by a corporation of *falancarii*. In 365, the price of the wine distributed there was fixed at 25 percent below the current market rate.[120]

Much admittedly remains uncertain about the extent of Aurelian's contribution, and about his precise intentions; and if only because of the time required for vines to grow and bear fruit, he cannot have lived to see the undertaking through to fruition.[121] What does seem clear are the following facts: the initiative is credited to Aurelian in the only relevant ancient source. The wine was distributed from his temple, and the profits from its sale went into a treasury, the *arca vinaria*, located in the same

---

[117] Funding for mortar production "customarily" came from the *arca vinaria* by 365 (*CTh.* 14, 6, 3); twenty years later, Symmachus referred to money missing from this treasury as "that which was supposed to be spent for public works" (*id quod operis publicis constabat impensum*; *Ep.* 9, 150, 1). Under Theoderic, the yearly sum allotted for the upkeep of the imperial palace and public buildings (*moenia*) at Rome came entirely from the *arca vinaria* (*Anon. Val.*, *MGH AA* 9, p. 324); cf. generally Chastagnol 1960, 341ff.

[118] *Aur.* 48: *argumento est id vere Aurelianum cogitasse, immo etiam facere disposuisse vel ex aliqua parte fecisse, quod in porticibus templi Solis fiscalia vina ponuntur, non gratuita populo eroganda, sed pretio*; cf. Virlouvet 1995, 51–9; Durliat 1990, 348–51; Chastagnol 1960, 321–5; Waltzing, *Étude* 2, 96–100.

[119] *CIL* 6, 1785, probably dating to *c.* 300; see Virlouvet 1995, 56–9; Rougé 1957, 320–8.

[120] *CTh.* 11, 2, 2; Chastagnol 1960, 322–3.

[121] Cf. Durliat 1990, 348–51, who also believes nonetheless that Aurelian took the initial steps. Beginning precisely in the later third century, the percentage of wine-amphorae reaching Rome, relative to those containing other goods, began a steep decline that reached its nadir between 350 and 400; some link with Aurelian's reform of the wine-dole, and the subsequent proliferation of wine arriving from upriver in wooden barrels, seems highly plausible; see Panella and Saguì 2001, 772–3; Panella 1999, 199–205.

place.[122] By the fourth century, it was a highly profitable enterprise, and the considerable revenues that accrued to the *arca vinaria* were largely or totally dedicated to public building projects. It is therefore no great stretch to see more than coincidence in the fact that the best candidate for the introduction of this system was also responsible for erecting the most extensive structure ever seen in Rome, before or since. Even if the Wall was completed before the new estates produced a drop of wine, the demands of its construction may well have contributed to the impetus behind the creation of the new treasury, assuming of course that this was an approximately contemporary development. If it was, the case grows for viewing the Wall as an important factor, even a defining one, in the development of an inter-related cluster of imperial initiatives that redefined the mechanics of government-sponsored building at Rome.

And if the *arca vinaria* came to maturity too late to be of use in funding the construction of the Wall, it almost certainly did underwrite later reconstructions, most notable among them the Honorian heightening of 401–3. Just the year before the project began, in fact, this treasury was a subject of some concern in the upper levels of the city administration. The son-in-law of Symmachus, Flavianus Nicomachus the younger, was accused of misappropriation of funds from the *arca vinaria* during his tenure as city prefect. The emperor himself demanded a full accounting, along with the speedy restitution of the missing money, the responsibility for which devolved upon the *comes sacrarum largitionum,* Flavius Macrobius Longinianus.[123] Symmachus in turn attempted to intervene on behalf of his relative, urging Longinianus to act with more restraint in his effort to recoup the money.[124] How the matter ended is uncertain, but curiously enough, the same Longinianus was the *praefectus urbi* who supervised the rebuilding of the Wall and put up the dedicatory inscriptions on its new gates only three years later. In the same three-year period, that is, we see him first making a strenuous effort to refill the *arca vinaria*, before turning almost immediately to supervising the largest construction

---

[122] The *HA* claims that Aurelian first intended to distribute the wine free, but was ultimately persuaded to sell it (see above n. 118); one may wonder, if the story has any truth to it, whether the cost of the Wall (and his other projects besides) did not lead to the change in plans, and perhaps even to the earmarking of the profits for building commissions.

[123] *CTh.* 12, 6, 26, of June, 400, addressed to Benignus, the *vicarius urbis*. Cf. Chastagnol 1950, 182–3; 1960, 345.

[124] Symmachus, *Ep.* 7, 96, 3: *interea nimis miror, quod in viro inlustri Flaviano domino et filio meo nec gradum honoris nec ius amicitiae cogitasti. Nam cum praestans auctoritas tua vinarii tituli debita flagitaret, usque ad officii multam contemptione praegressa est. Patienter admitte, neque praefecturam neque amantissimum tui virum tali contumelia debuisse perstringi.*

project to occur in Rome since the building of Aurelian's Wall. I am again tempted to see more than coincidence at work here, though the evidence hardly conduces to the coherent sequence of cause and effect that a minimally inspired raconteur might nonetheless readily create.

Once built, the Wall might if necessary even have paid for itself, had the *arca vinaria* at any given time disposed of insufficient funds for its upkeep. It was clearly paying for other buildings in the city by the early fifth century, when during the pontificate of Innocent I (401–17), a portion of the revenues collected at the Porta Numentana (*sic*) was earmarked for the endowment of the new titular church of Saints Gervasus and Protasus (now S. Vitale).[125] While customs dues had long been levied on traffic entering Rome, the line of demarcation had previously been marked only by widely spaced *cippi*; presumably, the less permeable obstacle presented by the Wall would have had a positive effect on the efficiency of customs collection, and thus on the city's bottom line.[126] Hence, the Wall need not be regarded as an unmitigated drain on a limited pool of financial resources. Over the long term, it may even have represented an investment of sorts.

In the end, the logistical assessment of the Wall's construction requires something of a balancing act. On the one hand, the relative paucity of explicitly relevant testimony often requires treating it as a product of its times, leaving the details to be extrapolated from what is generally known, or knowable, about administrative structures and conventions as they were in previous and subsequent periods. On the other, the Wall was no ordinary undertaking, and to undervalue its potential as an agent in the reshaping of the very political and economic ambit from which it sprang is to miss possibly the most interesting part of the story. The question thus becomes one of deciding when to proceed from the general to the specific, and when, or whether, to see in a few suggestive details the germ that heralded or even prompted the reconfiguration of the larger picture. And if a causal link between the Wall and the changes that occurred between the Severan period and the accession of Constantine cannot be regarded as definitively proven, the practical effects of its construction must nonetheless have mirrored them closely indeed, prompting a move – however temporary and *ad hoc* – in precisely the directions known to have been taken under Diocletian, his colleagues, and his successors.

[125] See *LP* 1, 222: *siliquas III, uncias III, portae Numentanae...*, with n. 15 on p. 223.
[126] Cf. Palmer 1980, 219–21.

It is less debatable that the construction of the Wall was an extraordinary endeavor, all the more so as it came after a period of relative inactivity,
and that drastic initiatives were required to put the necessary pieces in
place in the span of a few years. It also evident that scant decades after its
construction, both the financing of public buildings and the organization
of the labor force were nothing like they had been at the beginning of the
third century. I am sufficiently convinced that the construction of the Wall
required novel interventions in precisely these areas to see the event as a
watershed in the history of public building in Rome, and thus also to
consider it part and parcel of an extensive series of Aurelianic reforms that
saw the more important corporations bound to the service of the state, the
range of government-subsidized commodities expanded, and the creation
of a new treasury, the *arca vinaria*, to help defray the cost of public works
formerly underwritten to a greater extent by private munificence.

3 | Motives, meaning, and context: the Aurelian Wall and the late Roman state

The preceding look at the immense logistical hurdles inherent in the construction and maintenance of the Aurelian Wall raises another query as yet insufficiently explored, for all (or perhaps because of) its apparent obviousness: why was the thing built in the first place, and subsequently so laboriously rebuilt and renovated? As it turns out, the question of what the Wall was supposed to do is rather less straightforward than it might seem; and "defense," the preferred response to date, provides only a partial explanation. Although the political and strategic military dynamics of the late empire cannot be overlooked, they are perhaps more usefully seen as the foundation for the "what for?" inquiry, rather than the final word. The same can be said for the treatment of the Wall in its broader context, as part of a widespread spate of wall-building during the later third, fourth, and fifth centuries that culminated in an empire-wide revamping of classical urban paradigms. While the Wall's place in this process requires further assessment, both to elucidate the rationale for its construction, and to better establish the nature of its influence upon the development and subsequent proliferation of urban fortifications in late antiquity, the truly exceptional nature of both the monument and the city of Rome itself cannot be overstated. The fortification of the *caput mundi* was, in both practical and conceptual terms, an unparalleled endeavor. Rome was in many respects a world unto itself, maintained by a vast influx of supplies, money, and migrants, all fuelling the production of more symbolic and ideological "capital" than anything very tangible. Hence, a more nuanced and complete understanding of the motives governing the construction of the Wall will require additional consideration of Rome's internal politics and administration, and the complex motives involved in maintaining a city of as many as a million hungry, chronically under-employed mouths essentially for its own sake, as a showpiece and a figurehead for Romans, provincials, and "outsiders" alike.[1]

---

[1] The scale and complexity of the effort needed to supply the (chronically underemployed) urban plebs is addressed in e.g. Aldrete and Mattingly 2000 and Lo Cascio 1999. On Rome as "showpiece and figurehead," cf. Edwards and Woolf 2003, esp. 1–20; 203–21.

3.1   The motives for Aurelian's Wall

The traditional explanation for Aurelian's decision to build the Wall has stressed two related factors. First, the preceding decade had witnessed two large-scale barbarian incursions into the heart of northern Italy, the first since the attacks of the Marcomanni a century before, both of which had been repulsed with considerable difficulty, and only after wide swathes of territory had been ravaged. In the course of the most recent attack by the Iuthungi, in the winter of AD 270–1, the city of Rome itself had lain open to the prospect of imminent attack for a few terrifying weeks following the initial defeat of Aurelian's army at Placentia (Piacenza).[2] While the threat dissipated after Aurelian caught up with the invaders and inflicted two successive defeats upon them, the capital remained shaken, the scene of widespread discontent and unrest that culminated in open rioting.[3] In addition, Aurelian was preparing to set off for the east to put down the rebellion of Queen Zenobia of Palmyra, a task that required him to take many of the troops stationed in the west to the east, leaving the frontiers dangerously thinly manned. Thus, the Wall was to assuage the fears of the restive populace of the city, and to ensure Rome's security in a way that the depleted standing army could not, in the event of renewed hostilities.[4]

As far as it goes, the standard account is not without its merits. It is surely significant that Rome's defenses were erected in the immediate aftermath of the two most serious barbarian incursions witnessed on Italian soil in centuries. More generally speaking, it is likely not a chance occurrence that city walls began to spring up *en masse* in previously secure interior regions of the empire at precisely the time when its frontiers were first coming to be widely and repeatedly breached (a correlation discussed in more detail below). But while defense must have been one of the factors

---

[2] The chronology of the first year of Aurelian's reign in particular has caused substantial difficulties, and must remain speculative to a degree given the paucity of relevant sources. Still, scholars are now increasingly agreed that there was only one attack by the Iuthungi (and not two as was once widely believed, e.g. by Homo 1904, 59ff.), and that it took place in the first part of 271, perhaps in early spring; see e.g. Watson 1999, 46ff. and Appendix B; Kotula 1997, 64ff. For the earlier invasion of northern Italy by the Alemanni in 259–60, see Watson 1999, 34, and Homo 1904, 52 and 219, with the accounts in Zosimus (1, 37–8) and Aurelius Victor (*de Caes.* 33, 3), which are now vividly confirmed by an inscription found at Augsburg in 1992 (see *AE* 1993, 1231, with the bibliographical references in Witschel 2004, 251, n. 4).

[3] *HA Aur.* 18, 2–6; cf. *de Caes.* 35, 6.

[4] See *inter alia* Watson 1999, 143–4; Richmond 1930, 241–2 (reprised in Todd 1978, 71–2); Homo 1904, 80 and 219–20; and Groag 1903, 1,376; cf. also Cozza 1987, 46.

behind the genesis of the Wall project, there will have been others at work, too, some of which have yet to receive the attention they deserve. I have singled out several that seem to me the most notable.

The timing and circumstances of the project suggest that the Wall may have had a more immediate purpose than the provision of security, or a sense thereof, in the face of potential but unspecific external threats (the recent attackers were, after all, decisively beaten when the Wall was begun). While the textual sources are frustratingly vague, it is clear that there was widespread turmoil in Rome during the first half of 271, the roots of which probably ran deeper than the temporary panic occasioned by the threat of the raiders to the north. Tensions came to a head while Aurelian was still engaged with the Iuthungi, in the form of a revolt of the mint-workers in the capital.[5] Although the several ancient accounts of the event are confused and not infrequently contradictory, and the claim that 7,000 of Aurelian's troops died when he returned to quell the rebellion surely an exaggeration, this "war" was without doubt a major event.[6] In brief, it appears that the mint workers, under the leadership of Felicissimus, the supervisor (*rationalis* or *a rationibus*) of the mint, barricaded themselves on the Caelian hill, from which they were ultimately dislodged only in open battle with imperial forces. Further, some leading members of the senate were apparently complicit in the revolt, and these may have played some role in inciting a significant segment of the urban plebs against the absent emperor; in any case, the magnitude of the insurrection was such that the rebel forces presumably counted more than the employees of the mint among their number.[7] And while the stereotyped allegations of Aurelian's cruelty in the *HA*, Aurelius Victor, Eutropius, etc. are perhaps overstated, there can be little doubt that he returned to Rome facing a concerted challenge to his authority, which he wasted little time in

---

[5] The most closely contemporary accounts (all from the following century) of the revolt and its suppression are in the *HA*, *Aur.* 38, 2–4; Aurelius Victor, *de Caes.* 35, 4–6; and Eutropius, *Brev.* 9, 14. Helpful modern discussions include Watson 1999, 52–4; Kotula 1997, 76–81; Cubelli 1992, esp. 9–52.

[6] It is called the "mint-workers' war" in the *HA* (*Aur.* 38, 2): *fuit sub Aureliano etiam monetariorum bellum Felicissimo rationali auctore*; the term is taken up much later in the *Suda* (see under μονιτάριοι), where the revolt is referred to as a "civil war" (ἐμφυλίον ... πόλεμον). The figure of 7,000 soldiers killed appears in Aurelius Victor, *de Caes.* 35, 6; and *HA Aur.* 38, 2. Malalas' statement that the revolt took place in Antioch (*Chron.* 12), defended by M. Peachin, has been generally rejected, I think rightly; the evidence is discussed in Cubelli 1992, 19–25.

[7] On the complicity of members of the senate, and the probable involvement of a broader segment of the urban populace, see Watson 1999, 52–3; Cubelli 1992, 46ff. Palmer likewise concluded that "Aurelian's war against the moneyers led by the director of the fisc was a general riot" (1980, 220).

forcefully repressing.[8] To sum up, then, the summer of 271 found Aurelian still at Rome, where he had just finished suppressing a serious uprising with considerable bloodshed. Elements of the populace doubtless remained restive; and the emperor was faced with the prospect of an imminent departure, with the bulk of his troops, for what promised to be a lengthy and taxing campaign against Zenobia and the upstart *imperium Palmyrenorum.*

In discussing the situation, others have noted that Aurelian must have concerned himself with mollifying an unruly urban plebs, in the interest of consolidating his hold on the capital during his absence; and it has not passed unnoticed that the opening preparations for the Wall were apparently undertaken in precisely this period.[9] Aurelius Victor and the *HA* seem indeed to imply a correlation, by appending the notice of the building of the Wall directly to their accounts of the seditions in the city during the moneyers' revolt.[10] Hence, the project has been seen as an attempt to placate the populace, by demonstrating Aurelian's commitment to the city and its defense, as well as the permanence and authority of his regime. I would argue, however, that the Wall's more immediate benefit in the matter of "crowd control" was probably to provide regular, paid employment for thousands of potentially idle hands. Just as sailors on ships of war have long been tasked with menial labors – not always strictly necessary ones – to keep their minds and muscles focused away from mutiny, so too might the Wall have served to divert the energies of the masses away from more destructive channels.[11]

The impact of the undertaking on employment figures in the city should not be underestimated. In her seminal study, Janet Delaine estimated that some 10,000 laborers on average were employed during the main phase of construction on the baths of Caracalla, a structure considerably smaller than the Wall that was completed in a similar timeframe.[12] If this figure is anywhere near the mark, it may be imagined that the total

---

[8] E.g. Aurelius Victor, *de Caes.* 35, 4: *Hoc tempore in urbe Rome monetarii rebellarunt, quos Aurelianus victos ultima crudelitate conpescuit*; *HA Aur.* 38, 2: *quod acerrime severissimeque conpescuit* (Aurelianus); also *ibid.* 21, 5–6; *Epit. de Caes.* 35, 4; Eutropius, *Brev.* 9, 14: *Quos (monetarios) Aurelianus victos ultima crudelitate compescuit. Plurimos nobiles capite damnavit. Saevus et sanguinarius ac necessarius magis in quibusdam quam in ullo amabilis imperator...*

[9] See e.g. Watson 1999, 54 and 144; Kotula 1991, 80–1.   [10] *HA de Caes.* 35, 6–7; *Aur.* 21, 5–9.

[11] In a similar vein, Vegetius recommends regular physical labor, including the digging of ditches, as a primary means of forestalling mutinous tendencies among the rank and file of the army (*De re militari* 3, 4, 1ff.); cf. Squatriti 2002, 11–65.

[12] See Delaine 2000, 135–6; 1997, 195–201.

number of people employed on the Wall was still higher, in which case the workforce might have comprised, on a conservative estimate, something like 10 percent of Rome's adult male inhabitants.[13] Hence, in addition to keeping an enormous number of people busy, the project would have resulted in an infusion of substantial payments, in cash and perhaps also in kind, into many Roman households, an occurrence which can only have had positive effects on the morale – and presumably the loyalty – of a sizeable segment of the populace.[14] The stability of Aurelian's regime in the capital is therefore likely to have been quite materially enhanced by means of his massive public works project, on the eve of a lengthy absence from the symbolic heart of his power.

Of course, Aurelian had faced resistance among the upper classes as well, whose discontent would have been rather less susceptible to diffusion by the increased availability of manual labor and a daily wage. While claims that the internal politics of Aurelian's reign were characterized by the systematic abrogation of the prerogatives of the senatorial order should be treated with caution, various members of the senate were evidently suspected of complicity in the disturbances at Rome, and subsequently subjected to stern reprisals.[15] Rising as it did in the immediate aftermath of these events, the Wall may also have been intended as a testament to the overweening authority of the emperor, a show of force designed to chasten and overawe his detractors. In this regard, the project would have been all the more effective for being undertaken, as I think it was, without the traditional initiative of the senate, in whose collective face it was thus in effect thrown.[16] One may additionally wonder whether the property of any of the purged senators happened to lie in the path taken by the Wall, and whether any of the senatorial estates on the periphery of the city known to have come under imperial control might not have done so

---

[13] Following Delaine's calculations, the 10,000 workers required for the baths would have comprised something like 7–8 percent of the adult male population.

[14] Delaine's observations are again germane: she imagines that the money spent on public works at Rome under the Severans was often comparable to what was given to the populace in annual donatives, and concludes that "both were alternative ways of distributing the same kinds of sums within the imperial capital" (Delaine 1997, 222); see also Brunt 1980 (on the period of the Principate as a whole).

[15] *HA Aur.* 21, 6; *ibid.* 39, 8; Zosimus 1, 49, 2; cf. Amm. 30, 8, 8. For a reappraisal of traditional scholarly claims about Aurelian's unmitigated hostility toward the senate, themselves based chiefly on the hostile ancient sources, see Watson 1999, 161ff.

[16] Cf. Cassanelli *et al.* 1974, 35. A desire to downplay this awkward reality may explain the unique and (I think) highly self-conscious reference in the *HA* to the Senate's having been consulted (*adhibito consilio senatus*; *Aur.* 21, 9) about the Wall.

following the events of 271.[17] In any event, a senatorial family like the Anicii Glabriones must have felt the emperor's power with singular immediacy, as his Wall rose in the midst of their extensive estates on the Pincio.[18]

Taking this line of reasoning a step further, it can be argued that Aurelian was acting in part to embrace and envelop the city, appropriating it to himself by putting his Wall around it. The Wall may indeed have been built with an eye to keeping people in as well as keeping them out, serving as a bulwark against sedition and invasion alike. In this light, the care taken to limit access to the upper levels of the Wall from within to a few strategic and readily defensible points takes on new meaning. With a garrison loyal to the emperor in place on the Wall, those living within its perimeter would have been as much surrounded, even trapped, as they were protected. Henceforth, movements of people and supplies occurred at the sole discretion of the emperor and his chosen representatives. Parties entering and leaving the city could have been closely monitored, checked and – in a word – controlled. As the praetorian camp was incorporated in the circuit, soldiers could in fact have gone directly from their barracks to any point on the urban periphery without ever setting foot at ground level, in the narrow streets that the Roman plebs – with ample roof tiles to hand – had effectively held against them in the past.[19] The power, latent or otherwise, thus invested in the ruling establishment must have been apparent to all who cared to look, and a powerful psychological tool in the armory of the imperial authorities.

One additional consideration deserves mention. I have already suggested that the Wall had a positive effect on the efficiency of customs-collection, and traced its apparently close relationship with the earlier customs circuit of the city.[20] While I would not go so far as Palmer has

---

[17] The steady growth of the imperial patrimony is documented in Homo 1899. There exists a single fragmentary epigraphic mention of *horti aureliani*, though both the location of this property and the date and circumstances of its entry into the imperial domain are unknown (126–7).

[18] On the location and ownership of this property, which remained in private hands through the end of the fourth century, see *LTUR* 2, 156–7 (*Domus Pinciana*); *LTUR* 3, 51 (*Horti Aciliorum*); and R. Lanciani in *BullCom* 1891, 131–55.

[19] As occurred during the riots in 238, when soldiers sallying from the *castra praetoria* chased their civilian attackers far into the city, where they were in turn assaulted from above with all manner of projectiles, with unfortunate consequences for everyone involved: see Herodian 7, 12, 5.

[20] See Chapter 2.

in making customs-collection one of the Wall's two primary *raisons d'être* (alongside defense), there is reason to think that an overhaul of the existing customs apparatus may have been an intentional result of its erection.[21] Thinking again in terms of Aurelian's broader program of administrative reforms, it will be apparent that the reorganization and expansion of the food dole needed to be paid for. At a time when the imperial treasuries were chronically depleted, and the monetarization of the economy as a whole at a low ebb, the most airtight system possible for taxing the foodstuffs and other commodities entering Rome will have been an effective way of defraying these additional costs. Dues on staples such as pork, oil, wine, and grain could have been collected in kind at the gates of the Wall, and then quickly redistributed to the urban plebs.[22] Such an arrangement could also explain Aurelian's alleged decisions to remit outstanding debts (payable chiefly in debased and scarce coin) to the fisc, and to eliminate informants in the employ of the treasury, who would have become quickly obsolete if, with the appearance of the Wall, it became quite literally impossible to find ways around paying taxes on goods bound for the city.[23]

3.2   The meaning and message of Aurelian's Wall

While the motives for the Wall's construction hitherto proposed all have a distinctly practical bent, the fortification of the city must inevitably also have been replete with symbolic and conceptual ramifications, at home and farther afield, some of them perhaps desirable and intentional, others doubtless not. An ostensibly simple question lies at the heart of the matter: could Aurelian's Wall have been meant to impress Romans and non-Romans, friends and enemies alike with its size, grandeur, and permanence, or was it a necessary evil, a patent admission of weakness necessitated by the harsh political and military exigencies of the time?

---

[21] Palmer 1980, esp. 219; cf. Lanciani 1892, 93ff.   [22] Palmer 1980, 219.

[23] See *HA Aur.* 39, 3: *idem* (Aurelianus) *quadru[m]platores ac delatores ingenti severitate persecutus est. tabulas publicas ad privatorum securitatem exuri in foro Traiani semel iussit*; with the remarks in Palmer 1980, 220. Cf. Aurelius Victor, *de Caes.* 35, 7. Interestingly, in both Victor and the *HA*, the description of these events directly follows the notice of the Wall's construction, which may again imply a connection with its appearance. The poor state of Roman coinage in general upon the accession of Aurelian is summarized in Cubelli 1992, 1–5; the subject is treated in greater depth in e.g. Callu 1969.

A response must first be qualified with the frank admission that there are no ready answers, and really no sure way of going about getting them. The always parlous process of proceeding from physical remains to what the ancients were thinking (and "meaning") is made more difficult in the case of the Aurelian Wall by the scarcity of directly pertinent written testimony, above all for the first century of its existence. Little surprise, then, that past remarks about the psychological implications of the enterprise, often made in passing, have presented it as everything from a token of decay and institutional decrepitude to a triumphal declaration of strength and determination, with a full range of intermediate positions also well represented.[24] Further, the extent to which the Wall can be seen as a "positive" or "negative" statement cannot be divorced from more practical considerations: the relative importance of what the Wall was to do and what it was to "say," that is, must be taken into account. Those who have leaned to the "negative" psychological side are not surprisingly the ones who thought its character most pragmatic and defensive, and thus essentially a sign of weakness (one doesn't, after all, often build monumental symbols of one's own defenselessness). Also, it should be remembered that what the Wall was supposed to mean and the way it was actually perceived may not have been at all the same. For that matter, what it was

---

[24] A partial sampling of comments made in the past few decades will suffice to show how deep modern ambivalence runs. According to Williams, "…it was a weakened, traumatized empire, fearful of the future. This is graphically illustrated by Aurelian's greatest surviving monument, the 12-mile fortified wall he built around Rome, following its narrow escape from the Alemannic invasion' (1985, 30). So too for Watson, "The city walls of Rome represent at once both the most emblematic and the most enduring monument of Aurelian's age. Nothing else so eloquently demonstrates that, by Aurelian's day, the Roman empire was now on the defensive" (1999, 60). Christie goes still further: "In effect Rome's walls are a blatant statement of panic and of mistrust in the ability of the legions and gods to protect both the city and the empire" (2000, 310); a sentiment reprised in Coates-Stephens' reference to the "astonishing admission of the capital's vulnerability which their construction implied" (2001, 233). At the same time, particularly outside the Anglophone world, the Wall has also been treated in a more nuanced and generally positive fashion. For Cassanelli *et al.*, it was meant to impress and menace Rome's enemies, while reinforcing the emperor's position at home: "Il progetto delle nuove mura è una diretta conseguenza della politica aureliana di rafforzamento del potere imperiale all'interno e fuori: è una risposta a quelle popolazioni 'federate' che, come gli Iutungi, minacciano scorrerie a ricompensa dei tributi non corrisposti dall'imperatore" (1974, 35). Kotula has called it a "témoignage matériel et visible de la puissance du dominat de cet empereur" (1997, 80; cf. *ibid.* 165); and Strobel, while acknowledging a real defensive function, has nonetheless seen it as a "fundamentally demonstrative act" designed positively to reinforce the image of Rome as *caput mundi*: "Der Mauerbau Aurelians sollte sicher neben realen Sicherheitszwecken der stadtrömischen Bevölkerung das Gefühl einer zuverlässig garantierten Sicherheit vermitteln, ist aber m.E. auch als ein grundsätzlicher demonstrativer Akt zu sehen, die Unerschütterbarkeit der urbs Roma als das 'Haupt der Welt' zu manifestieren" (1993, 296).

meant for and the uses to which it was ultimately put may also have differed. In their ensemble, these caveats demonstrate the impossibility of treating the case of Rome in isolation. Neither the "practicality" nor the symbolic resonances of the Aurelian Wall can be assessed without reference to other walls, and indeed to the development of the urban enceinte writ large in the late-antique Mediterranean and beyond.

Prior to late antiquity, the last significant wave of wall-building in the interior provinces of the western empire had occurred under Augustus; and even then, the fortification of new and existing colonies, *municipia*, and *civitates* remained more the exception than the rule, a mark of particular favor on the part of the emperor, the sole authority with the power to sanction the construction of urban defenses.[25] In all of Gaul, for example, only 18 of more than 40 principal cities had anything resembling a functioning enceinte at any point in the first century AD, and the entirety of the south-west (Aquitaine), the area farthest from the Rhine frontier, was without a single walled city.[26] Many newly founded cities throughout the West, including provincial capitals, never received walls,[27] and in other cases, sections of Augustan ramparts were demolished to make way for new construction within decades of their erection.[28]

It is, of course, true that some "prestige" fortifications continued to appear in the first and second centuries around manifestly unthreatened cities;[29] and walled cities never ceased to proliferate in the frontier provinces of the empire, from Dura Europus and Hatra on the Euphrates to Trier, Tongres, and Cologne on the Rhine, where renewed threats could prompt bouts of wall-building, as at Augsburg during the Marcommanic Wars of the 170s.[30] On the whole, however, the unfortified profile of large sections of Britain, Gaul, Spain, North Africa, and Italy became only more

---

[25] Cf. Goodman 2007, 12–13; Esmonde Cleary 2003; Gros 1992, 218–20; Goudineau 1980, 244ff.; generally on these walls, see also Colin (1987), *Les enceintes augustéennes dans l'occident romain.*

[26] See Garmy and Maurin 1996, 188; Gros 1992, 218; Goudineau 1980.

[27] Examples include Carthage (founded by Caesar) in North Africa; Narbonne, Bordeaux, and Amiens in Gaul; and Camulodunum (Colchester) and London in Britain.

[28] In Italy, circuits were not completed at e.g. Carsula and Benevagienna (Gros 1992, 221). Partial demolitions of Augustan fortifications occurred before the end of the first century at Fréjus, Arles, and Nîmes in Southern Gaul alone (Goudineau 1980, 246–7).

[29] Esmonde Cleary 2003; Rebuffat 1986, 351–4.

[30] Trier: Cüppers 1973, 133–222; cf. Heinen 1985, 85–6 and 110–11; Tongres: Rebuffat 1986, 353; Cologne: Spiegel 2006; Hanel 2002; Dura: *Dura Reports,* seasons 7–8 (1939), esp. 40ff. on the multiple Roman repairs and additions to the earlier Hellenistic and Parthian fortifications; Hatra: Gawlikowski 1994; cf. Sommer 2005, 375–6; Augsburg: Ortisi 2001, 72–93, with Schwarz 2003, 644–7.

pronounced over the centuries of the *pax Romana*, when – again away
from the frontiers – new enceintes were infrequent and existing ones were
often allowed to fall into disrepair, or submerged under new constructions, or demolished whole or in part as cities expanded over and beyond
the line of their old ramparts.[31] For all that walls still entered into a certain
Roman urban ideal – one thinks of mural crowns on city *tychai*; the
representations of walled cities in first-century frescoes from Rome
(notably the Oppian Hill fresco) and Pompeii; and occasional numismatic
depictions of walled cities on local issues of coinage, chiefly in the eastern
empire[32] – the majority of the empire's urban dwellers, between the first
century AD and the third, nonetheless lived in effectively open cities.

Exceptions to the rule in the Italian peninsula include Aquileia, where
the badly degraded wall was allegedly extensively repaired in preparation
for the siege it faced in the civil war of 238; and Milan, where the rebellious
general Aureolus successfully held out against the besieging army of
Gallienus for months in 268.[33] Yet these were isolated cases, and only with
the chronic instability of the mid third century did things begin to change,
beginning with the fortification of Verona in 265 in the wake of the
Alemmannic incursion of 259–60. Outside Italy, new walls rose in
Athens, over-run by the Heruli in 267, and Antioch, which had been
devastatingly sacked in the 250s by the armies of the resurgent Persian
Empire.[34] At Thessalonika, the Hellenistic defenses of the city were rebuilt

[31] As occurred at Rome itself, where the Servian Wall was swallowed by new construction and
increasingly ruinous from the first century AD on (cf. Frézouls 1987, 273ff.); and elsewhere at
e.g. Minturnae, south of Rome on the Via Appia, where the republican enceinte was cut by a
theater early in the first century AD (see Laurence 1999, 151–3, with the references cited there).
Generally on the decline of urban enceintes under the high empire, cf. Goodman 2007, esp. 62,
85–6, etc.; Johnson 1983b, 69.

[32] Cf. generally Goodman 2007, 28ff.; on the Oppian Fresco, see La Rocca 2000; for numismatic
depictions of walled cities (and mural-crowned *tychai*), see Price and Trell 1977, figs. 496ff.

[33] On the restoration of the circuit at Aquileia by forces opposed to Maximinus, see Herodian 8,
2, who explains the poor condition of the wall with the memorable assertion that "under
Roman rule the cities of Italy no longer needed walls or arms." On Gallienus' siege of Milan
in 268, during the protracted course of which he was assassinated, see Aurelius Victor, *de Caes.*
33, 18–19, where mention is made of the use of "(siege) machines of every kind"
(*machinationibus omnis generis*) against the city; cf. Zos. 1, 40, 1ff.

[34] Debate continues about whether Antioch was sacked once or twice. Zosimus describes only
one terrible sack in 252/253 (*Historia Nova*, 1, 27, 2); the more closely contemporary
Ammianus mentions two separate events (Amm. 23, 5). Whatever the case, the emperor
Valerian soon began the reconstruction of Antioch, in the course of which work was begun to
turn the island at its center into (probably) a fortified citadel, seemingly never completed: see
Malalas, *Chron.* 12, 38 (Dindorf, 306), with Downey 1961, 257–8. Presumably, the enceinte of
the city was also repaired at this time, as it often was over the following centuries (cf. Downey
1961, 546–9). For other possible examples of mid-third century walls, see Rebuffat 1986, 354–5.

in timely fashion around 250, closely anticipating the first Gothic invasions and sparing the city, several times besieged, from sack.[35] Surviving traces of these walls often suggest hurried and rather *ad hoc* construction. The small circuit centered on the agora at Athens was cobbled together by citizen-laborers, using quantities of rubble from the destruction caused by the Heruli.[36] In Verona, the wall likewise incorporated a heterogeneous assortment of reused building materials, sculptural fragments, and inscriptions, probably taken chiefly from buildings razed in its path.[37]

All of this is to say that when the foundations of the Aurelian Wall were laid in 271, defensive fortifications did not yet feature prominently in the cityscapes of the Mediterranean interior of the empire. Like Dynastic Egypt, Achaemenid Persia, and Ottoman Anatolia, the Roman Empire in its heyday had quite successfully relied on strongly defended frontiers to guarantee its internal security.[38] The carefully crafted and visually striking, even ornamental circuits of the later republican and Julio-Claudian periods were largely defunct; and the few rough-and-ready walls built in the mid third century provided little precedent for urban enceintes as monumental assertions of the prerogatives of a strong central government. It is hence difficult to imagine that the inhabitants of Rome – or Athens, Antioch, Verona, etc. – would have been particularly prepared or inclined to attribute much in the way of triumphal ideological associations to city walls, structures until recently rendered obsolescent by an extended period of relative peace and prosperity. *A fortiori*, those responsible for the decision to build or rebuild the first of the new enceintes will have had little basis, in physical reality or in the popular consciousness, for putting a positive "spin" on their walls, for all that they might have wished to do so.[39]

---

[35] See Spieser 1984, 25–80, esp. 64ff.

[36] See Franz *et al.* 1988, 5–11 and 125–41 (a lengthy appendix devoted entirely to the "post-Herulian wall"); Thompson 1959, 63–5; with Zos. 1, 29, 3.

[37] See Cavalieri Manasse and Hudson 1999; Fogolari 1965, esp. 37–40; cf. Richmond and Holford 1935, 72ff. The date is given by a preserved dedicatory inscription (*CIL* 5, 3329).

[38] Cf. Tracy 2000, 71–3; Keegan 1993, 142ff. Of course, the frontiers were maintained by more than the force of Roman arms alone: diplomatic initiatives, for example, and the creation of "Romanized" buffer zones on both sides of the *limes* proper all played their part in preserving the inviolability of the interior provinces during the *pax romana*; see Mattern 1999, esp. 81ff.; Whittaker 1994.

[39] Though the unusual example of Nicaea shows that it was possible and desirable, as early as the 260s, to celebrate a new enceinte. Here, an impressive brick-faced wall built *ex novo* following the Gothic invasion of 256/7 was depicted repeatedly on coins issued first by Gallienus, and subsequently by two local usurpers, Macrinus and Quietus. Completed under Claudius II in 268/9, and commemorated in an extant dedicatory inscription, this wall was patently a symbol of power, patronage, and imperial legitimacy from the outset. Still, it rose in a more peripheral and exposed region of the empire, where something of the "frontier mentality"

The initial configuration of the Aurelian Wall points to similar conclusions. Its original elevation of 7–8 meters was no higher or more monumental than necessary to meet the practical requirements faced by its planners, among which defense against external threats must have presented the greatest challenge from an architectural standpoint, as considerably less would presumably have sufficed for crowd-control, customs-collection, and so on. Hence, it was designed to be proof against attack from lightly armed and equipped raiding parties unprepared for the conduct of protracted sieges.[40] Questions about their technological capabilities aside, the Germanic marauders who reached Italy in the third century were seeking not to occupy territory, but to amass maximum plunder as quickly as possible. As it was neither profitable nor safe to remain long in one place, a barrier capable of resisting a scaling attack for any length of time would have sufficed. The solid bulk of the Wall, screened by the powerful array of projectile weapons available to its defenders, will have presented a daunting obstacle for bands of warriors equipped with the weapons they carried and little else. Indeed, in the 270s, when most cities in the inner reaches of the empire remained unfortified, the mere presence of a wall was probably often sufficient deterrent to convince invaders to turn their attention to softer targets.[41]

The utilitarian configuration of Aurelian's Wall was well seen already by Richmond, who went the further step of contending that it was supposed to be unobtrusive, to blend in as much as possible with its surroundings, thereby downplaying the necessity of providing the Eternal City with a wall.[42] And though it would be difficult to prove that the Wall was made as unprepossessing as possible to minimize the psychological reverberations of its appearance – even in its original phase it would have been difficult to miss – it certainly does seem not to have been much emphasized during the first century and more of its existence. It is most conspicuously absent

---

likely prevailed, than any of the contemporary fortifications previously mentioned; and it is telling that the walls at Athens, Antioch and, for that matter, Rome were never shown on third-century coins, as far as I know. See Karnapp and Schneider 1938, esp. p. 3 for the coins, and p. 43 for the inscription; cf. also Foss and Winfield 1986, 79ff.

[40] Cf. Cozza 1987, 49; Richmond 1930, 241–5.

[41] There is nothing to show that prosperous walled cities like Milan and Aquileia, situated in exposed locations astride the main routes of ingress into peninsular Italy, were attacked, much less sacked, during the incursions of the 260s. At Augsburg, the capital of Raetia, destruction layers were left outside the walls during an invasion of the 240s, while the city center remained inviolate: see Ortisi 2001, 83–4.

[42] Richmond 1930, 245: "The world was not to know that its greatest City had become a fortified castle...The essential part of the plan was to build a wall which was strong, but inconspicuous."

from the Regionary Catalogues, the two detailed inventories of Roman topography produced in the first half of the fourth century.[43] In both documents, buildings outside the Wall are listed alongside others within, with no acknowledgement that an often impermeable barrier lay between, impeding progress along the itineraries traced out for each region. No mention is made even of the Wall's gates, which later became primary points of topographical reference for other features located in their vicinity, though much smaller landmarks on roads elsewhere in the city are often indicated.

Later in the century, the Roman senator Ausonius also ignored the Wall in his description of Rome, which heads his list of the empire's twenty greatest metropolises.[44] Interestingly, Ausonius had no qualms about beginning the section on his own city, Bordeaux, with a glowing account of its wall.[45] The fortifications of Trier, Milan, Aquileia, and Toulouse, the first three strategically located on access routes to the interior of the empire, are likewise lauded for their strength and majesty.[46] Yet there is not a hint that any of the five leading cities of the empire had any defenses whatsoever, though Constantinople, Antioch, and of course Rome had all recently been massively refortified.[47] If the towns of the northern frontiers and the continental interior could proudly vaunt their new armored shells, the far greater capitals of the Mediterranean littoral still could not, despite – or perhaps because of – the presence of enemies sometimes quite literally before their gates.[48]

In short, then, the internal evidence for the Wall itself, the example of existing urban defenses elsewhere, and the turbulent military and political situation prevailing in Italy at the beginning of Aurelian's reign together indicate that, in its earliest phase, Rome's enceinte was in large part envisioned as a practical measure taken in response to pressing needs

[43] Homo noted this omission, without attempting further explanation, save to claim it as an indication that the Wall did nothing to change the "pre-existing regional and administrative organization" of the city (1904, 304). The texts are published in full in VZ 1, 63–258.

[44] *Ordo nobilium urbium*, 1. On Ausonius, see generally Matthews 1975, 81–7.

[45] Ibid. 20: *quadrua murorum species, sic turribus altis/ardua, ut aerias intrent fastigia nubes....*

[46] Ibid. 6, 7, 9, 18, respectively.

[47] Ibid. 1–5; the five cities, listed in descending order of importance, were Rome, Constantinople, Carthage, Antioch, and Alexandria. Only Carthage and Alexandria, located on the still placid southern shore of the Mediterranean, remained comparatively unthreatened (and unfortified) in Ausonius' day.

[48] Ausonius was writing scant years after the Goths defeated the Romans at Adrianople, in the aftermath of which Constantinople was saved only by its walls, which the Goths failed to penetrate: see Amm. 31, 16, 7.

occasioned by pressures from outside ("barbarians"), and from within (sedition and popular unrest, fiscal difficulties). A prevailing sense of it as a drably functional thing also explains well its treatment in the upper echelons of Roman society, where it was almost completely ignored throughout the fourth century. Much would change before the Aurelian Wall developed into the embodiment of Rome's strength, permanence, and civic stature that it later became. This metamorphosis could come about only after a cognitive revolution that encompassed a pervasive reshaping of traditional urban paradigms across the empire, via a lengthy and complex process that the Wall helped to inform and define.

3.3   New walls, old realities, and the changing face of the late-antique city

Already at the end of the third century, there are signs that the Roman exemplar had itself become an impetus for change, a precedent and a paradigm for the renaissance of the urban enceinte. This is nowhere more apparent than in the case of the two cities that replaced Rome as the principal imperial capitals of the western empire, Milan and Trier. From the moment of the *translatio imperii* from Rome to the two new capitals, both places were unabashedly and programmatically compared to the ancient *caput imperii*, and their monumental architectural patrimonies extolled as new incarnations of the glories of old Rome.[49] In step with the rhetoric, the construction of Maximian's palace in close proximity to the circus at Milan replicated the ensemble of the Palatine and the Circus Maximus; and a spate of additional public building aimed further at recalling the glories of the erstwhile capital, as Ausonius conspicuously noted.[50] Yet the greatest building project in

[49] Cf. Settis 2001, 997–8; Cantino Wataghin 1996, 242–4. Trier is compared quite favorably to Rome in two panegyrics of the tetrarchic period; see *Pan. Lat.* 10 (2), 14, 3 (of *c.* 289, addressed to Maximian, currently in residence at Trier; the *gentium domina* is of course Rome): *Interim tamen te, gentium domina, quoniam hunc optatissimum principem in Gallis suis retinet ratio rei publicae, quaesumus, si fieri potest, ne huic invideas civitati, cui nunc ille similitudinem maiestatis tuae confert natalem tuum diem celebrando in ea consuetudine magnificentiae tibi debitae*; and 6 (7), 22, 4–5 (of 310, addressed to Constantine):...*sicut hic video hanc fortunatissimam civitatem, cuius natalis dies tua pietate celebratur, ita cunctis moenibus resurgentem ut se quodammodo gaudeat olim corruisse, auctior tuis facta beneficiis. Video circum maximum aemulum, credo, Romano, video basilicas et forum, opera regia, sedemque iustitiae in tantam altitudinem suscitari ut se sideribus et caelo digna et vicina promittant.*

[50] *Ordo nobilium urbium* 7, lines 37–45: *tum duplice muro amplificata loci species populique voluptas circus et inclusi moles cuneata theatri; templa Palatinaeque arces opulensque moneta et regio Herculei celebris sub honore lavacri; cunctaque marmoreis ornata peristyla signis*

Milan following the transfer of the court was the erection of a new enceinte, an initiative all the more noteworthy for occurring with a functional defensive circuit already in place.[51] At Trier, meanwhile, the enceinte made a sudden appearance on a commemorative double-solidus medallion struck in *c.* 316, just after Constantine had been conspicuously praised for restoring the *moenia* of the city in a panegyric of 310.[52] Though Trier had been a bulwark of the Rhine frontier since its founding under Augustus, its fortifications only began to receive laudatory attention in the early fourth century, when flattering comparisons with Rome became politically expedient. The walls of Milan and Trier, that is, were physically and ideologically rehabilitated precisely when these cities were attempting to usurp the legacy of Rome, now surrounded by the largest enceinte in the empire.

This "reflection" of Rome in the provincial capitals may thus lie at the root of the glorification of the urban enceinte that occurred there, a reshaping of prevalent ideas about what an imperial residence should look like that was later to be reflected back to Rome and Constantinople at the beginning of the fifth century, when these places too began to flaunt their walls as only frontier capitals had before. But for all that the precocious fortification of Rome may have contributed to the genesis of a new "bristling" image of the imperial capital(s), however, it cannot fully explain the renaissance of the urban enceinte that occurred throughout the empire in late antiquity, a process whose general parameters invite some additional comment.

A point of central importance, only now coming into focus thanks to a series of carefully observed and archaeologically based regional studies, is

---

moeniaque in valli formam circumdata limbo: omnia quae magnis operum velut aemula formis excellunt: nec iuncta premit vicinia Romae; cf. also the remarkable (if genuine) lines allegedly inscribed over the gates of Milan in the fourth century by the proconsul Marcellinus, quoted in Graf 1882–83, vol. I, 19: *Dic homo qui transis, dum portae limina tangis:/Roma secunda vale, Regni decus imperiale;/Urbs veneranda nimis, plenissima rebus opimis,/Te metuunt gentes, tibi flectant colla potentes./In bello Thebas, in sensu vincis Athenas.*

[51] The new wall, built *c.* 300, considerably expanded the earlier fortified periphery, incorporating regions of the city, including the neighborhood of the old circus, which were subsequently monumentally re-edified: see esp. Ceresa Mori 1993, 13–36; cf. Cantino Wataghin 1996, 248–9; Krautheimer 1983, 69ff. Ausonius' repeated mention of the wall(s) in the passage quoted in the preceding note is the more noteworthy for occurring amongst a list of monumental buildings directly likened to Roman exemplars; is it possible that the reference to the "double wall" (*duplice muro*, comprised of the older defenses and the new wall of Maximian) is likewise intended to recall the dual Servian and Aurelianic circuits at Rome?

[52] The obverse of the medallion shows the enceinte, whose profile is dominated by a gate (the *Incluta Porta*) facing onto the Moselle bridge (Baldwin 1921, 37–63; cf. Toynbee 1944, 189); *Pan. Lat.* 6 (7), 22, 4.

that the refortification of the western provinces of the empire which clearly did begin in the later third century cannot be explained as a desperate reaction in the face of overwhelming pressure from barbarian raiders. The effects of the allegedly devastating incursions into interior Spain in *c.* 260 and Gaul in 275–6, reported in a very few, very tendentious sources, now tend to be minimized, and are in any case insufficient to explain the first concerted campaign of wall-building, which occurred only after the end of the worst troubles.[53] The dating of circuit walls is notoriously fraught, and datable coins, ceramics, and other finds from foundation-levels of walls, in the happy cases where such things exist, generally provide only a rough *terminus post quem* for the beginning of construction, and nothing for its duration.[54] That said, the new generation of individual site-reports and regional surveys, focused above all on Gaul and Spain, now make it clear that there was a first wave of wall-building in these provinces that began around the 270s, gathered steam under Probus and then Diocletian and his colleagues, and was largely complete by the end of the first Tetrarchy in 305.

In Gaul, the walls of this tetrarchic group bear marked similarities to one another. They are thick, generally in the range of 4–5 m, with curtains often at least 9–10 m high, studded with closely spaced, projecting towers with solid bases. Their lower courses are realized to various heights in *opus quadratum* masonry, erected with varying quantities of spoliated materials re-employed with extreme care, re-cut where necessary and arranged with inscriptions and anomalous features on the inner, invisible facings of the blocks. Above the *opus quadratum*, the remaining elevations of the curtains and towers are constructed in small blocks of stone interspersed with multiple courses of bricks (sometimes five or more, though three is more common), spaced at usually regular intervals. The effect is highly striking, the more so when it includes complex geometric patterns, most notably at Le Mans, and remarkably uniform amongst the various circuits attributable to the late-third century.[55] In addition to Le Mans, these include the partially extant,

[53] See Brulet 1996; Garmy and Maurin 1996, 193ff.; Maurin 1992, 381–3; on Spain, cf. also Fernández-Ochoa and Morillo 2005, 299; Kulikowski 2004, 102. For the older view of chaos and catastrophe following upon the heels of barbarian hordes in 276, and prompting more or less desperate attempts at fortification, see e.g. Johnson 1983a, 113ff.; von Petrikovitz 1971; Butler 1959.

[54] For a resume of the difficulties inherent in dating urban fortifications, see Wacher 1998 (focusing on Britain).

[55] On the wall at Le Mans, see the superbly exhaustive study of Guilleux 2000, esp. 191ff. on the decorative facings; other such facings in Gaul and beyond are surveyed at 218–22.

archaeologically documented circuits at Amiens, Angers, Bordeaux, Bourges, Nantes, Périgueux, Poitiers, Orléans, Rennes, and Saintes;[56] the walls of Grenoble, datable by an extant dedicatory inscription to the joint reign of Diocletian and Maximian (286–93) should be added to this first group of fortifications, as probably should the circuit at Dijon.[57] As others have noted, these majestic and aesthetically striking ramparts hardly reek of panic and desperation; rather, they are technically impressive achievements, costly and highly visible public buildings that conferred an air of grandeur and civic stature, proclamations of urban sophistication and permanence in much the way that the baths, theaters, basilicas, and temples of the early-imperial period had been.[58]

After something of a hiatus in the construction of new enceintes for much of the relatively peaceful and prosperous fourth century,[59] a second wave of fortification commenced at the beginning of the fifth century, in this case in evident relation to a growing climate of insecurity punctuated by the massive Germanic incursions of 406–9, which marked the beginning of the end of the imperial order in Gaul. Enceintes built at this time are generally somewhat smaller, thinner, and less carefully crafted than the tetrarchic examples. Such circuits are particularly concentrated in Novempopulania in the extreme south-west, where they generally occupy the highest and most defensible areas of the towns they served, leaving out still more of the existing urban fabric than the tetrarchic walls, and seem indeed to have the character of fortified refuges. The walls of Bazas, Lectoure, Saint-Bertrand-de-Comminges and, farther north, Clermont-Ferrand are likely or certain to date to this period, while farther east in Gallia Narbonnensis, Arles, Nîmes, and Vienne, amongst others, have been proposed as likely candidates.[60]

Recent overviews of late-antique fortifications in Spain have produced very similar conclusions. There, too, a first group of massive, meticulously

---

[56] See the overviews in Loseby 2006; Heijmans 2006; Guilleux 2000, 243ff.; Garmy and Maurin 1996; Maurin 1992; cf. also Goodman 2007, 203–9. Where the older surveys of Johnson (1983a, 82ff.) and Butler (1959) base themselves on archaeological data, they remain useful.

[57] Grenoble: *CIL* 12, 2229, with Heijmans 2006, 68. According to Gregory of Tours (*HF* 3, 19), "the ancients" attributed the walls of nearby Dijon to Aurelian.

[58] Cf. Guilleux 2000, 259–62; Garmy and Maurin 1996, 191–2; Maurin 1992, 370–2 and 388–9.

[59] Fourth-century exceptions include Dax in the south, and Yverdon, Maastricht, Mouzon, and Tours in the north; on Dax, see Garmy and Maurin 1996, 85–121; for the rest, see Guilleux 2000, 244, with further references.

[60] On Novempopulania, see Maurin 1992, 384ff; for Narbonnensis, see Heijmans 2004, 112–24, where a fifth-century date is suggested for several other towns, including Narbonne itself; see also Heijmans 2006; for recent work on Saint-Bertrand, see Esmonde Cleary and Wood 2006.

assembled walls built with large amounts of spoliated stone was erected around a number of cities located chiefly in the northern part of the peninsula.[61] Like the Gallic exemplars, they are thick (5–6 m is common, and the walls of Lugo are as much as 7 m thick!), and feature a great number of projecting towers spaced usually less than *c.* 30 m apart, and sometimes as little as 10–12 m. The circuits at Gerona, Zaragoza, Iruña de Oca, Astorga, León, Gijón, Lugo, Braga, Tiermes, and Elorza all fit these criteria, and there is certain or probable archaeological evidence to date all of them between the last third of the third century and the beginning of the fourth.[62] The chronology of this first concerted program of fortification – with all due caveats about dating difficulties – thus mirrors the Gallic evidence quite closely, with a culminating point under the Tetrarchy following occasional signs of earlier beginnings from *c.* 270 on. Moreover, just as in Gaul, a relative lull in wall-building seems to have ensued in the fourth century, followed by a second series of fortifications in the early fifth. The new Iberian circuits are again generally less extensive and thinner than their tetrarchic antecedents, and demonstrate less care in the reuse of spoliated materials in particular, leaving them with a distinctly less polished appearance; probable examples include Mérida, Burgo de Osma, and Monte Cildá.[63]

In Italy itself, the legacy of the civil wars of the first century BC, along with centuries of Greek colonization in the south, had left the peninsula with a relatively high concentration of urban enceintes,[64] some of which were wholly or partially reutilized in late antiquity, generally following extensive restoration or reconstruction. As the late-antique repairs often involved only the upper sections of these circuits, leaving the older foundation levels undisturbed, they can be particularly hard to date, as at e.g. Pavia.[65] Where more precise dating is possible, however, the chronological pattern documented in Spain and Gaul recurs yet again. In the wake of the construction of the Aurelian Wall, new walls were built

---

[61] New investigations carried out over the past two decades have largely supplanted the older works of e.g. Johnson 1983a, 124–31, Balil 1970, 603–20, and Richmond 1931. The best overview is Fernández-Ochoa and Morillo 2005, which contains extensive references to earlier studies, many of them conducted by the authors themselves; for a more detailed picture, see the various contributions in Rodríguez Colmenero and Rodá de Llanza (2007); cf. also Kulikowski 2006, 136–7; 2004, 101–9.

[62] Fernández-Ochoa and Morillo 2005, esp. 319ff.

[63] *Ibid.* 339–40; on Monte Cildá, see Iglesias Gil and Gutiérrez 2007.

[64] Cf. Gros 1992, esp. 216.

[65] The incorporation of *spolia* dating up to the later third century furnishes only the roughest *terminus post*; see Bullough 1966, 87–90.

at Rimini, likely beginning under Aurelian, and at Milan and Susa during the Tetrarchy; while at Lucca, the old enceinte was extensively renovated under Probus, as recent archaeological investigations have proven.[66] Epigraphic evidence adds the central-Italian towns of Fanum Fortunae and Pisaurum to the list, both of them refortified under Aurelian himself.[67] Thereafter, relative inactivity in the fourth century preceded a second efflorescence of fortifications across the peninsula in the first half of the fifth. Monumental new walls rose around Ravenna, Albenga, and Terracina – the last two examples testifying to the remarkable efforts made even by relatively small towns to transform themselves into imposing citadels – and significant work was carried out at e.g. Naples, Aquileia, and Bologna as well, though the details are murkier.[68]

The relative anomaly is Britain, where a number of cities, including the provincial capital at London, were provided with new defenses already in the Severan period. All the same, a number of new and distinctly more imposing urban fortifications were built in the later third century, and considerable efforts were made in the fourth century to enlarge and improve existing walls, which were often thickened and bolstered with projecting external towers.[69] The majority of the monumental "Saxon shore forts" along the Channel coast were also built near the end of the third century, in what appears to have been a centrally co-ordinated effort. While these impressive compounds may perhaps be seen as responses to coastal raiding, they may just as well or better relate to Britain's troubled political situation in the later third century, when the allegiance of the

---

[66] Milan: Ceresa Mori 1993; Susa: Christie 2006, 326–31; Rimini: Gobbi and Sica 1982, 26–7; Lucca: Ciampoltrini *et al.* 2003.

[67] See above Chapter 2, n. 54.

[68] Ravenna: Gelichi 2005; Christie 1989; Christie and Gibson 1988; Terracina: Christie and Rushworth 1988; Ortolani 1988; Albenga: Pergola 1993–94; Lamboglia 1957, 37–9. In the case of Naples, debate continues about the extent of the late-antique additions to the existing pre-Roman circuit, but one major building campaign certainly took place under Valentinian III in *c.* 440, according to an extant dedicatory inscription (*CIL* 10, 1485); see also Arthur 2002, 34–8; Pani Ermini 1993–94, 195–8; Napoli 1969, 740–52. At Aquileia, where the chronology of the extant sections of two distinct circuits is similarly confused, several major fourth- and fifth-century reconstructions clearly occurred, perhaps following a first major (re)building campaign of the mid third century; see Christie 2006, 291ff.; Pavan 1987, 17–55; Brusin 1967, 38ff.; cf. also Cantino Wataghin 2005, 107–8. The late-antique walls at Bologna, the first to encircle the city, were built *ex novo*, apparently in time to resist the siege of Alaric at the beginning of the fifth century; see Brogiolo and Gelichi 1998, 55–6.

[69] For the general trends in British wall-building, as well as detailed information on individual circuits, see Esmonde Cleary 2007; 1987; Wacher 1998 (with particular reference to difficulties in dating British walls); 1995, 70–81; Casey 1983. Notable examples of *ex novo* circuits of the later third century include Caistor-by-Norwich, Cambridge, Canterbury, and Gloucester.

province went more frequently to usurpers (Postumus and his successors, and then Carausius and his) than to the "legitimate" rulers of the empire.[70]

In the face of the chronological and typological parallels between urban enceintes over such a broad swathe of the western provinces, a number of recent scholars have been inclined – I think rightly – to postulate a centralized, imperially sponsored initiative to fortify urban centers of strategic importance beginning in the later third century. In addition to similarities in construction, logistical factors have been adduced in support of direct imperial intervention: the resources of the central administration, it is argued, would have been required to finance these massive projects to ensure their completion in relatively expeditious fashion.[71] Active participation by the imperial administration also seems the best explanation for the extensive demolitions required for the construction of the new walls, which usually truncated the existing urban nuclei of the sites they encircled, provoking sometimes radical topographical upheavals.[72]

The desire to reassert imperial control over the former provinces of the breakaway *imperium galliarum*, which was finally suppressed by Aurelian in 274, was perhaps one motivating factor behind the initial impulse to fortify. A second, more comprehensive explanation has been sought in the reorganization of the defense, administration, and supply network of the provinces that reached maturity under the Tetrarchy. In addition to the subdivision of the early-imperial provinces into smaller, more manageable units, the system of military supplies (the *annona militaris*) was comprehensively reformed, road networks were improved, and – very probably – a network of fortified cities was instituted at strategic points.[73] As well as serving as bastions in a system of "defense in depth" that recognized the permeability of the frontiers, such centers would also have been depots for

---

[70] Generally on the "Saxon shore forts" (in quotations because the phrase itself connotes a defensive effort against Saxon raiders that has now been called into question), see Pearson 2003; Johnson 1976. For alternative explanations of the purpose of these structures, which may indicate the presence of towns as much as military garrisons, see Allen and Fulford 1999; Fulford and Tyres 1995; Cotterill 1993.

[71] See e.g. Fernández-Ochoa and Morillo 2005, 333–4; Wacher 1998, 48–50.

[72] E.g. Guilleux 2000, esp. 262; Maurin 1992, 383. For Italy specifically, cf. also the more cautious assessment in Christie 2001, 112ff.

[73] Generally on these reforms, see e.g. Potter 2004, 263–98; Williams 1985, 102–14; specifically on the role of fortifications and other infrastructure in the imperial reorganization, see Fernández-Ochoa and Morillo 2005, 329–39; Bleckman 2004, esp. 80–4; Kulikowski 2004, 108; Guilleux 2000, esp. 245–6; Williams 1985, 91–101.

the storage of goods essential for supplying new, mobile field armies (the *comitatus*) based well behind the "front lines" along the Rhine and Danube rivers.[74]

But just as in the case of the administrative and financial reforms discussed in the previous chapter, there is good reason to believe that the program of urban fortification generally attributed to the period of the Tetrarchy actually began somewhat earlier. Amongst the enceintes discussed above, those at Dijon, Le Mans, Saintes, Lucca, Rimini, and elsewhere are all best dated to the reigns of Aurelian and Probus, which is to say to exactly the period when the Aurelian Wall was being built.[75] As the temptation to trace direct technical parallels between the Wall and a subsequent generation of enceintes is better avoided, as others have demonstrated to their peril,[76] chronological coincidence alone is best left to bolster the *a priori* likely proposition that Rome's new ramparts were neither unrelated to the sequential proliferation of walls in the provinces, nor unknown to those responsible for building these provincial walls. What seems clear, in any event, is that with regard to the construction of city walls, too, Aurelian and his Wall at Rome appear at the dawn of an enterprise that was fully realized only under Diocletian and his colleagues. The circuits that sprouted thickly in a number of provinces beginning in *c.* 270 are unsurpassed as testimonials to the range and scope of the ramified, authoritarian bureaucratic apparatus that would characterize the rejuvenated Roman state as it emerged from the troubles of the third century.

The imperial authorities must also have provided some of the impetus behind the rash of wall-building in the early fifth century, if several decrees in the Theodosian Code are any indication. In 396, Arcadius and Honorius ordered all of the *rectores provinciarum* to ensure that the citizens of the cities under their control built new walls if necessary, or otherwise restored existing ones; and in 412, the *praefectus praetorio Illyrici* was similarly commanded to set all the citizens of Illyricum to work

---

[74] See the sources cited in the preceding note.

[75] Indeed, as far as the emperor Julian was concerned, the cities of the West had been fortified under Probus, who is credited with walling 70 cities in Gaul alone (*Convivium*, 314b). On the dates of the five walls cited, see above notes 55, 56, and 66.

[76] For such attempts, see Todd 1978, 79ff.; Wiseman 1956, 146–7; the allegedly similar features they observe in various walls in Gaul and Spain, notably projecting, closely spaced towers with solid bases, are too common across the empire, too tactically expedient, and too frequently attested before the construction of the Aurelian Wall to be convincing proof of direct imitation of Rome. Todd's suggestion that the plan of the Wall was itself directly influenced by the example of Palmyra, where Aurelian went only after work at Rome was well underway, is similarly unconvincing (Todd 1983).

building walls.[77] In practice, however, the resources and effective reach of the state had dwindled to the extent that individual cities probably often had to manage on their own,[78] a phenomenon reflected in the considerably more heterogeneous and often – with significant exceptions, the imperial capital at Ravenna above all – less technically accomplished walls built at the time in the West in particular, many of which probably should be seen as responses to looming crisis.

In any case, the central fact remains that, as a result of their proliferation between the third and fifth centuries, circuit walls came to be considered essential urban features, to the point that cities were ultimately defined as such on the basis of whether or not they were provided with an enceinte;[79] and though the preceding survey has focused on the West, the same is manifestly true for the eastern empire, as others have shown.[80] Where once it had been forums, baths, and theaters that represented the essence of classical urbanism across the Roman world, it was now walls that did so. Like the public buildings of the high empire, enceintes had real and important functions; and for their utility as well as their ubiquity and monumentality, they were inextricably linked with the "idea and the ideal" of the late Roman metropolis.[81] The broadening connotations of the word

[77] On the decree of 396 (*CTh* 15, 1, 34), see above Chapter 2, n. 102; on that of 412, see *CTh* 15, 1, 49: *Constructioni murorum et conparationi transvectionique specierum universi sine ullo privilegio coartentur, ita ut in his dumtaxat titulis universi pro portione suae possessionis et iugationis ad haec munia coartentur...*

[78] In 440, Valentinian III essentially acknowledged the inability of the central government to provide for the defense of the cities of the Italian littoral, threatened by a Vandal fleet, whence he restored the right to bear arms to all citizens and ordered them to defend themselves: see *Nov. Val.* 9.

[79] In the early-seventh century, Isidore of Seville began his chapter on public buildings with a lengthy discussion of walls, noting first that "the walls themselves are the city" (*nam urbs ipsa moenia sunt*; *Etym.* 15, 2, 1), and later explaining that a town without walls was only a *vicus*, and not a *civitas* (*ibid.* 15, 2, 11–12). Gregory of Tours, writing at the end of the sixth century, was at a loss to explain why the town of Dijon, being surrounded by an impressive defensive wall that he describes in detail, was known as a *castrum* and not a *civitas* (*HF* 3, 19). In describing the opposing fortunes of Rome's two ports, Procopius said that the flourishing Portus had "an exceedingly strong wall," before delivering a succinct epitaph for Ostia: "a place of great consequence in olden times, but now entirely without walls" (*BG* 1, 26, 9; trans. Dewing). Cassiodorus also famously alluded to the importance of city walls, noting that they were an adornment in peacetime, and a precaution in times of war (*Var.* 1, 28). For a partial sense of the growing secondary literature on the subject, see Liebeschuetz 2001, 49–52 (on the East), and 74ff. (on the West); Bachrach 2000; Ward-Perkins 1998, 409–10 and *passim*. On Italian walls, see above all Christie 2006, esp. 281–399, which contains a wealth of observations on defensive strategies and urban fortifications in late-antique and early-medieval Italy with which I quite uniformly concur, and which might usefully be read alongside the following section; see also Christie 2001; Pani Ermini 1993–94; Ward-Perkins 1984, 191ff.

[80] See Saradi 2006; 1995; Crow 2001; Liebeschuetz 2001, esp. 49–52.

[81] The phrase is borrowed from the title of Brogiolo and Ward-Perkins 1999.

moenia in late antiquity is an evocative indicator of the physical, symbolic, and ideological impact such structures came to have, as a term that had once meant "circuit walls" alone became a metonym for "public buildings," the essence of the city as a whole.[82] Urban defenses became, in short, a simple fact of life, the real guarantors as well as the symbolic embodiment of the prominence and prosperity of a city. Implicit in this proposition is, of course, the assumption that city walls were militarily viable, and that their growing popularity reflects their effectiveness at keeping hostile forces out of the areas they enclosed. To provide a better idea of the extent to which this was so, a brief digression on late-antique siegecraft, technology, and military strategy is warranted.

With regard to the technical capabilities of Rome's adversaries, Roman writers give a generally negative impression, with the notable exception of the Sassanian Persians in the east.[83] Barbarians are repeatedly maligned for their lack of skill in the conduct of sieges, while the effectiveness of well-maintained and garrisoned fortifications is a recurring motif. Ammianus Marcellinus memorably depicts the Gothic chieftain Fritigern, watching helplessly as waves of overzealous warriors "ignorant of siegecraft" (*ignaros obsidendi*) were slaughtered before the walls of Adrianople. Fritigern pungently reminded those around him that he was "at peace with walls," and suggested that the bulk of the Gothic forces move on to less defended regions ripe for richer pickings.[84] The theme is later echoed in Procopius' description of Belisarius' scornful laughter, as he watched the conduct of the Gothic siege engines before the walls of Rome.[85]

To be sure, peoples living beyond the frontiers were not as inept and uninformed as the ethnographic biases and literary tropes of their Roman chroniclers often made them out to be; nor can they have been totally unaware of the machines and techniques current among their Roman neighbors, particularly as so much of the Roman army in the fourth and

[82] On the semantic evolution of *moenia*, see above Chapter 1, n. 72.
[83] E.g. Anon. *DRB* 18, 4. The remarkable finds from Dura Europus provide a uniquely detailed archaeological picture of sophisticated Persian siege-technology in action in the mid third century: see James 2005; 2004.
[84] Amm. 31, 6, 4: *Tunc Fritigernus frustra cum tot cladibus colluctari homines ignaros obsidendi contemplans relicta ibi manu sufficiente abire negotio imperfecto suasit pacem sibi esse cum parietibus memorans suadensque, ut populandas opimas regiones et uberes absque discrimine ullo vacuas praesidiis etiamtum adorerentur.*
[85] Procop. *BG* 1, 22, 2; cf. *BG* 1, 17, 7; Amm. 31, 15, 15; 31, 16, 7. See also *BV* 1, 5, 8, where Procopius writes that Geiseric had all city walls in the Vandal kingdom of Africa razed, save the enceinte of Carthage, in order that none of the cities might be held against him in the future.

fifth centuries was made up of barbarian levies.[86] As early as Trajan's time, the Dacians are said to have had apparently sophisticated artillery and siege engines.[87] The use of simpler scaling ladders in (generally unsuccessful) attacks on Roman cities is well attested, and the Huns are said to have employed rams and towers in addition to ladders against Naissus in 442, and "all types of engines" in the taking of Aquileia in 452.[88] Still, there is no reason to believe that roving bands of warriors regularly employed the elaborate siege trains, complete with the massive towers, artillery, prefabricated rams, etc. so common in the wars between Romans and Persians.

From the period before the advent of gunpowder, there are, in fact, few exceptions to the rule that the fabrication and use of complex siege equipment, which required soldiers or specialists skilled in military engineering, was largely the prerogative of centralized states possessed of considerable resources and logistical capabilities.[89] Moreover, it is almost impossible to maintain a stationary army in the field for any length of time without access to a productive surplus of foodstuffs and organized lines of supply;[90] and prior to the dissolution of the western empire in the fifth century, invading forces generally did lack the logistical apparatus to maintain a siege when supplies in the immediate vicinity of their target were exhausted. Hence, *mutatis mutandis* when the Goths had the resources of Italy at their disposal in the sixth century, they regularly conducted sieges against Byzantine garrisons during Justinian's wars of reconquest.[91] So, too, in Merovingian and especially Carolingian France, lengthy and "technological" sieges were common.[92] But if the Germanic

---

[86] On barbarian siege capacities, see Elton 1996, 82–6; Thompson 1982, 6ff. (a particularly negative assessment); cf. Bachrach 2000, 196–7.

[87] Dio Cassius, 68, 9, 5–6 (stating that the siege engines used by the Dacians were made and manned primarily by Roman deserters). Tacitus also describes a siege of a legionary fortress by *Batavi* and *Transrhenani*, again claiming that the "uncustomary" deployment of siege engines, specifically towers, was managed only with the help of Roman deserters and prisoners (*Hist.* 4, 23).

[88] Cf. Elton 1996, 84. On Naissus, see Priscus, frag. 6, 2; for Aquileia, see Jordanes, *Getica*, 221: *qui (Hunni) machinis constructis omniaque genera tormentorum adhibita...*, with Duval 1976, 291–4.

[89] See Landers 2003, 125–96; cf. Keegan 1993, 140.

[90] A central theme in e.g. Lynn 1993; on late antiquity and the early Middle Ages, see esp. W. Kaegi, "Byzantine Logistics: Problems and Perspectives" (1993, 39–56); B. Bachrach, "Logistics in Pre-Crusade Europe" (2002, 57–78); see also Roth 1999, 314–19.

[91] Procop. *BG* 2, 12, 1ff. (an attack on Rimini with sophisticated siege towers); see also 2, 21, 1ff.; 3, 5, 1ff.; 3, 6, 1ff.; 3, 10, 5ff.; 3, 11, 19ff; 3, 12, 12ff.; 4, 23, 1ff.; etc. For a more extensive account of defensive strategy in post-Roman Italy, see now Christie 2006, 348ff.

[92] See Bachrach 1972; cf. Halsall 2003, 215–27 (a somewhat less sanguine view of the importance of walled cities and siege warfare in e.g. early-medieval Francia, particularly for the pre-Carolingian period).

successor kingdoms in the West included substantial siege capabilities in their Roman inheritance, it remains safe to say that existing standards were rarely surpassed after the fall of the empire, much less before.

This is important to note because walls seem to have been effective even in resisting adversaries as logistically and technologically advanced as the Persians (or the Romans themselves). The overwhelming impression one gets from reading late-antique authors, and above all the detailed narratives of Ammianus and Procopius, is that strongly defended sites were capable of putting up prolonged resistance in the face of all efforts to effect their capture, and that sieges were enormously costly and arduous undertakings.[93] This is true regardless of the methods employed by besiegers; and the picture remains quite consistent over time in part because there were no really revolutionary developments in basic military tactics, strategy, and technology from late antiquity through the early Middle Ages.[94] Siege towers, bolt- and stone-throwers, ladders, rams, mining operations, and massive earthworks, along with a panoply of contrivances designed to counter them, were the state of the art in the third century, and remained so in the ninth. The late-antique handbooks in which the appearance and use of such devices were described likewise continued to be the seminal texts on the subject for many centuries.[95] The end result was a near stalemate between offensive and defensive technologies, with a slight edge perhaps going to defenders. It was not until the advent of cannon in the late Middle Ages that attackers got weapons consistently capable of breaching even the strongest curtain walls.[96]

---

[93] The Persian siege of Amida occupies nearly an entire book of Ammianus' *History*. The city was finally taken after many months, and only at great cost (Amm. 19, 1ff.). The Persians were likewise successful at Amm. 20, 7, 7ff.; while they failed at 20, 7, 17–18, always after lengthy and difficult sieges. For successful Roman sieges, see Amm. 24, 2, 9ff.; 24, 4, 2ff.; 24, 5, 11; unsuccessful: Amm. 20, 11, 6, ff.; and 21, 11, 2ff., the latter detailing Julian's failed attempt to take Aquileia, garrisoned by two legions still loyal to Constantius, despite a wide array of siege machinery. The Byzantine siege of Petra is one of the longest described in Procopius (*BG* 4, 11, 11–12, 27). When the city was finally taken, the Byzantine commander allegedly razed the walls to forestall future trouble (*BG* 4, 12, 28); cf. also *BP* 1, 7, 12ff.; 2, 13, 16ff. In the seventh century, fortified sites remained crucial to Byzantine strategic thinking in Italy: see (Pseudo-) Maurice, *Strategicon* 10, 2, with Brown 1984, 83.

[94] Bradbury 1992, 6ff. and *passim*; cf. Christie 2006, 348ff.; Bachrach 1994, 119–33; on the earlier period, see also Dixon and Southern 1996; Baatz 1983.

[95] For contemporary descriptions of siege equipment, see Amm. 23, 4, 1ff.; Vegetius, *Epit.* 4, 13ff.; *Anon. De rebus bellicis* 18, 1ff.; Procop. *BG* 5, 21, 4ff.

[96] J. Keegan goes furthest in asserting the superiority of defensive technology, concluding that of all options available to besiegers before the coming of gunpowder, "None, except starvation, offered a certain, or even a very effective, means of bringing a fortification to surrender" (Keegan 1993, 151); cf. Hughes 1974, 67ff.; de la Croix 1972, 39ff.

Urban enceintes consequently continued to be built and maintained in theaters of armed conflict, and it is no exaggeration to say that walls, or rather walled cities, defined the conduct of warfare in western Europe and beyond throughout late antiquity and the early Middle Ages. The nature and intensity of potential threats could, of course, change, as occurred when Germanic peoples in the West became gradually more ambitious in their territorial designs and more accomplished in their methods. Still, siege warfare was almost always more the norm than the exception, and fortified cities and *castra* were the central points around which political and military thinking centered.[97]

And though centuries of peace in interior provinces like peninsular Italy, southern Gaul, and Spain had resulted in a temporary and anomalous decline in the importance of urban fortifications, the dynamics of warfare in these regions were again decisively conditioned by the defensive walls that cities sprouted in late antiquity. By the early fifth century, the majority of the wealthiest and most populous urban centers had been fortified. When they could be taken, they were; and when hostile forces were either unequipped or unwilling to engage in protracted sieges, they settled for whatever was available outside the walls. This remained true throughout the early Middle Ages, when the strategic map of the former western empire was still shaped by cities endowed with surviving late-Roman walls. In 762, the campaign of Pippin I to subdue the duke of Aquitaine revolved around the lengthy siege of Bourges, the fourth-century walls of which were breached only with diverse siege engines and prodigies of military engineering.[98] In 846, by contrast, lightly armed Saracen raiders could only plunder the churches and shrines outside the Aurelian Wall, which they apparently did not bother even to attack in force.[99]

This last episode leads into a final point about the "practical" aspects of Rome's defenses. Throughout the period under discussion, the Aurelian Wall repeatedly proved its effectiveness in keeping attackers at bay.[100] Even

[97] Bachrach 2001, esp. 98–103; 1994, 119–33; Loseby 1998, 249–52; Bradbury 1992, esp. 1–19; specifically on Italy, see Christie 2006, 300–99; Christie and Rushworth 1988. Ammianus tells the interesting story of a turncoat Roman who advised the Persian king Sapor to change tactics completely, by avoiding long sieges of cities and strongholds near the frontier, and heading straight for the wealthier and less defended territories behind (18, 6, 3). The implied originality of the suggestion further attests to the prevalence of siege warfare at the time; and the inhabitants and defenders of the Roman frontier indeed promptly obliged the Persians by retiring inside their walls and avoiding pitched battles (18, 7, 1).
[98] The siege is reconstructed in detail in Bachrach 2000, 210–18.
[99] *LP* 2, 100–1; 106–7.   [100] *Contra* Pani Ermini 1995, 175–6; cf. below n. 112.

at its original height, it successfully withstood the only two sieges it faced, both of which occurred during the reign of Maxentius. Indeed, Lactantius makes direct reference to the near impossibility of storming the Wall, even with Roman legions presumably skilled in siegecraft.[101] It was only when Maxentius broke with the precedent established during the previous sieges, by leading his army out of the city to face a pitched battle with Constantine's forces at the Milvian Bridge, that he was decisively routed.[102] The picture remains much the same for the period following the Honorian reconstruction. Alaric besieged the city three times between 408 and 410, and succeeded in entering on the third attempt only – the sources are unanimous on this point – with help from the inside.[103] During the Gothic Wars in the sixth century, the Wall was repeatedly defended for extended periods against numerically superior forces. Procopius often refers to the respect it commanded from attackers, never more poignantly than when he has Totila say that he meant to raze the Wall, that it might never again cause him the problems it had previously.[104] So, too, at the end of the sixth century and again in the eighth, the Wall still sufficed to keep the most belligerent of the Lombard kings, Agilulf and Liutprand, out of the city.[105] There are exceptions to be sure, most notably the Vandal sack of 455, and the taking of the city by Ricimer's army in 472 (in the former instance, little effective resistance was mounted, while in the latter, Rome's defenders held out for five

---

[101] See Lactantius, *DMP* 26–7, esp. 27, 2, where the hopelessness of Maximian's attempt to breach the walls of Rome with a relatively small army is emphasized: *Ille* (Maximianus) *interea coacto exercitu invadit Italiam, ad urbem accedit senatum extincturus, populum trucidaturus; verum clausa et munita omni offendit. Nulla erat spes inrumpendi, oppugnatio difficilis, ad circumsedenda moenia non satis copiarum...* Cf. *de Caes.* 40, 7, with Barnes 1981, 30–31.

[102] Cf. Lenski 2008, 209–10.

[103] Procopius gives two alternate versions of the capture of the city. In the first, "Trojan Horse" variant, Alaric made a present of 300 Gothic youths to serve as slaves in Roman households, who had been instructed to open the Porta Salaria at a pre-arranged time. In the second, the Roman noblewoman Proba, in despair at the suffering of the people and seeing that the situation was hopeless, had her own slaves open the gate to avert further hardships (both at *BV* 1, 2, 14–27). In any case, there is nowhere a hint that the Wall was successfully stormed: cf. Sozomen, *Historia Ecclesiae*, 9, 9, 4; etc. Additional general sources for the events of the period are listed below at n. 106.

[104] *BG* 3, 16, 22ff. Moreover, Procopius is adamant that on the two occasions when the Goths did manage to take the city, they effected their entrance by treachery alone, both times with the complicity of Isaurian garrison-troops: for the first betrayal, *BG* 3, 20; for the second, *BG* 3, 36.

[105] The determined siege it faced from the latter has already been described above in Chapter 1. On the events of Liutprand's tempestuous reign, cf. Noble 1984, 23ff.; and 44–5 on the siege of Rome. On Agilulf's earlier armed sallies into the vicinity of Rome, cf. Markus 1997, 99ff., with the letters of Gregory I cited in Chapter 4, nn. 158–60.

months before capitulating).[106] Still, the overwhelming implication of the
historical record is that the Wall was for many centuries a practicable and
even formidable means of defense.

3.4   Honorian Rome and Celestial Jerusalem

Hence, when Longinianus was supervising the radical restructuring of the
Aurelian Wall that began in 401, urban enceintes were demonstrably useful
(as they continued to prove with unnerving frequency), and increasingly
ubiquitous. And though the prevailing view that the rebuilding was undertaken to keep barbarians out again oversimplifies a potentially more interesting reality, the story of the Wall's heightening must remain partially
rooted in the political and military circumstances of the time. When
Alaric crossed the Alps with his army in 401 and defeated a Roman force
on the river Timavus, Rome and the Italian peninsula were faced with the
greatest threat from a hostile (and non-Roman) army seen since the third
century.[107] Even after the Goths were turned back beyond the Alps
following the bloody and inconclusive battle of Pollentia on Easter Sunday
of 402, the latent menace remained a constant source of concern.[108] The
move of the imperial court from Milan to the marshy fastnesses of Ravenna
at precisely this time may indicate that "barbarian" siege capabilities were
increasingly feared, and it surely reflects grave concerns at the highest levels
of the administration.[109] No less deliberate was the timing of the
heightening of the Aurelian Wall, which also commenced in the months
between Alaric's arrival in Italy and the battle of Pollentia. Honorius' gifted
court poet Claudian even said as much in explicitly connecting the Gothic
presence with the renovation of the Wall, in his panegyric of 404 on the
emperor's sixth consulship (*de sexto consulatu Honorii*).[110]

---

[106] On the Vandal sack, see esp. Prosper, *Epitoma Chronicon, anno* 455 (Mommsen ed., 483–4);
cf. Procop. *BV* 1, 5, with Bury 1923, vol. 1, 325; on the events of 472, see MacGeorge 2002,
esp. 242–55; Humphries 2000, 526–8; Jones 1964, 240–4; Bury 1923, 337ff.

[107] Valuable historical accounts of the years leading up to the sack of Rome in 410 include:
Blockley 1998, esp. 118–28; Chaffin 1993; Matthews 1975, 273ff.; Courcelle 1964, 31–77.

[108] Allegations of widespread discontent over the Roman general Stilicho's failure to destroy
Alaric, while doubtless exaggerated by chroniclers after his death in 408 and his posthumous
vilification, probably contain an element of truth; the evidence is discussed at length in
Cameron 1970, 156ff.; cf. Chaffin 1993, li; Matthews 1975, 273ff.

[109] Cf. Blockley (1998, 120), who flatly states that the move was "a result of this war."

[110] *De VI cons. Hon.* 531–2: *Addebant pulchrum nova moenia vultum/audito perfecta recens rumore
Getarum. . . .*

It is one case where there is good reason to accept the literal truth of Claudian's remark, as Rome's situation at the beginning of the fifth century had changed markedly since the later third, in ways that suggest ample practical motives for the heightening of its enceinte. In the first place, the prospect of an extended siege was more real than it had been under Aurelian, when mobile field armies could still have been expected to rush to the relief of the capital. In addition, Rome was facing an imminent threat from an external enemy for the first time since Constantine had disbanded the Praetorian Guard and the *equites singulares Augusti*, thereby drastically reducing the number of resident troops available to protect it.[111] The hasty and ill-conceived attempt to introduce reinforcements from Dalmatia into the city before Alaric's second siege in 409 (the force was intercepted and destroyed en route) indicates that the standing garrison at Rome was indeed perceived by contemporaries as insufficient for its defense.[112] As the Ravennate government's failure to intervene effectively against Alaric demonstrates, the city was indeed, as never before, on its own.

It should come as no surprise, then, that economy of manpower was evidently at a premium in the defensive scheme of the reconfigured Wall. In addition to increasing the range and efficiency of projectile weapons –

[111] On the composition of the Praetorian Guard and the *equites singulares*, and their dissolution by Constantine following his defeat of Maxentius, see Coulston 2000; Speidel 1994, esp. 151–7.

[112] See Zos. 5, 45, 1; the strength of the relieving force is given as 6,000. Zosimus says further that Pope Innocent I, evidently under no illusions about the strength of the existing garrison, actually visited the imperial court at Ravenna to request reinforcements for the city. Procopius implies that the Romans had grown more pessimistic about the defensive viability of their enceinte in the following century, when he says that Belisarius' preparations in anticipation of the Gothic siege of 537–8 were met with considerable skepticism on the part of the locals, who noted that Rome could not be supplied with food by sea, and that the length of its wall, and the flatness of the ground on which it stood, made the city extremely difficult to defend (*BG* 1, 14, 16). This passage has led one scholar to suggest that the Wall was, even from the beginning, "a celebratory monument of a great emperor, more than a valid and strategically viable defensive structure" (Pizzi 1998, 59). This, however, is going too far. First of all, for all that Rome was undoubtedly a difficult place to defend, the putative objections Procopius puts in the mouths of the Romans are patently a literary embellishment of the "insurmountable" challenges that his hero Belisarius ultimately overcame. Second, it would be truly remarkable, as noted above, if a wall begun in the first year of a tumultuous five-year reign, and in the immediate aftermath of devastating barbarian invasions, was initially intended as a "celebratory monument of a great emperor." And finally, most obviously of all, Belisarius did successfully defend the Wall for a year, with an army very probably smaller than the standing garrison of the capital in Aurelian's day. In sum, while manpower must have been a constant worry, all the more so as the population of the city declined, it by no means follows that the Wall was militarily ineffective.

the ubiquitous and effective hand-launched stone perhaps above all – the raised towers and curtains rendered far more problematic the use of scaling ladders, which attackers of the period could certainly have been expected to employ.[113] Ladders of the new requisite length were more difficult to make, less stable, and required many more men to transport and deploy, thus inhibiting the rapid and efficient movement of sizeable numbers of attackers to wall-top level. The tactical advantage thereby conferred on Rome's defenders was significant, all the more so if, as I think, the garrison was grown too small to guard the Wall in strength for the entirety of its twelve-mile circuit.

The blocking of many of the original passages through the Wall, particularly the *posterulae*, in the same building campaign also makes good sense as a measure intended to reduce the number of people necessary to mount an effective defense. All gates, clearly, were potential points of weakness that required more defenders than comparable lengths of solid curtain. Further, the potential military utility of the posterns as sally-ports was hardly likely to be exploited by an already understrength garrison. Thus, *pace* Richmond, the tactical circumstances of the early fifth century also provide a more convincing context for the heightening than those of the early fourth, when the city was still garrisoned by its full complement of praetorians.[114]

Yet the most striking implications of Claudian's allusion to the Wall lie less in its factual content than in the very fact of its existence. To my knowledge, Claudian was the first ever to describe the Wall in unambiguously laudatory terms, and he did so in his semi-official capacity as spokesman for the imperial court in the West.[115] With the *De sexto consulatu*, the essentially triumphal conception of urban enceintes earlier attested in the provinces made its way to the heart of the empire, in the form of an ostensibly shameless acknowledgement, conspicuously included in a product of imperially sanctioned propaganda, that the

[113] Cf. Richmond 1930, 74–5; on the role of the thrown stone in Roman siege warfare, see Baatz 1983, 136.

[114] Richmond's otherwise reasonable remark that "the Wall became such a barrier as no besieging army could hope to cross without the most elaborate preparations, which could be adequately thwarted by a minimum garrison" (1930, 253) hardly works for Maxentius' administration, when Rome's garrison was not at all the "minimum garrison" that it likely had become a century later (see above n. 111). On the formidable presence of the heightened Wall, cf. Cozza 1987, 49.

[115] Claudian's first "celebration" of the Wall actually dates to 395, when he referred to the "tower-bearing banks" of the Tiber in his panegyric for the consuls Probinus and Olybrius, cited above at Chapter 1, n. 26.

fortifications of the *caput mundi* had been hastily improved because of the fears inspired by a hostile army at large in the Italian peninsula. As words and sentiments were not often fortuitously chosen in the panegyrical tradition to which Claudian's poem belongs, his implicit acceptance of Rome's vulnerability, albeit only as a foil for the emperor's successful defense of the city, comes as a watershed moment. For all that the Wall might still have been a necessary evil, it had become possible and evidently desirable to present it as something more, to stress its presence as a token of the emperor's tutelary patronage over the city that remained the most potent symbol of the empire's enduring greatness.[116] For the first time, that is, we are asked to see the Aurelian Wall as a prime indicator of the networks of association and patronage between the emperor and the *urbs Roma aeterna* that comprise the central thrust of Claudian's panegyric.[117]

The piece is devoted entirely to Honorius' *adventus* into Rome in 404, a ceremony that by its very nature gave perimeter walls a privileged place. The arrival of a late-antique emperor at a city, especially a capital, was a ceremonially charged occasion conducted and described in increasingly stylized idioms.[118] It was a defining moment in the projection of the emperor's majesty; and nowhere was the act of entry more potently reified than on the threshold between intramural and extramural space. The mention of the Wall in a piece devoted to an *adventus* is thus an evocative nexus between the representation and the reality, an architectural extension of the dynamic interplay between "art and ceremony" so integral to the creation of the imperial persona in late antiquity.

The ceremony proper was a carefully scripted occasion – in Ammianus' famous description of Constantius II's arrival in Rome in 357, the emperor himself might have been an early avatar of performance art,[119] – disseminated in lasting form by written descriptions and visual depictions of the event. When Constantius bowed his head in token of his lofty stature as he passed beneath the gateway of the city, the Wall was already a dramatic

---

[116] Claudian's *oeuvre*, like that of many of his near-contemporaries, is replete with allusions to Rome's history and assertions of its enduring stature (cf. Ausonius, *Ordo*, 1: *prima urbes inter, divum domus, aurea Roma...*), notable among them the encomiastic passage at *De consulatu Stiliconis* 3, 130–66; cf. Cameron 1970, 349–89. Fourth- and fifth-century literary constructions of "Eternal Rome" are collected in Paschoud 1967, and more recently in Brodka 1998; on Claudian, see Brodka, 91ff.; Paschoud, 151–5.

[117] On the political context of the *De VI consulatu*, see Dewar 1996, esp. xxix–lii; MacCormack 1981, 50–5.

[118] The fullest treatment of the subject is MacCormack 1981, 17–89; see also McCormick 1986, esp. 84–91 on entries at Rome; Humphries 2007, esp. 30–3.

[119] Amm. 16, 10, 5ff.

presence, as it remained fifty years later when Honorius ducked under the Porta Flaminia.[120] What is new is the publicized (and published) association between the Wall itself and the triumphal entry of the victorious emperor into his capital. For the first time, Rome's defenses were directly adduced for the glorification of the emperor, in the process assuming their place generally in the "popularization" of urban enceintes begun earlier on the frontiers, and more pointedly in a developing canon of walls seen as triumphal symbols of *adventus*. Moreover, an implicit parallel was created with the *adventus* of another figure of compelling interest to the Theodosian dynasty: already in the fourth century, an established iconographical connection existed between the increasingly numerous depictions of Jesus' entry into Jerusalem and scenes of imperial *adventus*, in which city walls featured prominently.[121]

Although Claudian, sparing at best in his use of Christian themes, says nothing of the sort, there is good reason to think that the rebuilt Wall immediately became a topographical expression of a new strain of "political theology" just then reaching maturity. Under Theodosius and his sons, the legacy of imperial Rome was pervasively assimilated into a new eschatological framework. The resting place of Peter and Paul was to be more eternal than ever, in its guise as the Christian capital of an ascendant Christian empire.[122] While this triumphant strain of Christianity, with its direct links to the imperial establishment, traced its origins to the era of Eusebius and Constantine, the connection between church and state that Rome was uniquely poised to capture had never been stronger than it became in the period between the last years of Theodosius' reign and the Gothic sack of the city in 410.[123] Little wonder, then, that another novel association was gaining currency at precisely the time when Aurelian's

---

[120] The device of inclining one's head while passing under gateways is attested as early as Cicero (*De orat.* 2, 267), and conspicuously present in Ammianus' account of the *adventus* of Constantius (16, 10, 10): *Nam et corpus perhumile curvabat portas ingrediens celsas et velut collo munito rectam aciem luminum tendens nec dextra vultum nec laeva flectebat tamquam figmentum hominis...* The assumption that Honorius did likewise is mine. It is clear from Claudian's account of Honorius' journey from Ravenna to Rome that the emperor took the Via Flaminia, descending through the Tiber valley past Narni (Narnia), and crossing the *pons mulvius* on his way into Rome (*De VI cons.*, 494ff.); cf. McCormick 1986, 86; Liverani 2004, 352ff.

[121] See Bühl 1995, 300–7.

[122] Generally on the conceptual evolution of this "New Rome," see Roberts 2001; Brodka 1998, esp. 127–254; Pietri 1976; Paschoud 1967, esp. 188–322.

[123] While Eusebius was the first to assert programmatically the concept of a Christian Roman Empire, notably in the *Vita Constantini* and the *Oratio de Laudibus Constantini* (cf. Barnes 1981, 245–71), more time was required before his vision became anything like reality. Among

Wall was monumentalized, as Rome began to emerge as the analogue of the heavenly city of Jerusalem, the ideal Christian metropolis most famously and influentially described in Chapter 21 of the *Apocalypse of John*.[124] As in the case of terrestrial Rome, the most prominent feature of the Celestial Jerusalem, depicted countless times in an unbroken iconographical continuum stretching from late antiquity to the present, was its awe-inspiring enceinte. The passage is important enough to be quoted in full:

And he took me in spirit over a great and high mountain and showed to me the holy city of Jerusalem descending from the heavens from God, containing the radiance of God; its light was like a most precious stone, like jasper-stone, in the likeness of crystal; and it had a great and high wall and it had twelve gates and over the gates twelve angels and inscribed names, which are those of the twelve tribes of Israel. (It has) three gates on the east and three on the north and three on the south and three on the west; and the wall has twelve courses, and above these the twelve names of the twelve apostles of the Lamb. And the one who spoke with me had a golden measuring-rod, that he might measure the city and its gates and its wall. And the city is arranged in a square, and its length is as much as its width. And he measured the city with the rod for twelve thousand stades; its length and width and height are equal. And he measured its wall at one-hundred forty-four cubits, by the measure of man, that is of the angel. And the structure of its wall was of jasper, but the city itself was limpid gold like to limpid glass. The courses of the wall of the city are adorned with every precious stone; the first of the courses jasper, the second sapphire, the third chalcedony, the fourth emerald, the fifth sardonyx, the sixth carnelian, the seventh chrysolite, the eighth beryl, the ninth topaz, the tenth chrysoprase, the eleventh dark amethyst(?), the twelfth amethyst. And the twelve gates are twelve pearls, each gate made from a single pearl. And the square of the city is limpid gold like to clear glass (Apoc. 21: 10–21).[125]

---

the many important works relevant to the religious and political dynamics of Theodosius' reign, see e.g. McLynn 1994, 291–360; Matthews 1975; Ensslin 1953.

[124] See Casartelli Novelli 2000; Uglione 1987, esp. 203–6; Paschoud 1979, esp. 59ff.; Pietri 1976, 1636ff.

[125] *Et sustulit me in spiritu super montem magnum et altum et ostendit mihi civitatem sanctam Ierusalem descendentem de caelo a Deo, habentem claritatem Dei; lumen eius simile lapidi pretiossisimo, tamquam lapidi iaspidi, in modum crystalli; et habebat murum magnum et altum et habebat portas duodecim et super portas angelos duodecim et nomina inscripta, quae sunt duodecim tribuum filiorum Israel. Ab oriente portae tres, et ab aquilone portae tres, et ab austro portae tres, et ab occasu portae tres; et murus civitatis habens fundamenta duodecim, et super ipsis duodecim nomina duodecim apostolorum Agni. Et, qui loquebatur mecum, habebat mensuram arundinem auream, ut metiretur civitatem et portas eius et murum eius. Et civitas in quadro posita est, et longitudo eius tanta est quanta et latitudo. Et mensus est civitatem arundine per stadia duodecim milia; longitudo et latitudo et altitudo eius aequales sunt. Et mensus est murum eius centum quadraginta quattuor cubitorum, mensura hominis, quae est*

I think this passage was on the minds of the authorities (Honorius, Stilicho, perhaps also the *praefectus urbi* Longinianus) responsible for the decision to heighten the Wall. Otherwise, it certainly came to be closely identified with Rome's new fortifications, or vice versa, in very short order.

The nature of this connection requires a good deal of explanation, beginning with several brief remarks on the Book of the Apocalypse. This ultimate section of the New Testament describes, in a series of extraordinarily vivid images, the end of the current age; the coming of an Antichrist; and a thousand-year reign of the celestial city, descended from the heavens as the abode of God's faithful, and the seat of "his" kingdom on earth. It is a challenging, often bafflingly ambiguous story laced with perplexing imagery, which may explain why its early history was plagued by squabbles over its orthodoxy. It was nonetheless firmly canonical by the end of the fourth century, when it seems to have enjoyed a sudden surge in popularity (the first sign of a trend that continued throughout the Middle Ages and beyond), perhaps in part because of the success of a new allegorical exegesis favored by thinkers as influential as Ambrose, Augustine, and Jerome.[126] Rather than a description of the end of the world, the book came to be understood as a symbolic rendering of earthly affairs, whence the Celestial Jerusalem became a model for the ideal community of the Church. The heavenly city, that is, was no longer a thing to be expected at the end of time, but a present reality, an evolving creation of the faithful taking shape within the confines of the Christian Roman Empire, itself destined to reign on in glory.[127]

Whatever the explanation, visions of the celestial city had clearly begun to capture the earthly imagination as never before in the years preceding

---

angeli. Et erat structura muri eius ex iaspide, ipsa vero civitas aurum mundum simile vitro mundo. Fundamenta muri civitatis omni lapide pretioso ornata: fundamentorum primum iaspis, secundus saphirus, tertius chalcedonius, quartus smaragdus, quintus sardonyx, sextus sardinus, septimus chrysolithus, octavus beryllus, nonus topazius, decimus chrysoprasus, undecimus hyacinthus, duodecimus amethystus. Et duodecim portae duodecim margaritae sunt, et singulae portae erant ex singulis margaritis. Et platea civitatis aurum mundum tamquam vitrum perlucidum.

[126] Origen was the first to offer a symbolic interpretation, followed by the Donatist Ticonius, whose views were seminal in shaping the thought of his countryman Augustine; on the exegesis and reception of the text generally, see Mazzuco 1983, 45–75. Y. Christie, amongst others, has directly linked the emergence of the new exegetical tradition to a sudden increase in apocalyptic imagery, which dates precisely to *c.* 400 (!); see Y. Christie 1979, esp. 110–11. The iconographical evidence is assessed in more detail below.

[127] See e.g. Quacquarelli 1987, 186ff.; Léon-Dufour 1987, esp. 166; Mazzuco 1983, 61–3; cf. also Hellemo 1989, 138–45.

and immediately following the rebuilding of the Aurelian Wall in 401–3, when imagery inspired by the Apocalypse of John burst upon the scene.[128] Though representations of the New Jerusalem had appeared occasionally at Rome perhaps as early as the third century, the motif came into its own in a group of sarcophagi datable to the end of the fourth century.[129] Attested also at Ancona and Milan, in addition to the several examples from Rome, the type features depictions of Christ and his apostles in majesty, set against the background of the promised city, indicated by an enceinte that came, in a sort of visual shorthand, to stand for the city as a whole.[130] Given the description in the Apocalypse, it could hardly have been otherwise; and from this time on, a towering and ornate wall became the primary iconographical trope used to identify the seat of Christ's coming kingdom on earth.

The tradition rapidly made its way into more monumental public commissions at Rome, where Celestial Jerusalems suddenly emerged as a regular feature of church decoration, in the apse mosaic at Sta. Pudenziana (Figure 3.1), executed in the first years of the fifth century, and even more tellingly at Sta. Maria Maggiore, built *c.* 432–440 (Figure 3.2).[131] Here, the scene of Jesus before the temple is set in Rome at the temple of Venus and Roma, the symbol *par excellence* of imperial Roman tradition, now seamlessly incorporated into the historical framework of the Christian scriptures.[132] In close counterpoint on the opposite spandrel of the triumphal arch, there stands an image of the Jerusalem of the Apocalypse. Thus, "Rome's claim to eternal rule is the instrument through which Christ

---

[128] The phenomenon is well documented in Colli 1983. On Rome specifically, see Casartelli Novelli 2000, 153–71, with the catalogue in Pani Ermini 2000, vol. II, 253–313. Cf. also Campanati 1999; Quacquarelli 1987, 189–90; Y. Christie 1979, 110–11. The trend is closely paralleled in contemporary literature, with Paulinus of Nola, Prudentius, and Pope Damasus all evoking ethereal fortresses in their writings; in addition to the works cited above, see Van der Meer 1938, 71; cf. *ibid.* 436–7 on the "invasion" of apocalyptic subjects around the year 400.

[129] A painting in cubiculum 3 of the so-called hypogeum of the Aurelii, of the later third century, appears to show the celestial city. It certainly appeared in a (lost) mosaic in St. Peter's, dating to before *c.* 360 (Colli 1983, 123ff.); and in another lost mosaic at Sta. Costanza, of mid-fourth century date (Campanati 1999).

[130] See Colli 1983; Sansoni 1969, 3ff. and *passim*; Lawrence 1927.

[131] It was depicted also at Sta. Sabina, on the triumphal arch, in a mosaic no longer extant (Colli 1983, 133).

[132] R. Warland has recently made a convincing case for the temple shown being that of Venus and Rome (Warland 2003). Though the argument is presented as a breach with a *communis opinio* that made the setting Jerusalem, the fact was already noted by F. Paschoud (1967, 9–10; cf. also De Seta 1989, 11ff.).

Figure 3.1 Celestial Jerusalem, apse mosaic, Sta. Pudenziana.

Figure 3.2 Celestial Jerusalem, triumphal arch, Sta. Maria Maggiore.

becomes the ruler of the world," an idea given concrete form in the juxtaposition of the real city of Rome with the Celestial Jerusalem.[133]

Very much a product of its time, this rendition of Jerusalem is dominated by an enceinte that rises high enough to occlude all but the highest gables within. The circuit is roughly circular, and punctuated with square towers that project a story above curtains liberally studded with radiant gems. A Latin cross features prominently in the semicircular arch of the one gateway shown. The visual predominance of the wall relegates intramural topography to an ancillary (and nearly invisible) position, thereby distancing the image both from the "classical" Greco-Roman iconographical tradition of the walled city seen in e.g. the city-fresco from the Oppian Hill in Rome, where the urban nucleus is shown from a bird's-eye perspective, neatly bounded but not at all obscured by its prominent circuit of walls;[134] and from the depiction of the real city of Jerusalem at the center of the sixth-century Madaba Map mosaic, where the walled circuit also delimits the city without occluding intramural topography – much of it identifiable – which is again represented from an overhead perspective.[135] It is a distinctly late-antique vision of a city, in short, where the enceinte has become the undisputed protagonist, as it is in the illustrations of the *Notitia Dignitatum*, for example, or the Peutinger Table or the *corpora* of the *agrimensores*;[136] but it is also something more specific. In its general contours and its particulars alike, the vision of Celestial Jerusalem at Sta. Maria Maggiore bears a notable resemblance to the newly elevated Wall of Rome.

Like the ideal enceinte of the ideal city, the Aurelian Wall had grown tall to the point of hiding from view nearly all of what lay inside it, becoming in the process the "face" of the city, the dominant feature of its external aspect, just like the defenses of its celestial alter ego. And like the walls of Jerusalem shown at both Sta. Maria Maggiore and Sta. Pudenziana, Rome's Wall was roughly circular, a broad similarity that

---

[133] Warland 2003, 133 and *passim.* Cf. also Casartelli Novelli 2000. Already for Prudentius, Rome's Wall symbolized the triumphant unity of the Christian Church (*Contra Symmachum* 2, 610–12): *Vivitur omnigenis in partibus haud secus ac si cives congenitos concludat moenibus unis urbs patria atque omnes lare conciliemur avito.*

[134] On the Oppian Fresco and its various analogues, see La Rocca 2000; more generally on classical representations of walled cities, see most recently Goodman 2007, 28–37.

[135] The firm grounding of the Jerusalem of the Madaba Map in the topography of the real sixth-century city is emphasized in e.g. Tzafrir 1999; on the marked dissimilarities between the Madaba Map Jerusalem and the depictions of Celestial Jerusalem at Rome and elsewhere, see Pullan 1999.

[136] Cf. Goodman 2007, 29ff.; Christie 2006, 187; 2001.

Figure 3.3 Celestial Jerusalem, triumphal arch, S. Lorenzo.

becomes much the more striking when it is remembered that the city of the Apocalypse is described in no uncertain terms as square. Indeed, the few representations of Jerusalem from Rome dating prior to *c.* 400 all had a quadrangular perimeter; and elsewhere, particularly north of the Alps, square Jerusalems always remained current, though round ones are increasingly attested in later centuries.[137] Yet New Jerusalem became consistently and serially circular at Rome in the fifth century, as it remained thereafter, in the sixth century at S. Lorenzo and at S. Prassede in the early ninth, where the jeweled circuits so clearly inspired by the Apocalypse in other respects have walls shaped like the real enceinte that rose in their midst (Figures 3.3–3.5). Thus, in the signal iconographical divergence from biblical precedent that began at Rome immediately after the Honorian heightening of the Wall, there comes a strong indication

---

[137] The point is best illustrated by a perusal of the catalogue at the end of Gatti Perer 1983, which contains detailed entries also for the examples subsequently cited; cf. also the catalogue in Pani Ermini 2000, vol. 2, 253–313. At Rome, the Jerusalem in the third-century hypogeum is square (see above n. 129), as it is on the city-gate sarcophagi, where the shape of the objects themselves lent itself particularly well to the quadrangular perimeter of the walls represented thereon.

Figure 3.4 Celestial Jerusalem, triumphal arch, S. Prassede.

Figure 3.5 Celestial Jerusalem, S. Prassede, detail.

that the Roman Wall had become both the model for, and the embodiment of, the biblical one.[138]

The impression is strengthened by additional correspondences in matters of detail. The towers of the circuits represented at Sta. Maria Maggiore, S. Lorenzo and S. Prassede all have hipped roofs (a four-faced pyramidal shape) of exactly the type first used in the heightened towers of Rome's Wall. The gates shown at Sta. Maria Maggiore and S. Lorenzo also recall the new gates of the Aurelian Wall, with the inscribed crosses on their keystones. As inscribed "Christian" keystones were by no means a ubiquitous feature of late-antique walls, real or represented, the parallel is the more noteworthy.[139]

The "Christianization" of Rome's Wall is further attested by other crosses outlined in the brickwork of the heightened curtains, several of which appear in the vicinity of other designs traced into the brick facings that have much puzzled past scholars (Figure 3.6). The proximity of a number of these radiate circles, lozenges, and half-ovals to the crosses makes them less whimsically casual than the term "caprices" (*capricci*) tentatively suggested by Cozza implies, the more so as similar designs are still more closely integrated with crosses in near-contemporary enceintes at places such as Terracina and Thessalonika (Figures 3.7–3.9).[140] Cozza himself thought them perhaps symbols of light ("sunbursts," rising suns or similar) and victory (palm fronds) used to complement the generic Christian symbolism of the associated crosses.[141] This is surely on the

---

[138] Hence, I believe that the heightened Wall was a seminal factor in the evolution of a new, round paradigm for the heavenly city that became widespread during the Middle Ages, when Rome and Jerusalem were being compared with increasing regularity (on which see De Seta 1989, 12ff.).

[139] In the illustrations of the *Notitia Dignitatum*, for example, there is no sign of crosses over city gates: the best example is the heavily fortified city used to illustrate the *tractus italiae*, which features a church prominently embellished with four golden crosses on its interior, but no corresponding Christian symbols over the two gates shown: see *Notitia, Occ.* 28 (Neira Faleiro p. 423). Amongst surviving late-antique gates elsewhere in Italy, the majority do not preserve extant traces of "Christian" keystones, though one – inscribed with a cross – does appear over a blocked gate in the wall at Terracina, where it is best explained as a direct borrowing from the Roman exemplar; see Ortolani 1988, 70.

[140] On Terracina, Christie and Rushworth 1988; and Ortolani 1988, 78, who I think overestimates the "spontaneous" nature of what he persists in calling "capricci" in the true sense of the word, though acknowledging their potential "religious-apotropaic" resonances. Yet surely the process of incorporating oddly shaped motifs into regular courses of brick or *vittatum* curtains represents rather more, in terms of advance planning and effort, than a moment of levity on the part of an individual mason. On Thessalonika, see Crow 2001, 93–8; Spieser 1984, esp. 66–7, with plates V, 1 and (better still) VII, 2.

[141] Cozza 1987, 26ff.

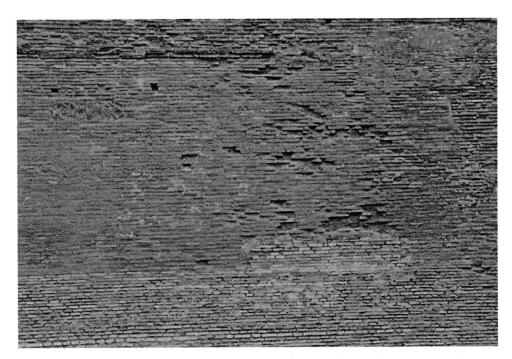

Figure 3.6 Curtain L25–26, decorative motifs. The cross shown in Figure 1.20 is just to the right.

Figure 3.7 Terracina, city wall, radiate motifs.

Figure 3.8 Terracina, city wall, "sunburst."

Figure 3.9 Terracina, city wall, tower D.

right track, as I think is his perception of "light" in the radiate spokes emanating from a central point that characterize many of these motifs.[142] If so, might they not also be explained, appearing as they do in the Wall of the new terrestrial incarnation of the Celestial Jerusalem, as intimations of coruscating jewels cut in various shapes?

It is an interesting coincidence that these figures are most closely paralleled in the nearby walls of Terracina, which are probably almost exactly contemporary with the decoration of Sta. Maria Maggiore. The roughly contemporary wall of Ravenna, one of the few other brick enceintes in Italy, also incorporates decorative "lunettes" not dissimilar to those at Rome and Terracina, as does the brick circuit at Dyrrachium/ Durres in Albania, this too datable to the fifth or early sixth century.[143] At

---

[142] "Light" symbolism – halos, sunlight, etc. – became a mainstay of Christian iconography in the fourth century, when it was used amongst other things to embody Nicene Christology: see Hellemo 1989, 32–9.

[143] On Ravenna, see Christie and Gibson 1988, 190; on Dyrrachium, Gutteridge, Hoti and Hurst 2001, esp. fig. 10 at p. 399.

Terracina, the radiate designs are moreover set in curtains where alternating courses of limestone and brick impart a striated appearance vaguely reminiscent of the banded walls described in the Apocalypse, a likeness more readily apparent at Thessalonika and Constantinople, whose fifth-century circuits were faced, in typical east Roman fashion, with alternating bands of stone and brick.

Across the empire, in fact, pronounced courses of contrasting stone and brick had become an increasingly common feature of circuit walls, beginning already in the later third century in places such as Britain and especially Gaul, where they remained current throughout the Middle Ages, when the enceinte of the Celestial Jerusalem was unquestionably the model.[144] Though the appearance of numerous exemplars prior to the Peace of the Church in 313 cautions against hasty attributions of Christian significance to such structures, as perhaps do the potential structural benefits of the "banded" facing technique,[145] it does not seem a great stretch to imagine that they eventually came to invite comparison and assimilation with the biblical paradigm in the new aesthetic milieu of the fourth and fifth centuries, as Celestial Jerusalem became an iconographical mainstay and real walls began to teem with symbols, at least some of which were patently Christian in inspiration. One of the best examples of the type is the late-fourth-century wall at Carcassonne, which happens, in another suggestive coincidence, to be among the early examples of a defensive wall adorned with decorative "capricci" similar to those described above.[146]

None of this, of course, proves that the radiate motifs were meant to be jewels, an admittedly challenging premise that involves difficulties beyond

---

[144] On the third-century Gallic enceintes, see above at nn. 55–6; in England, the late-third century Saxon shore forts feature similar banded facings: see Johnson 1976, 34–62. On medieval Gallic walls and Celestial Jerusalem, see Van Emden 2000, esp. 551ff. Architectural resonances of the *Apocalypse* are in fact legion, from Constantinian Jerusalem (the real one), to Carolingian Aachen, to the England of Edward I. The associations precociously developed in the Wall of Honorian Rome flourished even into the modern era, when the rebuilt "mural crown" of Augsburg could still be likened to the walls of Celestial Jerusalem in the seventeenth century. On Augsburg, see Roeck 1989; more broadly, see De Seta 1989; Rossi and Rovetta 1983; Heitz 1979; Müller 1961, esp. 53–114 on German cities and Heavenly Jerusalem in the Middle Ages.

[145] Technical analyses of these walls usually focus on the function of the brick bands in particular as bonding and/or leveling courses (see e.g. Ousterhout 1999, 157ff.); while there may be truth to the idea, it by no means excludes the possibility of an aesthetic or symbolic component: "form," in short, may admirably have complemented "function" as the Christianization of the empire progressed.

[146] The decorations include several lunettes in the "Tour de la Marquière": see Johnson 1983a, 112; cf. Braund 1973; Christie and Rushworth 1988, 85. For the dating, see Heijmans 2004, 121; Fourdrin 2002, 311.

mere stretching of the evidence, among them the need for a coextensive reinterpretation of the many similar designs found in contemporary religious architecture (much of which was in fact already inspired by the New Jerusalem paradigm).[147] It should be said, too, that radiate "suns" and the like are occasionally attested earlier in manifestly non-Christian contexts (e.g. Severan Leptis Magna; third-century Cologne);[148] though their dramatic surge in popularity and concomitant juxtaposition with crosses, from the fourth century on, would seem to herald the arrival of a truly new phenomenon. All told, the idea perhaps need not be dismissed out of hand as a working hypothesis, if only because it calls attention to the underappreciated fact that fifth-century enceintes were being thus decorated in the first place. Whatever exactly they represent, the flourishing embellishments in the walls at Rome, Terracina, Thessalonika, and elsewhere betoken a developing sense that urban defenses were supposed to be ornate and inherently "Christian." To this extent, it is difficult not to imagine some connection with the description in the Apocalypse of John that so inspired later generations of builders, along with the authors of the Jerusalem-mosaics at Rome.

In short, then, it is clear that the Jerusalem of the Apocalypse, distilled into the essence of its wall, was on the ascendant in Rome at the beginning of the fifth century, at the same time that Rome's identity as an ideal Christian capital was being ever more stridently trumpeted, in part by recourse to analogies with the New Jerusalem.[149] As the

[147] See *inter alia* Rossi and Rovetta 1983; Grabar 1946, vol. 2, 109–11. Such motifs occasionally appear also in other more utilitarian structures, notably in restorations to the Roman aqueducts (see Coates-Stephens 2003b, 166, with fig. 1; *LTUR Suburbium* 1, fig. 32; Cozza 1987, 29, with figs. 23 and 26); and rather more frequently in churches at Rome, particularly those of the fifth century (Cozza, 26ff.).

[148] See the illustrations in Ortolani 1988, 79; cf. also Guilleux 2000, 218–22. I suspect that the famous decorated tower at Cologne (the Römerturm) represents a third-century restoration of the original enceinte, this datable on dendrochronological grounds to the beginning of the second century; cf. Spiegel 2006, 18.

[149] I am tempted to wonder whether the twelve gates of the Jerusalem of the *Apocalypse* did not also inspire comparisons with the Wall. The grouping of three gates in each side of Jerusalem's wall, taken up in everything from illustrated manuscripts to the tripartite *Westwerke* of medieval cathedrals and abbeys, could have been applied, with only a bit of stretching, to the outer perimeter of the post-Honorian Wall, when its many smaller apertures had been walled up. Interestingly enough, the portrayal *cum* personification of Rome in the Peutinger Table shows exactly twelve roads leaving the city: that the figure is achieved only by a selective representation of gates (the Portuensis and Metronia are omitted; the Praenestina and Labicana are separated, etc.) suggests to me that it stems from a conscious decision on the part of the redactor, aimed at an idealized representation of reality. The document itself, in the form in which it was transmitted in the medieval manuscript tradition, is usually dated between the

center of earthly Christianity and the terrestrial embodiment of the celestial city, Rome might have required the preternaturally prepossessing ramparts it then acquired even without the ominous notes of the "Gothic rumor." At any rate, the public acclamation of the Wall, its religiously charged decorative features, and the sudden efflorescence of depictions of Jerusalem's wall all suggest that the parallels between the two cities and their enceintes were much on the minds of contemporaries.

And if Roman prestige suffered a temporary setback following Alaric's sack of the city in 410, the vehemence of the various reactions to the event demonstrates above all how powerful the ideal of a Christian Rome already was. Augustine's *magnum opus*, the *De civitate Dei*, is an immensely complex book, but on a very basic level, it was written expressly to counter the perception that the heart and citadel of the Christian world had fallen, a notion to which even the dour sensibilities of Jerome proved susceptible.[150] Indeed, Augustine's effort to distance irremediably the earthly city of Rome from the celestial kingdom of the redeemed ultimately came to rather little, inasmuch as it was in the generations immediately following the sack that the portrayal of Rome as the center of Latin Christendom took on the essential characteristics it was to retain for the next millennium and more.[151] Leo I made the classic and enduring statement of Rome's place as *caput mundi* and *sedes Petri* alike in his eighty-second sermon, in the course of which he associated Christian Rome directly with the "heavenly kingdom." How truly remarkable, then, that in practically the same breath he recalled

second half of the fourth century and the first half of the fifth; for the *status quaestionis*, see Bosio 1983, 147–62.

[150] Generally on the *De civitate Dei* and its place in the polemics that followed upon the sack, see P. Brown 2000 [1967], 287–312; Pelican 1987; Paschoud 1967, 239–45; Courcelle 1964, 67–77. While Jerome does not quite equate the fall of the city with the demise of the faith, his horror at the event and his sense of its profound repercussions are nonetheless vivid: see e.g. *Ep.* 123, 16 (written before the fall): *quid salvum est, si Roma perit?*; *Ep.* 128, 5: *Pro nefas, orbis terrarum ruit, in nobis peccata non corruunt. Urbs inclita et Romani imperii caput, uno hausta est incendio. Nulla regio, quae non exules eius habeat. In cineres ac favillas sacrae quondam ecclesiae conciderunt, et tamen studemus avaritiae...*; cf. also *Ep.* 127, 12 (the famous *capitur Urbs, quae totum cepit orbem* passage); *Ep.* 126, 2; *Ep.* 130, 5, etc.

[151] Cf. Pietri 1976, esp. 1, 645–51; Paschoud 1967, 319–22; Ullmann 1960, 25–51. And for all that Augustine's later countryman Fulgentius shared his self-conscious interest in distinguishing between real Rome and celestial Jerusalem, the words attributed to him by his biographer, as he stood gaping in the forum around the year 500, only emphasize the real extent of their conceptual amalgamation: *Fratres, quam speciosa potest esse Hierusalem coelestis, si sic fulget Roma terrestris!* (*S. Fulgentii episcopi ruspensis vita*, PL 65, col. 131).

Romulus' first wall of the city, by way of reminding his listeners how much greater the Rome refounded in the blood of Peter and Paul was than the one originally born in fratricide.[152] The polyvalent allusion to the equally superior grandeur of Rome's new "Christian" ramparts is unmistakable.

3.5   *Sedes Petri; caput mundi?* Rivals of Rome and the imitation of the Aurelian Wall

Remaining on the theme of the *longue durée*, we may imagine that the emotive impact of the Aurelian Wall continued to grow in step with the identification of Rome as the leading light of the Christian world. Certainly its physical presence, scrupulously maintained over the centuries, must have loomed ever greater as the urban sprawl that once surrounded it crumbled and receded. Indeed, the power of the Wall, and that of the image of the Christian citadel it came to represent, were of a sort to be felt even far beyond the visible horizon. Examples from two distant places will suffice to hint at the reach of its legacy. The first is Ravenna, where the growing pretensions of secular and religious grandeur that accompanied its establishment as a principal seat of imperial government in 402 soon led to increasingly strident claims of rivalry with Rome.[153] Here, a century after Rome's Wall was heightened, and scant decades after its own enceinte

[152] *Sermo* 82, 1 (combining the versions given in manuscripts β and γ; see *CCSL* 138A, 509): *Isti* [sc. Peter and Paul] *sunt sancti patres tui verique pastores, qui te regnis caelestibus inserendam multo melius multoque felicius condiderunt quam illi quorum prima studio moenium tuorum fundamenta locata sunt, ex quibus is qui tibi nomen dedit fraterna te caede foedavit. Isti sunt qui te ad hanc gloriam provexerunt, ut* gens sancta, populus electus, *civitas* sacerdotalis et regia, *per sacram beati Petri sedem caput totius orbis effecta, latius praesideres religione divina quam dominatione terrena.* Similar sentiments appear in *Sermo* 83; and they are closely echoed by Leo's secretary, Prosper of Aquitaine: see *Carmen de Ingratis,* 40–2: *sedes Roma Petri, quae pastoralis honoris facta caput mundo, quidquid non possidet armis religione tenet.*

[153] See Gillett 2001, esp. 155–7; Marcus 1997, 143ff.; cf. generally Gelichi 2000. As Gillett rightly says, Ravenna did not definitively supplant Rome as the seat of imperial government in the West until the last quarter of the fifth century; and it was from exactly this period that Ravenna began to be compared programmatically with Rome, after tentative beginnings earlier in the century. Personifications of Ravenna modeled on the *tychai* of Rome and Constantinople first appeared on silver coinage in 475 (Gillett, 155; cf. MacCormack 1981, 235ff.); and at the beginning of the sixth century, Theoderic was famously shown, in a mosaic in his palace, flanked by equally imposing figures of Rome and Ravenna (see Agnellus, *LP* 94, with Gillett, 156; La Rocca 1993, 473; MacCormack 1981, 235).

had been massively reworked, the vision of the New Jerusalem so commonly evoked at Rome was reproduced; and nowhere are the Roman exemplars more closely mirrored than in the Ravennate churches of San Vitale and Sant'Apollinare in Classe.[154] Like the claim made later in the century by the archbishops of Ravenna to wear the *pallium* traditionally reserved for the bishops of Rome,[155] it is a concerted statement about the status of the city and its church, and their place in the broader order of things, all captured in two scintillating city walls.

The second is Constantinople. Even at first glance, it is suggestive that the great land walls of the city were built within a decade of the rebuilding of the Aurelian Wall, particularly since the genesis of the project must now be placed in even closer chronological proximity to the heightening of the Roman Wall than was previously thought, thanks to the discovery of a remarkable new inscription in 1993, which quite convincingly dates the start of construction to *c.* 404–5.[156] Scant months after the delivery of Claudian's fulsome encomium on the enlarged walls of Rome in the *de sexto consulatu Honorii*, that is, ground was broken for the new walls of Constantinople.

Further scrutiny only increases the suspicion that the "New Rome" on the Bosporus was reacting consciously to the example furnished by the original, by demonstrating quite simply that there was no immediate practical need for a new wall at Constantinople at the time of its construction. Like Rome, the city already had a functional enceinte, built in the course of its refounding under Constantine, which enjoyed from the outset a considerable defensive advantage over the circuit at Rome because of the far shorter perimeter of its landward approaches. Further, there is no indication that the city faced any greater peril when the wall was built between *c.* 405 and 413 than it had more or less constantly

---

[154] The circuit at Ravenna was greatly expanded in the half-century that followed the transfer of the imperial court in 402, and there are signs of continued rebuilding and restorations at the end of the fifth century under Odoacer: see Christie and Gibson 1988; cf. Gelichi 2000, 116ff.

[155] Gregory I strongly opposed this presumption on the part of Ravenna's bishops; see Marcus 1997, 150–3.

[156] The inscription records a restoration of the circuit undertaken following an earthquake in 447, and states explicitly that the wall had originally taken nine years to construct. In light of the law in the *Codex Theodosianus* that suggests that the towers of the wall were fit for habitation by 413 (*CTh.* 15, 1, 51, cited in full above at Chapter 2, n. 58; cf. *CTh* 7, 8, 13), already identified by Speck (Speck 1973, 135–43) as a solid *terminus ante* for the enceinte, construction should thus have begun in *c.* 404–5: see Lebek 1995, 110–19; Bardill 1999, 676. Van Milligen's study of the fortifications of Constantinople (of 1899) has at last been supplanted by the new monograph of Astutay-Effenberger 2007; see also Crow 2007, 262–8; Ahunbay and Ahunbay 2000; Foss and Winfield 1986, 41ff.; Müller-Wiener 1977, 286–300.

since the defeat at Adrianople in 378, and the decision to rent out the towers of the new wall to private citizens immediately upon their completion is hardly redolent of dire military necessity.[157] Then, there is the most remarkable fact of all: the new wall enclosed a predominantly rural landscape of monasteries, cemeteries, and aristocratic villas.[158] In seeking to explain such a singular happenstance in an age more often characterized by urban contraction, Cyril Mango was left to suggest that the greatest enceinte ever seen on the European continent was built to enclose three cisterns, none of which existed until years – many decades in two of the three cases – after its completion.[159] I submit that the distant specter of Rome's improved Wall was the more compelling stimulus, and that Constantinople's new defenses were intended to be bigger, more awe-inspiring and, to be sure, more militarily effective as well.[160]

It may not be a terrible oversimplification to say that the matter in large part boils down to a case of one-upmanship between the two leading cities of the Roman world. While the extent of the competition between Rome and Constantinople, and the depth of the vitriol it aroused at various times can be endlessly debated, it is beyond doubt that a rivalry existed, which was institutionalized following the death of Theodosius I in 395 and the final partitioning of the empire between his sons.[161] And though Rome effectively disappeared as a secular rival to Constantinople soon thereafter, the epic struggles for ecclesiastical primacy between the two cities were just beginning, the endless particulars of which need not be rehashed here. Following as it did almost immediately upon the division of the empire

---

[157] *CTh.* 15, 1, 51 (quoted in full above at Chapter 2, n. 58).

[158] See Mango 1985, 46ff. The more traditional view that the growing population of the new capital required more space than had been included inside the Constantinian circuit is reprised in Dagron 1974, 519–25, who acknowledged nonetheless that the space enclosed was vastly larger than the *abitato* of the time.

[159] Mango 1985, 49.

[160] As they are amply described in the sources cited above, I omit a full description. Suffice it to say that the main wall was generally slightly higher that the Aurelian Wall, and fronted by far more impressive outworks, comprised of a lower second wall, or *proteichisma*, complete with towers, and a massive ditch beyond. Cf. Ward-Perkins 2000, e.g. 66–8: "Nevertheless the Theodosian land-walls of Constantinople, though considerably shorter than those of Rome ... are undoubtedly the most impressive (and successful) defences ever erected in the Roman period."

[161] A good general survey of prevailing views of Rome in the eastern capital, where it was programmatically evoked and imitated, is Dagron 1974, 48–76; cf. also Carile 2002; Ward-Perkins 2000, 63ff. Iconographical echoes of Rome in fourth-century Constantinople are treated at length in Bühl 1995.

and the monumental "facelift" undergone by the old *caput mundi*, the building of Constantinople's enormous new wall is best construed as an act aimed at demonstrating the literally unassailable pre-eminence and permanence of the "New Rome" in military, political, and religious affairs alike.

In the conscious emulation of Rome's defenses at Constantinople, and for that matter in the bare fact that the two greatest cities in the empire were almost simultaneously given far more imposing perimeter walls, there appears the ultimate testimonial to the radically changed place of the urban enceinte in the late-antique Mediterranean. A century earlier, both places had, with little fanfare, been fortified in a way designed to assure a modicum of safety for their inhabitants and little more. Yet by the beginning of the fifth century, for all that perimeter walls may have remained an unfortunate and even growing necessity, they could be presented as something very different: Rome and Constantinople began, in short, to proclaim their privileged status by means of their enlarged walls, and not in spite of them.[162] As walls became more ubiquitous and ideologically acceptable, the two leading cities of the empire girded themselves with new, superlative exemplars of defensive fortifications, leaving other places – notably including the second cities of the West and the East, Carthage and Antioch – to follow suit.[163]

But make no mistake: the city of Rome itself provided the example for others to follow. Just as the construction of the Aurelian Wall came at the beginning of the first major flurry of urban fortification in the later third century, so too its heightening closely anticipated a second wave of wall-building in the early fifth. The adoption of the Roman model at e.g. Milan and Trier in the earlier period, and later at Ravenna and Constantinople, thus points to the role of the Aurelian Wall in shaping the very urban paradigm that ultimately contributed to its own preservation through the centuries. By the end of antiquity, the ideal of the city, the ideal of the capital, and beneath it all the ideal of Rome were inextricably tied to the image of the bristling citadel. The tenacity with which a drastically

---

[162] Neil Christie observes the same trend in the epigraphic record, where celebratory/dedicatory inscriptions from city walls become much more common in the fifth century than before (Christie 2006, 289–90).

[163] Cf. Christie 2006, 298. Carthage was encircled by a new enceinte in *c.* 425; see Heijmans 2004, 122–3; Christie 2001, esp. 114–16; Wells 1980. Also during the first half of the fifth century, the Daphne Gate at Antioch was rebuilt with massive square towers in fine marble, liberally studded with gilded decoration, in direct imitation of the Porta Aurea in the land walls of Constantinople, according to John Malalas: see *Chron.* 14, 13 (Dindorf ed. 360).

shrunken population at Rome continued to maintain its enormous Wall in the early Middle Ages strongly indicates that its importance as a token of civic stature was more keenly felt than ever, at a time when the city was not coincidentally coming into its own as the citadel of a *Respublica Christiana*. This, however, is a matter to be left for the final part of this study. Before examining how the Wall left its mark on the presentation of post-imperial Rome, we must first consider the marks it left on the city itself.

4 | The city, the suburbs, and the Wall: the rise of a topographical institution

The second part of this study is animated by the central question, hitherto almost untouched, of what the Aurelian Wall "did" to Rome. In part, I want to consider the effects of the Wall on the fabric of the city, on the way it looked and the way it functioned, and thus on the activities of people living within and around it, whose lives it touched in a variety of ways. But I am equally concerned with the Wall's impact on the concept of Rome in late antiquity and the early Middle Ages, and its place in the cognitive landscapes of Romans and outsiders, which in turn conditioned the representations of "Rome" exported abroad and vaunted at home. In what follows, we will consider some of the more salient results of the immuring of Rome, first in terms of topography and infrastructure, and then in the following chapter in relation to prevailing conceptions of urban space and the limits thereof, before turning in the final chapter to the place the Wall had come to occupy after a half-millennium spent seeping into the spirit and fabric of the city, when as the pre-eminent embodiment of "Rome" – as reality and as ideal – it became instrumental in the creation of a new papal capital that was simultaneously the regional hub of a nascent ecclesiastical state, and the quasi-mythical focal point of an immeasurably vaster spiritual empire.

These are subjects that demand the juxtaposition of textual sources and archaeological evidence, which means they also require some coming to terms with the inescapable dichotomy between Rome as a literary construct and Rome as an artifact: between the picture of the city as it was conceived, described, and constructed in writing, and the situation on the ground, insofar as this is recoverable. Yet for all that their relationship to each other and to the "real Rome" of the first millennium AD is notoriously difficult to define, these are both facets of a single reality, an ensemble in which bricks and mortar were always inextricably intertwined with the written word, just as what the city actually was was inseparable from what it was variously supposed to be.

4.1   *Urbs* and *suburbium*

Rodolfo Lanciani famously compared imperial Rome to Victorian London, the capital city of the dominant world empire of his own day, which he knew from experience as a practically boundless metropolitan conglomeration, a monumental urban center and seat of government surrounded by densely packed suburbs stretching for miles in all directions, all linked in an indissoluble unity.[1] Expanding on his analogy, we might try to imagine how things would have gone in London if, during the early years of the Second World War, say, an enceinte had been built around the center of the city, in a rough circle with a radius of two miles centered on London Bridge.[2] I imagine that neither London nor Londoners would ever have been quite the same again; and I think the appearance of the Aurelian Wall at Rome was a cataclysm of comparable magnitude, the repercussions of which have not ceased to be felt more than seventeen centuries later.

Lanciani's analogy raises the broader issue of the relationship between the city of Rome and its suburbs. There is no single answer to questions of where the city ended and where its suburbs started, where the suburbs ended, nor indeed about how each of these concepts was defined in the period in question. The Romans themselves, in fact, hardly ever used the term *suburbium*, preferring instead its adjectival derivative *suburbanus*, employed in reference to discrete locales.[3] Roman jurists and modern scholars alike have suggested a variety of possible responses, all of them significant in one way or another. Differences generally boil down to a matter of semantics and perspective.

Several things can, however, be said with some certainty. First of all, in the imperial period, there was no single, universally applicable boundary between the *urbs* and its surroundings, theoretically as well as topographically speaking.[4] The *pomerium* was one fixed limit, the customs-circuit another, and the Servian Wall a third; but already by the early empire, jurists recognized the *de facto* reality that the urban center had expanded well beyond these limits, which prompted them to offer the alternative

---

[1] Lanciani 1897b, 265ff.   [2] Cf. Lanciani 1892, 101.

[3] See Volpe 2000, 183; Champlin 1982, 97.

[4] Useful overviews of the relationship between center and suburbs include, in addition to the articles cited in the preceding note, Goodman 2007, esp. 7–59 on Rome; Witcher 2005; Panciera 1999, 9–15; Frézouls 1987; and Quilici 1974 (the last two with strikingly different views of the extent of "urbanization" of the Roman periphery); cf. also Patterson 2000, Coarelli 1997b, 89ff.; Carandini 1985.

definition of *continentia tecta* or *continentia aedificia*.[5] Thus defined, the *urbs* proper became the extent of the area covered by densely packed urban-style housing, a boundary by definition of a labile and highly fluid nature. Of course, the perimeter of the fourteen Augustan regions extended the limits yet further, rendering in some sense urban a periphery stretching beyond even the area ultimately enclosed by the Aurelian Wall. In topographical terms, the situation is no less ambiguous.[6] There were large open spaces in the very heart of the city, among which the area occupied by Nero's Domus Aurea springs immediately to mind. Just beyond the monumental center, there were in some places the parks and gardens of the aristocracy, while in others there were busy markets, warehouses, residential neighborhoods, and of course the cemeteries, stretching in places for miles, with tombs, columbaria, hypogea, and shrines piled nearly – and sometimes literally – on top of each other.

Thus, as a number of others have said, imperial Rome was an "open city," spreading and diffusing itself gradually into a hinterland itself packed with zones of intensive agricultural production, cemeteries, aristocratic villas, etc., all of which depended upon the center for their existence.[7] The story of the Wall's impact on the city, then, is really that of how it came to insert itself into this organic unity, and of how and to what extent it altered the materiality, function, and definition of two spaces thenceforth distinguishable, at least to the modern eye, as "inside" and "outside." For in the modern period, the legacy of the Wall has undeniably loomed remarkably large. For all that it is often taken for granted or overlooked, it has fundamentally conditioned discussion and classification of "city" and "suburb," most obviously because it is so often the frame chosen to surround representations – pictorial and scholarly alike – of the city of Rome.[8] It is a tradition with storied roots, stretching back at least to the plans of the city redacted with increasing frequency beginning in the

---

[5] See Goodman 2007, 13–18 and 46–59; Frézouls 1987, esp. 377–84.

[6] Much important work on the Roman periphery has been done in recent years; contributions most relevant to late antiquity and the early Middle Ages include: P. Pergola, R. Santangeli Valenzani and R. Volpe 2003; Marazzi 2001a; 1998; 1988; Spera 1999; Coarelli 1986, esp. 35–58. Behind all of it lies the *magnum opus* of G. Tomassetti (Tomassetti 1975–1980 [1910–1926]), which is at last being supplemented and largely supplanted by the *Suburbium* continuation of the *LTUR*, now nearing completion (see V. Fiocchi Nicolai, M. Grazia Granino Cecere, Z. Mari, Rome, 2001–).

[7] The interconnectivity of periphery and center has been emphasized by nearly all the scholars mentioned in the previous notes; the term "open city" is used in e.g. Frézouls 1987 and Quilici 1974.

[8] The phenomenon is eloquently introduced in Quilici 1974, 410–16; cf. Marazzi 1988, 258.

later Middle Ages, most of which leave the area outside the perimeter of the Wall largely or totally blank. *Hic sunt dracones...* In their pioneering studies of the Roman *campagna*, Nibby and Ashby likewise made the Wall the starting point of the *suburbium*;[9] and Lanciani did the same with the *Forma Urbis*, though of course the Wall does not correspond precisely with any of the definitions of the *urbs* current from the republic through the high empire. The trend remains in full force today, as for example in the enormously important *Lexicon Topographicum Urbis Romae*, which takes the Wall as its outer limit, though the majority of the entries contained therein originated long before it came to exist (and hence, the *Suburbium* continuation of the *Lexicon*, just now appearing, also takes the Wall as its starting point).[10] Much work on Roman roads likewise begins from the gates of the Aurelian Wall, which the main arteries predate by many centuries.

Up to a point, this is fair enough. Discussions of the *urbs* have to end somewhere, and those about the *suburbium* need a beginning. Yet the fact remains that the omnipresence of the Wall tends to lead to the dangerous impression that Rome was always a compact unit shaped (exactly) like the perimeter of its Aurelianic enceinte. To anticipate my conclusions somewhat, I do think that the Wall entered on the trajectory that led to this modern paradigm in precisely the period covered in the present survey, and that the process by which it did so is one of the most remarkable aspects of its history. It by no means follows, however, that the Wall was perceived in like manner in the years immediately following its appearance, a caution to be borne in mind as we begin from the beginning, with the "landing" of the Wall on the "open city" of Rome in the third century.

4.2   The immediate topographical impact of the Wall, local

It would be difficult to exaggerate the effect of the Wall's construction on the topography of the several intensively developed quarters through which it ran. Countless buildings were leveled; entire residential and commercial neighborhoods were split in two, as were luxurious villas

---

[9] See e.g. Ashby 1927 and 1902–1910; Nibby 1848–9.

[10] See above n. 6; see especially the introduction in *LTUR Suburbium* 1, 1–5. The contributors to the recent *Suburbium* colloquium (Pergola *et al.* 2003) were also asked to use the Aurelian Wall as the inner limit of their studies. Tomassetti's survey is a notable exception that, in taking the Servian Wall as its starting point, more successfully captures the blurry blending of city and *campagna* by rooting its suburban itineraries farther into the urban nucleus.

and sprawling estates of the wealthy; venerable family tombs were immured or buried and lost forever from view, and so on. Numerous examples of private residences, public buildings, and tombs either razed or altered beyond recognition have already been mentioned in Chapter 2, to which the addition of a few representative vignettes will suffice to convey a sense of the sudden violence of the intervention on the cityscape.

A series of excavations on the grounds of the former Villa Patrizi, just outside the Porta Nomentana, has documented several sprawling villas of the early empire, furnished with ample residential spaces, peristyle court-yards, and gardens.[11] Various rooms along the inside of the Wall that probably belonged to one or more of these villas, among them a bath building with a preserved marine floor mosaic, were destroyed and filled with rubble during its construction.[12] The main nucleus of the villa, situated about 50 m outside the Wall, appears to have gone out of use at approximately the same time: there are no signs of fourth-century habitation, and two third-century coin hoards were found, one of them containing *antoniniani* that cannot have been deposited more than a decade or so before the building of the Wall.[13] Not far to the east, near the junction between the Wall and the Castra Praetoria, construction crews

[11] The best overview of the extramural villas is in Lanciani's publication of the remains that came to light during the building of the headquarters for the state railroad company: see Lanciani 1918, esp. 25ff.; cf. *LTUR Suburbium* 1, see under *Antoniae Caenidis praedium; Ti. Alieni Caecinae praedium;* see also G. Gatti in *BullCom* 1909, 133ff. In the 1960s and again in the 1990s, the area was studied anew by teams from the British School: see Gilkes *et al.* 1994 and Bird *et al.* 1993.

[12] See Bird *et al.* 1993, esp. 64–6; on the mosaic, probably also datable within the century immediately preceding the Wall, *ibid.* 100–3. On the probable association of these rooms with the extramural complex, see Gilkes *et al.* 1994, 128–9, with fig. 1.

[13] Generally on the phases of occupation and abandonment, see Gilkes *et al.* 1994, 128–9; on the coins, *BullCom* 1909, 136; cf. Lanciani 1918, 29. One of the two hoards contains thirty-seven *denarii* dating through the reign of Elagabalus (218–22); as their intrinsic worth was far higher than the debased *antoniniani* that came into use from the reign of Caracalla, they are liable to have been hoarded and kept out of circulation for much of the third century, leaving the year 222 a very rough *terminus ante* that might well reflect a date closer to the building of the Wall. The second hoarded consisted of *antoniniani*; it is sadly only passingly mentioned in the period reports I have found, where the "second half" of the third century is the most precise *terminus* offered (*BullCom* 1909, 136); hence my assumption that the latest examples date from the 250s to no later than the reign of Aurelian and the presumptive abandonment of the site. An additional rough *terminus post* for the end of these villas comes from the series of stamped lead pipes found in the area, which peters out in the early third century, after a regular sequence of first- and second-century examples; see Lanciani 1918, 25–9. The latest bears the name of T. Flavius Titianus, in all probability the person of that name attested as proconsul of Africa under Caracalla; see G. Gatti in *BullCom* 1907, 230–1; *CIL* 2, 4076 and 4118.

hacked their way through an elegant house built in the first century AD, recycling its bricks for the curtain of the Wall built on the spot, but leaving in place and burying everything that did not serve for the new construction, including the intrinsically more valuable marble columns and paved floors. Excavations of an ornate nympheum abutting the inner face of the Wall near the Porta Tiburtina likewise turned up sculpted busts and marble fixtures that were simply left *in situ* and buried.[14]

These examples, wholly characteristic of the picture that emerges from scattered reports of five centuries' worth of digging in the vicinity of the circuit, are chosen with an eye to illustrating one additional point, already hinted at long ago by Lanciani but in need of repeating. In short, the space cleared during the building of the Wall was far wider than the 4 m of its foundation trench.[15] Beyond mere trimming back of adjacent sections of buildings, the scope of the demolitions was extended to encompass the creation of tactically expedient zones of open space, both inside and out. There is good reason why all the excavated remains in close proximity to the Wall mentioned above come from its internal side. All of them were buried beneath mounds of earth from the foundation trench, piled up in a carefully compacted artificial rampart that Lanciani measured in several places at approximately 3 m deep at the base of the Wall.[16] There was no need to raze to the ground the structures interred in this rampart, which was obviously envisioned as a permanent construction which the buried remnants would if anything have helped to stabilize. Beyond its sloping face, which was probably at least as wide as the foundation trench itself, there will have been additional space cleared to serve as an access road or *intervallum*, essential for the rapid and efficient deployment of troops around the perimeter of the Wall, as well as for the transport of the supplies and laborers required for the building and subsequent maintenance of the Wall itself.[17] Lanciani's

---

[14] This and the preceding example are well summarized in Lanciani 1892, 104–6. This article, which I cite frequently though it is now in many respects dated, deserves a lasting place in the historiography of the Wall, as the first serious effort made to think about what the Wall "did" to the city. On the nymphaeum, see also *BullCom* 1886, 309; *Notizie* 1886, 271; *ibid.* 1884, 392, etc.

[15] See Lanciani 1892, 88; and in *Notizie* 1880, 127–8.   [16] Lanciani 1892, 110.

[17] Similarly, access roads were nearly always built and maintained alongside aqueducts, inside the city as well as in the open country beyond, to ensure the sort of ready maintenance that was surely envisioned also in the case of the Wall; see above Chapter 2, n. 20; cf. also Coates-Stephens 2003, 427.

estimate of 5 m of total cleared space behind the Wall is a bare minimum that I would tentatively increase to 8–10.[18]

The situation at Rome is remarkably closely paralleled at Dura-Europos, where the western flank of the city wall was reinforced with a massive earthen *agger* soon before the destruction of the city in 256 at the hands of the Sassanian Persians. Initially, the 5 m wide "Wall Street" between the rear of the fortifications and the external walls of the buildings lining the street was filled nearly to wall-walk level with dirt and rubble, and the internal walls of the adjacent structures – most notably the synagogue complex – reinforced with further deposits of earth to buttress them against the lateral pressure exerted by the fill; when this reinforcement proved insufficient, further earth was added to the internal buttresses. Finally, at a later moment, the remaining sections of the structures projecting above the earthen rampart were razed and added to the *agger* itself (the buried sections were left in place), as were the remainder of the buildings over the entirety of the blocks contiguous with the fortifications.[19] The result was a sloping berm some 20 m wide, with a further 30 m of open space just behind, which together formed a defensive zone approximately 50 m wide.

Outside the Aurelian Wall, still more extensive demolitions must have occurred, though the details of the situation in the late third century are impossible to recreate because of later interventions that decisively altered the aspect of the terrain. The removal of large quantities of earth and rubble from the vicinity of the Wall, best associated with the mention of *egestis immensis ruderibus* at the beginning of the fifth century on the Honorian dedicatory inscriptions, lowered the ground around much of the circuit well below the level of Aurelian's time, leaving the sills of *posterulae* floating in mid-air and effectively erasing the third century from the archaeological record.[20] In 403, in any case, the ground outside the

---

[18] On the ring road and the apparently arbitrary figure of 5 m, see Lanciani 1892, 88; as this feature will have been beyond the sloping rampart that Lanciani himself documented, 5 m in total seems low. Motives of security likely also dictated the removal of privately owned structures in such close proximity to the rampart-walk and its defenders. Careful study of the late-third century enceinte at Le Mans has suggested a similar figure of 5–6 m width for the road running behind the wall, which in this case abutted the rear of the fortifications directly, with no intervening earthen rampart; see Guilleux 2000, 120.

[19] See Kraeling 1979, 4–6, with Plan 4 (on the synagogue in particular); closer to Rome, there are traces of a sizeable *agger* composed largely of rubble from razed buildings at e.g. Bordeaux: see Garmy and Maurin 1996, 70–1.

[20] See Chapter 1, n. 60. Though the cryptic phrase has been subject to varying interpretations, I believe Homo had it basically right when he long ago suggested that Honorius improved the

Wall was as nearly sterile, and thus inhospitable for attackers, as possible. By the sixth century, Procopius leaves no doubt that the Wall was also fronted by a substantial ditch, from which it was separated by an open "killing zone" wide enough to accommodate a sizeable segment of the Byzantine garrison, trapped between the ditch and the Porta Salaria after an abortive sally.[21] This may be the *fossa* said to have been begun under Maxentius, subsequently completed and perhaps restored on more than one occasion; it at any rate dates before Belisarius, who is specifically said to have re-dug an existing feature.[22]

Though the original provisions may not have been as elaborate (and there is no indication that a ditch was included at first), a wide apron will at least have been scraped bare down to ground level, perhaps correspond- ing approximately with the space later cleared of "ruins" under Honorius. Given especially the modest elevation of the Wall in its first phase, any standing structures left nearby would have posed a serious threat to defenders at wall-top level. Further, the initial design of the towers, expressly intended to facilitate the deployment of *ballistae* and handheld projectile weapons (bows, javelins, stones) from their flat roofs and the capacious windows of the lower chambers, would make little sense if the uninterrupted fields of view required for the proper use of these weapons had not been realized from the beginning. Though the case for the importance of defensive artillery in the design of the Wall may have been overstated in the past by Richmond in particular, for whom the First World War, with its legacy of trench warfare, defensive artillery and machine-gun emplacements, interlocking fields of fire, etc. was

---

defensibility of the Wall by removing large quantities of earth and accumulated rubbish from its base (though I agree with Coates-Stephens [2004, 87] that *ruderibus* more likely means "ruins" of pre-Aurelianic structures than "rubbish" *per se*), in places going well below Aurelianic levels and exposing parts of the foundations (Homo 1904, 271; *contra* e.g. Richmond 1930, 35). As Homo says, this is much the best explanation for how the sill of the *posterula* between the Portae Tiburtina and Praenestina-Labicana comes to be so far above current ground-level; cf. Caruso and Volpe 1989–90, 76–8. The smaller *posterula* by the Viale Cristoforo Colombo is likewise suspended in mid-air, leaving the foundation of the Wall beneath exposed, revealing a projecting section of a prior construction that would have been cut away had it been above ground in Aurelian's time.

[21] *BG* 1, 18, 19ff.

[22] *LP* I, 290: (Belisarius) *custodiis et munitionibus vel fabricis murorum aut reparationem fossati circumdedit civitatem Romanam et munivit*; cf. Procopius, *BG* 1, 14, 15. Prudentius, writing almost exactly at the time of the Wall's heightening in *c.* 400 (the precise date is disputed), mentions passing through the Wall on his way to the Tomb of St. Hippolytus on the Via Tiburtina, which is said to lie "not far from the outer rampart" (*Haud procul extremo . . . vallo*; *Peristephanon* 11, 153). With due allowance for poetic vagaries, the description would seem to indicate the presence of an earthwork at this relatively early date.

particularly vivid, there is no question that *ballistae* figured prominently in the minds of Romans concerned with the defense of fortified positions.[23] If nothing else, the psychological impact of these weapons, with their superlative range, accuracy, and power, was evidently immense, and frequently noted by Roman writers: the author of the *De rebus bellicis* described a bolt-thrower, suggestively called the "lightning ballista" (*ballista fulminalis*), used specifically to defend walls; while Belisarius, according to Procopius, took care to furnish the towers of the Wall with *balistrae* (*sic*) when he occupied the city in 536.[24] The best *a priori* assumption is thus that Aurelian's scheme envisaged the use of such devices – in addition to far larger numbers of handlaunched weapons – and that appropriate demolitions were conducted in front of the Wall to ensure their efficacy.

The villas on the site of the Villa Patrizi may be relevant here, in which case they would allow for something other than the usual argument from silence. There, standing walls immediately inside the Wall are preserved beneath the fill, while outside there is a lacuna of several tens of meters before the remains pick up again, which will correspond with the extent of the later earthmoving campaigns and *fossae*.[25] Despite the fact that the Wall proper left the central nucleus of these several villas untouched, they were seemingly abandoned and never again occupied, though many suburban villas farther outside the Wall experienced even a modest boom in the fourth century.[26] Moreover, valuable stashes of coins deposited easily within living memory of the Wall's construction were not recovered.[27] One possible explanation is that already under Aurelian, these structures 50 m and more outside the Wall had been flattened to the

[23] On the first-period towers as platforms for *ballistae*, see Richmond 1930, 76–80; cf. Cozza 1987, 29. Generally on Roman artillery, see the sources cited above at Chapter 1, n. 29.

[24] Anon. *De rebus bellicis* 18: *Huiusmodi ballistae genus murali defensioni necessarium supra ceteras impetu et viribus praevalere usu compertum est . . .*; Procop. *BG* I, 21, 14; cf. also I, 23, 9–12, where Procopius describes in lurid detail the plight of a Goth in full armor affixed to a tree by a bolt from one of Belisarius' *ballistae*. Archaeology has likewise revealed traces of towers designed and employed for the deployment of artillery, from Britain (the fort at High Rochester was equipped with a *ballistarium* – a platform for *ballistae* – according to two preserved inscriptions commemorating its construction and restoration; see *RIB* I, 1280–81) to the Euphrates, where at the city of Hatra, a stone-throwing catapult (an *onager* or *scorpio*) was found among the ruins of a tower destroyed during the Persian sack of the city in the mid third century (Baatz 1978).

[25] See Gilkes *et al.* 1994, fig. 1.

[26] On the "boom," see Volpe 2000, 205ff.; Spera 1999, 383ff.; Marazzi 1988, 274–80; Coarelli 1986, 35ff.

[27] Above n. 13.

foundations, the remnants of which were interred with so little trace that the recovery of the money was impossible. The best comparative evidence comes from Gaul, where there is archaeological evidence to indicate that the late-third century circuit at Le Mans was fronted by a glacis some 80 m wide, often cut through densely built urban zones; a still-higher figure of *c.* 100 m has been suggested for the approximately contemporary wall at Bordeaux.[28]

Even if less drastic demolitions were envisioned for Rome than in the more exposed and less populous *civitates* of Gaul, the central point stands that the Wall will have created, from its inception, a gash far wider than it was high. Chiefly in the more densely packed quarters, its immediate topographical signature will hence have been even more pronounced horizontally than it was vertically, a swathe conservatively estimated at 40–50 m wide (and possibly substantially larger) blazed through every-thing in its path, which grew thereafter literally wider and deeper with the passage of time.[29] The evocatively immured buildings that remain today actually, with a touch of irony, fared better than their neighbors. They are the tip of the iceberg, the visible signs of a destruction better attested by the greater void that surrounds them.

4.3 The immediate topographical impact of the Wall, regional

Moving beyond the 50+ m strip of the city directly involved, or rather engulfed, in the erection of the Wall, it may be asked what happened to the areas that bordered it on both sides. As space does not permit a detailed examination of all the regions traversed (a book in itself), I propose to focus on two widely separated sectors, one briefly and the second at

---

[28] Le Mans: Guilleux 2000, 121–3; Bordeaux: Garmy and Maurin 1996, 71–3 and esp. 190–1.

[29] In calling similar attention to the need for strategic demolitions outside new late-antique enceintes, Neil Christie has noted the need for more studies on their spatial extent. Neither ancient sources nor archaeological work to date permit much in the way of conclusions about how much space was thought strategically necessary (or actually cleared), a question of obvious moment for late-antique urban history in general; see Christie 2001, 118. My sense is that the 25 m minimum I allow for Rome is much more likely to underestimate the reality than to overstate it. The total suggested minimum of 40–50 m is the rough sum of this figure plus the 4 m of the foundation, plus 10 meters more for the internal *intervallum*. By way of comparison, recent work on the closely contemporary circuit at Lugo in NW Spain suggests a total cleared area 60m in width, measured from the outer lip of the *fossa* to the inner edge of the *intervallum* (Alcorta Irastorza 2007, 287 and *passim*).

greater length, which between them capture a range of the possible, pointing to issues of broader relevance that might serve as starting points for studies of other parts of the city.

The first is the area of the Esquiline. In a recent article, Robert Coates-Stephens documented the appearance here, over the course of the fourth century, of a sizeable number of large urban *domus* belonging to members of the senatorial elite, most built *ex novo*.[30] Coates-Stephens focused on the prevalence of spoliated materials – inscriptions, statues, columns, and the like – incorporated into these new constructions, on the basis of which he advanced the hypothesis that the demolitions occasioned by the construction of the Wall lay at the root of the phenomenon. In this scenario, the edifices razed would have left a glut of surplus building materials, more or less ready to hand, which was then progressively tapped for many years to come. Perhaps; it might be added that if as much land was cleared as I think, it becomes increasingly likely that sufficient *spolia* resulted to serve the needs of several generations of landed proprietors, especially if the recuperation, storage, and reuse of these materials was managed in controlled fashion.[31] It is an idea, certainly debatable, with potentially important ramifications for wider questions about the use of *spolia* in late antiquity in general, and the (seminal?) impact of the many roughly contemporary urban enceintes on the process. It deserves further consideration that it cannot receive here.

What is clear is the fact that a number of new aristocratic houses rose on the Esquiline, beginning a generation or so after the building of the Wall. Suddenly, the intramural reaches of the hill took on a more urban aspect, with walled residential compounds dotting what had previously been a predominantly open landscape of cemeteries and gardens (the *horti maecenatis, liciniani, lamiani*, etc.). Yet there is no indication whatsoever of a corresponding phenomenon on the far side of the Wall: henceforth, at any rate in this north-eastern quadrant of the city, if one was to have a house near the urban center, as distinguished from an outlying country seat, it was preferably located inside the Wall. It is a pattern that generally holds for the rest of the circuit as well, where immediately outlying areas were characterized if anything by the abandonment of existing residences more

---

[30] Coates-Stephens 2001, 217–38.

[31] Cf. Coates-Stephens 2001, esp. 232ff.; Neil Christie has also hinted briefly at similar considerations, including the stockpiling of *spolia* (Christie 2001, 118–19). More generally on the use of *spolia* in Rome from the fourth century on, see the sources cited below at Chapter 6, n. 57.

than the construction of new ones, as with the cluster of villas outside the Porta Nomentana.[32] At the same time, the truly suburban *villae rusticae* situated especially between about the third and sixth milestones of the consular roads, a mile and more beyond the Wall, continued to flourish.[33]

On current evidence, in fact, it would seem that small-scale, intensive farming made a comeback in the immediate urban periphery during the later empire, resulting in a sort of "rural involution" usually explained as a process whereby ever-larger holdings of absentee proprietors, or *massae fundorum*, were subdivided into smaller plots worked by tenants.[34] In part, this view stems from the surprising lack of late-antique "seigniorial" dwellings attested in Rome's immediate vicinity, relative to the great amount of land under cultivation, according to sources such as the *Liber Pontificalis*. I would add a point of clarification: it is not that evidence for houses of the estate-owning class is generally limited, but rather that it is (extremely) limited precisely over the mile or so just beyond the Wall. In the city, all sorts of thriving aristocratic houses are known from the fourth century, among which the many on the Caelian may be added to the examples from the Esquiline.[35] The most impressive fourth-century villa sites also come from the same eastern side of the city, but much farther out beyond the third milestones on the Viae Praenestina, Labicana, Latina, Appia and Ardeatina.[36] In between there is remarkably little, even in the way of modest farmhouses. The same is true in the north, where between the Tiber and the Via Nomentana, only one possible late-antique villa is attested near the Wall (less than 100 m outside the Porta Salaria, between Via Viterbo and Via Rieti), while a number of other sites in use in the early and middle empire disappeared completely.[37]

The example of the Esquiline thus introduces the Wall as a powerful pole of attraction that stimulated settlement – especially upper-class settlement – within its confines, possibly with the corollary effect of creating a sort of residential no-man's-land for some distance outside. This centripetal pull may indeed offer the best explanation for the

---

[32] See above, with n. 13. The decline in the numbers of villas situated within a mile of the Aurelian Wall, still at peak levels in the early empire, is clearly apparent in the various contributions to Pergola *et al.* 2003.

[33] On the clustering of aristocratic estates at this distance from the city, see Marazzi 2001a, 724–5; Volpe 2000, 200–5; Coarelli 1986, 41.

[34] Marazzi 2001a, 731ff.; 1988, 262 (the term "rural involution" is coined here); Volpe 2000, 209; Carandini 1985, 67–8.

[35] See e.g. Pavolini 1993; and more generally Guidobaldi 1986, updated in 1999.

[36] See Spera 1999, 383ff.; Coarelli 1986, 35ff.; and esp. the contributions in Pergola *et al.* 2003.

[37] See Pavolini *et al.* 2003, esp. figs. 2 and 5.

perplexing disparity between ongoing textual indicators of large-scale cultivation in Rome's immediate periphery on the one hand, and the depopulation and abandonment adumbrated in the archaeological record on the other.[38] There need not have been a net demographic decline, but rather a simple shift of the population inside the Wall, causing a reduction in the desirability of the land immediately outside for residential uses, and prompting its return to intensive agricultural production geared to meeting the needs of the lucrative urban market.[39]

A similar demographic shift is better documented in Trastevere, where it clearly did extend also to members of less elevated social strata. In this and several other respects, the Transtiberine salient of the Wall makes for a particularly good case study that merits attention at greater length.

In the first three centuries of the empire, the geographically diffuse fourteenth Augustan region on the right bank of the Tiber had boomed. In the flood plain between the Janiculum and the river, residential and commercial quarters spread out amongst extensive tracts of gardens and cemeteries, resulting in a populous swathe of territory stretching from the Vatican in the north to Pietra Papa (roughly across the river from S. Paolo *fuori le mura*) and beyond in the south.[40] Only a small fraction of this area was included in the wedge of land enclosed by the Wall,[41] the appearance of which precipitated an immediate topographical convulsion of which clear traces remain.

The key source is Lanciani's report on discoveries made toward the end of the nineteenth century during operations to systematize the banks of the Tiber, at the point where the northern stretch of the Wall meets the

---

[38] In addressing this dichotomy between the textual and archaeological records, R. Santangeli Valenzani has argued that the "missing settlers" came seasonally down from the Appenines, leaving little archaeological trace with their temporary camps (Santangeli Valenzani 2003a). I would suggest that many of these invisible workers, chiefly those employed in fields in the immediate urban periphery, were actually concentrated inside the Wall.

[39] Cf. Marazzi 2000, 39. Even if the "ruralization" of this intermediate zone began as early as the second century, as e.g. Marazzi would like (2001a, 731ff.; 1988, 261ff.), it was a gradual development that the Wall would still have tended to accelerate considerably, if it did not cause it outright. The fourth century also saw the first installation of Christian cemeteries in close proximity to the Wall (earlier foundations were most often situated *c.* 2–3 km outside), a phenomenon perhaps also symptomatic of a demographic shift that opened up new extramural spaces for communal burials, as Fiocchi Nicolai has proposed (2000a, 354).

[40] A comprehensive overview of Roman Trastevere is sorely lacking. At present, see Tucci 2004; Azzena 1996; Rodriguez Almeida 1981, 140–7; Palmer 1981; Tomassetti 1975–80, vol. 6, 303–63; Savage 1940; Lugli, *Monumenti* III (1930–8), 628ff.

[41] Cf. Homo 1904, 233. On the Transtiberine salient of the Wall, see above all Cozza 1987–8 and 1986.

river near the Villa Farnesina. The results of three dense pages in the *Notizie degli Scavi* can be summarized as follows.[42] Of two principal structures identified in the area, one, the *cellae vinariae novae et arruntianae*, a wine-warehouse of Trajanic date, was cut in two by the Wall. The second, a large house of the first century AD, which Lanciani thought combined elements of an urban *domus* and a suburban villa, lay completely outside. Both complexes evidently went immediately out of use with the building of the Wall: there is no evidence of later repairs or additions to either one, nor are there any signs of habitation in their extramural vicinity in late antiquity. Meanwhile, inside the Wall, the remaining part of the *cellae...arruntianae* was demolished, the level of the ground raised with earth from the foundation trench, and a neighborhood of densely packed housing immediately built, much of it on land that Lanciani emphasizes showed few if any traces of human presence prior to this period. These houses were repaired and inhabited for centuries thereafter, even after the events of the fifth and sixth centuries.

A bit perversely, Lanciani's account was included merely by way of introduction to his description of the immured tomb of Platorinus, subsequently treated at rather greater length. Later Richmond, who knew the report and quoted it extensively, proceeded to draw on it primarily for its use in dating the Transtiberine walls.[43] The immediate interests of each scholar lay elsewhere, and the conclusion perhaps even seemed too obvious to mention; in any case, the extraordinary ramifications of these data were left hanging, for here is an unmistakable demonstration of the Wall as the agent, the prime mover, behind the reconfiguration of an entire neighborhood. On the inside of the new circuit, an urban quarter of wall-to-wall housing was suddenly built where there had been none before, while pre-existing structures outside were abandoned, and the land given over to farming.[44] What had once been a busy suburb became half city and half country, diverse worlds brought into existence and perpetuated by the sheer divide of the Aurelian Wall.

The scenario may well have repeated itself at the southern junction between the Wall and the river, though the details are hazier. Another warehouse on the riverfront was bisected, and its extramural section left to

---

[42] *Notizie* 1880, 127–9.   [43] Richmond 1930, 16–18.

[44] Such is Lanciani's conclusion about the subsequent use of the space outside the Wall; whether it is an argument from anything more than silence is not clear (*Notizie* 1880, 128–9). The sequence of coins found outside the Wall ends, after three centuries, with the reign of Maxentius.

decay.[45] By the sixth century, a pointed topographical reference demonstrates that this zone "outside the walls by the Porta Portuensis" pertained to private gardens (*horti*), which produced revenues in part destined for services at its owner's tomb.[46] The chronological sequence is admittedly diffuse, and the archaeological data for the area inside the Wall insufficient to show whether external abandonment was paralleled by internal development. Still, the situation in its broad outlines is suggestively similar to what went on farther north, where all indicators point to a pattern of concentration of settlement inside the circuit and "ruralization" outside that recalls in more vivid detail the sequence of events already postulated for the Esquiline.[47]

The Wall is connected with further significant topographical realignments in Trastevere, notably in regard to the roads and bridges that linked the region with the rest of the city. The subject requires an extension of spatial perspective to include communications between the right and left banks of the river, and thus also the parts of the city on the opposite (left) bank equally implicated in the repositioning of these features. As the continuation of the fortifications on the left bank of the river brought changes to the far side well beyond the walled salient, "Trastevere" will continue to be used in the broad sense of the term, roughly corresponding with the fourteenth urban region, which extended north into the Ager Vaticanus. Beginning here, the three bridges directly involved – one destroyed, one moved, and one built new – are discussed in order, descending with the current.

Just downstream from the modern Ponte Vittorio Emanuele, the piers of a Roman bridge rose high out of the water until their destruction in the nineteenth century. The structure currently goes by the name Pons Neronianus (or Neronis), though the toponym is not attested before the

---

[45] See *FUR*, tav. 39. The warehouse was built in good brickwork generically attributed to the "imperial period" (*Notizie* 1892, 116); a cut was made in the Wall at exactly this point, but the brief report unfortunately makes no mention of finds from the surrounding area (*BullCom* 1892, 286–7); for other scattered finds (pipes, etc.) *c.* 150 meters inside the Wall, see *Notizie* 1893, 420.

[46] *CIL* 6, 8401 (*anno* 578): *deputavimus in ista sepultura nostra ex t(esta)m(enti?) pagin(a?)M ad oblation(em) vel luminaria nostra (h)orti Transtiberini uncias sex foris muros iuxta porta(m) Portuense(m), quod fuit ex iure q(uon)d(am) Micini cancel(lari) inl(ustris) urb(anae) s[e]d(is), patris me[i].*

[47] Procopius described Trastevere in terms that mirror the archaeological indicators, noting that the construction of the Wall was followed by the development of "dense housing" (οἰκίας συχνὰς) inside the area enclosed (*BG* 1, 19, 10); see below n. 77. Tantalizing further traces of fourth-century abandonment in southern Trastevere are summarized in Azzena 1996, 952.

Mirabilia of the twelfth century.[48] It may have been built already under Caligula to connect the city with his gardens and circus in the Ager Vaticanus (which likewise took Nero's name in the Middle Ages), and it certainly existed by the reign of the latter, who located his new baths on the street running east from the bridgehead. This street, the so-called Via Recta, was the principal transverse axis in the northern Campus Martius, connecting the Tiber with the Via Lata (Flaminia), the main road to the forum area from the north.[49] A route of probably still greater importance ran south from the bridge to the city center by way of the Circus Flaminius, along the way conditioning the architectural orientation of the whole western sector of the Campus Martius.[50] If Coarelli *et al.* are right, this colonnaded street was from early republican times the urban extension of the Via Triumphalis, in which case a river crossing on the site of the Pons Neronianus will have existed well before the bridge of the first century AD.[51] Thus by the imperial period at the latest, and probably much earlier, the whole street system of the Campus Martius was focused on the site of this river crossing (Figure 4.1).

[48] VZ 3, 26. Concise and up-to-date summaries of the bridge appear at *LTUR* 4, under *pons Neronianus*; and Galliazzo 1995, 23–4. While there remains more controversy over the identification of several of Rome's ancient bridges than there perhaps should be, the brief overview in the latter (pp. 5–28) has, I think, the essentials of the situation absolutely right (as e.g. the *LTUR* still does not).

[49] Its westernmost tract, of which ample traces are known, corresponds with the modern Via dei Coronari. The name "Via Recta" is a modern derivation from a corrupt reading of *Via Tecta*, a street of obvious importance mentioned several times in Martial and Seneca, and applied to this indeed "straight" road by nineteenth-century topographers. Palmer has argued in favor of the old identification, against a developing consensus that makes the street running south from the bridge to the Circus Flaminius the Via Tecta (see the following note); see Palmer 1990, 58–9, with the *status quaestionis* in *LTUR* 5, under *via Tecta*. Palmer's interpretation of the relevant texts is questionable, and the archaeology contrary, as numerous remains of colonnades have appeared along the road to the Circus Flaminius: see Coarelli 1997a, 120; Quilici 1983, 62; Lanciani 1883/1891, 23ff. on the "Via Recta," and 76ff. on the Via Tecta. Regardless, the "Via Recta" was a route of first-rate importance, whatever it was called in antiquity.

[50] See La Rocca 1984, 65–7; Coarelli 1977, 818–19 and 842–6; Castagnoli 1947, esp. 156. On the case for attributing the toponym Via Tecta to this route, see also Coarelli 1997a, 118ff., with a summary rebuttal of Palmer 1990 at n. 11.

[51] For its identification with the Via Triumphalis, see Coarelli 1997a, 127ff.; 1977, esp. 820–1; and La Rocca 1984, 65–7, all expanding on the earlier views of Lanciani (1883/1891, 15ff.) and Castagnoli (1947, 156; cf. 1992, 29–30). Following Castagnoli, Coarelli imagines a ferry across the river from perhaps the fourth century BC (1977, 842, with n. 87), in connection with the Via Triumphalis itself, which he believes crossed the river here by the end of the fourth century BC at the latest (1997a). E. La Rocca also suggests a wooden precursor to the Pons Neronianus (1984).

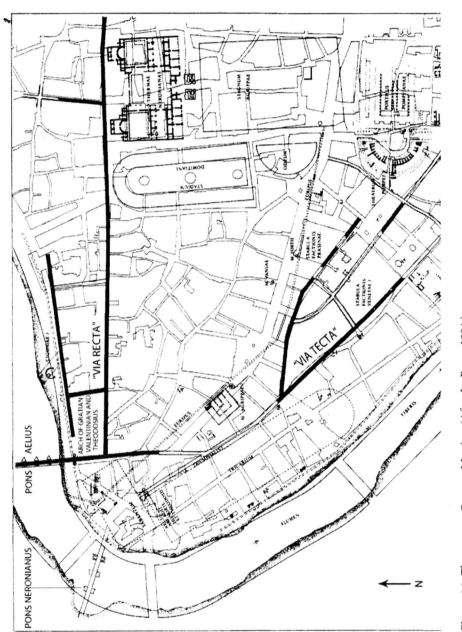

Figure 4.1 The western Campus Martius. (After La Rocca 1984.)

While the location and identification of streets on the Transtiberine side present more difficulties, it is clear that the republican road leading west through the Ager Vaticanus, the Via Cornelia, must originally have been connected with this bridge, as must the ancient Via Triumphalis that led north to Veii.[52] These two ancient arteries, the primary ones in the region, both ran in the immediate vicinity of the Pons Neronianus, perhaps still as one street before diverging just to the north. Thus, anyone seeking to reach either one from the northern part of the city will have crossed here, the only possible place above the Pons Agrippae, more than a kilometer downstream. The paved street found leading away from the Transtiberine bridgehead will in one way or another have permitted easy access to both.[53] So things remained until Hadrian built his mausoleum, which he connected to the city with a new bridge, the Pons Aelius, not far upstream from the existing one. Possibly the Via Aurelia Nova crossed the river here from the beginning, on its way west to join the main trunk of the road (the Aurelia Vetus) that left the city through the Porta Aurelia (S. Pancrazio) on the Janiculum.[54] Otherwise, its urban tract in the second century coincided with that of the Via Cornelia over the Pons Neronianus, perhaps the best conclusion given that the Pons Aelius seems originally to have functioned in strict connection with the mausoleum, of which it may initially have been little more than an appendage.[55] From then on, the regional outlook remained basically unchanged for some time, with two bridges from the city, the primary Neronianus and secondary Aelius, offering access to the three principal roads on the right bank, the Cornelia, Triumphalis, and Aurelia Nova.

Then one day, the Pons Neronianus ceased to function. It is now widely acknowledged that this development had occurred by the beginning of the fourth century, as the bridge cannot be associated with any of those listed

---

[52] The best recent overview is Liverani 1999a, 34–40, who commendably synthesizes scattered archaeological reports on remains of streets in the area. Cf. 2003, 399–413; Castagnoli 1992, 29–34.

[53] On the findings, see Liverani 1999a, 39.

[54] It is interesting but hardly conclusive that the Aurelia Nova is first attested shortly after the erection of the Pons Aelius, in an inscription (*CIL* 14, 3610) dedicated to C. Popilius Pedo, *curator operum publicorum* in 150 with joint responsibility for the Aurelia Nova and the Vetus, as well as the Cornelia and Triumphalis. Generally on the road, the course of which remains largely a mystery, see Tomassetti 1975–80, vol. 2, 541–5; and the brief overview in Verrando 1981, 257–9. While each seems to think the Aurelia Nova of considerably greater antiquity than the Pons Aelius, they both imply without further explanation that the road crossed on this bridge.

[55] See L. Borsari in *Notizie* 1892, 412–28; cf. Lanciani in *BullCom* 1893, esp. 22ff.; Le Gall 1953, 211–15.

in the Regionary Catalogues (occasional suggestions to the contrary not-withstanding).[56] It was definitely ruinous by the time Procopius was writing, when the Pons Aelius was manifestly the only functioning bridge in this part of the city.[57] By this point, then, and in all likelihood by the end of the third century, the northern half of the Campus Martius was connected to the Ager Vaticanus (or *Vaticanum*, as the region was by then known) only by the Pons Aelius, a bridge whose one advantage over the older, more central, and infinitely better-connected Pons Neronianus was its protected bridgehead on the right bank, at the foot of Hadrian's mausoleum. The most likely conclusion is that the Wall immediately put the older bridge out of commission, though it is possible that it remained serviceable until the reign of Maxentius; the case for prolonging its use further is weak indeed.[58] The otherwise inexplicable decision to privilege the Pons Aelius makes good sense if the exposed position of the Pons Neronianus made it an unacceptable defensive liability, and if Hadrian's mausoleum was integrated with the circuit, via the Pons Aelius, from the beginning.

The fortification of the riverbank and the end of the Pons Neronianus thus forcefully reoriented the primary axis of communications between the northern Campus Martius and the Vatican, redrawing the topography especially of the more densely urbanized left bank in the process. From one day to the next, the point where the two most important axes in the Campus Martius converged became a dead end. All traffic on both main arteries was henceforth detoured to the Pons Aelius, making an awkward dogleg north that a glance at a map will show led away from the principal roads and edifices across the river. The relatively insignificant access road

---

[56] The *terminus ante* is given by the earlier of the two lists, the *Curiosum*, which is best dated to the early part of Constantine's reign at the latest: see VZ 1, 66ff. The lone noteworthy voice of dissent is that of Le Gall, who identified the Pons Probi of the Catalogues with a late restoration of the Pons Neronianus, thus claiming that the bridge was extensively rebuilt precisely when it was more likely being dismantled; see Le Gall 1953, 210–11; 305–11; followed by D'Onofrio 1978, 47–8; 1971, 43–5. Le Gall based his assertion on the claim that the triumphal arch of Arcadius, Honorius, and Theodosius was associated directly with the entrance to the bridge. The building (or rebuilding) of the arch, in fact, had nothing to do with the Pons Neronianus, as Lanciani already realized (*BullCom* 1893, 20; see also Liverani 2004, 352; *LTUR* 1, under *Arcus Arcadii, Honorii et Theodosii*).

[57] The total absence of any reference to another bridge near the Pons Aelius is proof enough. A functioning Pons Neronianus could not have escaped mention at e.g. *BG* 1, 22, 14ff., where the defenses in the area of the mausoleum feature in an extended narrative, which includes discussion of the garrisoning and successful defense of the river wall against a Gothic attack.

[58] Cf. Liverani 1999a, 37; in *LTUR* 4, 111; Galliazzo 1995, 24. For Prudentius, writing *c.* 400, "Hadrian's Bridge" was already the sole means of reaching St. Peter's: *ibimus ulterius qua fert via pontis Hadriani* (*Peristephanon* 12, 61).

to the Pons Aelius consequently became the fulcrum of the neighborhood
in the fourth century, and was restructured accordingly: stately porticoes
were built on both sides of it, in conjunction with the new triumphal arch
of Gratian, Valentinian, and Theodosius that spanned it near the river.[59]
It was thus integrated, in form and function, with the remainder of the
colonnaded triumphal route from the circus Flaminius, the Via Tecta,
which from time immemorial had proceeded directly to the bridgehead
of the Pons Neronianus; the name *porticus maximae* was henceforth
applied to the redirected street in its ensemble.[60]

Meanwhile, the final sections of the two ancient avenues to the Pons
Neronianus disappeared literally off the map. From the end of the empire
to the present, both streets have continued to exist up to – and not a step
beyond – the point where they encountered the single new road to the
Pons Aelius.[61] With the exception of a short stretch of the "Via Recta" on
the west side of the road to the mausoleum, even their Roman paving has
disappeared without a trace, leaving a gaping lacuna that has prompted
extended bouts of head-scratching in the past, and led the presumed
course of both roads to the bridge to be variously denied, though the
arguments used in support of the one from silence have never been
convincing.[62] Yet there is a much simpler explanation: these tracts of road

---

[59] The completion of the *porticus maximae* is commemorated in the inscription of the arch itself,
known from the transcript included in the Einsiedeln Itineraries (see *CIL* 6, 1184, of *c.* 380):
*Imperatores caesares ddd nnn Gratianus Valentinianus et Theodosius pii felices semper Auggg
arcum ad concludendum opus omne porticuum maximarum aeterni nominis sui pecunia propria
fieri ornariq. iusserunt.* There has been speculation that the inscription describes merely a
restoration of an older structure (e.g. Coarelli 1997a, 120; 1977, 845; La Rocca 1984, 66),
but this does full justice neither to the inscription, nor to the topography of the western
Campus Martius which both scholars have done so much to illuminate. The colonnaded Via
Tecta led to the site of the Pons Neronianus long before the Pons Aelius was built; and there
is no reason to think that the side street to the latter bridge was similarly embellished from
the beginning. For more on these points and generally on the topography of the region,
before and after the Wall, see Appendix D.

[60] On the designation *porticus maximae*, see the preceding note. Lanciani and Coarelli both note
the new importance of this axis in late antiquity, as the new continuation of the old Via
Triumphalis, and subsequently the main route to the Vatican; neither, however, considered the
important issue of why it came to be preferred over the Pons Neronianus (above n. 51).
Its acknowledged sudden rise to prominence makes Coarelli's suggestion that the portico to
the Pons Aelius existed prior to the erection of the triumphal arch in 380 all the more
surprising. On the antiquity of the Via Tecta and its connection with the Pons Neronianus,
see e.g. Coarelli 1997a, 127ff.

[61] In modern terms, the Via dei Coronari ("Via Recta") and the Via dei Banchi Vecchi (Via
Tecta) end exactly at the Via del Banco Santo Spirito, the axial prolongation of the Pons
Aelius/Ponte S. Angelo.

[62] See Appendix D.

were rendered useless with the end of the Pons Neronianus, and supplanted by the newly aggrandized street to the mausoleum, where their paving (and the columns of the Via Tecta?) very possibly ended up. There is certainly no lack of remains of this latter tract, preserved beneath the modern surface of what soon became the final stretch of the most important corridor in Rome, the link between the old city on the left bank and the new city of St. Peter at the Vatican.[63]

In addition to being diverted, all inbound and outbound traffic on the Viae Cornelia, Triumphalis, and Aurelia Nova, once served by two bridges, was funneled onto the more cramped of the two. If traffic jams did not immediately result, they soon will have with the explosive rise to prominence of the complex around St. Peter's in the fourth century, which left this strategic node more frequented than ever even as the best river crossing fell out of use.[64] The new situation is mirrored precisely in the unusual range of toponyms – a virtual traffic jam in itself – soon applied to the bridge and the gate leading to it, among which Aurelia, Cornelia, and S. Petri are all attested by the seventh century.[65] The names of the ancient suburban roads diverted here, that is, were intermingled with the legacy of the newer and still more important destination at the grave of Peter. One might imagine that the scene that took place on the spot over a thousand years later, when the parapets of the Pons Aelius collapsed under the crush of pilgrims heading to St. Peter's during the Jubilee of 1450, was not without some late-antique precedent.[66]

[63] The modern Via del Banco Santo Spirito. Cf. Coarelli 1997a, 120; Lanciani 1883/1891, esp. cols. 17ff. and 76ff. Four of the eleven itineraries in the Einsiedeln list start from the Porta S. Petri on the bridge, two of them passing through the arch of Gratian, Valentinian, and Theodosius (itineraries 2, *A porta Sancti Petri usque ad portam Salariam*, and 10, *A porta Sancti Petri usque porta Asinaria*).

[64] The two modern bridges placed immediately above and below the site of the Pons Neronianus (the Ponte Vittorio Emanuele and the Ponte Principe Amedeo, respectively) are optimally situated to connect the city with the Vatican, a role which they have indeed taken over almost completely from the Pons Aelius.

[65] The Porta S. Petri and Porta Aurelia are both given in Procopius (e.g. *BG* 1, 19, 4); and *porta Cornelia* occurs alongside *porta Sancti Petri* in the seventh-century list of Rome's gates transcribed by William of Malmesbury (VZ 2, 141). Procopius' (repeated) use of the name Porta Aurelia for this gate, as well as the one on the Janiculum, is emphatically not an "error" as Dewing says in the *Loeb* edition (vol. 3, p. 185). Before Procopius, the gate was already called the *domni Petri apostoli porta* in the *Cosmographia* of "pseudo-Eticus" (VZ 1, 315), which must date between 417 and 534 (and likely before 500; see VZ 1, 312–13); cf. Liverani 2003, 404–7; Le Gall 1953, 289.

[66] 172 people died in the incident, in the wake of which the bridge was extensively repaired; see Borsari in *Notizie* 1892, 417; cf. Gregorovius 1973, 1887; Lanciani in *BullCom* 1893, 19. During the first jubilee of 1300, on Dante's famous testimony, the crowds on the narrow

All of the remaining five river crossings below the Pons Neronianus were concentrated within the new land walls of Trastevere, a fact worthy of note in itself. The building of the Wall directly involved the northernmost of these crossings, the bridge built by Agrippa to his Transtiberine gardens, which carried with it the *specus* of the Aqua Virgo. This was originally located just below the meeting of the Wall with the river at the Villa Farnesina, where the remains of two ancient bridges separated by only 140 m have led to confusion over the identification of both. As I think the debate now definitively resolved (*pace* Coarelli and Cozza), I present only the essentials of the sequence of events adumbrated by the diverse remains.[67]

The first Pons Agrippae, constructed probably between 19 and 10 BC, was repaired in 147 under Antoninus Pius in an intervention recorded in the inscribed *Fasti* found at Ostia, at which point it took the new appellation Pons Antonini.[68] When the Wall was later built, it rose literally on top of the bridgehead on the right bank, at the point where it made a right angle at the river, which it paralleled heading downstream, within the enclosed salient, for 140 m. Here, a second bridge was built on the site of the modern Ponte Sisto, joining the Transtiberine fortifications with the river wall on the left bank, which thence turned upstream for 2.6 km to the Porta Flaminia (Figure 4.2). Immediately above the new bridge, there was thus a walled "corridor" of river, protected at its upper extremity by the pillars of the old Pons Agrippae.[69] While the pillars were left standing, the superstructure was systematically dismantled, and the spoliated blocks from the old bridge re-employed in the superstructure of the new. This left the riverbed beneath the old one clear of all debris, and led the old name Pons Antonini to be transferred along with the *spolia*, which perhaps included an inscription of 147 left visible in the new construction.[70] The official name of the bridge, however, given in the

bridge were such that distinct lanes were created for traffic headed in opposite directions (*Inferno* 18, 28–33); cf. Gregorovius 1973, esp. 1412.

[67] Since Le Gall resurrected the idea, originally suggested by Gatti (*Bullcom* 1887, 306–13), that only one of the two structures was a bridge, the identification of the Pons Agrippae has become a sticky problem (1953, 210–11 and 305–11). Though flawed, his arguments continue at times to crop up, most recently in Coarelli's entry in the *Lexicon* (*LTUR* 4, see under pons Agrippae; pons Aurelius, pons Valentiniani); see also e.g. Coarelli 1997a, 124; 1977, 824–6; Cozza 1987–88, 138; 1986, 104–7. For the rather lengthy rebuttal required to do justice to the views of these important scholars, see Appendix E.

[68] The relevant entry in the fragment, published by G. Calza in *Notizie* 1939, 361–5, reads thus: [–] *K. Febr. imp. Antoninus Aug(ustus) pontem Agrippae dedic(avit)*. The year is AD 147.

[69] Remains of this section of the river wall were found in several places; its presence is a key piece of evidence that has been ignored by Le Gall and his supporters; see Appendix E.

[70] See Appendix E.

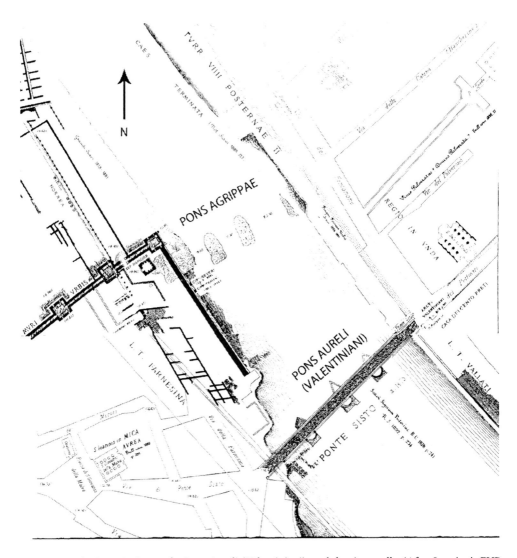

Figure 4.2 The Pons Agrippae, the Pons Aureli (Valentiniani), and the river walls. (After Lanciani, *FUR* tavv. 20–7.)

Regionary Catalogues, was the Pons Aureli, after the same emperor who finished the Wall itself, Marcus Aurelius Probus.[71]

---

[71] The use of the emperor's *nomen gentilicium* will have served, by design or otherwise, to distinguish it from the other bridge he dedicated farther downstream, which took his *cognomen* to become the Pons Probi (see below); cf. Taylor 1995, 89. The name Pons Aureli is given in Polemius Silvius (*pons Aurilius*, VZ 1, 308), as well as in the *Curiosum* (*pons Aurelius*, VZ 1, 149). It was later known also as the Pons Valentiniani, after a restoration carried out in that emperor's name in *c.* 366, attested in a dedicatory inscription from the superstructure of the bridge found on the riverbed (*CIL* 6, 31402; cf. Lanciani in *BullCom* 7 [1878], 245–6).

I therefore think it certain that the building of the Wall encompassed the intentional destruction of the Pons Agrippae, and its
replacement by the Pons Aureli, the latter apparently still under construction at Aurelian's death. The change naturally provoked additional
alterations in street networks and traffic patterns on both sides of the
river, though the construction of a replacement crossing nearby will
have made the effects less pronounced than those accompanying the
end of the Pons Neronianus. A new element in the picture is the
cutting of the Aqua Virgo, as a result of which altered arrangements
and generally a great deal of effort will have been required to supply
buildings in the affected areas of Trastevere with water. Some structures were doubtless left without, while others might have gained
access for the first time, if the channel of the aqueduct was indeed
diverted from the old bridge to the new.[72] One of the more visible
localized results (the data from the right bank are again sparser than in
the Campus Martius) was possibly the abandonment of the *thermae
Severianae* near the Porta Settimiana, which a passage in the *HA* seems
to show were left without water by the southward migration of the
Aqua Virgo.[73]

Moving downriver to the Aventine, we come to the Pons Probi, the last
of the three bridges directly implicated in the building of the Wall, and the
second built new at the time. First mentioned in both Regionary Catalogues, it was later famously rebuilt amidst scandal during the prefecture
of Symmachus in the 380s, when it took the name Pons Theodosii, in
which guise it continued in use into the Middle Ages, serving the area of

---

[72] Rabun Taylor has considered the implications of these various dislocations in greater detail,
and plausibly reconstructed sections of the new course taken by the street in the Campus
Martius (and, he assumes, the aqueduct) that previously went to the Pons Agrippae (Taylor
1995, esp. 85 and 88, with fig. 3). While the aqueduct may well have been diverted, it should be
said that there is no absolute proof that it was. Lloyd's earlier study of the Aqua Virgo, in fact,
ends with the destruction of the Pons Agrippae, implying (though it is never said explicitly)
that it no longer crossed the river thereafter (Lloyd 1979, esp. 200ff.). In this event, the
northern part of Trastevere would have been more drastically affected, left to rely on the Aqua
Traiana for whatever water continued to arrive (the other aqueduct coming from the west, the
Aqua Alsietina, served southern Trastevere; see Rodriguez Almeida 1981, 144–7).

[73] *HA Sev.* 19, 5: *Opera publica praecipua eius extant Septizonium et thermae Severianae,
eiusdemque etiam ianuae in Transtiberina regione ad portam nominis sui, quarum forma
intercidens statim usum publicum invidit.* I agree with Taylor (1995, 89–90, *contra* Richardson
1992, 395) that the phrase *forma intercidens* is better construed as a reference to a deliberate
"cut" in the aqueduct than to its "collapse"; the latter reading improbably requires that the
baths were abandoned soon after their construction, in preference to repairing a break in an
important aqueduct that served the entire surrounding region as well.

the Ripa Romea on the right bank of the river, today's Ripa Grande.[74] With occasional exceptions, the Pons Probi/Pons Theodosii has justly been identified with one of two groups of possible bridge-pilings visible in the Tiber until their demolition in the nineteenth century, the first near the northern extremity of the Aventine, and another approximately 200 m farther downstream.[75] In either case (the one upstream is much the better candidate), it originally connected south Trastevere with the Marmorata quay and the assorted warehouses between the Aventine and Testaccio.[76] As little can be said for certain about its effect on local topography, it suffices at present to note that it existed, and that it was completed under Probus, whose *cognomen* distinguished it for posterity from the other bridge dedicated upstream at the same time, the Pons Aureli.

Hence, by the beginning of the fourth century at the latest, every bridge in the city was located comfortably within the protected salient of the Wall on the right bank, with the lone exception of the Pons Aelius, shielded by Hadrian's mausoleum. The construction of yet another bridge inside the Wall testifies further to the development of this area into the newly privileged space revealed in the centripetal patterns of settlement outlined above. In the end, the various scattered hints combine in an ensemble, threadbare but internally consistent, that suggests that the destructions, dislocations, and new construction attendant upon the building of the

[74] See *Curiosum* (VZ 1, 150); *Notitia* (VZ 1, 183); the name appears also in Polemius Silvius (VZ 1, 308); following its restoration under Theodosius, it is attested as the *pons marmoreus Theodosii* in the *Mirabilia* (VZ 3, 26); and the *pons Theodosii in Riparmea* (i.e. *ripa romea*) in the *Graphia* (VZ 3, 84). For the later sources regarding the Pons Theodosius, cf. Le Gall 1953, 305–11 (the contention that it was built *ex novo* in the 380s aside). Generally on the Pons Probi, see also Galliazzo 1995, 24–5; on the scandals that attended the extensive reconstruction of the bridge under Theodosius, see Chastagnol 1960, 350–3.

[75] Both plotted in the *FUR*, tav. 34. The first are marked *vestigiae pontis*, while the second are the "antiche ruine" plotted by Nolli on his plan of 1748.

[76] There is admittedly no proof that the names Pons Probi and Pons Theodosii refer to the same structure. Still, the medieval Pons Theodosii was definitely in the area of the Ripa Grande, and the Pons Probi of the *Notitia* and *Curiosum* cannot with any plausibility be associated with any of Rome's other bridges. Accepting the prevalent view that they were one and the same, they are better associated with the northern group of remains. A major road led directly from the Transtiberine side of the piers toward the summit of the Janiculum (see *FUR* 34); and a fragmentary imperial dedication discovered during the demolitions (see Lanciani in *BullCom* 1877, 167, no. 141) suggests at least that the rubble once belonged to an important public work. This leaves the rubble farther south, which does not seem to have been connected with any streets, free to be identified as the supports that carried the Aqua Traiana over the river (for which a convincing case is made in Taylor 1995, 91ff.). Lanciani, Le Gall, and Galliazzo (above nn. 74–5) were likewise all inclined in favor of the northern location for the bridge.

Wall made intramural Trastevere an urban space as never before, setting it on the path to becoming what it was when Procopius described it in the sixth century:[77] a densely settled wedge, clustered within the contours of its fortified periphery, and indissolubly attached to the urban nucleus on the left bank, which it came to resemble far more closely than the rest of the fourteenth region left beyond the enceinte.

4.4 The immediate topographical impact of the Wall, citywide

As the preceding regional overviews already begin to demonstrate, the repercussions of Rome's enclosure made themselves felt well beyond the immediate vicinity of the new enceinte. Continuing the progression from the local to the more macroscopic, there are a number of issues bearing broadly on the city and its hinterland to discuss, amongst which pride of place goes to the interconnected questions of communications, transport, and trade. The topic leads immediately back to the Tiber, Rome's principal avenue of long-distance communications and commerce, and to the ensemble of Aurelian's alimentary reforms outlined in Chapter 2. An immediate disclaimer: much of what follows may not properly reflect the Wall's impact on the city *per se*; here, the old uncertainties recur about the extent to which the Wall anticipated, caused, or reflected other symptoms of change. I begin simply by presenting a series of events between them illustrating a truly revolutionary re-ordering of the storage and distribution of foodstuffs, which was, in a manner that remains to be clarified, fundamentally connected to (in anticipation of, in conjunction with, or resulting from) the construction of the Wall.

One of Aurelian's initiatives, according to the *HA*, was the increase of the daily bread-ration by an ounce.[78] While Coarelli's argument against the resulting *communis opinio* that makes Aurelian the first ever to distribute bread in place of unmilled grain appears sound, it is fair to say that the tentative beginnings made perhaps under Alexander Severus

---

[77] *BG* 1, 19, 10: ζεύξαντες οὖν ταύτῃ τὸν ποταμὸν γεφύρᾳ, ξυνάπτειν τε τὸ τεῖχος ἔδοξαν καὶ οἰκίας συχνὰς ἐν χωρίῳ τῷ ἀντιπέρας δειμάμενοι μέσον τῆς πόλεως τὸ τοῦ Τιβέριδος πεποίηνται ῥεῦμα ("It seemed good, spanning the river in this place with a bridge, to join the wall together; and building dense houses in the land on the far side, they [the 'ancient Romans'] put the stream of the Tiber in the middle of the city.")

[78] *HA Aur.* 47, 2.

were taken up on a much grander scale beginning in the 270s.[79] The distribution of loaves to the plebs must thus have brought the mills on the Janiculum to new prominence at this time, and cemented their place within the ambit of public policy and institutional control.[80] Ever since Procopius, the extension of the Wall to the summit of the Janiculum has in fact been explained as an expedient intended in part to protect these mills, which it reached just far enough to enclose.[81] Assuming this postulate to be true, it indicates that the course of the Transtiberine walls was conceived with the reformed system of the *annona* in mind; and it further provides a convincing context for the construction of the Pons Probi. An imperial intervention in the processing and transport of enough grain to feed hundreds of thousands would explain well the positioning of a new bridge on a direct line between the spot where imported grain was unloaded, at the Marmorata quay, and the Janiculum.[82] There is thus the hint of a connection, and a close chronological coincidence, between provisions made for defense, transport-infrastructure, and the provisioning of the city, which resulted in the creation of a protected corridor between Rome's principal port and the mills across the river.

[79] See Coarelli 1987, 445–56. Recent finds at the one known mill on the Janiculum fully support his proposed late-Severan date for the introduction of the first public mills in Rome (see below n. 81). Still, as subsidies of oil and pork, the other commodities first distributed under the Severans (oil: *HA Sev.* 18, 3; pork: *HA Alex. Sev.* 26, 2), apparently had to be reinstituted by Aurelian after their discontinuation during the difficult middle decades of the third century, it is all the more probable that the immense task of organizing the milling of sufficient bread for *c.* 200,000 daily rations was left to Aurelian definitively to accomplish. Coarelli himself stresses the massive difficulties, tantamount to the re-ordering of the whole distributive apparatus of the *annona*, that the substitution of loaves for grain required (*ibid.* 451ff.); I think the transition unlikely to have been fully accomplished under Alexander Severus, much less under his short-lived successors. The ancient sources list bread prominently among the items of the *annona* reconstituted by Aurelian, though the notice that he added an ounce to the "bread" of the city may imply that loaves had already been distributed at some previous point (as Coarelli argues, *ibid.* 453; cf. 446, n. 83, with *HA* 47, 2); see also *HA Aur.* 48, 1; *ibid.* 35, 1–2; and the *Chronographus* of 354 (VZ 1, 279); cf. Durliat 1990, 42–51.

[80] *HA Aur.* 47, 2.

[81] *BG* 1, 19, 6ff. One mill complex on the Janiculum, located just inside the Wall by the Porta Aurelia (S. Pancrazio), has been identified and reasonably fully excavated: see Wilson 2000; Bell 1993; cf. Cozza 1987–88, 167–9, with fig. 46. Its close proximity to the Wall has several times been cited as evidence that the contours of the circuit were conditioned by the presence of these mills (by e.g. Bell).

[82] The road leading from the presumed Pons Probi toward the Janiculum is an important piece of evidence here; see De Caprariis 1999, 219–20; Coarelli 1987, 450; Rodriguez Almeida 1981, 140–1; Wikander 1979, 21. Perhaps the road also should be placed on the list of additions to the urban infrastructure made under Aurelian and Probus, a dedicated "grain street" that kept the enormous volume of new commercial traffic clear of the Via Aurelia (*Vetus*), which ran nearly parallel only a short distance away; cf. Wikander.

A second and more remarkable chain of circumstances begins with the sudden and total abandonment of the manmade mountain of broken amphorae (Monte Testaccio) located in the midst of the commercial district south of the Aventine. Thorough analyses of the accumulation, composed entirely of containers used for the transport of olive oil, show that sherds continued to be deposited until the sole reign of Gallienus (260–8).[83] The abrupt end has been documented and indeed stressed in the fundamental study of Rodriguez-Almeida, who strangely made little further effort to consider why amphorae were no longer deposited here, and where all the later ones got to, even after acknowledging that Rome's urban masses remained dependent on foreign imports (including oil transported in amphorae) for centuries to come.[84] In relation to the end of Testaccio there is to be juxtaposed a second fact, mentioned only in passing by Lanciani and until very recently ignored. The hill in the northern Campus Martius now called Montecitorio is composed of broken amphorae approximately dated to the fourth and fifth centuries.[85] Picking up where Lanciani left off, Francesca de Caprariis has demonstrated that the modern toponym itself is attested in its oldest form as the *mons Acceptorius*, presumably after the corporation of *acceptores*, the agents responsible for the storage and administration of the foodstuffs destined for public distribution.[86]

De Caprariis' study is especially noteworthy for being the first to propose the further connection between the fortification of the city, the end of Testaccio, and Aurelian's alimentary reforms.[87] There is much circumstantial evidence to recommend the thesis. In the same short span of years, the banks of the river were fortified, new crossings were provided

---

[83] Aguilera Martín 2002, 212ff.; Blázquez *et al.* 1994; Rodriguez Almeida 1984, 109ff., esp. 135–9.

[84] Rodriguez Almeida 1984, 165ff. He, in fact, asserts that imports to Rome effectively stopped cold between Gallienus and Diocletian, during the "turbulent" reigns of Aurelian and Probus, a proposition that appears to me highly suspect. To begin with, Rome's increasing reliance on oil from North Africa from the third century on should caution against placing undue emphasis on the effects of events in Spain; and there is no cause to think that imports of African oil ceased at any point in the later third century: see e.g. Mattingly 1988, esp. 54–6; cf. Panella 1999, 196–8. Even if we accept that Rome went without imported oil for decades, this still raises the root question of why oil amphorae were no longer discarded at Testaccio by the fourth century, and where they all ended up. On the amphorae arriving in Rome in the fourth and fifth centuries, see e.g. Keay 1984, with the summary at 433–4, where the shift from Spanish to African sources of production for the urban market over the course of the third century is again stressed (without any hint of a third-century stoppage in imports).

[85] R. Lanciani, in *REL* 17 (1908), 92, cited in De Caprariis 1999, 230.

[86] De Caprariis 1999, 230–1.

[87] She is followed by Aguilera Martín 2002: see e.g. 66 and 218.

to the walled salient on the right bank, and vast quantities of agricultural staples began to be shipped, stored, and distributed in places where they had not been previously, at least in the same quantities. Grain henceforth went to the mills on the Janiculum, whence it was returned to the city for distribution via the five river crossings inside the Transtiberine walls, two of them built new and dedicated under Probus. Loaves of bread were distributed at numerous points around the city, called *gradus* or "steps" by the fourth century, while the central node from which all unmilled grain had been distributed, the *porticus minuciae frumentariae*, became defunct.[88] There is reason to think that the remaining three staples were all subsequently delivered to the vicinity of Aurelian's temple, two of them for the first time. With regard to pork, the Regionary Catalogues locate for the first time the *forum suarium* in the same area of the Campus Martius; and though the existence of a *forum suarium* is securely attested from the beginning of the third century, the scale and importance of the commerce at this complex must have increased notably with Aurelian's reintroduction of free distributions of pork.[89] As for wine, the government-subsidized ration was stored and sold at the new temple of Sol by the fourth century at the latest.[90] Finally, something substantial occurred to make the containers in which oil arrived disappear from the vicinity of Monte Testaccio. In the fourth century, a new mountain of sherds, subsequently remembered with the name of the administrators of the *annona*, arose in the immediate vicinity of Aurelian's temple.

---

[88] See De Caprariis 1999, 231; Coarelli 1987, 453; Rickman 1980, 197. On the mechanics of bread distribution by the later fourth century and the network of *gradus*, see Tengström 1974, 82–8; cf. Rickman 1980, 208.

[89] Durliat believes that Aurelian was the first altogether to institute free distributions of pork (1990, 49–51). In light of Coarelli's arguments and the reference to pork distributions under Alexander Severus (*HA Alex. Sev.* 26, 2, with Coarelli 1987), I would modify Durliat slightly to say that Aurelian re-instituted and regularized the pork dole, imparting the essentials of the form it retained into the fifth century. Though the location of the *forum suarium* is never specified before the Regionary Catalogues, there is no particular reason to believe that it was located elsewhere prior to Aurelian. Its new prominence is amply attested by a flurry of epigraphic and literary testimony over the course of the fourth century, well summarized by L. Chioffi, *LTUR* 2, 347, see under *forum suarium*. A. Moneti, in fact, wanted to place the *forum suarium* of the Catalogues in the portico of the temple of Sol itself, a hypothesis that, if correct, would decidedly widen the apparent scope of Aurelian's intervention in the supply of pork (Moneti 1990). However, the number of structures listed between the temple and the *forum suarium* in the Regionary Catalogues makes this interpretation difficult, as Chioffi has noted. For more traditional views of the location, layout, and functions of the temple of Sol, see Virlouvet 1995, 51–9; Palmer 1990, 45–6; Hülson 1895 (none of whom imagines a direct connection with the *forum suarium*).

[90] As early as *c.* 300, if the standard dating of *CIL* 6, 1785 is correct (see above Chapter 2, n. 119).

Lanciani's passing reference unfortunately gives no indication of what these vessels contained; if it was not wine, oil remains as the likely candidate.[91] Since the wine stored at the temple of the Sun arrived in wooden barrels (*cupae*), the probability that at least some of the amphorae deposited in Montecitorio held oil seems all the greater.[92]

The first point to emerge from this brief overview is that the end of Testaccio is a symptom of broader, systemic changes in the administration of the city. In a sense, so too is the Wall. Of course, it would be facile to suggest *tout court* that the fortification of Rome necessitated the relocation of its most important ports and storage facilities; and even the attempt to trace causal links between the building of the Wall and other symptoms of change is fraught with difficulty. Hence, beginning with Testaccio and then proceeding to the Campus Martius, I will limit myself to some preliminary remarks about the extent to which Rome's new enceinte, as a physical barrier, can be seen as an agent in the transformations outlined above. In several instances, I believe it is possible to show that the presence of the Wall played an active part in shaping the contours of the "commercial revolution" that subsequently unfolded.

Although a number of warehouses around Testaccio, notably the Horrea Lolliana, were separated from the Tiber by the 800 m stretch of wall built along the riverbank, this in itself need not have caused significant disturbances. There is no proof that any of these structures were supplied principally from adjacent docks on the river to begin with, and the primary port facilities just upstream at the Trajanic quay remained unobstructed.[93] It is indeed striking that the quay and the porticus Aemilia

---

[91] By the fourth century, oil was distributed from *mensae oleariae* scattered around the city, which numbered some 2,300 according to the *Regionary Catalogues* (VZ 1, 164; *ibid.* 188); see also *CTh* 14, 24, 1, *De mensis oleariis*; and cf. Pavis d'Escurac 1976, 197–201. Presumably, however, the individual distribution sites were supplied from (one?) central depot, where oil imports were delivered and stockpiled.

[92] *CIL* 6, 1785; cf. Virlouvet 1995, 56–9; Coarelli 1987, 448; Rougé 1957, 320–8. The textual evidence is corroborated by a sharp decline in the numbers of imported wine amphorae at Rome, beginning in the late third century and continuing through the fourth: see Panella and Saguì 2001, 772–3; Panella 1999, 199–205.

[93] The Horrea Lolliana appear on fragment 25 of the Severan marble plan. The two small stairs shown leading from the warehouse to the riverbank, the latter apparently not provided with docking facilities, do not to my mind constitute good evidence that the warehouse was supplied primarily from this direction (as De Caprariis [1999, 219] seems to imagine). The other warehouses on the same fragment lack stairs to the river altogether. Further, what limited routes of access existed between the river and the warehouses in this sector seem to have been preserved after the fortification of the riverbank. Two small apertures were detected in the river wall in, strikingly enough, the approximate vicinity of the Horrea Lolliana (see Meneghini 1985, 38; Gatti 1936, 69; *contra* De Caprariis, who asserts that this stretch of the river wall was entirely without gates), which may even correspond with the stairs shown in the plan.

behind it, which together comprised the heart of the emporium, extended almost exactly to the point where the river wall ended; or rather, that the Wall was made to cross the river just before it would have begun to obstruct them.[94] And in fact, the area of the emporium remained bustling well into the fifth century, though the archaeological data for the region fronted by the river wall are too sparse to permit conclusions about whether commercial activity continued unabated there, too.[95]

The best case for the direct impact of the Wall seems to have eluded all mention. A survey of the riverbed made in the 1980s using sidescan sonar revealed the presence of pilings on the riverbed between the ending of the river wall on the left bank and the termination of the southern branch of the Transtiberine salient. These remains are most plausibly associated with a barrier designed to cover the riverine approaches to the city, best dated to the time of the Wall's construction.[96] Early-modern maps reveal the remnants of two unusually large towers on both sides of the river in this location, where Leo IV is said to have built two reinforced towers in the mid ninth century, probably by way of restoring or augmenting an earlier defensive arrangement.[97] The existence of such a barrier from the 270s on

---

[94] The best overview of the emporium and its surroundings is now Aguilera Martín 2002, 51–124. Extant remains of the quay date to the major renovation and expansion of the emporium district carried out under Trajan; see Rodriguez Almeida 1984, esp. 67ff.; Carettoni *et al.* 1960, 83–4; Le Gall 1953, 194–6; Gatti 1936. Meneghini has misinterpreted Bruzza's description of the remains he observed along the Marmorata quay in 1870 (published in Gatti 1936, 67ff.), and hence claimed that a later brick wall along the top of the Roman river-embankment in front of the Emporium formed part of the Aurelianic defenses of the city, and that the apertures visible in the sole remaining depiction of the structure (an anonymous nineteenth-century watercolor), which gave access to the Roman stairs ascending from the quay, were originally provided to allow passage from the quay through the enceinte; see Meneghini 1985, 35ff.; also Meneghini and Santangeli Valenzani 2004, 189–91. Bruzza's description and the plan supplied by Gatti (1936, fig. 1) actually make it clear that the original river wall ended with the remains of the semicircular tower, presumably the one reconstructed by Leo IV in *c.* 848 (see below n. 97), that stood across the river from the termination of the Transtiberine walls. I would suggest that the brick wall upstream was constructed under Pope Urban VIII in the 1640s, to connect the defenses on the left bank with the point where his new walls in Trastevere met the river.

[95] An extended tract, some 200 meters long, of the warehouses along the riverbank north of the porticus Aemilia was excavated in the 1980s. The complex remained fully functional until the end of the fourth century, with ongoing signs of commercial activity, albeit on a diminished scale, through the fifth. see Moccheggiani Carpano, M. Incitti and R. Meneghini, in *BullCom* 1986, 560–95, esp. 593–5; Moccheggiani Carpano, in *BullCom* 1985, esp. 86–8; cf. Meneghini in *BullCom* 1987–88, 360–2.

[96] See Cozza 1987–88, 139ff.; cf. Hertz 1991, 305ff.

[97] *LP* II, 115; see the plans of e.g. Bufalini 1551 (*Le piante* 2, tav. 208); Du Pérac 1577 (*Le piante* 2, tav. 249); Greuter 1618 (*Le piante* 2, tav. 292); de Paoli 1623 (*Le piante* 2, tav. 305); cf. Cozza 1987–8, 143. The probable remains of the tower on the left bank were observed by Bruzza in 1870: see Gatti 1936, 67–70.

will inevitably have occasioned a fundamental change in the way river-borne commerce from the ports of Ostia and Portus entered the city. Very simply, the large barges, or *naves caudicariae*, which had formerly carried commodities like grain and oil directly to the emporium must henceforth have been unloaded farther downstream, as it will have been extremely difficult, if not impossible, to tow them past the point where the river entered the circuit of the Wall.[98] Precisely this problem presented itself in the case of the obelisk famously shipped to Rome from Alexandria in 357, according to Ammianus Marcellinus. The difficulty of getting the massive transport barge *through the walls* was such that the obelisk was unloaded three miles south of the city on the via Ostiensis, and laboriously dragged the far greater distance to its destination at the Circus Maximus by road.[99]

Additional epigraphic and textual evidence points to the same conclusion, albeit in more circumstantial fashion. In the high empire, the Pons Sublicius, the first above the emporium, was specified as the boundary between two distinct modes of shipping, above which *lyntrarii* piloting smaller boats that could be poled easily upstream took over from the *navicularii caudicarii* who manned the heavy barges towed up from the ports.[100] By the early fourth century, however, the *navicularii* are called simply the *codicari nabiculari* (*sic*) *infernates*, indicating that they operated "below" some unspecified point that I think is most likely to have been the Wall itself.[101]

The resulting need to transport the commodities necessary for the survival of the city to the emporium and other points of debarkation inside the Wall would therefore have greatly expanded the mission of the smaller boats capable of being maneuvered upstream. Perhaps the best explanation for Aurelian's alleged introduction of a new association of

---

[98] Such an operation would have required anchoring the heavily loaded boats, disengaging the tow ropes from the teams of men or animals pulling them, and somehow conveying ropes and boats upstream through the pillars of the barrier to meet teams of haulers on the inside of the Wall. The mechanics of towing barges from the ports to the city are detailed in Le Gall 1953, 256–9; Tengström 1974, 57–9 (who allows a greater role for animals on the Tiber towpaths than did Le Gall); Aguilera Martín 2002, 29–43.

[99] Amm. 17, 4, 14: ... *tandemque sero impositus navi per maria fluentaque Thyrbridis velut paventis, ne, quod paene ignotus miserat Nilus, ipse parum sub emeatus sui discrimine moenibus alumnis inferret, defertur in vicum Alexandri tertio lapide ab urbe seiunctum, unde chamulcis impositus tractusque lenius per Ostiensem portam piscinamque publicam Circo illatus est Maximo.* The phrase *moenibus...inferret* surely indicates the perceived impracticality of bringing the obelisk literally through the walls.

[100] The key text is *CIL* 6, 1639, which mentions *codicari nav[iculari] infra pontem S[ublicium]*; cf. Le Gall 1953, 257. On the various types of boats used on the Tiber, see *ibid.* 216–31; Rougé 1966, 193–4.

[101] *CIL* 14, 131, a dedication to Constantine in the name of the members of this *collegium*.

navicularii amnici is the sudden need to transport the wares carried by
naves caudicariae from new points of offloading farther downstream into
the city proper.[102] Though generally poorly documented, there are
remains of port facilities south of the Wall on both sides of the river,
where the transfer of supplies from the larger class of shipping to the
smaller could have occurred in late antiquity.[103] Such an arrangement
would also go some way toward explaining why oil imported from Spain
and increasingly North Africa was no longer offloaded in the vicinity of
Testaccio: if oil amphorae had subsequently to be transferred to smaller
boats at a point well downstream of the emporium, the additional labor of
transporting them upstream past the emporium to the vicinity of
Aurelian's temple (and Montecitorio) would have been comparatively
insignificant, and perhaps justified in the context of Aurelian's sweeping
effort to centralize the administration of state-subsidized commodities in
the northern Campus Martius.[104]

As for the increased prominence of the Campus Martius in the
reformed system of the *annona*, there are several factors quite independent
of the Wall that may have contributed to a partial shift away from the
emporium and Testaccio. The *HA* stresses Aurelian's effort to stimulate
wine production in the Italian peninsula north of Rome; by the time it was
written in the fourth century, wine was evidently arriving from these
regions, by way of the Tiber, in quantity.[105] If the invasions under
Gallienus had indeed disrupted Spanish oil production significantly, there
was perhaps an effort to produce more of this upriver as well.[106] Umbria
was long famous for its livestock, and the valley of the river Clitumnus

---

[102] *HA Aur.* 47, 3. For an alternate view of the significance of this passage, see Rougé 1966, 194–6.

[103] Numerous remains of docks and warehouses lined the left bank of the Tiber, south of the
Wall, for several kilometers: see Moccheggiani Carpano 1975–76; cf. Castagnoli 1980, 37–8;
Le Gall 1953, 196ff. and 258. The potential importance of the large quay on the right bank at
Pietra Papa, to which Le Gall was unwilling to attribute a significant commercial role, has
been reasserted in Palmer 1981, 382ff., *contra* Le Gall 1953, 258–9. Certainly the *vicus
Alexandri* at the third milestone on the Via Ostiensis, where the obelisk was unloaded in 357
(above n. 99), must have been equipped with a sizeable quay.

[104] It is also conceivable that some commodities offloaded south of the Wall entered the city
by road, via the Porta Ostiensis on the left bank and the Porta Portuensis on the right. There
is, in fact, a small, unexplored mound just east of Testaccio ("piccolo Testaccio"), and thus
nearer the Porta Ostiensis, perhaps composed of transport containers brought by land,
perhaps after the walling of the riverbank (though there are as yet no data to support this
conjecture); see De Caprariis 1999, 219; cf. Aguilera Martín 2002, 215–18.

[105] The area of production is said to extend from Etruria *usque ad Alpes maritimas* (*HA Aur.* 48, 2).

[106] Constant local, small-scale production of oil for the urban market is assumed in e.g. Mattingly
1988, 49–50, who further notes the likelihood that the primary zone of manufacture was
upriver in the Sabina.

continued to be singled out for praise in late antiquity.[107] As hogs for the pork dole carried to the city by river will have lost far less weight – and value – than those herded overland from the pig-producing centers in southern Italy, Umbrian pork must have held its attractions for the administrators of the *annona*.[108] All such supplies arriving from the Italian interior would have been most conveniently unloaded in the northern river ports, and stockpiled in the Campus Martius.

This said, I am nonetheless inclined to think that the essential components of the reformed *annona* were located within the perimeter of the fortifications by design. While grain, oil, and meat had always been stored in quantity within areas of the city later enclosed by the Wall, dedicated initiatives were evidently required to locate new facilities for the storage and distribution of wine inside the circuit at Aurelian's temple of the Sun, and to extend the Wall to the point occupied by the mills on the Janiculum. Further, in the decades following the erection of the Wall, the centralization of commercial space initiated by the urban authorities likely developed momentum of its own, as others involved in the import and sale of valuable commodities gradually moved their operations inside the circuit.[109] Where it might once have seemed expedient to base storage depots outside the customs circuit, we may imagine that the conversion of this boundary into a defensive perimeter increased the appeal of its interior, particularly when, in the early fourth century, hostile armies began appearing outside the ramparts with some frequency.[110]

---

[107] The modern Clitunno; see Claudian, *De VI cons.* 506–8: *quin et Clitumni sacras uictoribus undas,/candida quae Latiis praebent armenta triumphis,/visere cura fuit.* Cf. Le Gall 1953, 263–4, with n. 6 on p. 263 for earlier literary references to the area as a center of pasturage for highly prized sacrificial animals.

[108] On the difficulties of transporting pigs overland from southern Italy, a primary zone of pork production for the urban market in late antiquity, see Barnish 1987, 160 and *passim.*

[109] As e.g. De Caprariis has suggested, calling the Wall "un ostacolo fisico che dovette gradualmente portare all'interno della città funzioni ed operazioni che prima si svolgevano altrove" (1999, 231).

[110] According to Lactantius, the army of Severus ravaged the Italian countryside in 307 during the retreat following its unsuccessful siege of the capital (*De mort. pers.* 27, 6: *Vastata est igitur ea pars Italiae qua pestiferum illud agmen incessit…*), an event that must have provided a strong incentive for local merchants to move their operations inside the Wall. The intramural concentration of commercial centers may have been further encouraged by imperial mandate, the better to regulate and tax imports of products earmarked for the urban market; cf. Palmer 1980, 219ff. As the same corporations responsible for providing state-subsidized goods in late antiquity also contributed to the "free market" at Rome by selling their surpluses at market prices (see Lo Cascio 1999), it seems the more likely that commercial activity will have gravitated toward, or piggybacked on, the central nodes of the *annona* in the Campus Martius.

The best documented example is that of wine, for which the area called the *septem caesares*, located in southern Trastevere well beyond the line later taken by the Wall, was a principal marketplace in the early empire.[111] In late antiquity, there is no further mention of the place. Meanwhile, the *cellae vinariae novae et arruntianae*, built under Trajan, were destroyed by the wall itself.[112] The possibility that at least some of the wares once stockpiled in these locations ended up in the vicinity of Aurelian's new temple *cum* wine depot deserves serious consideration. Something similar may have occurred in the case of the second-century warehouses and the adjacent mounds of sherds and assorted refuse (Monte Secco) still visible in the nineteenth century just north of the city on the right bank of the Tiber, which were perhaps also abandoned after merchants formerly based in the area moved across the river to the Campus Martius.[113]

Finally, it is worth noting that in the first period of the Wall's history, an intramural location would have detracted relatively little from the efficiency of communications and trade with the outside world. The pointed effort made to keep the principal port of the city unobstructed has already been mentioned. Farther north along the banks of the Campus Martius, the river wall was perforated by six *posterulae*, more than enough to permit access to all the primary docking facilities known to have existed.[114] Indeed, the provision of six gates in 2.6 km of riverfront strongly indicates that already in the planning stages of the Wall, a high volume of commercial traffic in the Campus Martius was envisioned. In leaving the 800 m of wall south of the emporium without comparable entrances, the Wall's planners may thus have given physical expression to an increase in the relative importance of the northern ports for the provisioning of the city.

With the exception of the destruction of the Pons Neronianus, all primary land routes to the city were likewise left open and functioning. This is by no means to discount the effect of the Wall on communications, particularly local communications, for it will certainly have blocked

---

[111] See Palmer 1981, 368–9.   [112] Lanciani, *Notizie* 1880, 127–9.

[113] See the brief notice of Lanciani in *Notizie* 1884, 392–3, which unfortunately does not provide any information about the date of the accumulations; cf. De Caprariis 1999, 231–3. If a second artificial mound near the Ponte S. Angelo (Monte Giordano) is likewise comprised of pot-sherds, a hypothesis to my mind more plausible than its traditional identification with the remains of the amphitheater of Statilius Taurus, we would have a further sign of the commercialization of the area as a whole. Only future excavation, however, can clear up the composition and chronology of the formation, currently totally unknown; see generally the brief summary of Asso 1953.

[114] Corvisieri 1878, *passim*; cf. De Caprariis 1999, 220ff.; Castagnoli 1980, 35ff.

countless routes of access – paths, alleys, open fields – that had previously allowed free passage between the heart of the city and its immediate surroundings, provoking locally significant dislocations and chanelling all movement between city-center and suburbs onto the roads that traversed the Wall.[115] All the same, gates were provided for all the consular roads, numerous secondary arteries, and even some barely glorified footpaths.[116] The proximity of many smaller posterns to one another and to larger gates is a clear testament to the care taken to preserve the existing street network: rather than deviating people a few tens or hundreds of meters, alternate apertures were regularly opened instead.[117] All told, the initial impact of the Wall on long-distance trade and travel was substantially mitigated by the effort made to leave accessible the many roads that connected the city with its intercontinental hinterland.[118]

In the end, though the relative impact of public policy and private initiative on the process is debatable, as is the power of the Wall *per se* as a pole of attraction, I would conclude that the presence of the enceinte was a contributing factor in the centralization of markets and warehouses within its precincts. The limited archaeological and textual data relevant to trade, commerce, and (to a lesser extent) communications thus tend to support the example of the preceding regional overviews, all of which suggest that the appearance of the Wall precipitated a diffuse topographical groundswell that altered patterns of settlement and favored – or even provoked – a growing polarity between an urban interior and an external periphery increasingly voided of a permanent population. It is a paradigm that applies best to the years between 270 and 410, after which Rome's relationship with its enceinte entered a new phase, as the urban center retracted from the contours it had once filled, and from the Wall itself.

---

[115] Archaeological evidence for the existence – to say nothing of the obstruction – of such minor routes is very sparse. In most cases, it is not clear even whether remains of streets (not to mention unpaved paths) traversed by the Wall were still in use when it was built; possible examples appear in the *FUR*, tavv. 2; 20; and 39; others revealed by excavation are published so cryptically in the *Bullettino Comunale* and *Notizie degli Scavi* that their relationship to the Wall is indeterminate: see e.g. *Notizie* 1907, 681 (a street between the Portae Appia and Ostiensis); *ibid.* 1913, 43 (near S. Saba on the Aventine).

[116] The minimum width for a road allowed by law was 8 Roman feet, or 2.4 m, and this is precisely the size of the road leading to the Porta Ardeatina postern, for example, where the gate itself, at 2.7 m wide, corresponds fairly closely with the dimensions of the street (cf. Spera 1999, 41–2; Quilici 1974, 713ff.). Yet the second postern on the far side of the Viale Cristoforo Colombo is barely half as wide, as are both posterns between tower D4 and the Castra Praetoria, and evidently also the one observed by Richmond below S. Giovanni: all glorified footpaths, in sum.

[117] Cf. Lanciani 1892, 102.   [118] Cf. Cassanelli *et al*, 1974, 39–40; Lanciani 1892, 101–02.

4.5   Big walls, small town: Rome after empire

Into the fifth century, dense concentrations of residential and commercial building frequently extended at least as far as the Wall, which was thus "lived" by a sizeable segment of the Roman populace on an everyday basis. Pronounced change came with the demographic collapse that began in earnest in the first quarter of the fifth century, and continued through the period of the Gothic wars in the mid sixth century.[119] As centers of population receded, the circuit stood starkly immobile and eventually quite isolated. Still there for all to see and experience, it had henceforward to be sought out, instead of inserting itself bodily into daily life. With the decline of imperial government in the West, moreover, the authority that had built the Wall, maintained it, and sanctioned its existence ceased to be, leaving both its upkeep and its legacy to be claimed by others. One result of all this is that there is less to be said about its effects on the evolving topography of the post-imperial city *stricto sensu*, inasmuch as this incarnation of Rome developed for the most part well inside its perimeter. At the same time, the shrinking *abitato* was never independent of the enceinte: regularly maintained and no less impermeable than before (just the opposite, in fact), the Wall exercised a constant pull on the parameters of urban life, mediating and channeling flows of goods and humans that sustained city and hinterland alike. To better understand how this was so, a bit of background on the form and functioning of Rome during the transition from late antiquity to the early Middle Ages is required, particularly as the traditional picture has recently changed in ways that suggest a closer integration between the Wall and the urban collective.

---

[119] The range of opinion on population figures for Rome is vast; I have followed something of a developing consensus that the population of the city in the early imperial period stood in the vicinity of 750,000 to 1,000,000 souls, a figure not substantially reduced probably until the beginning of the fifth century, when the Gothic sack and the subsequent loss of the African grain supply to the Vandals kicked off a steady and rapid decline. With particular reference to late antiquity, see Purcell 1999, 138ff.; Lo Cascio 1997, esp. 40ff.; Durliat 1990, 94–123; Barnish 1987, 161ff.; cf. Christie 2000, 311–12. For the fourth century, an estimate ranging between Lo Cascio's minimum of 600–700,000 inhabitants and Durliat's maximum of 900,000 (he prefers *c.* 800,000) should hit close to the mark. For the eighth and ninth centuries, I believe Meneghini and Santangeli Valenzani's recent figure of 50–60,000 best accounts for the evidence presently available (2004, 22–3). I am not at all convinced by L. Gatto's recent attempt to question the standard view – amply supported by literary, documentary, and archaeological sources – that Rome experienced a demographic collapse over the course of the fifth and sixth centuries that saw the population of the city reduced by something like 90% (Gatto 1998).

In the first place, zones of occupation were substantially more diffuse from the sixth century through the tenth than was once thought. The vision of a dense nucleus along the Tiber in the Campus Martius applies far better to the situation in the twelfth century and later than to the early Middle Ages, when settlement was still scattered widely across the vast area enclosed by the Wall, albeit in the midst of sizeable "rural" interstices.[120] As archaeologists and historians have devoted more attention to signs of early medieval activity, in sum, more have turned up.[121] Clusters of housing existed on the Esquiline, around the Lateran, at the foot of the Caelian by the Porta Metronia, and in the vicinity of the old imperial fora, to name but some examples.[122] Ongoing cleaning and maintenance in the fora of Trajan, Nerva, and Caesar into the ninth century,[123] and the explosion of churches and charitable complexes in and around the Forum Romanum beginning in the seventh century indicate that large numbers of people continued to congregate in these areas.[124] Several important aqueducts were likewise maintained at least through the ninth century, serving diverse regions of the city: the Traiana in the west, the Virgo in the north, the Alexandrina in the south, and the Claudia in the east furnished water for numerous monasteries, baptisteries, baths, mills, and private residences along their urban tracts.[125] The street network, too, shows considerable signs of continuity, with many of the major thoroughfares of the Roman period either preserving their original paving, or following

[120] According to Krautheimer's classic vision, the population of Rome was already concentrated in the Campus Martius by the later sixth century, and surrounded by an enormous intramural *disabitato* composed of imposing ruins and rural vistas and speckled with only the most exiguous nodes of settlement (Krautheimer 1980, 68 and *passim*). While there is no doubt that the population and the physical extent of the city were vastly shrunken, the studies cited in the following notes, amongst others, have demonstrated that Krautheimer overestimated both the density of population in the Campus Martius in the early Middle Ages, and the extent of desolation elsewhere. Even in the tenth and eleventh centuries, the Campus Martius was not yet the nucleated hub of urban life in Rome that it later became (Hubert 1990, 96 and *passim*).

[121] For up-to-date summaries, see Paroli 2004; Meneghini and Santangeli Valenzani 2004; Delogu 2001; cf. also Bauer 1996, 117–24.

[122] Santangeli Valenzani 2004 and 2000; Pani Ermini 2001, 306ff.; Meneghini and Santangeli Valenzani 2001, 21–7; Meneghini 2000a and 1999; Coates-Stephens 1996; Hubert 1990, esp. 74–83.

[123] Meneghini and Santangeli Valenzani 2007, 115–58; 2004, 257–88; 2001, 25–33; Santangeli Valenzani 2001a and 1999; Meneghini 2000b.

[124] Reekmans 1989, 876–80; Delogu 2000a, esp. 94–6; Giuntella 2001, 681ff.; Pani Ermini 2001, 313–14.

[125] See Coates-Stephens 2003a and 2003b; cf. also Meneghini and Santangeli Valenzani 2004, 65–70.

the same course through successive elevations necessitated by rising ground levels.[126] Thus, the Wall was not so universally removed from frequented areas of the city after all, nor was the *abitato* an isolated world insulated from its distant shell, suspended in a void.

In addition to the people living nearby, many others, Romans and outsiders alike, still routinely passed through the gates of the Wall in considerable numbers. The flow of goods in and out of Rome never ceased. Through the seventh century, grain, wine, and oil continued to arrive from as far away as Sicily, Africa, and the Levant.[127] Then, with the final dissolution of long-distance trade networks following the Arab conquest of Carthage in 698 and the Byzantine appropriation of church properties in Sicily and southern Italy three decades later, the interdependence between the city and its regional hinterland became if anything more pronounced:[128] the products necessary for its survival now came by necessity from (relatively speaking) just outside the gates. Roman artisans, meanwhile, were producing jewelry and accessories for export to their new Lombard neighbors.[129] Cult practice in the Christian era gave Romans further compelling reasons to frequent the Wall. Extramural burials remained the norm until the later sixth century, and common into the seventh. Alongside the cemeteries, renowned churches and martyrial shrines punctuated the extramural countryside, drawing crowds of locals and pilgrims alike.[130] All of this is to say that the Wall was still regularly experienced by a steady stream of people whose movements, essential to the functioning of the city as a whole, continued to be channeled selectively around and through its contours. It is a premise to be borne in mind as we turn to consider the extent of its imprint on the infrastructure and layout of the post-imperial city over the *longue durée*.

---

[126] Pani Ermini 2001, 299ff.; Meneghini and Santangeli Valenzani 2001, 20–1; Delogu 2000a, 90.

[127] The celebrated excavations at the Crypta Balbi have turned up thousands of imported amphorae of seventh-century date from all of these regions; the size of this sample alone requires a new appreciation of the persistence of Mediterranean-wide networks focused on Rome: see Paroli and Vendittelli 2004; Saguì 2002; Arena *et al*, 2001; Panella and Saguì 2001, 791ff. Finds of imported seventh-century ceramics even at rural sites in the Roman *campagna* support the evidence of the Crypta Balbi, and testify further to the diffusion of imported commodities from the city center back out into its surroundings: see Messineo 2003, 34; di Gennaro and dell'Era 2003, 117.

[128] The events of the period are considered further in Chapter 6, below; on the sudden contraction of Rome's economic, cultural, and political horizons at the beginning of the eighth century, see Santangeli Valenzani 2003b; Panella and Saguì 2001, 813–15; Marazzi 2001a; 1993; 1991; Wickham 2000b, esp. 356–66; Delogu 2000a, 100 and *passim*; Arthur 1993.

[129] See Ricci 1997.

[130] The "Christianization" of extramural space is considered at length in Chapter 5, below.

4.6   The topographical *Nachleben* of the Aurelian Wall

As it was by way of the roads that connected it with remaining clusters of population that the Wall still "touched" even the areas most remote from it, issues of transport and communications come to the fore for the period spanning the fifth through the ninth centuries. The closure of its many *posterulae* marks an important turning point. In all probability by the close of the Honorian building campaign in 403, and certainly before the first Gothic siege of Rome in 536, all or nearly all of these secondary apertures had been walled up, along with the larger gate (the Porta Chiusa) by the Castra Praetoria.[131] The Porta Ardeatina was also out of use by the seventh century at the latest,[132] and the Pinciana was immured between the Gothic Wars and the compilation of the Einsiedeln Itineraries toward the end of the eighth century.[133] Thus, even before the siege of 410, at a time when population levels remained high, nearly half of the known routes of access to the city in the main tract of the Wall on the left bank of the river were likely no longer passable.

It is a dramatic change: instead of the relatively dense pincushion of roads radiating out from the center that pierced the Aurelianic enceinte, circulation was henceforth relegated to something like twelve primary arteries, plus the three in Trastevere, nearly all of them the principal consular roads of republican date.[134] Though the long-distance traffic that had always gravitated to these major thoroughfares was little affected,[135] the network of communications between the city center and its regional hinterland once served by the blocked streets was significantly curtailed, and this at a time when Romans were coming to depend more and more on local production for their survival, and to frequent the suburban graves

[131] Though there is no proof for the date of the closure of the *posterulae*, the technique of the brick-faced fill, and the fact that many of them were left considerably above ground level during the clearing operations that accompanied the Honorian heightening of the Wall, suggest a probable *terminus ante* of 403, as I have previously assumed (see above n. 20; cf. Richmond 1930, 229ff.). As the Porta Chiusa is Honorian, it was clearly open into the fifth century, but it must have been closed by the time Procopius was writing, as it is never mentioned in his narrative, while all the other gates in the northern sector of the Wall, where the Gothic attacks were concentrated, appear frequently.

[132] This conclusion results from its absence in the seventh-century list of Rome's gates reproduced by William of Malmesbury.

[133] Mentioned often in Procopius, it is omitted from the description of the Wall appended to the Itineraries.

[134] With the closure of the Pinciana and Ardeatina, the total drops to 13, or one gate for every Roman mile of solid curtains.

[135] Cf. Esch 2003 and 2001.

of the Christian dead in growing numbers. The result, apparent in both archaeological and textual sources, was a reconditioning of patterns of movement, and the infrastructure that supported them, around the urban periphery.

Outside the Wall, a spider-web pattern replaced the pincushion, as a flourishing network of cross-streets grew and ramified amidst the extensive swathes of territory, now deprived of direct access to the city, that lay between the few remaining radial axes of the consular roads. To be sure, "horizontal" connectors between the "vertical" arteries leading out of the city had always existed, but the vitality of these streets in late antiquity and the early Middle Ages is remarkable.[136] Older routes were maintained and often enlarged, and others were built new.[137] To some extent, this is a function of the vitality of the *suburbium*, dotted by a dense patchwork of Christian *loca sancta* visited by growing numbers of the faithful;[138] but there is an underlying structural factor also at work. Beginning with the construction of the Wall, and to a greater degree following the closure of the *posterulae*, the only way to connect numerous cultivated areas, dwellings, and cult centers in the suburbs with the intramural community was to link them with the roads that passed through the remaining gates.

Something very different occurred inside the circuit, where capillary circulation between radial arteries if anything dwindled. The roads most frequented and best maintained were those that offered direct access to gates in the Wall, while the secondary streets branching off the main avenues tended to fall into decrepitude.[139]

---

[136] This is one of the important conclusions to emerge from the recent *Suburbium* conference (Pergola *et al.*, 2003). In addition to the individual contributions cited subsequently, see the summary remarks of F. Bisconti, at p. 503.

[137] The south-eastern sector of the suburbs is the best studied. On the dense fabric of connecting streets between the Viae Latina, Appia, Ardeatina, and Ostiensis, see De Rossi and Granelli 2003, 332ff.; Spera 1999, 386ff., esp. 398; 406–7; 416–18; 421ff.; etc. The phenomenon also extended to other parts of the urban perimeter, however: see Calci and Mari 2003, 178ff.; and in the same volume, Pavolini *et al.*, 2003, 80ff.

[138] The impact of religious geography on the development of these cross-streets is frequently emphasized in the contributions cited in the preceding note; see also Fiocchi Nicolai 2000a and 2000b, 348–56; cf. Pani Ermini 2001, 298–9.

[139] By the end of the early Middle Ages, this situation had reached an advanced state, as Hubert has shown. From the tenth through the thirteenth centuries, it was precisely the Roman roads leading out of the city, classed generally as *viae publicae*, that were maintained, restored, and kept accessible to wheeled traffic; the tortuously winding alleys (*viae vicinales*) branching off of them were usually little more than footpaths designed to permit access to nearby housing clusters (Hubert 1990, 105ff.).

The Caelian hill is a representative example that has been comparatively thoroughly investigated.[140] Of the three streets that remained in use by the eighth century, out of a formerly dense network, the two most important led directly to gates in the Wall: the *via Caelemontana – clivus Scauri* from the Lateran and the Porta Asinaria to the eastern slopes of the Palatine and the Circus Maximus, and the *via capitis Africae*, the axial prolongation of the road from the Porta Metronia that connected this gate with the area of the Coliseum and the forum beyond. These routes were maintained, and when necessary elevated and repaved, throughout the early Middle Ages, but the side roads amongst the decrepit *insulae*, workshops, and aristocratic *domus* that flanked them were progressively abandoned beginning in the fifth century.[141] What new construction occurred from the later fifth century, nearly all of it religious in character, clustered along these two axes, especially at the point where they met at right angles at the summit of the hill, by the arches of the still-serviceable Aqua Claudia.[142]

Elsewhere, the medieval heart of the Esquiline was the *clivus Suburanus*, the common continuation of the streets from the Portae Tiburtina and Praenestina that terminated at the Forum. The numerous early-medieval churches and monasteries in the region were almost without exception ranged along this one surviving road, from the preserved Roman paving of which the seventh-century foundation of S. Lucia *in selci* derived its name in later centuries,[143] as did a sizeable number of contemporary religious institutions similarly identified by their proximity to paved roads.[144] The proliferation of churches, *diaconiae*, and houses in and around the imperial fora – the most "viable" area of all, situated at the confluence of the remaining roads that led out of the city in all directions – from the seventh century on has already been noted.[145]

---

[140] On the excavations of the past two decades, see Pavolini 2004; 1993.

[141] Pavolini 2004, 428–31; 1993, 63ff.

[142] *Ibid.* Among the new foundations were S. Stefano Rotondo (*c.* 460–70), the church and *diaconia* of S. Maria in Domnica (originally of the seventh century?), the later monastery of S. Tommaso *in formis*, and presumably the smaller (unlocated) church of S. Stefano *in capite Africae*.

[143] The location of a *diaconia* in the eighth century, the church on the site was built under Honorius I (625–38); see *LP* I, 323, with Serlorenzi 2004, esp. 363–8.

[144] That the four titular churches on the same road (S. Pietro in Vincoli, S. Martino ai Monti, S. Prassede, and S. Eusebio) were all distinguished with the locator *in silice* attests further to the real and perceived importance of this Roman street in the early Middle Ages, as does the construction of two *diaconiae*, several monasteries, and the newly monumentalized churches of S. Prassede and S. Martino ai Monti, all between the seventh and ninth centuries: see Saxer 2001, 561–2; Reekmans 1989, 887–8.

[145] See above nn. 122–4.

Such indications regarding the parameters of intramural viability are the more noteworthy for their bearing on the shape of the *abitato* as a whole. As the instances just cited already begin to indicate, the relatively few preserved arteries offering transit through the Wall were indeed those along which settlement tended to concentrate.[146] As private dwellings remain poorly attested, however, despite recent advances, the location of ecclesiastical foundations becomes a valuable supplementary indicator of residential concentrations, for the dual mission of the Church to care for souls and bodies undoubtedly occasioned a correlation between the positioning of its physical infrastructure and the places where people were living. While this proposition holds to some degree for churches in the post-imperial period, the better demographic yardstick is the network of charitable centers, the *xenodochia* and *diaconiae* where the resident poor and pilgrims alike were fed, bathed, and sheltered. Unlike most of the titular churches, they were established when extensive population decline and the "mural" constriction of road networks had already occurred, and should therefore more faithfully reflect the changed realities of the post-imperial city.[147] Moreover, beyond responding to existing demographic circumstances, these complexes will have drawn people to their environs and – unlike churches *per se* – physically sustained them.[148]

And, in fact, an overwhelming majority of *diaconiae* rose on the primary axes of communications through the city, above all on the north-south route between St. Peter's and St. Paul's, and a second that branched off the first west of the forum, which it traversed on its way to the Lateran.[149] Over two-thirds of the *diaconiae* in existence when the

[146] See generally Coates-Stephens 1996, esp. 239–45, with distribution maps of textually and archaeologically attested housing for the period 500–1000; cf. Santangeli Valenzani 2004, 55–6.

[147] No *xenodochia* can be documented in the city of Rome before the fifth century, and they seem to have become common only toward the end of the century, and increasingly in the sixth: see Stasolla 1998, esp. 5–14; Santangeli Valenzani 1996–97. The first explicit mentions of *diaconiae* at Rome appear only from the 680s, in a series of references in the *LP*, the first in the life of Benedict II (*LP* I, 364; cf. *LP* 1, 367; 369; 410). Marrou and Bertolini were hence led to opine that the institution took root in Rome then (Marrou 1940, esp. 95–101; Bertolini 1947). Durliat now prefers to put the origins of the *diaconiae* back to *c.* 600 or a bit before (Durliat 1990, 164ff.; on the *status quaestionis*, see Delogu 2000a, 101); while he may well be right, the fact remains that all attested *diaconiae*, like the *xenodochia*, date after the heightening of the Wall, the closure of its *posterulae*, and the onset of large-scale demographic decline.

[148] A close correlation between the locations of *diaconiae* and centers of population was already noted by Bertolini (1947, 67–72); cf. Santangeli Valenzani and Meneghini 2004, 78–80.

[149] The routes corresponding with the first, second, and ninth of the Einsiedeln Itineraries (*a porta sancti Petri usque ad sanctum Paulum*; *a porta sancti Petri usque ad sanctam Luciam in Orthea*; *a porta sancti Petri usque porta Asinaria*, respectively). That the itineraries were

Einsiedeln Itineraries were compiled lay along these two poles, which in the Itineraries are suggestively circumscribed by the three gates they traversed: the Portae S. Petri, Asinaria, and Ostiensis.[150] Of the remainder, all but one were positioned on the main routes to other gates traced in the remaining itineraries.[151] A similar pattern is observable in relation to the intramural *xenodochia*, also generally located in close proximity to the roads most traveled.[152] The main concentrations of church buildings designed to provide for the sustenance of the urban populace, that is, clustered along thoroughfares defined and privileged by their connection with the Wall.

Causes for this phenomenon are not far to seek. *Xenodochia* provided by definition for (amongst other things) the reception and lodging of travelers and pilgrims, who obviously had good reason to be found on the roads that joined Rome to the outside world.[153] There was an additional motive for establishing *diaconiae* on the roads leading out of the Wall, which by virtue of their superior width and Roman paving – which often outlasted the early Middle Ages, particularly away from the alluvial zone near the river – were also those best suited to wheeled transport. One of the principal missions of the *diaconiae* was the distribution of grain, which from the mid eighth century came increasingly from church properties, the *domuscultae*, located on the old consular roads in a band from five to fifteen miles outside the Wall.[154] The inter-related functions of the intra-mural centers of distribution and the extramural zones of production were

---

formulated primarily as a practical guide to the city, rather than a catalogue or "mental map" of Roman topography (the latter view presented in e.g. Santangeli Valenzani 2001b), seems to me certain, as does the ensuing conclusion that the routes outlined correspond with the principal axes of movement between center and periphery in the latter part of the eighth century, as Lanciani (1883/1891) already assumed; see also Del Lungo 2004, 88ff.; Delogu and Belardini 2003, esp. 214–17.

[150] See Saxer 2001, 587ff.; on the Wall as a topographical matrix for the itineraries, cf. Bauer 1997, 224–5.

[151] Saxer 2001.

[152] Giuntella 2001, 678ff. (on both *xenodochia* and *diaconiae*); Santangeli Valenzani 1996–97, 214ff. From the mid eighth century, *xenodochia* were, in fact, increasingly amalgamated, physically and administratively, with *diaconiae*, which in this period became the principal foci of ecclesiastical charity, benefiting from a surge in papal patronage that saw many existing locations restored, and others built new: see Giuntella 2001, 671–7; Santangeli Valenzani 1996–7, 212–14 and 219–20; Durliat 1990, 173ff.

[153] Cf. Stasolla 1998, 20ff.

[154] On the organization of the *domuscultae* and their role in the provisioning of Rome, see esp. Marazzi 1998, 235ff.; cf. 1991, 251ff.; on their location, see also De Francesco 2003, 536. The *diaconiae* not connected with major thoroughfares leading through the Wall are almost all near the river, where the unusually dense cluster of eight around the ports by the Tiber island must in part result from the proximity of this additional "road" of supply, as Marrou already recognized (1940, 97–8).

thus linked also in physical geography, always via the critical intermediate nodes of circulation focused on individual gates in the Wall.

Though the map of early-medieval settlement in Rome remains largely to be drawn, a case can thus already be made, as might indeed be imagined *a priori*, that frequented zones tended to parallel the thoroughfares running between the city center and its suburban hinterland, as well as – away from the Tiber – those aqueducts that remained serviceable.[155] The example of Pompeii, subject of the most detailed studies on communications, spatial organization, and settlement patterns available for any Roman town, supports our *a priori* hypothesis. Pompeii was never densely settled in comparison to e.g. Rome and Ostia (atrium houses were always preferred to multi-story *insulae*, and cultivated space abounded within the walls), and as Ray Laurence has shown, the streets connected to the primary gates in the walls were in fact the most frequented, and boasted an unusually high concentration of both housing and commercial enterprises (bakeries, *fullonicae*, metalworking concerns, inns, and taverns).[156] Early-medieval Rome came in some respects to resemble first-century Pompeii more than imperial Rome: as a result of diminished population density, the later inhabitants of Rome, from the top of the social scale on down, were largely free to situate themselves in the most advantageous sites within the sprawling ambit of the semi-deserted intramural expanses. As more data are collected, it should become more apparent that the most desolate parts of the *disabitato* were those farthest removed from good roads and sources of potable water; and that foci of occupation more often than not clustered around the points where they converged.[157] Wells and aqueducts functioned independently of the enceinte, but the streets manifestly did not. The reduction of points of access through the Wall to a bare

---

[155] Next to the river and the aqueducts, the third primary source of water was wells. For the distribution of known wells, see the map in Coates-Stephens 2003a, 93, which shows a remarkable concentration in the forum area, a particularly well-connected zone of dense habitation no longer served by aqueducts. In part the product of an anomalously intense level of archaeological exploration, the sheer number is nonetheless telling. On the importance of wells in early-medieval Rome, cf. Squatriti 1998, 22.

[156] Laurence 1994, 88–103 and *passim*. Cf. also Laurence 1999, esp. 148–61, on the pronounced impact of through-roads frequented by travelers on the configuration of monumental topography in Roman towns.

[157] This is precisely what occurred on the Caelian, where the wide spaces between the few surviving roads were effectively deserted, as Pavolini has recently stressed (2004, 431). Naturally, other factors had an effect on patterns of settlement, not least among them the location of prominent nodes in the religious geography of the city, discussed more in the next chapter. On the distribution of intramural churches, see Reekmans 1989, figs. 2–3 and *passim*; also e.g. Pietri 1976, esp. 3–29; 461–514.

minimum was thus the germ of its most pronounced and enduring effect on the topography of the city at the end of antiquity and the beginning of the Middle Ages.

A further, not entirely unrelated observation to be made is that the bare fact of the Wall's existence provoked more activity on the urban fringes than is likely otherwise to have occurred there. Several letters written by Gregory the Great around the year 600 demonstrate that the city had until his time been possessed of a permanent garrison, under the command of the local legates of the Exarch at Ravenna, the *magister militum* and the *praefectus praetorio*.[158] The *legio theodosiacorum*, named after the son of the Byzantine emperor Maurice, was charged specifically with the task of manning the Wall.[159] Gregory actually complains of the laxity shown by the troops in the performance of their duties, but the point remains that the Wall was the focus of a stable military presence at the end of the sixth century: the fortified periphery itself, that is, gave rise to a permanent population of sorts.[160]

Traces of this population are to be sought chiefly around the gates. As access to the upper levels of the Wall was gained exclusively via the stairs in the gate-towers, the tactical importance of which was underlined by the construction of fortified enclosures at the rear of many gates in the fifth century, it is highly probable that the barracks of those tasked with its defense were situated nearby. At the Porta Appia, a large building in *opus vittatum* dated to the sixth century has indeed been provisionally identified as a barracks, a plausible explanation for the appearance of such a sizeable structure in a militarized zone on the urban periphery.[161] Perhaps this is where the resident Byzantine troops were quartered whose presence may be

---

[158] Gregory Mentions a *praefectus praetorio* Gregorius and a *magister militum* Castum, who had served with distinction in the defense of Rome against the Lombards, only to see their troops removed from their command and stationed in Narni and Perugia (*GR* 5, 36): *Sed de gloriosis viris Gregorio praefecto praetorio et Casto magistro militum non mediocriter sum afflictus, qui et omnia quae potuerunt fieri nullomodo facere neglexerunt et labores vigiliarum et custodiae civitatis in obsessione eadem vehementissimos pertulerunt et post haec omnia gravi dominorum indignatione percussi sunt.*

[159] *GR* 2, 45: *Theodosiaci vero, qui hic remanserunt, rogam non accipientes vix ad murorum quidem custodiam se accomodant, et destituta ab omnibus civitas, si pacem non habet, quomodo subsistet?*

[160] Gregory complained to the emperor in 595 about the removal of Rome's garrison to Narni and Perugia ("that Perugia may be held, Rome has been abandoned..."; though for how long this new disposition remained in effect is unknown: *Deinde corrupta pace de Romana civitate milites ablati sunt; et quidem alii ab hostibus occisi, alii vero Narniis et Perusiae positi, et ut Perusia teneretur, Roma relicta est* (*GR* 5, 36). Even thereafter, the city retained enough defenders to prevent Agilulf from taking it: *Et quia nos qui intra civitatem fuimus Deo protegente manus eius* (Agilulf) *evasimus...* (*ibid.*)

[161] See Spera 1999, 418, with catalogue entry UT 35, on p. 49.

further inferred from the Greek inscription on the interior keystone of the gate, which I would date to the sixth century.[162] With the final heightening of its towers and the other architectural modifications undertaken in its latest construction phases, likewise best attributed to the sixth century, the Porta Appia may thus be imagined to have taken on the appearance of a miniature citadel, surrounded by ancillary structures utilized by its garrison.

A second hint of peripheral settlement comes from nearby at the Porta Latina, just inside of which the church of S. Giovanni in Porta Latina was built in the first half of the sixth century.[163] It is a curious development, occurring as it did in a region never densely populated even in the high empire (or at any time thereafter, up to the present). While the extramural stretches of the Via Latina were quite rich in cemeteries, martyrs' shrines, and churches likely to draw substantial crowds of the faithful,[164] this does not explain the decision to build another church in a seemingly isolated and undistinguished intramural location, far from the holy sites and relics that abounded a mile and more outside the Wall. Given that the only known, substantial "inhabited" structure within an extensive radius was the Wall itself, it is possible that the church was intended in part for the use of soldiers (and customs officials?) based around the Porta Latina.

Yet the construction of this church may also imply the existence of a civilian population, as may the approximately contemporary churches installed just outside the Portae Tiburtina and Salaria.[165] In the first place, the garrison on the Wall can be expected to have attracted a cadre of service personnel and "camp followers" concerned with meeting the needs of the soldiers stationed there. Perhaps the frequent repairs carried out on the Wall also occasioned the creation of semi-permanent settlements of laborers at various times. Second, the productive land just outside the Wall was worked by a labor force that I imagine to have lived primarily within its protective confines.[166] Anyone seeking to reach such extramural fields

---

[162] See Appendix C.

[163] The proposed dates range between 500 and 550; see Appendix B, n. 5.

[164] See the comprehensive list of sites on the Via Latina in the CD-Rom gazetteer that accompanies the *Suburbium* volume (Pergola *et al.*, 2003); in addition to the more famous sites like S. Stefano, S. Eugenia, and SS. Gordianus et Epimachus, more than twenty anonymous shrines are recorded; I thank R. Coates-Stephens for pointing this out to me.

[165] See Reekmans 1968, 184 and 196. There is also the church of S. Giovanni e Paolo by the Porta Aurelia on the Janiculum, mentioned for the first time in the Einsiedeln Itineraries; see Reekmans 1989, 899; and the oratory of S. Euplo, just outside the Porta Ostiensis, mentioned in the eighth-century inscription from S. Maria in Cosmedin cited below at n. 170.

[166] See above nn. 32–34. For continued attestations of extramural zones of production, see below n. 169.

will have been best off living as close as possible to the gate nearest their property, thereby saving a long walk along the inside of the Wall in many cases made longer by the closure of the *posterulae*. Finally, it is worth mentioning L. Pani Ermini's suggestion that the growing monumental Christian infrastructure in the suburbs might have prompted a centrifugal movement of associated personnel, "tied through building projects, services, cottage industry, commerce and whatever else was required to the many (extramural) sanctuaries," whom she seems to imagine dwelling just inside the Wall.[167] All told, then, there is good reason to think that the fortifications, in addition to drawing concentrations of inhabitants, will have conditioned the distribution of other people independently occupied in the urban periphery.

Hard data in support of these hypotheses are hard to come by, but certainly their scarcity need not reflect an equally desolate reality. As the dwellings of all but the most elevated classes were, by the later sixth century, built increasingly in perishable materials notoriously difficult to locate archaeologically, buildings like the two relatively monumental, stone-built structures erected near the Portae Appia and Latina may represent only the tip of the iceberg of civilian as well as military settlement.[168] Some corroboration comes from the clusters of private housing that arose around the Porta Maggiore and the Porta Metronia in the ninth and tenth centuries,[169] which are certainly more likely to have been

---

[167] "...legata per lavori edilizi, per servizi, per produzioni artigianali, per commerci e per quant'altro necessario, ai molti santuari..." (Pani Ermini 1999, 39 and ff.). It should be said, however, that many of the important suburban shrines were located a rather inconvenient walking distance outside the Wall, and further that extramural monasteries, assistential structures, baths, *habitacula*, etc., were filled with a stable population of caretakers and dependent recipients of Church charity permanently resident outside the Wall; see e.g. Pani Ermini 1989, 861; Reekmans 1968, esp. 189ff.

[168] Outmoded generalizations about wooden hovels replacing grand *domus* and *insulae* in the early Middle Ages aside, there is no doubt that building in wood became substantially more prevalent; at Rome, raw clay seems also to have been increasingly used. Already in 397, the emperors had to mandate the removal of "huts or shacks" presumably made of such ephemeral materials from the Campus Martius (*CTh.* 14, 14: *Eos, qui in campo Martio casas seu tuguria conlocare temptaverint...*). Especially for previously undeveloped areas like those around the Portae Appia and Latina, where there were neither older buildings to occupy nor ready sources of *spolia*, the association of a working-class population with "perishable" housing seems permissible. On residential building in early-medieval Rome, in addition to the works cited above in nn. 122–4, see Santangeli Valenzani 2002, 419–26.

[169] At the Porta Maggiore, early-medieval remains are attested to go with the property documents that show growing settlement here from the mid ninth century (see Coates-Stephens 1996, 242 and esp. 2004, 115–25; also Hubert 1990, 76); for the Porta Metronia, we are limited to textual sources of the tenth and eleventh centuries, which mention a number of habitations in the vicinity (Hubert 1990, 77–9, with n. 50).

attracted by ready access to plots of cultivated land outside the circuit (along with, in these cases, the proximity of functioning aqueducts) than by the presence of whatever permanent garrison, if any, remained along the Wall.[170]

Indicators of this type nuance the picture of intramural settlement in important ways, not least by reaffirming the role of gates as foci of concentrated activity. Still, they are the exceptions that prove the rule that the Wall was sparsely populated around most of its perimeter. If the topographical signature of the circuit was initially most pronounced horizontally, its defining characteristic beginning in the fifth century was its verticality. When it was made simultaneously higher and more sparing of access, the monumental physicality of the Wall *per se* was enhanced, just as the sharp contours of the flanking swathe it had once cut through its environs began to broaden, fade, and ultimately blend into the encroaching countryside. Thereafter, the gates and curtains of the enceinte stood out more with each passing generation. Scrupulously maintained in their full "imperial" glory, they were a living testament to the high-water mark reached by the physical fabric of the imperial capital, at a time when the surrounding vestiges of imperial Rome looked ever-less defined, more rural, and quite literally lower and humbler. Nor was this effect lost on contemporaries. As we shall see, the perceived importance of the Wall grew in lock step with its corporeal prominence. The more the city drew away from it, the more tenaciously Romans used it in the definition of their surroundings.

---

[170] Agricultural activities on some scale are indicated at the Porta Maggiore by the discovery of several millstones, perhaps belonging to the tenth-century watermill described in the documents reported in Hubert 1990, 76. Throughout the early Middle Ages, the land outside a number of other gates (the Portae Appia/S. Sebastiano, Ostiensis/S. Paolo, Portuensis, etc.) remained the site of intensive farming, of which several eighth-century inscriptions detailing donations of properties by Roman nobles to the Church furnish the most telling proof: see De Francesco 2003, 537–43; and on the most famous among them, still located in the narthex of S. Maria in Cosmedin, Bertolini 1947, 142–5. For mention of *horti* outside the Porta Portuensis in the sixth century, see above n. 46.

5 | Sacred geography, interrupted

From the moment of its construction, the Aurelian Wall began markedly to affect the manner in which Romans lived and worked and moved, and thus to alter the physical contours of the city, as the previous chapter has, I hope, shown. It remains to be seen how the new fortifications came to affect the less tangible aspects of Rome's urban identity: the characterization and classification of urban space, and the body of convention, civic and religious – the two are effectively inseparable – that had long distinguished a city center which in reality transitioned quite imperceptibly into its surroundings. The following, then, is an attempt to explore how the Wall first altered and ultimately (re)created prevailing notions of urban boundaries, beginning under the last pagan emperors and continuing into the age of papal supremacy.

Along with these changed boundaries came new and different prescriptions for the use of territory on both sides of the line, above all in matters of sacred cult, which evolved beyond recognition in the first centuries of the Wall's existence. But for all that pagans and Christians took conspicuously different approaches to the distinction between urban and suburban space, and the activities appropriate to each sphere, they were nearly unanimous in their choice of the enceinte as the intervening threshold. As the clear and enduring separator between these "inner" and "outer" zones, the Wall gave physical form and context to a sequence of shifting religious and cultural paradigms that redefined the relationship between interior and exterior space, each of which was in turn privileged over the other. In the process, city and suburbs crystallized into more readily differentiated entities, which proceeded along increasingly divergent historical trajectories as "Rome" grew to be coextensive with its walled perimeter.

5.1 *Muros dilatavit, pomerio addidit*: the immuring of the *pomerium*

The Aurelian Wall became a fulcrum in Rome's sacred landscape in *c.* 274, even before its completion, when according to the *HA* Aurelian expanded the *pomerium*, an undertaking described – tellingly – immediately after the notice of the Wall's construction: "Adhering to the counsel of the Senate, he (Aurelian) expanded the walls of the city of Rome. Yet he did not add to the *pomerium* at that time, but afterwards."[1] Several scholars have denied that Aurelian did any such thing, oddly assuming that the *pomerium* had reached its greatest extent under Vespasian in AD 75, and thereby in effect denying its strict correlation with the perimeter of the new Wall, which manifestly diverged in places from the *pomerium* of the high empire.[2] Yet there is every reason to believe that Aurelian did enlarge the area of the *pomerium*, and that he indeed made it coterminous with the defenses of the city.

The notice in the *HA* is itself good evidence to this effect. The author makes a point of saying that the *pomerium* was not expanded when the Wall was begun, but only somewhat later, apparently in conjunction with the defeat of Zenobia and the reunification of the empire.[3] This clarification has no sense at all unless the late-fourth-century audience of the *HA* was expected to associate the *pomerium* directly with the Wall, and to know that it had been expanded beyond its Vespasianic limits, these clearly delineated by the boundary *cippi* last renewed under Hadrian, of which some surely remained visible. The *pomerium* was thus greater than it had been in Hadrian's time, and readily enough conflated with the enceinte to prompt the specification that Aurelian waited some time after construction on the Wall commenced to expand it. It is difficult to escape the further conclusion that the two circuits were made effectively identical, nor is there any reason to doubt that the development occurred under Aurelian.

Archaeological data also broadly back the case for a third-century enlargement of the *pomerium*, particularly on the eastern flank of the city,

[1] *HA Aur.* 21, 9:...*adhibito consilio senatus muros urbis Romae dilatavit. Nec tamen pomerio addidit eo tempore, sed postea.*
[2] See e.g. Dmitriev 2004, 572–7 (a particularly garbled account); Liverani 2004, esp. 358; Coarelli 1997a, 90–2; Syme 1978, esp. 222–3. Lugli accepted an Aurelianic expansion in the Campus Martius, but pointedly denied any correlation between Wall and *pomerium* (*Monumenti* II, 98). Homo thought Aurelian made the *pomerium* co-extensive with his Wall, as – cautiously – does Andreussi (Homo 1904, 305–6; Andreussi 1988, 232; cf. also Labrousse 1937, 172–3).
[3] Such is the apparent implication of the digression that immediately follows, where the author recalls the custom that only emperors who had enlarged the confines of the empire with the addition of "some piece of barbarian land" had the right to add to the *pomerium*, whence Aurelian could not properly have done so until his triumph in 274; see *Aur.* 21, 10: *pomerio autem neminem principum licet addere nisi eum, qui agri barbarici aliqua parte Romanam rem p. locupletaverit.*

where burials continued at numerous sites inside the line later followed by the Aurelian Wall through the second century and into the third, at which point they tailed off markedly. Though it can no longer be taken completely for granted that the presence of burials inevitably indicates an extrapomerial location, as cemeteries inside the Claudian *pomerium* around the Portae Flaminia and Salaria manifestly continued to function for some time after Claudius, a suggestive pattern nonetheless emerges: in peripheral areas of the city later enclosed by the Wall, most if not all of them outside the pre-Aurelianic *pomerium*, the deposition of corpses effectively stopped upon its construction.[4] Along the Via Appia, for example, human remains continued to be interred in the tombs of the wealthy families that lined the road at least through the second century, after which burials tailed off, never to be resumed.[5] Something similar occurred at another cemetery inside the Porta Ardeatina, straddling the modern Viale delle Terme di Caracalla.[6] The scenario seemingly repeated itself between the Portae Tiburtina and Praenestina-Labicana, where the Wall divided a sprawling cemeterial zone in regular use for the three centuries prior to its construction, at which point the acres of tombs on the inside were covered over with dirt and rubble and transformed into gardens, according to Lanciani, and burials became far less frequent, if they did not stop altogether.[7] In short, over the entirety of the area

---

[4] Coates-Stephens has justly called attention to continuing burials inside the Claudian *pomerium* around the Portae Flaminia and Salaria, a phenomenon with weighty implications for the current understanding of funerary practice at Rome that has yet to be properly explored (was intrapomerial burial permissible – or at any rate practiced – under certain circumstances...?); see Coates-Stephens 2004, 61. As Coates-Stephens thinks the Porta Maggiore area was already included within the Claudian *pomerium*, the numerous second- and third-century burials at the cemetery within lead him to conclude that intrapomerial burial in fact occurred on a massive scale (*ibid.* 60–2; 76–7; 106–9). If this area remained extrapomerial until Aurelian, however, as I think it may have, it would be easier to continue to see intrapomerial burial during the imperial period as exceptional. The issue of the eastern extension of the Claudian *pomerium* hinges on two questionable pomerial *cippi*, one allegedly observed by Ligorio near the Porta Chiusa, and another extremely fragmentary one found during the demolition of the "tre archi" bridge not far inside the Porta Maggiore, where it was reused in the Middle Ages (Coates-Stephens 2004, 40; see also Labrousse 1937, 180ff.; cf. *BullCom* 1909, 132). Given that the mutilated "tre archi" stone was not found *in situ*, the case for a Claudian extension of the *pomerium* as far east as the Porta Maggiore (and the nearby cemetery) remains to my mind open to question.

[5] See Lugli, *I monumenti* I, 432ff.; cf. *LTUR* 4, 294.

[6] See Quilici 1987, esp. 732–3, with prior bibliographical references; cf. also Patterson 2000, 96.

[7] See Lanciani in *BullCom* 8 (1880), esp. 51–2; *LTUR* 4, 276–7, see under *Sepulchrum: Aurelii*. Coates-Stephens has argued *contra* Lanciani that the cemetery continued to function as such into the fourth century (2004, 76–7 and 106–9). Though the garbled reports of nineteenth- and twentieth-century excavations in the area permit little certainty, the indicators seem to me

encircled by the Wall – and only this area – instances of burial datable between the later third century and *c.* 410 are far more rare than they were previously, and seem largely to be confined to the *ad hoc* and perhaps clandestine reuse of existing sepulchers.[8] There is thus all the more reason to think that Aurelian extended the *pomerium* to the Wall, and that the force of the ancient prohibition against burial within its confines, themselves redrawn and thereafter embodied by the Wall, remained fully in vigor.[9] Indeed, if Coates-Stephens is right that the busy cemetery inside the Porta Maggiore was already inside the Claudian *pomerium*, one might even propose, in light of its progressive abandonment from the later third century on, that the traditional role of the *pomerium* was reasserted upon its amalgamation with Aurelian's new fortifications.[10]

Nor is there anything particularly surprising in what amounted to a restoration of the longstanding equivalence between the physical and sacral boundaries of the *urbs*. From earliest memory, the *pomerium* had been inextricably bound up in the definition of the urban perimeter, and the archaic rites performed at the founding of a new city, when the *sulcus primigenius* was ploughed where the walls were later to rise.[11] For Romans of the historical period, the term itself was derived from its association with the urban enceinte; according to Varro, it came from *post murum*, thus reflecting the standard positioning of the *pomerium* along the inner

---

insufficient to prove large-scale continuing use after the 270s; a single Christian epitaph was found, along with the occasional chi-rho symbol, which should date to the time of Constantine or later. Yet these are few in number, and might well belong to the period of Alaric's sieges of the city in 408–10, when other similarly hasty depositions first occurred inside the Wall (see below n. 35); Coates-Stephens acknowledges the possibility that the late burials "were carried out in a time of crisis: perhaps plague, famine or siege, when the normal restrictions on burial were relaxed" (*ibid.* 107); the years 408–10 again come to mind.

[8] See *LTUR* 4, see under *Sepulchrum: Aurelii*; *ibid.*, see under *Sepulchrum: Domitii*; Quilici 1987, 733. For previous examples of intrapomerial burial under the republic and earlier empire, see Simonelli 2001, 144–6.

[9] On the force of the ancient prohibition, see Lambert 1997, 285ff.; Toynbee 1971, 48–9; on Rome, cf. also Homo 1904, 228–31. The ban was reaffirmed several times in the third and fourth centuries, and was still valid in the sixth, when a law of 290 was included in Justinian's Code (*CJ* 3, 44, 12; cf. below n. 36).

[10] In this case, known instances of intrapomerial burial in Rome from the century preceding the building of the Wall would greatly outnumber those from the century that followed; on the late burials, see above n. 7.

[11] See e.g. Aulus Gellius, *Noct. Att.* 13, 14, 1: *"Pomerium" quid esset, augures populi Romani, qui libros de auspiciis scripserunt, istiusmodi sententia definierunt: Pomerium est locus intra agrum effatum per totius urbis circuitum pone muros regionibus certeis determinatus, qui facit finem urbani auspicii*; cf. Andreussi 1988, 220ff.; Rebuffat 1986, 348–9; Rykwert 1976, 129ff.

facing of a circuit wall.[12] At Rome, it had corresponded closely – though not everywhere exactly – with the Servian Wall by the end of the republic, an association that blurred as the city grew and the *pomerium* came to be expanded into regions outside the old circuit, including Testaccio and parts of the northern Campus Martius.[13] What then more natural, than that the builder of Rome's new enceinte, the self-proclaimed *restitutor* of Roman tradition, should have taken the opportunity to recreate the archaic nexus between *muri* and *pomerium*?[14] Practically from its inception, in sum, the Aurelian Wall in effect "equaled" the religious frontiers of the urban center; thereafter, it came to represent many other things besides, as we shall see.

5.2   The Wall, the law, and the definition of urban space in the fourth century

In 1891, Christian Hülson published a bronze slave collar belonging to a certain Asellus, the slave of an official attached to the administration of the *annona* at Rome.[15] Hülson dated the collar roughly between the reign of Constantine and the beginning of the fifth century, on the basis of its resemblance to a number of similar examples, all likely produced in the fourth century, when they apparently came into vogue following Constantine's ban on the branding of slaves.[16] The collar of Asellus differs from the others in one crucial respect: its inscription specifies the wall of the city as the limit beyond which its bearer was forbidden to pass: "I am Asellus, the slave of Praeiectus, an official of the *praefectus annonae*.

---

[12] Varro, *De lingua Latina* 5, 143: *terram unde exculpserant, fossam vocabant et introrsum iactam murum. Post ea qui fiebat orbis, urbis principium; qui quod erat post murum, postmoerium dictum eiusque auspicia urbana finiuntur;* specifically on Rome, cf. Livy, *Ab urbe cond.* 1, 44, 1ff.; on the debate over whether *post murum* indicates an intramural or extramural position, see Simonelli 2001, 135.

[13] Testaccio: Labrousse 1937, 174–8; Campus Martius: Andreussi 1988, 233–4; Coarelli 1977, 821–3; on the Esquiline, see above. Meanwhile, the Aventine was included in the *pomerium* only under Claudius, though it lay inside the Servian circuit; see Labrousse.

[14] The term *restitutor* appears with notable frequency on Aurelian's coinage, both in the previously attested form *restitutor orbis*, and the unprecedented *restitutor saeculi*: see Watson 1999, 174–5; Homo 1904, 126, n. 1. On Aurelian's conservatism, particularly of the religious variety, cf. Watson 1999, 201–2; 207; etc.

[15] *Röm. Mitth.* 6 (1891), 341–3.

[16] *Ibid.* 342–3. Other examples were published by G. B. De Rossi (De Rossi 1874; also in *BullCom* 1887, 265–6 and 286–96). For the proposal that collars were introduced after Constantine banned branding, see De Rossi 1874, 60.

I have gone outside the Wall; capture me, because I have fled, and return me to Flora at the To(n)sores."[17] Asellus, in other words, would have become a fugitive the moment he set foot outside the Aurelian Wall.

As far as I know, there is no record at Rome of any fixed boundaries used to regulate the comings and goings of slaves before the construction of the Wall, nor do the remaining fourth-century collars, all of which seemingly belonged to slaves in the employ of private owners, prescribe a set line of demarcation. On the basis of this admittedly unique text, however, it appears that Aurelian's Wall had soon developed into precisely such a boundary specifically for those slaves attached to the urban administration, or more particularly to that of the *annona*.[18] Within a century of its construction, that is, the Wall was being used by the administrators of the city as a means of controlling the movements of their human assets. Here is convincing testimony to the effect that the Wall was used expressly to keep certain groups of people inside the city, in addition to preventing others from entering. The collar of Asellus is, moreover, an initial indication that, from an official standpoint, Rome's enceinte had become a means of defining and circumscribing the confines of the city proper, separating a particular sort of urban space from what lay beyond.

A law in the Theodosian Code promulgated in 382 more clearly demonstrates the extent to which, within a century of its completion, the Wall had developed into an autonomous mechanism of spatial definition. The reigning emperors declared that no senator was, under any circumstances, to wear military attire "inside the walls" (*intra moenia*).[19] In essence, the mandate is but an updated reiteration of ancient prohibitions against bearing weapons and other trappings of military authority inside the

---

[17] *ASELLUS SERVUS PRAEIECTI OFFICIALIS PRAEFECTI ANNONIS FORAS MURU EXIVI TENEME QUIA FUGI REDUC ME AD FLORA AD TOSORES.* The "return address" is very probably in the vicinity of the temple of Flora on the Aventine (as opposed to the one on the Quirinal), a location near the Wall where we should expect to find slaves in the service of the *annona*; see *LTUR* 5, 77, under *To(n)sores.*

[18] Such also is the conclusion of Hülson, (n. 15), 342.

[19] *CTh* 14, 10, 1: *Sine exceptione temporis matutini, dumtaxat intra moenia constitutus, nullus senatorum habitum sibi vindicet militarem, sed chlamydis terrore deposito quieta coloborum ac paenularum induat vestimenta.* In this context, the term *moenia* must refer to an enceinte *per se*, as the alternate translation, "the buildings of the city," is surely too vague to make good sense: I do not see, that is, how the law would have been envisioned in theory, or applied and enforced in reality, if not in relation to a fixed and visible line of demarcation. And though it is addressed to the urban prefect of Constantinople, I cannot imagine that the same statute, or one very much like it, did not apply at Rome, the only capital explicitly named in any of the four laws in the chapter (*CTh* 14, 10) devoted to dress codes in the *urbs*: see below nn. 21 and 22.

pomerium,[20] whence it is the more remarkable that a defensive circuit replaced all mention of the *pomerium* in the new law, thus becoming the sole physical and legal point of reference by which a custom many centuries old was thereafter to be reified and preserved.

Further legislation followed in short order forbidding the wearing of breeches, boots, all garments made of skins, and long hair "inside the city" (*intra urbem*).[21] Considering their close association with the law on senatorial dress, and given further that phrases like *intra urbem* and *in civitate* were practically synonymous with "inside the Wall" in the following centuries, the most likely assumption is that these additional sartorial strictures also took the Wall as their limit.[22] So, too, in terms of the practical application of these statutes, the gates of the Wall present themselves as much the most logical location for their enforcement, where individuals who failed to conform would most easily have been weeded out, and inside of which offenders were unambiguously culpable. By the time of Theodosius, then, long hair, leather breeches, and martial attire went no further than the gates of Rome, immediately inside of which began the privileged zone where distinctively urban modes of dress and deportment were made to prevail.

The famous law of 342 declaring that pagan temples outside the Wall were to be left unharmed suggests that, still earlier, some idea of the enceinte as a spatial terminator unto itself had already come into being.[23] The peculiar phrasing of the law seems to imply a conscious topographical distinction between the intramural and extramural reaches of the city, even possibly a sense that buildings in the two zones separated by the Wall pertained to diverse architectural patrimonies. In this context, it is worth

---

[20] The traditional character of the *pomerium* as the separator between civil and military spheres of competence is well and succinctly outlined in Andreussi 1988, esp. 223–8; cf. Simonelli 2001, 139–51.

[21] All traditional "barbarian" fashions; cf. Pharr 1952, 415, nn. 3 and 6. See *CTh.* 14, 10, 2 (*anno* 397): *Usum tzangarum adque bracarum intra urbem venerabilem nemini liceat usurpare;* the sanction was repeated two years later (14, 10, 3): *Intra urbem Romam nemo vel bracis vel tzangis utatur;* and in 416, leather clothing ("even on slaves") and long hair were added to the list of items banned from "inside the most sacred city" (14, 10, 4): *Maiores crines, indumenta pellium etiam in servis intra urbem sacratissimam praecipimus inhiberi.*

[22] The heading of the chapter comprising the four laws cited in notes 19 and 21, *De habitu, quo uti oportet intra urbem,* further implies that the same definition of the *urbs*, specified in the first law of 382 with the term *moenia*, applied in all four cases. For the subsequent use of *intra urbem* and similar phrases at Rome, see below, esp. Section 5.4.

[23] *CTh* 16, 10, 3 (addressed to the prefect of Rome): *Quamquam omnis superstitio penitus eruenda sit, tamen volumus, ut aedes templorum, quae extra muros sunt positae, intactae incorruptaeque consistant.*

repeating the observation of Theodora Heres, who remarked that in late
antiquity, monumental structures specifically inside the Aurelian Wall
were most often built in brick, while *opus vittatum* prevailed outside.[24]
The rule does not always hold, nor can it be unequivocally proclaimed that
the Wall was the sole or principal point of reference that dictated the
choice of building materials. Nonetheless, different technical standards do
seem to have prevailed for buildings in an area of the city center that
generally corresponded with the defensive perimeter, which cannot readily
be explained on purely practical or logistical grounds.[25] Perhaps *opus
latericium*, the preferred medium of early-imperial monumental architecture, was thought more appropriate to the intramural urban center.[26]
Whatever the explanation, the explicit intra-/extra-mural distinction
drawn in the law of 342 reveals the existence of a conceptual framework
that could, at least in theory, have produced zones of architectonic differ-
entiation based on the Wall *per se*.

The appearance of the Wall in fourth-century law thus swells the list of
diverse functions, once imputed to older administrative boundaries
between *urbs* and suburbs, which it subsumed unto itself. To the examples
of the customs-circuit, mentioned several times previously, and the *pomerium* as a determinant of funerary practice, we may now add the traditional
significance of the latter as the line within which "urban" dress codes (and
building codes?) were expected to prevail. In the collar of Asellus, there is
the further hint of a wholly new sort of regulation, very plausibly inspired
by the presence of the new fortifications themselves. As it altered the
appearance of the urban center and the practical exigencies of life in and

[24] Heres 1982, 60; cf. also Bertelli 2001, 154.

[25] Indeed, the many sites where tufa was quarried – along the banks of the Aniene, just north of
the city; east and south of the Lago di Bracciano; in the vicinity of the Colli Albani, etc. – were
often as close or closer to the city center than the primary sites of brick production
(on which see above Chapter 2); on the provenance of the tufa used at Rome in late antiquity,
see Bertelli 2001, 151ff. Nor can the choice of materials be linked with issues of wealth, class,
patronage and the like: the regular use of *opus vittatum* in many of the great extramural
churches (S. Agnese, S. Sebastiano, S. Lorenzo, S. Pancrazio, St. Peter's and St. Paul's...), and in
"secular" structures as important as the Villa of Maxentius shows that there was no particular
stigma attached to its use. The few exceptions of note include the intramural churches of
S. Vitale (early-fifth century) and S. Giovanni in Porta Latina (sixth century), both in *opus
vittatum*; and the extramural brick mausoleum of Constantia adjacent to S. Agnese, of
mid-fourth-century date.

[26] At Santa Maria Maggiore, built under Sixtus III (432–40), the foundations were built in *opus
vittatum*, while the visible walls above ground level were all in *opus latericium*; here perhaps is a
hint that *latericium* was a "prestige" building technique preferred over *vittatum* for an
important intramural commission.

around it, that is, the Wall began also to prescribe the limits within which assorted legal and cultural traditions of imperial Rome held continued sway, and thus to recreate the *urbs* proper in its own image, or better its shape.

In the end, Aurelian's assimilation of the *pomerium* with the Wall made it all the easier to abrogate the symbolic resonance of the former, while preserving the force of its constraints on the regulation of urban space. Little wonder that Rome's newly Christian masters availed themselves of the opportunity to substitute the more religiously neutral, and indeed increasingly "Christianized,"[27] Wall for the indelibly "pagan" boundary it mirrored. The *pomerium* was not forgotten by the later fourth century, as the erudite digression on the subject included by the pagan author of the *Vita Aureliani* in the *HA* shows;[28] rather, it was willfully ignored. Thereafter, the Wall featured more and more prominently in the articulation of urban space, as the Christian Church asserted itself as the primary constituted authority over nearly every aspect of Roman life, and reinvented the city as the capital of an *imperium christianum*. If we are to explain how the equation between the Wall and the *urbs*, forged amidst the legal and cultural institutions of the late empire, flourished and ramified in the mutated urban matrix of the early Middle Ages, we must first explain how the enceinte became a focal point in the sacred geography of Christian Rome.

5.3   Spheres of sacrality and the circumscription of *Roma Christiana*

In 416, Pope Innocent I sent a peevish reply to a series of questions posed to him by Decentius, the bishop of Eugubinum (Gubbio).[29] One of Decentius' queries concerned the *fermentum*, the host consecrated by the pope at Sunday mass, and carried to the priests officiating at the same time at titular churches elsewhere in the city, whose duties prevented them from receiving communion directly from their bishop. By way of defending what was strictly a papal prerogative, Innocent informed Decentius that he sent the *fermentum* only to the *tituli* "inside the city" (*intra urbem*); and that it was not to be carried further afield to surrounding parishes (*parrochiae*) and cemetery-churches (*cimeteria*), which were

---

[27] See above Chapter 3.4.   [28] *HA Aur.* 21, 10–11.   [29] See Cabié 1973.

staffed by resident clergy possessed of the distinctive privilege of conse-
crating the host themselves.[30] All the priests in the predominantly rural
diocese of Gubbio, implies the pope, were to enjoy the same degree of
independence from their episcopal seat.

The passage is precious for its bearing on Roman practice. The polar
opposition between funerary and intra-urban space leaves no room for
doubt: the *de facto* line of demarcation between *urbs* and the surrounding
zone of *cimeteria* was the Aurelian Wall, just beyond which expanses of
Christian burials began.[31] Thus, in the organizational scheme adumbrated
in Innocent's letter, the Wall also separated two discrete spheres of ecclesiastical administration. Masses conducted outside of it were performed by
priests whose liturgical duties – and by extension their relationship to the
pope and the Church of Rome, in the geographically narrowest sense of
the phrase – differed markedly from those of the titular priests who
officiated *intra urbem*.[32] In ecclesiastical as well as secular legislation, the
enceinte had begun to delimit the physical compass of the "city of Rome";
and already under Innocent I, *urbs* and *muri* were, technically speaking,
effectively the same thing.

As the Wall's early rise to prominence on the horizons of Christian
Rome is integrally related to the resting places of the Christian dead, the
subject of funerary topography requires closer attention. A sample at last
count comprising approximately 500 intramural burials leaves no doubt
that the inhumation of corpses inside the Wall was an exceptional occurrence until the middle of the sixth century.[33] Though the catacombs went
progressively out of use from *c.* 400, open-air cemeteries, often associated
with the great suburban cemetery-basilicas and a host of smaller martyrial
churches and shrines, grew and multiplied until the period of the Gothic
Wars (536–52).[34] Many of them remained in use for some time thereafter,
at least into the seventh century, though the sudden increase in urban
burials from the mid sixth century indicates that the Gothic Wars were

---

[30] Cabié 1973, lines 92–101: *De fermento vero quod die dominica per titulos mittimus, superflue
nos consulere voluisti, cum omnes ecclesiae nostrae intra civitatem sint constitutae. Quarum
presbiteri, quia die ipsa propter plebem sibi creditam nobiscum convenire non possunt, idcirco
fermentum a nobis confectum per acolitos accipiunt, ut se a nostra communione maxime illa die
non iudicent separatos. Quod per parrochias fieri debere non puto quia nec longe portanda sunt
sacramenta nec nos per cimeteria diversa constitutis presbiteris destinamus et presbiteri eorum
conficiendorum ius habeant atque licentiam.*

[31] Cf. Fiocchi Nicolai 2000a, 354; Pani Ermini 1999, 42.

[32] See Chavasse 1993, esp. 64–6 and 253–5; cf. Saxer 1989, 924ff.; Cabié 1973, 51–3.

[33] Meneghini and Santangeli Valenzani 2004, 105.

[34] Nieddu 2003; Fiocchi Nicolai 2001, 121ff.; 2000a.

indeed a turning point, after which burials *intra muros* were never again uncommon until the final dissolution of papal power in Rome in 1870.[35] The physical evidence thus concords both with the continued injunctions against urban burial repeated by secular and religious authorities alike,[36] and with the archaeological picture from the rest of Italy and Gaul, where intramural burial became common only from the sixth century.[37]

The substantial lag between the Christianization of the empire and the rupture with "pagan" funerary practice represented by the migration of human remains into cities is a complex subject that remains to be fully explored, though it has benefited from a surge of recent interest.[38] For present purposes, it suffices to say that the Christian authorities at Rome almost always respected the limit of the Aurelianic *pomerium*, now embodied by the Wall, for over two centuries; and that all of Rome's Christian cemeteries, including those early examples that predated the Wall, were situated outside of it. Over the course of the fourth and fifth centuries, new and expanded burial grounds crowded ever-closer to the circuit, without transgressing its confines.[39]

There was thus a preponderance of Christian *loca sancta* within three miles of the Wall, where Rome's masses and luminaries – martyrs, confessors, popes, and clergy – alike were buried from the beginnings of the faith into the sixth century.[40] Following the "peace of the Church" in 313, the Roman suburbs were first to be transformed by a panoply of

[35] Meneghini and Santangeli Valenzani 2004, 103–25; 1993; Fiocchi Nicolai 2003, 944–7; 2001, 134ff.; Vismara 1999; Cantino Wataghin 1999, 148–50; Osborne 1985, 281ff. The archaeological record thus supports Procopius, who alluded to the haphazard disposal of corpses inside the Wall during the Gothic siege of 537 (*BG* 2, 3, 19), after which the traditional prohibition seems never to have regained its erstwhile force. Zosimus describes a similar situation in his account of the Gothic siege of Rome in 408 (Zos. 5, 39); and it is indeed to this event that the scattered and rather *ad hoc* fifth-century tombs in the city are often attributed: see e.g. Meneghini and Santangeli Valenzani 2004, 125; Fiocchi Nicolai 2001, 136.

[36] A law against urban burials promulgated in 290 was included in Justinian's law-code (*CJ* 3, 44, 12); and in 563, the Church Council of Braga again strongly discouraged the practice, though admitting of certain exceptions. On the Roman juridical tradition on burials *in urbe* and its relevance to late-antique and early-medieval realities, see Vismara 1999; Cantino Wataghin 1999, 147ff.; Lambert 1997.

[37] See Fiocchi Nicolai 2003, esp. 947ff.; Cantino Wataghin 1999, 158ff.; Cantino Wataghin and Lambert 1998, 89–114; Lambert 1997, 289ff.

[38] The recasting of traditional relationships between the living and the dead during the transition from antiquity to the Middle Ages has been addressed to some extent by all the scholars of funerary topography cited in the preceding note; see also Picard 1998, 311–20; Brown 1981, 3–8.

[39] See e.g. Fiocchi Nicolai 2000a, 354.

[40] The popes, of course, continued to be buried outside the Wall (at St. Peter's) through the early Middle Ages; see Picard 1969.

monumental edifices that rose around the shrines of the illustrious dead. By Constantine's death in 337, as many as six cavernous cemetery-basilicas were complete or under construction, in addition to St. Peter's and the smaller foundation at the grave of St. Paul, the majority erected at the instigation of the imperial family.[41] Inside the city, only the Lateran basilica, itself in a peripheral region adjacent to the Wall, visibly proclaimed the ascendancy of the Church.[42] Under Constantine's immediate successors, still more churches punctuated the countryside around the graves of the martyrs, soon covering nearly all the major approaches to the city, at a time when the first titular churches were just beginning to make tentative inroads on the intramural cityscape.[43]

These peripheral shrines were the vibrant epicenter of Christian Rome in the fourth century, nodes of concentrated sanctity where the faithful most poignantly and visibly embodied the ideal community of the Church on the festival days of Rome's legion of martyrs, and constant foci for the private devotions of streams of residents and pilgrims seeking immersion in the aura of the saints.[44] In the 360s, Jerome and his school friends famously spent their Sundays groping about the stygian recesses of the catacombs, which they circled the city to visit.[45] Over the following two decades, Pope Damasus (366–84) imbued the crypts of the martyrs with an architectural presence worthy of their popular profile by widening, embellishing, and illuminating heavily frequented spaces, and appending commemorative epigrams to the most celebrated tombs.[46] Around 400, the Spanish poet Prudentius followed in Jerome's footsteps, pausing frequently to marvel at Damasus' elaborate interventions along what was

---

[41] The remaining six, all inaugurated by mid-century at the latest, are S. Agnese, S. Lorenzo, SS. Pietro e Marcellino, S. Sebastiano, the anonymous basilica on the Via Praenestina, and the recently discovered basilica on the Via Ardeatina, likely the foundation of Pope Marcus (AD 336). On the new and monumental Christian presence in the suburbs, see Fiocchi Nicolai 2003, 926ff., 2001, 53ff.; Pani Ermini 1995, 176ff.; 1989; Reekmans 1968. For the Via Ardeatina basilica, see Fiocchi Nicolai, Del Moro, Nuzzo and Spera 1995–96.

[42] Cf. Krautheimer 1980, 21ff. The only other intramural Constantinian foundation was the nearby church of S. Croce in Gerusalemme, inconspicuously installed in a hall of the Sessorian Palace.

[43] Fiocchi Nicolai 2001, 59–60; Reekmans 1968, 182–3.

[44] Cf. Trout 2005; Fiocchi Nicolai 2003, 933ff.; Brown 1981, 40–9.

[45] Jerome, *In Hiezechielem* 12, 243–9 (*CCSL* 75, 556–7): *Dum essem Romae puer et liberalibus studiis erudirer, solebam cum ceteris eiusdem aetatis et propositi, diebus Dominicis sepulcra apostolorum et martyrum circumire, crebroque cryptas ingredi quae, in terrarum profunda defossae, ex utraque parte ingredientium per parietes habent corpora sepultorum, et quia obscura sunt omnia, ut propemodum illud propheticum compleatur. Descendant ad infernum viventes....*

[46] See Fiocchi Nicolai 2001, 79ff.; Saghy 2000; Curran 2000, 146–55.

by then a well-traveled sacral highway.[47] Even after the urban interior had
become saturated with churches by the later fifth century, the prestige of
the suburban sites and the attraction of the abundant relics housed there
ensured for them a continuing prominence that was soon institutionalized
via networks of stational liturgies, which bound the city center to its
intensely sanctified periphery.[48]

Rome's extramural environs, then, were the heart of a new geography of
the sacred, the native ground of the "cult of the Saints." Though it has not
escaped notice that this privileged territorial halo began with the defensive
perimeter,[49] the power of the Wall's corporeal presence, and the conceptual resonances it spawned, have been insufficiently emphasized. The
Aurelian Wall bodily anchored the radiating vistas of the Christianized
suburbium that stretched away from its gates in every direction, becoming
in the process a towering landmark in a reconditioned ensemble of urban
and suburban space. It was the starting point for the newly numinous,
and – crucially – it was perceived as such by contemporaries.

A first hint comes in Prudentius' description of the crypt of the Martyr
Hippolytus, located outside the Porta Tiburtina on the site of today's
church of S. Lorenzo. In a passage replete with images of spatial transition,
written in the form of an itinerary, Prudentius began by placing the shrine
"not far from the outer rampart in the pomerial fields," where "a crypt
opens up, submerged in hidden caverns." The implied passage through the
Wall is more explicitly mirrored a few lines later in the depiction of the
antechamber of the crypt, in which "the day enters the first doorway, as far
as the top of the yawning aperture, and lights up the threshold (*limina*) of
the vestibule."[50] In approaching the holy precincts of the martyr's grave,
the pilgrim traversed a series of thresholds – strongly reminiscent of
Damasus' evocative *sanctorum limina* – that began with the Wall itself.[51]
Later in the century, Sidonius Apollinaris echoed Prudentius in a letter to
his friend Herenius describing his arrival at Rome in 467, when he was

---

[47] See esp. *Peristephanon* 11 and 12, with Roberts 1993, 148–87.
[48] A topic discussed in more detail below. See Chavasse 1993; Saxer 1989, 932ff.; Osborne 1985, 284ff.; cf. Pani Ermini 1999, 40ff.
[49] See e.g. Pani Ermini 2001, 267–8; Fiocchi Nicolai 2001, 217; Marazzi 2000, 39; Spera 1999, 382.
[50] *Peristephanon* 11, 153–58: *Haud procul extremo culta ad pomeria vallo/mersa latebrosis crypta patet foveis./Huius in occultum gradibus via prona reflexis/ire per anfractus luce latente docet./Primas namque fores summo tenus intrat hiatu/inlustratque dies limina vestibuli.* Cf. Roberts 1993, 160–1.
[51] See (e.g.) *Epigrammata Damasiana* 32, 3–5: *hic quicumque venit sanctorum limina quaerat;/ inveniet vicina in sede habitare beatos,/ad caelum pariter pietas quos vexit euntes.*

struck by the same concentric layering of the "thresholds of the saints" over the "pomerial" boundary at the Wall.[52]

The responses of Prudentius and Sidonius to the charged liminality of the Wall, their sense of it as the inner confine of a numinous Christian realm, find a compelling architectural parallel in the colonnaded walkways built to link the extramural churches of Rome's leading holy patrons, Saints Peter, Paul, and Lawrence, with their respective gates in the Wall.[53] The porticoes leading to St. Peter's and St. Paul's are first mentioned in Procopius, whose account they predate, as in all probability does the third, to S. Lorenzo, though it appears in writing only in the eighth century.[54] They were most likely standing by the end of the half-century between the pontificates of Hilarus (461–8) and Symmachus (498–514), when the popes embellished all three shrines with constellations of baths, hostels, monasteries, and "dwellings for the poor,"[55] in addition to episcopal residences at St. Peter's and S. Lorenzo, thereby imparting to these complexes the character of quasi-autonomous settlements which they retained through the Middle Ages, during the course of which all were endowed with defensive circuits of their own.[56] By the early-sixth century at the latest, the Wall had thus become the starting point for "sacred ways" to the most prominent extramural sanctuaries, and the threshold between the ancient city within and the "capitals" of the new community of the saints beyond.[57] To step through the Wall was to enter – literally and very physically – into the precincts of Rome's three most celebrated martyrs.

[52] Sidonius Apollinaris, *Ep.* 1, 5, 9: *Ubi priusquam vel pomoeria contingerem, triumphalibus apostolorum liminibus adfusus omnem protinus sensi membris male fortibus explosum esse languorem*; for yet another use of *pomeria* as a metonym for city walls, cf. Paulinus of Pella on the defense of Bazas in SW Gaul in 414 (*Eucharistikon*, 383–5): *Vallanturque urbis pomeria milite Halano acceptaque dataque fide certare parato pro nobis...*
[53] See Fiocchi Nicolai 2001, 116; Reekmans 1989, 909–10; 1968, 195–201.
[54] St. Peter's: *BG* 1, 22, 21; St. Paul's: *BG* 2, 4, 9; S. Lorenzo: *LP* I, 396 and 508.
[55] *Pauperibus habitacula*; see *LP* I, 263.
[56] Generally on the development of the three complexes, see Pani Ermini 2000, 19–25; Reekmans 1989, 909–14; 1968, 195–207; Belli Barsali 1976. The wall around the Vatican was, of course, built by Leo IV (847–55), and that at St. Paul's by John VIII (872–82), while S. Lorenzo was fortified rather later, in *c.* 1200.
[57] Cf. Fiocchi Nicolai 2000b, 229. It is quite possible that the porticoes, in particular the one leading to St. Peter's, were built still earlier, perhaps even before the end of the fourth century, when the colonnaded extension of the Via Triumphalis that terminated at the Pons Aelius was completed in *c.* 380 (see Appendix D). As the covered walkway on the far side of the river between the mausoleum of Hadrian and the basilica was effectively an extension of this route, one might speculate that it was an approximately contemporary project. A similar colonnade rose at nearly the same time at Milan, the primary imperial residence, departing the wall at the Porta Romana and flanking both sides of the road to Rome for 600 m, where it ended in a triumphal

Along the route to St. Peter's, the architectural nexus between the locus of the saint and the city walls was reaffirmed in writing. By the start of the Middle Ages, the visitor to the basilica was confronted by a forest of inscriptions installed in and around the colonnade, six of which were included in a seventh-century epigraphic compendium preserved in a ninth-century manuscript.[58] One text, perhaps placed above the Porta S. Petri, at the approaches to the Pons Aelius, proclaimed:

Peter the gatekeeper has fixed his shrines before the gates
who could deny that this citadel is in the likeness of the heavens? On the other side
the atria of Paul surround the walls (*muros*)
between them is Rome: therefore here sits God.[59]

Another, conjecturally displayed along the portico itself, read:

Now truly like the heavens is famous Rome whose fortifications (*claustra*) proclaim that God is within.[60]

In a variation on the association between the Wall and the enceinte of the Celestial Jerusalem that gained currency from the time of the Honorian heightening in 401–3,[61] the fortified urban nucleus appears here as a terrestrial proxy for the "citadel" of heaven itself. Suspended between the axes of the colonnades running to the churches of Peter and Paul, the twin protectors of heaven and Rome, the Aurelian Wall was the single most visible and compelling symbol of Rome's unique sanctity: it was the bristling cranium of the *caput ecclesiae*, and the "frame" within which the immanence of God became manifest.

---

arch perhaps dedicated under Gratian (see Caporusso 1991, 251–7); in 382–6, Ambrose annexed to the portico the monumental new *basilica apostolorum* (later S. Nazaro), thereby creating an arrangement suggestively similar to the example (precedent?) of St. Peter's.

[58] See *ICUR* 2/1, 99, nos. 7–12. De Rossi was confident that none of the inscriptions transcribed in the original collection dated later than the seventh century (most, in fact, fall between the fourth and the sixth), whence he derived his rough *terminus ante* for the document; more precise chronological indicators for the six inscriptions in question are lacking (95–7). The language of 7, echoed in 12 (see below nn. 59–60), leaves no doubt about its positioning at or near the Porta S. Petri; of the remaining four texts, three can be placed in the general vicinity on internal grounds, leading De Rossi (99) to imagine very plausibly that all six were observed in the area of the gate and the colonnade leading to St. Peter's.

[59] *ICUR* 2/1, 99, no. 7: *Ianitor ante fores fixit sacraria petrus/quis neget has arces instar esse poli/ Parte alia pauli circumdant atria muros/hos inter roma est hic sedet ergo deus.* Pani Ermini (2000, 24) asserts that the inscription describes the ninth-century walls at the Vatican and St. Paul's, when in fact *muros* clearly means the Aurelian Wall; hence, she also (ignoring De Rossi) dates it three centuries too late.

[60] *Ibid.* no. 12: *Nunc caelo est similis nunc inclyta roma vere/cuius claustra docent intus inesse deum.*

[61] Above Chapter 3.4.

For if the Wall was in one sense the threshold opening onto the *sanctorum limina*, it was also only the innermost bastion in a system of defense in depth, the visible analogue of the protective cordon of saints that at Rome, as at so many other Christian cities, comprised a primary line of fortification for the urban nucleus within. Even before Alaric's sack of Rome, Paulinus had scoffed at the Romans for putting their faith in legions and Honorius' heightened Wall alone, when only steadfast piety could be trusted to save them from the barbarian menace.[62] The saints themselves were the strongest "ramparts" and "towers," without whose beneficent intercession manmade defenses were useless.[63] Similarly for Prudentius, it was the blood of the martyrs slain at Zaragoza that had "shut out the race of invidious demons from all the gates, and pushed the black shades from the purified city"; while the shrine of the martyr Agnes at Rome, "founded within sight of its towers," likewise did more to protect the city than the Wall itself.[64] It was the beginning of a long tradition of metaphorical "martyrial walls," described in technical terms redolent of the fortifications they encircled, that saw the *muri, propugnacula, turres,* and *valla* of saintly relics juxtaposed with the real ones just behind.[65] Four centuries later, Milan and Verona were still shielded as much by their coronas of saints as by their late Roman walls; for the authors of the *Versum de Mediolano civitate* (*c.* 740) and the *Versus de Verona* (*c.* 800), these dual circuits were indeed the outstanding characteristic of their respective cities, the yardstick of their grandeur, and the underpinning of their claims to pre-eminence.[66]

[62] *Carm.* 26, 103–05: *fidant legionibus illi/perfugioque parent reparatis moenia muris,/nulla salutiferi quibus est fiducia Christi.* . .; cf. Courcelle 1964, 32–5.

[63] *Ibid.* 233–4: *dei tu dextera, Felix/esto, precor, nobis tu munitissima turris*; and (again in reference to the shrine of St. Felix at Nola), 426–9: *manus inpia sacris/finibus absistat, quibus est tua gratia vallum,/atque tuam timeant hostes quasi daemones aulam,/nec cruor haec violet quae flamma vel unda refugit*; see also *Carm.* 19, 329–42 (on the foundation of Constantinople): *nam Constantinus proprii cum conderet urbem/nominis et primus Romano in nomine regum/ christicolam gereret, divinum mente recepit/consilium, ut quoniam Romanae moenibus urbis/ aemula magnificis strueret tunc moenia coeptis,/his quoque Romuleam sequeretur dotibus urbem,/ ut sua apostolicis muniret moenia laetus/corporibus. tunc Andream devexit Achivis/ Timotheumque Asia; geminis ita turribus extat/Constantinopolis, magnae caput aemula Romae,/ verius hoc similis Romanis culmine muris,/quod Petrum Paulumque pari deus ambitione/ compensavit ei, meruit quae sumere Pauli/discipulum cum fratre Petri.*

[64] On Zaragoza, see *Peristephanon* 4, 65–8: *Omnibus portis sacer immolatus/sanguis exclusit genus invidorum/daemonum et nigras pepulit tenebras/urbe piata*; cf. Roberts 1993, 190; on Rome, see *Peristephanon* 14, 1–4: *Agnes sepulchrum est Romula in domo/fortis puellae, martyris inclytae./ Conspectu in ipso condita turrium/servat salutem virgo Quiritum*, with Roberts 2001, 553–4.

[65] Cf. Gauthier 1999, 208; Fasoli 1974, 29–34.

[66] See Pighi 1960, with La Rocca 2003, 412ff.; and Picard 1998, 349–65; cf. also Trout 2005, esp. 140ff.; Ward-Perkins 1984, 219–20 and 224–7.

But nowhere was the link between physical and metaphysical fortifications more prominently realized than at Rome, which remained unsurpassed among the cities of the West both for the majesty of its defensive circuit and the quantity of its saintly patrons. The connection between this potent cache of apotropaic personae and the Wall was made manifest on the city gates, many of which were rechristened with the names of the martyrs upon whose shrines they opened.[67] By the 530s, the Porta S. Petri had been joined by the Portae S. Pauli (Ostiensis) and S. Pancratii (Aurelia).[68] A century later, the number had swollen to include the Portae S. Valentini (Flaminia), S. Silvestri (Salaria), S. Lorentii (Tiburtina), and S. Iohannis (Asinaria).[69] By virtue of their new designations, these gates proclaimed themselves adjuncts of the sanctified buffer zone of extramural cemeteries and churches, reinforcing the Wall itself with a concentrated dose of holiness, and affixing it to its serried outworks of saintly relics.

Under no illusions about the source of their enceinte's true strength, the Romans went so far as to dissuade Belisarius from meddling with the buckled curtain between the Portae Flaminia and Pinciana, familiarly known as the "Broken Wall," which he had planned to rebuild in the course of his siege preparations at the end of 536.[70] St. Peter, they said, had pledged to attend personally to the defense of this vulnerable point. The dangerously bulging section was left in place, where it remains today as the *muro torto*.

5.4 The Wall, stational liturgy, and the boundaries of the urban church

The Aurelian Wall, then, grew steadily greater than the already impressive sum of its parts. It was at once an intrinsically sacred presence and the topographical fundament of Christian Rome, whence it should come as no

---

[67] Cf. Fiocchi Nicolai 2001, 117; Pani Ermini 1999, 42; 1995, 202.

[68] On the first mention of the Porta Sancti Petri in the *Cosmographia* of "Pseudo-Eticus," probably a work of the fifth century, see above Chapter 4, n. 65; cf. Procop. *BG* 1, 19, 4. For the Porta S. Pauli, see Procop. *BG* 2, 4, 3 and 3, 36, 7–10; *LP* I, 298; and for the Porta S. Pancratii, Procop. *BG* 1, 18, 35 and 1, 28, 19.

[69] These new names are all given in the *Itinerarium Malmesburiense* (VZ 2, 141–53), alongside the three previously attested in Procopius. The *porta sancti Iohannis* appears earlier in the *LP* life of Sabinianus (604–6); see *LP* I, 315.

[70] Procop. *BG* 1, 23, 3–8.

surprise that the organization of the local church hinged on the Wall long
after Innocent I wrote his letter to Decentius of Gubbio. While the use of
the *fermentum* fell into desuetude (by the eighth century, the custom
was retained only on Easter), the distinction *intra urbem* – *in cimeteria*
(i.e. *intra* vs. *extra muros*) continued to dominate the spatial horizons of
ecclesiastical administrators for centuries, as Antoine Chavasse has
adroitly shown through his analyses of the tripartite structure of the
Roman liturgy.[71] A brief resumé of Chavasse's organizational schema
should suffice to highlight the centrality of the Wall.

The backbone of the liturgy was the regular Sunday masses performed
by priests attached to each of the twenty-five intramural *tituli*, where the
inhabitants of the city congregated each week.[72] The extramural *cimeteria*,
or *parochiae*, remained a zone apart, though the decimation of the suburban population during the Gothic Wars appears effectively to have ended
the regular congregational services, presided over by resident priests,
envisioned by Innocent I. Thereafter, the popes had to make exceptional
arrangements to ensure continued observances over the graves of the
martyrs. John III (561–74) stipulated that wine, bread, and candles
for masses *ad corpum* be supplied from the Lateran; later, Gregory III
(731–41) made provision on a reduced scale for the celebration, "in the
cemeteries located roundabout Rome," of the birthdays (*natalicia*) of their
eponymous martyrs.[73] Under the latter, that is, it was but once a year that
candles and consecrated host were sent from the Lateran to each cemetery,
and a priest provided *pro tempore*, in order that the martyr's day not pass
unobserved. It was a stark contrast with the situation inside the Wall,
where the *tituli* still bustled with constant activity.

Stational services conducted (usually) by the pope in person comprised
the third element of the liturgical calendar; as the means *par excellence* by

---

[71] Chavasse's collection of articles on the Roman liturgy in the early Middle Ages has been
published as a book (Chavasse 1993), which for the sake of convenience is cited in all
subsequent references. The work is suggestively subtitled *Une liturgie conditionée par
l'organisation de la vie* in urbe *et* extra muros. On the division of the liturgy into 1) Sunday
masses performed by priests in urban *tituli*; 2) services performed in honor of Rome's martyrs,
again generally by priests; and 3) stational services directed by the pope, cf. also Saxer 1989,
917–18. On the gradual decline in the use of the *fermentum* between the fifth and eighth
centuries, see Chavasse 1993, 66–7; Saxer 1989, 928ff.

[72] Chavasse 1993, 254ff.

[73] *Ibid.* 57–9 and 317–20. On John III's initiative, see *LP* I, 305; on that of Gregory III, *ibid.* 421:
*disposuit ut in cimiteriis circumquaque positis Romae in die natalicorum eorum luminaria ad
vigilias faciendum et oblationes de patriarchio per oblationarium deportentur, ad celebrandas
missas per quem praeviderit pontifex qui pro tempore fuerit sacerdotem.*

which the leaders of the Roman Church staked out its geographical aegis, they merit a closer look. From the later 400s on, the popes crossed back and forth from one end of the city to the other on their way to preside at these *stationes*, where masses were held to mark important dates in the Church calendar.[74] On such occasions, the pope set out from the Lateran on horseback for the prescribed church, preceded by a panoply of banners, lamps, incense, and crosses, and followed by the remainder of his entourage.[75] Grand showpieces of ecclesiastical pomp, these processions, and the ensuing services, were the glue that made the most diffuse urban church in Christendom cohere. By insinuating themselves into every nook – and congregation – of the city, the popes in a sense recreated the primitive unity of the apostolic Church, while simultaneously proclaiming the territorial hegemony of its triumphant successor.

A perusal of the Roman liturgical handbooks, or "sacramentaries," of the sixth, seventh, and eighth centuries demonstrates that the location of the various stations was chosen above all with an eye to achieving the widest possible spatial distribution, within the enceinte.[76] Stations were held at all the *tituli*, as well as at the six leading "devotional" churches: the Lateran, S. Maria Maggiore, and S. Stefano on the Caelian inside the Wall, and St. Peter's, St. Paul's, and S. Lorenzo – and only these three places – outside. Chavasse's study of the liturgical calendar for the six weeks of Lent is particularly revealing.[77] Among the thirty-seven stations (more than half the yearly total) indicated for the period, twenty-two weekday services were performed in twenty-two of the twenty-five *tituli*, while gatherings on the six Sundays and nine salient weekdays occurred in the six larger churches. The stations for each week invariably took place in sites far removed from one another, requiring the pope repeatedly to traverse the

---

[74] Pope Hilarus (461–8) seems to have given the stational liturgy the essentials of the form it retained for centuries; and he furnished a traveling stock of liturgical vessels for the masses, stational and otherwise, performed at all the titular churches, which was stored at the Lateran and S. Maria Maggiore; see *LP* I, 244–5, with Chavasse 1993, 47ff. and 255; Saxer 1989, 938ff.; Baldovin 1987, 143–53. The stations were 66 in number in the seventh century, after which very few new ones were added (Chavasse 1993, 258). For a convenient summary overview of Roman liturgy, stational processions, and topography over the *longue durée*, see also de Blaauw 1994, 27–72.

[75] See Saxer 1989, 951–2 and 973ff.

[76] Cf. Chavasse 1993, 233–5. Chief among these texts are the so-called Leonine Sacramentary (probably of the sixth century); the Gregorian Sacramentary (seventh century); and the Gelasian Sacramentary, preserved in its mature form in several eighth-century manuscripts: see Chavasse, esp. 153–229.

[77] Chavasse 1993, 231–46.

"four corners of the city" as Easter approached.[78] If one connects the dots of the succeeding stations with lines (as Chavasse has done),[79] the result is an arresting image of a snarl of intersecting vectors framed by the outline of the Aurelian Wall. It is as though a rubber ball had bounced back and forth between its irregular contours, over-reaching them only to arrive at St. Peter's, St. Paul's, and S. Lorenzo.

It is therefore all the more striking to recall that the three extramural stational churches were precisely the ones connected to the city via the covered colonnades. Further, the late-fifth century popes who programmatically expanded the facilities at all three shrines – and very possibly built the colonnades, too – were the same individuals responsible for the definitive assimilation of these centers into the administrative sphere of the "urban" Church. Following the decision of Hilarus to include St. Peter's, St. Paul's, and S. Lorenzo in the stational calendar in the first place, his immediate successor Simplicius (468–83) arranged for titular priests from the adjacent ecclesiastical regions (6 and 7, 1, and 3 respectively) to perform Lenten services at these sites, which like the great devotional churches *in urbe* were without resident clergy.[80] In short, the only extramural churches treated like their intramural counterparts, in terms of their use for stational gatherings and their rotating allotment of urban priests, were the ones physically attached to the Wall. The confines of the *urbs* – which is to say the Wall – were extended to embrace the three suburban sites that the pope and members of the clergy were duty-bound to enter in the course of the annual liturgical cycle.[81] It is hard to imagine more convincing testimony to the pre-eminence of the enceinte as the topographical denominator of the Church of Rome in the early Middle Ages.

---

[78] *Ibid.* 236; cf. also Baldovin 1987, 153–5.   [79] *Ibid.* 237–44.

[80] See *LP* I, 249, with Chavasse 1993, 57; on Hilarus' seminal role in the creation of the stational liturgy, see above n. 74. Only with the pontificate of Gregory I (590–604), according to the *LP*, were regular masses *super corpus* instituted at St. Peter's and St. Paul's (*LP* I, 312); in the eighth century, the weekly masses at St. Peter's were still performed on a rotating basis by priests, and later "cardinal bishops," attached to the urban Church: see *LP* I, 421 and 478.

[81] This is not to say that the pontiffs and Roman clergy did not officiate elsewhere in the suburbs. Gregory I, for example, delivered several of his homilies in cemeteries *extra muros* in 590–2. However, as Gregory himself stressed, his presence at these occasions was purely a matter of choice, and indeed *contra morem* (*Hom.* 21, 1): he was only expected to preside at the regular stations at the three major basilicas; cf. Chavasse 1993, 122; 257–8. The *LP* similarly makes a point of saying that Pope Sergius (687–701), while still a priest, made a diligent (and apparently unusual) effort to say masses at various cemeteries (*LP* I, 371): *Hic tempore presbiteratus sui inpigre per cymiteria diversa missarum sollemnia celebrabat.*

Other written sources heighten the impression that the physical compass of the Church bifurcated along the perimeter of the Wall. The two seventh-century catalogues of Rome's cemeteries and churches punctiliously differentiate between intramural and extramural features. Each of the places listed in the *Notitia ecclesiarum urbis Romae* was outside the circuit, with the exception of the church of S. Giovanni e Paolo on the Caelian, which was mentioned before all the others and pointedly said to be *in urbe Roma*.[82] As for the *De locis sanctorum martyrum quae sunt foris civitate Roma*, the itinerary of (extramural) martyrs' shrines was reworked in the later eighth century to include a roll of churches enumerated under the rubric "these churches are located inside Rome."[83] Every one of the twenty-one structures named stood inside the Wall, the point where *intus Romae* began and *foris civitate* ended. Herman Geertman has called attention to signs of a kindred distinction in accounts of papal donations to Roman churches – notably but not exclusively including the comprehensive recap of Leo III's donation of golden crowns and baskets (*canistra*) to "all the churches" (*universas ... ecclesias*) of Rome in 807 – according to which *diaconiae, xenodochia,* and a particular class of intramural monasteries were consistently distinguished from their extramural equivalents, when the latter were mentioned at all.[84] In light of the indications furnished by the Roman Sacramentaries, Geertman's conclusion that the "external" patrimony of the Church was administered independently of its holdings inside the Wall gains further in plausibility.[85]

Following its precocious appearance in the civil law of the late empire, in sum, the Wall featured still more prominently in the calculations of those responsible for shaping the administrative infrastructure and geographical parameters of the Roman Church, at a time when the city as a whole was increasingly permeated by its ecclesiastical establishment.

---

[82] VZ 2, 72.

[83] VZ 2, 118: *Istae vero ecclesiae intus Romae habentur;* on the (separate) composition and dating of the list of intramural churches, see Geertman 1975, 158–63.

[84] See *LP* II, 18ff., with Geertman 1975, esp. 111–14 on *diaconiae;* 123–4 on monasteries; and 127 on *xenodochia.* In the account of the donation of 807, monasteries that followed the Latin rite and were unattached to the service of the most prominent basilicas were grouped together, with no mention made of the numerous otherwise similar foundations outside the Wall (*LP* II, 22–4).

[85] Geertman proposed that *diaconiae* and *xenodochia* inside the Wall were governed from the Lateran, while a separate administrative apparatus oversaw those in the vicinity of St. Peter's (1975, 114 and 127).

5.5 *In urbe, extra muros*

But for the authors of the more or less official Church sources that dominate the historical record for the several centuries after Procopius, the Wall came to stand for the territorial nucleus of Christian Rome in something more than a juridical or technical sense. These texts, whose numerous topographical references overwhelmingly concur in their illustration of what was meant by "inside" and "outside" the city, often reveal the Wall almost in the guise of a natural feature, a geographical constant that imposed itself with growing force on the consciousness of those tasked with describing their physical environment.

The *LP* contains the largest sampling of relevant terminology for the period of its compilation, beginning in the first half of the sixth century and ending in the second half of the ninth. A lexical survey of the document in its entirety suggests several points of note. To begin with, there is the frequent incidence of "internal" topographical designators such as *in urbe, intra urbem,* and *in civitate,* which more definitively prove what has previously been suggested regarding the occasional use of similar terms in the fourth and fifth centuries: the "city" of Rome – the *urbs* or *civitas* proper – was understood to begin and end with its defensive perimeter. Of 29 discrete locales, the large majority churches and other religious foundations, said to be *in urbe* (or the like), only one sat outside the Aurelian Wall. Likewise, all the places described as "outside the city," usually in the standard formulation *miliario* [x] *ab urbe,* with the distance measured in traditional fashion from the Forum, lay beyond the Wall. The lone exception is the *basilica beati Apollenaris,* located near the end of the colonnaded walkway to St. Peter's at a place called *ad Palmata,* which is described in the biography of its founder Honorius I (625–38) as being *in urbe Roma.*[86] This curious anomaly is to my knowledge without parallel either in contemporary Roman sources,[87] or certainly in the remainder of the *LP,* where the Vatican area is consistently treated as extra-urban.[88]

---

[86] *LP* I, 323: *Item fecit [Honorius] basilicam beati Apollenaris martyris in urbe Roma, in porticum beati Petri apostoli qui appellatur ad Palmata...*

[87] I have yet to find a single example of an extramural site situated *in urbe* in the *Registrum* of Gregory I and other papal letters, the *Ordines Romani,* the *Liber Diurnus,* the so-called Leonine, Gelasian, and Gregorian sacramentaries, etc.

[88] When the Lombards under Desiderius threatened Rome in 772, for example, pope Hadrian I commanded the valuables from St. Peter's and St. Paul's to be brought "inside the city" for protection (*LP* I, 494): *Nam ecclesias beati Petri ac Pauli exornare fecit eius sanctitas et cuncta earum cymilia et ornatus in hanc civitatem Romanam introduxit.* Likewise, before the Saracen

The aberration hence seems to prove the rule, especially given the proximity of the *basilica beati Apollenaris* to the portico, which evidently could indeed, in the eyes of one seventh-century cleric at least, be perceived as an extension of the Wall, and thus of the *urbs* itself.

Interestingly, the practice of describing intramural structures as *in urbe*, never very common, petered out almost completely by the later seventh century. – 25 of the 29 places so labeled in the *LP* occur before the pontificate of Agatho (678–81), though the amount of text devoted to the succeeding two centuries greatly exceeds all of what came before. Thereafter, when specific indications for the placement of buildings inside the Wall were given at all, they referred solely to ecclesiastical regions, local "neighborhood" toponyms (*in platana, ad duos amantes, in septem vias,* etc.), streets, or prominent landmarks.

Just as *in urbe* was disappearing from the pages of the *LP*, however, the Wall and its gates began coming into their own as points of spatial reference, nearly always for sites located beyond them. The first edifice sited in relation to a city gate was the *oratorium beato Euplo*, built under Theodore I (642–9) just outside the circuit along the Via Ostiensis, *foris porta beati Pauli apostoli.*[89] The Wall *per se* did not appear in a similar context until the life of Gregory II (715–31), where the church of S. Lorenzo is said to be *foris murum.*[90] Thereafter, gates and Wall alike rapidly developed into landmark features in *LP* excurses on extramural topography. Of the 58 passages that state an extramural foundation to be outside the Wall or a particular gate, fully 50 date between the pontificates of Hadrian I (772–95) and Benedict III (855–8). A remarkable number – 29 of the 58 – pertain to S. Lorenzo, which seems to have achieved the "outside-the-walls" epithet it still maintains at a relatively early date;[91] the remaining 29 passages are thinly spread amongst a number of churches, cemeteries, monasteries, and *diaconiae*, all situated within three Roman miles of the Wall.

At the same time, phrases of the *in urbe* type continued to be applied to the urban collective (as opposed to individual structures), often as

incursion of 847, Pope Sergius II was advised to bring the "treasuries" of the same churches *intro...Roma* (*LP* II, 99).

[89] *LP* I, 333.
[90] *LP* I, 397: *Sancti Laurenti pariter ecclesiam foris murum sitam...reparavit.*
[91] I have no good explanation for the disproportionate occurrence of *foris muros* in relation to S. Lorenzo. Other important suburban churches, among them S. Pancrazio, S. Valentino, and even St. Peter's are only sporadically designated as extramural. More surprisingly, St. Paul's, so commonly known to subsequent ages as *fuori le mura*, is never so described in the *LP.*

a means of differentiating between the city and an outside world that brought recurring natural and human threats to, and sometimes over, the urban threshold. Whether it was an armed incursion or the sudden impetus of a Tiber flood, the accounts of such events reveal the Wall as the unmistakable – and very logical – line of demarcation between the city and the chaotic reaches beyond. In 756, the Lombard King Aistulf ravaged the territory "outside the city" (*extra urbem*), but was ultimately unsuccessful in his attempt to besiege and capture "this Roman city" (*hanc Romanam urbem*).[92] Likewise, when Toto of Nepi and his followers occupied Rome in 768, they entered "through the gate of Saint Pancras into this Roman city."[93] When floodwaters inundated Rome, these, too, were said to have entered the city when they broke through one of its gates. The great flood of 791 erupted through the Porta Flaminia, which it ripped from its hinges.[94] Under Sergius II (844–7), the swollen Tiber flowed "through the *posterula* that is called Saint Agatha's into the city of Rome," a description repeated essentially verbatim in reports of later floods under Benedict III (855–8) and Nicholas I (858–67).[95] In all of these instances, the frontier of the *urbs* is clearly the Wall itself.[96]

Of course, such threats were hardly new to the eighth and ninth centuries, and already in the account of the siege-plagued pontificate of Silverius (536–7), a direct contrast could be drawn between *in civitate* and *foris muros*.[97] *In urbe*, that is, had long been the antithesis of *foris muros*.

---

[92] *LP* I, 451: *Omnia extra urbem ferro et igne devastans atque funditus demoliens consumsit, imminens vehementius hisdem pestifer Aistulf ut hanc Romanam capere potuisset urbem.*

[93] *LP* I, 468:...*ingredientesque per portam beati Pancratii in hanc Romanam urbem....*

[94] *LP* I, 513; cf. I, 399.

[95] *LP* II, 91–2: *Et ingressus est per posterulam quae appellatur sanctae Agathae in Romanam urbem*; cf. *LP* II, 145 (Benedict III); and II, 153 (Nicholas). The *posterula sanctae Agathae* perforated the river wall in the northern Campus Martius.

[96] Papal letters transcribed in the *Codex Carolinus* give the same impression: during the Lombard siege of 756, Aistulf is said to have demanded that the Porta Salaria be opened to him, that he might enter the city (*Aperite mihi portam Salariam, et ingrediar civitatem*); while his forces "wasted all properties outside the city (*extra urbem*) far and wide with fire and the sword" (*Et omnia extra urbem praedia longe lateque ferro et igne consumpserunt...*; see *CC* 8, p. 495). In 771, when the opponents of Pope Steven III closed the gates of the Wall against him, they likewise acted to prevent his entry *in civitatem*. For all the importance – and physical proximity – of the Vatican, where Steven was compelled to reside, its extramural position rendered it definitively suburban: *turmas facientes et portas civitatis claudentes, fortiter resistebant et nobis comminabantur atque in civitatem nos ingredi minime permittebant; CC* 48, p. 567, 4–5.

[97] When Belisarius arrived at Rome, "the Goths who were in the city or outside the walls fled and left all the gates open and fled to Ravenna" (*LP* I, 291): *Noctu ipsa quo introivit Vilisarius patricius, Gothi qui erant in civitate vel foris muros fugerunt et omnes portas apertas dimiserunt et fugerunt Ravennam.*

The great change of the eighth century came in regard to the Wall's visibility. It was noticed, as it were, more than ever before in tales of current events, and cited with much greater frequency – quantifiably so, as shown above – in descriptions of the Roman landscape. It is true that the papal biographies of the eighth and ninth centuries tend toward greater prolixity than their predecessors, whereby they afford the Wall more space to develop into a protagonist on the local scene than the terse entries of earlier years. Floodwaters break down parts of it, and allegedly even overtop it during particularly memorable events;[98] the minority party in a factional struggle seeks refuge on its parapets from the masses below;[99] various popes barricade the gates in preparation for siege,[100] and so on. Its new prominence also corresponds remarkably closely with the beginning of the narrative tradition on papal repairs to the circuit. The biography of Gregory II, the first pope said to have conducted a significant campaign of restoration, is in fact the first to locate a building (S. Lorenzo) *foris muros*.[101] Moreover, the subsequent surge in "extramural" toponyms documented above is chronologically bracketed by the reigns of Hadrian I and Leo IV, the two popes credited with the most extensive mural repairs, which are described in unprecedented detail in their respective biographies.[102] The authors of papal history, in short, had good reason to be more attentive to the Wall after *c.* 715.

Nonetheless, I very much doubt that the sudden debut of the Wall as a reference-point for the location of buildings in its vicinity was, strictly speaking, a calculated propagandistic initiative, or to put it another way, that the compilers of the *LP* were directed to mention the Wall as much as possible in such contexts. Rather, the sum total of the evidence in the *LP* points to the following two conclusions. First, when describing their surroundings, literate members of the Roman clergy thought frequently in terms of a spatial dichotomy centered on the defensive circuit. Second, these lettered clerics began in the eighth century to "see" the Wall in a way they had not before, and to call it to mind as a matter of course when talking about sites in the immediate urban periphery.

---

[98] See the passages cited above at nn. 94–5.   [99] *LP* I, 470.   [100] *LP* I, 478 and 493.

[101] If we add the few places described as *iuxta* or *infra muros* to the 58 citations of extramural structures, the following figures result for Wall-based addresses in and around Rome: before 715 (the first year of Gregory II's pontificate), 4 in *c.* 280 pages of text and commentary, in Duchesne's edition; for the period 715–872, 59 in *c.* 320 pages. On Gregory's repairs to the Wall, see *LP* I, 396.

[102] See *LP* I, 501 and 513; *LP* II, 115.

With the passage of time, the Wall likely came to circumscribe Rome in the popular imagination as well, though the available ecclesiastical sources (and, for that matter, the legal texts of the preceding epoch) are, of course, a questionable barometer of prevailing popular conceptions. In Italy, the city with the most socially inclusive documentation for the early Midde Ages is Lucca, where the episcopal archive contains a treasure trove of eighth- and ninth-century contracts, charters, deeds of sale and lease, etc., which together reveal a great deal about the manner in which urban space was perceived and categorized. Although the documents pertain to trans-actions that in one way or another involved the Church, they very fre-quently concern the holdings of the laity, and presumably speak in terms current among the (lay) propertied classes. A thorough survey of the archive has shown that at Lucca, *infra civitatem* quite unambiguously meant "inside the wall."[103] Even buildings adjacent to the inner facing of the enceinte were *infra civitatem*, while those beyond were either *extra civitatem* or *extra*, *prope*, or *foris murum*. As in the *LP*, *infra murum* was almost never used: *infra civitatem* alone sufficed to mark a spot as intramural.[104]

When a similar corpus of notarial documents becomes available for Rome beginning in the tenth century, the resulting picture of spatial con-sciousness is effectively identical. As Hubert has demonstrated, properties – dwellings, orchards, pastures, gardens, mills – situated anywhere inside the sprawling ambit of the Wall were simply *infra urbem* or *positum Romae*, usually without further specification.[105] *Infra muros* is, again, extremely rare. Holdings outside the circuit, meanwhile, were either *extra urbem/ muros*, or more often *extra (talem) portam*. For the centuries of the high Middle Ages, it is thus quite safe to accept Hubert's verdict that "the overall perception of space was not so much based on the landscape as on the symbolic limit of the enceinte."[106] What should be added, however, is that this mural-centric Roman universe has every appearance of predat-ing the earliest extant deeds and charters of the tenth century. Its origins should extend through the period covered by the Luccan archive, on the likely assumption that the circuit at Lucca did not attract more precocious notice than the Aurelian Wall; and it might be imagined that Romans

---

[103] See De Conno 1991, esp. 73–9; cf. La Rocca 2003, 425–7.   [104] De Conno 1991, 74.

[105] For this and the immediately following observations, see Hubert 1990, 63–73.

[106] Hubert 1990, 69–70; cf. 69: "À n'en pas douter, les Romains voyaient en elle [l'enceinte] une frontière entre deux mondes . . . l'espace rural ne commençait pour les contemporains que les portes passées."

had begun to divide their real estate in like terms already in the aftermath of the protracted sieges of the fifth and sixth centuries, which must have brought the internal-external dichotomy into sharp relief for all. Certainly this dichotomy was keenly felt in the *LP*, for all that the text directly represents only the views of a very particular segment of Roman society.

In addressing the enduring influence of the Aurelian Wall on the definition of local boundaries, it must finally be stressed that post-imperial Rome differed from Lucca, and indeed all the cities of Western Europe, in several crucial respects. Rome was unique for the length and total area of its enceinte, which dwarfed all remaining pockets of (relatively) dense settlement;[107] and for the wealth, power, and sheer size – in architectural as well as human terms – of its ecclesiastical establishment. The *LP*'s insistence on the effort expended by eighth- and ninth-century pontiffs to maintain the Wall is the more remarkable for the pronounced disparity that had arisen between the dimensions of the circuit and the size of the urban population, which stood at several tens of thousands of souls by the eighth century.[108] The Roman enceinte had undeniably become an artifact, a relic of past imperial grandeur initially designed to envelop something like twenty times more people than it later surrounded. Its survival, and indeed resurgence, in the straitened conditions of the early Middle Ages defies a narrowly practical explanation, on the premise that maintaining and defending nearly 19,000 meters of fortifications with a lesser number of adult male inhabitants is not a narrowly practical undertaking. The question then becomes one of why the leading local power – the Church by the eighth century – insisted on the preservation of a boundary so out of proportion with its surroundings; or to put it another way, of what the Wall meant to the Church, and why it was made to absorb so many very finite human and material resources.

5.6   The decline of the *suburbium* and the rise of the world's largest reliquary

To some extent, the early-medieval upkeep of the Wall can be seen as an expedient used by various popes to proclaim their expanded capacities as

---

[107] Cf. Hubert 2001, 159.

[108] I estimate an early-medieval population in the neighborhood of 50,000 total inhabitants; see above Chapter 4, n. 119.

temporal sovereigns and protectors of the Christian capital, an issue discussed in the following chapter. Yet its continued importance was surely also a function of the richness and density of the sacred landscape it enclosed. Even as population figures first shrank dramatically and then stagnated, intramural Church foundations continued to expand and multiply, whereby the ratio of consecrated ground to inhabitants increasingly favored the former, to an extent unparalleled elsewhere. As a great repository of the sacred, the Wall contained enough of value amply to justify its resuscitation at the hands of Rome's newly empowered religious authorities.[109] It remains to be stressed, however, that the enceinte was more than an armored shell for the hallowed sites it encompassed: in the eighth century, it became more than ever a guiding presence, as it began visibly to condition what amounted to a radical overhaul of the metaphysical topography of the saints, and to occasion by the very fact of its presence an intramural concentration of the holy treasures that had previously sanctified the *suburbium.*

Foremost among these treasures were the bones of local saints and martyrs interred in the peripheral cemeteries. The popularity and prestige of such relics surged throughout Western Europe beginning in the eighth century, when they were increasingly treated as valuable commodities, imbued with a potent aura of the divine that – significantly for anyone seeking a sudden infusion of spiritual capital – accompanied them wherever they went.[110] Rome, of course, had much the largest stock of venerable corpses, an endowment that materially enhanced its stature as the capital of Western Christendom, while at the same time making it the preferred target for growing crowds of people seeking, with or without the consent of Church authorities, to obtain relics.[111]

Not coincidentally, Roman relics began in the mid eighth century to be transferred in bulk from neglected and war-scarred suburban cemeteries into the city, where they enriched a bevy of churches and monasteries pointedly chosen for their intramural location. In the aftermath of the Lombard siege of 756, when many cemeteries had been robbed of their prestigious remains, Paul I (757–67) undertook the first intramural

---

[109] Cf. Reekmans 1989, 902.   [110] See e.g. Caroli 2000; Geary 1990, 28–43.

[111] See Smith 2000; Llewellyn 1993, 183–90; Geary 1990, 45–9. For a first-person perspective on a notorious but hardly isolated case involving unauthorized Carolingian borrowing of Roman relics, told by Einhard, the instigator of the translations himself, see the *Translatio et miracula sanctorum Marcellini et Petri auctore Einhardo* (*MGH SS* 15, 1, 238–64).

translation *en masse* of saintly relics, which he distributed to "*tituli,* monasteries or *diaconiae* and other churches" situated "inside this Roman city."[112] Though Hadrian I and Leo III subsequently aimed to revitalize the *suburbium* by restoring a plethora of churches and cemeteries, their intervention failed to arrest a plurisecular process of abandonment and decay;[113] and the volume of translations if anything increased under their successors.

Paschal I (817–24) seems to have been especially tireless in seeking out relics and conducting them "within the enclosure (*claustra*) of this blessed city."[114] After reconstructing the *titulus* of S. Prassede on the Esquiline, he straightaway filled it with vast quantities of bones rescued from "ruined cemeteries."[115] Thereafter, following his restoration of the *titulus* of S. Cecilia, the same pope was (miraculously enough) led by a vision to uncover the corpse of the martyr herself, which was thought to have been carried off to Pavia by the Lombards in 756.[116] Paschal's immediate reaction upon the discovery of such valuable remains was to take them from the cemetery of Praetextatus, "located outside the Porta Appia," and

---

[112] *LP* I, 464: ...*protinus eadem sanctorum corpora de ipsis dirutis abstulit cymiteriis. Quae cum hymnis et canticis spiritalibus infra hanc civitatem Romanam introducens, alia eorum per titulos ac diaconias seu monasteria et reliquas ecclesias cum condecenti studuit recondi honore*; see also Paul's letter to John, abbot of the (intramural) monastery of Saints Steven and Silvester (*PL* 89, col. 1191): *Unde conspecta eorumdem sanctorum locorum desidiosa incuria, et ex hoc valde ingemiscens, atque plurima doloris attritus moestitia, aptum prospexit, Deo annuente, eosdem sanctos martyres et confessores Christi, et virgines ex iisdem dirutis auferre locis. Quos et cum hymnis et canticis spiritalibus in hanc Romanam introduximus urbem, et in ecclesiam, quam noviter a fundamentis in eorum honorem construxi (intra moenia scilicet in domo quae mihi parentali successione obvenit, in qua me natum constat atque nutritum) eorum sanctissima collocans condidit corpora*; cf. *CC* 42, p. 556. The first mention in the *LP* of a transfer of suburban relics to an intramural site occurs in the life of Theodore (642–9), where the martyrs Primus and Felicianus are said to have been taken from graves on the Via Nomentana and placed in S. Stefano Rotondo (*LP* I, 332); the only other episode prior to the time of Paul I occurred under Leo II (682–3; *LP* I, 360). The legend that Boniface IV transferred cartloads of relics to the Pantheon upon its conversion to a church in *c*. 609, which apparently results from a late interpolation in the *LP* (see Davis 2000, 64), is almost certainly apocryphal; cf. McClendon 2005, 31. For an itemized listing of seventh- and eighth-century translations, see Saxer 1989, 1020–3.

[113] Cf. Geertman 1975, 105.

[114] See *Paschalis papae I epistolae*, 1 (*PL* 102, col. 1086): *Et quia convenit nostro apostolico moderamini, ut diversa corpora sanctorum, quae diu inculta jacuerunt, cum summa vigilantia ob honorem omnipotentis Dei intra hujus almae urbis claustra honeste congregare*; cf. *LP* II, 52.

[115] *LP* II, 54. A contemporary inscription (dated 20 July 817) still preserved at S. Prassede asserts that fully 2,300 saints were placed in the church, hundreds of whom are listed by name; see Ferrua 1957–58; cf. Osborne 1985, 292–3.

[116] *LP* II, 56.

bring them "inside the walls of this Roman city," where they were placed with appropriate pomp in the eponymous martyr's church.[117]

The Wall was similarly depicted as the common destination for inward-bound relics in the biography of Leo IV, where reference to the "many bodies of saints" translated "inside the walls of this venerable city" interestingly enough follows immediately upon the account of Leo's repairs to the city walls.[118] The narrative sequence thus recalls the examples of S. Prassede and S. Cecilia, where architectural improvements had been triumphantly punctuated upon completion with the installation of relics transplanted from the suburbs. Though the many saints translated by Leo IV were earmarked in like fashion for the rebuilt church of SS. Quattro Coronati, the papal biographer noted this fact only after situating them with respect to the enceinte. More than a fence or a frame, the Wall is in this instance revealed as a sacred monument unto itself, a macrocosm of the restored churches inside and (like the churches) a destination in its own right for the relics it housed and protected.

The testimony of the papal biographers thus leaves no doubt that an intramural location was a primary criterion in the selection of sites chosen to receive relics. The few exceptions to this rule are limited to remains transferred to the new urban nucleus growing up around the Vatican, which were in fact always distinguished from the rest.[119] In part, the mass translations of the eighth and ninth centuries consequently appear as a practical measure designed to consolidate and protect a precious resource, and thus to afford Church authorities greater control over the burgeoning trade in sacred antiquities: it was manifestly more difficult to steal relics

---

[117] *Ibid.: Quae cuncta suis pertractans manibus collegit et cum magno honore infra muros huius Romanae urbis in ecclesia nomine ipsius sanctae martyris dedicata, ad laudem et gloriam omnipotentis Dei, eiusdem virginis corpus, cum carissimo Valeriano sponso atque Tyburtio et Maximo martyribus, necnon Urbano et Lucio pontificibus, sub sacrosancto altare collocavit.*

[118] *LP* II, 115: *Ipse vero…papa multa corpora sanctorum quae diu inculta iacuerant, summo studio summoque cordis affectu, ad honorem omnipotentis Dei, infra huius alme urbis menia congregavit mirifice.*

[119] The first pope responsible for large-scale translations inside the Wall, Paul I, also brought the remains of Petronilla from the Via Appia to St. Peter's; yet the detailed description of this translation was made to stand alone, to be followed several lines later by the blanket reference to the many bodies taken *infra hanc civitatem Romanam* (*LP* I, 464). The only other pontiff to convey relics to the Vatican was Gregory IV, who enriched the oratory dedicated to his eponymous predecessor Saint Gregory I with the remains of the martyrs Sebastian, Tiburtius, and Gorgonius (*LP* II, 74). There is no indication that he took any relics inside the circuit; while the other popes to do so in quantity (Paschal I, Sergius II, Leo IV) brought nothing to the Vatican. The relatively rare relics installed at St. Peter's thus seem exceptional cases, spawned by very particular papal projects that required breaking with a practice otherwise scrupulously observed.

from frequented churches inside the Wall than from deserted and over-grown extramural cemeteries, and those who succeeded in doing so would still have had to transport their prizes through one of the city gates, now guarded by customs officials appointed by the pope.[120] Yet the focused migration of saintly multitudes inside the defensive circuit also betokens a more complex and ideologically charged agenda, calculated by its propon-ents to reconfigure the map of Roman sacred geography. By transforming the area circumscribed by the refurbished enceinte into the most relic-strewn ground in Christendom, the popes anchored what had become a papal citadel on a peerless foundation. In the process, the fortified nucleus was sundered from an extramural periphery that, once denuded of its holy dead, largely departed the purview of the urban authorities and became definitively "rural" in a way that equally bucolic reaches inside the Wall never did.[121]

For whatever became of the bricks and mortar of the ancient capital, with its gaping voids irremediably beyond the capacity of the Church to fill, it would henceforth be packed with the soaring and incorruptible silhouettes of the saints. This dense grouping of holy pinnacles was in turn neatly bounded by a mural crown that, more than any other surviving feature of the Roman cityscape, preserved an air of grandeur commensur-ate with their stature. The prevailing vision of this reality is incarnated with lapidary clarity in the mosaic decoration commissioned for the triumphal arch of S. Prassede by Paschal I,[122] where that leading architect of the translations chose to reprise the venerable theme of the Celestial Jerusalem *cum* Rome, with one crucial variation. The stately buildings that once filled the city-center, in the fifth- and sixth-century antecedents at S. Maria Maggiore and S. Lorenzo (Figures 3.2–3.3), have completely given way to the towering figures of the twelve apostles, surrounded by a typically close approximation of the Aurelian Wall (Figures 3.4–3.5). The paradigm of the Christian capital chosen by the pontiff to crown the relics he had brought inside the enceinte was made up of exactly two elements: a

---

[120] The collection of customs-dues (*actionarica*) at the city gates was entrusted to agents confirmed by papal mandate, according to a formula preserved in the *Liber Diurnus* (Codex Claromontanus 97; Foerster, p. 268): *Constat nos magnitudidini* (sic) *vestrae commisse actionarica de diversas portas huius romae urbis ad peragendo in fide dominicale de hac transacta inditione.* ...

[121] Cf. Delogu and Belardini 2003, 212ff. On the close correlation between the translation of relics and the diminished vitality of the Roman suburbs, see Pani Ermini 1989, 867–77; Osborne 1985, 286–98. On the continuing perception of the Wall as the dividing line between urban and rural space in the high Middle Ages, see Hubert 1990, 70 (quoted above at n. 106).

[122] See above Chapter 3.4, with figs. 3.4–5.

great wall and a grouping of larger-than-life saints. One need look no
further than this image to see where the true wealth and glory of papal
Rome was construed to reside.[123]

Ultimately, then, the Wall lost its character as the starting-point for a
numinous halo, thronged with divine intercessors and pilgrims, that had
once made the suburban periphery the spiritual heart of the urban center.
By the mid ninth century, the circuit had swallowed up the riches of the
suburbs and superimposed their collective legacy on the already storied
ground of the (intramural) urban Church, whereby it engendered a
remarkably dense concentration of holy loci (and objects) that, like an
isolated galaxy, looked even more dazzling against the surrounding void.
Once the inner rampart in a system of metaphysical "defense in depth,"
the circuit was left to become the sole bulwark and frontier of Christian
Rome, a majestic vessel that alone sufficed to impart corporeal form to a
place no longer defined as much by its monumental infrastructure as by its
population of saints and martyrs.

---

[123] The connection between the image of Jerusalem and the Rome of Paschal I was made manifest
(should the point have been lost on anyone) by the dedicatory inscription in the apse just
behind, which trumpeted the pope's translation of relics to the site: *…qui corpora condens
plurima sanctorum subter haec moenia ponit* (*LP* II, 63, n. 10). Generally on the mosaic, cf.
Thunø 2002, 176–8; Mauck 1987.

6 | The Wall and the "Republic of St. Peter"

6.1 The Aurelian Wall and the post-Roman "state," from Justinian to Charlemagne

With the final triumph of Justinian's armies over the Goths and the restoration of Italy to "Roman" rule in the early 550s, the administration of Rome passed into the hands of representatives of the imperial government in Constantinople. The transition to Byzantine rule in the reconstituted province received its legal underpinnings with the "Pragmatic Sanction" of 554, which included amongst its provisions a section on the upkeep of the ancient capital, aimed chiefly at the preservation of vital infrastructure.[1] The banks of the Tiber, the forum, the seaports, and the aqueducts were specifically recommended to the care of the supervising authorities, alongside "public buildings" in general, amongst which Rome's battered walls must have figured prominently. Though the titles and responsibilities of the various officials employed in the urban administration did gradually evolve, the governance of the city and the maintenance of its physical building stock remained for the next century and a half – at least in theory – the task of civil servants in the employ of the central government in Constantinople.

The Pragmatic Sanction was addressed to the victorious commander Narses and to Antiochus, *Praefectus per Italiam*,[2] who together exercised effective authority in the vacuum left by the collapse of the Gothic regime. As a more permanent and articulated bureaucratic apparatus took shape over the following decades, despite the chaos occasioned by the

---

[1] *Constitutio Pragmatica*, 25 (*CIC Nov.*, App. VII, p. 802): *Ut fabricae publicae serventur. Consuetudines etiam et privilegia Romanae civitatis vel publicarum fabricarum reparationi vel alveo Tiberino vel foro aut portui Romano sive reparationi formarum concessa servari praecipimus, ita videlicet, ut ex isdem tantummodo titulis, ex quibus delegata fuerunt, praestentur;* generally on Byzantine public building at Rome after 554, see Coates-Stephens 2006, esp. 299–304; cf. Humphries 2007, esp. 53–8.

[2] *Constitutio Pragmatica*, 27 (*CIC Nov.*, App. VII, p. 802).

Lombard invasion, the positions occupied by these two individuals were institutionalized in lasting form.[3] The office of supreme military commander was entrusted to the person of the exarch, a title certainly attested by the 580s, who had his seat in Ravenna.[4] Civic governance remained the preserve of the praetorian prefects of Italy, whose mandate evidently extended over Rome by the pontificate of Gregory I, the same period in which the position of the *praefectus urbi,* traditionally the apex of the urban administration, likely not coincidentally disappeared.[5] During the course of the seventh century, with the gradual "militarization" of Byzantine Italy, the praetorian prefecture fell into desuetude (the last mention comes in 639), leaving the exarch in sole control by mid-century if not earlier.[6]

Responsibility for the direct supervision of the city of Rome was in turn delegated by its absentee overlords to a cadre of subsidiary officials, attested in the seventh century under the generic title *iudices,*[7] as well as with more precise terms like *chartularius, sacellarius, tabellio,* and so on. The title of *dux,* generally borne by the commander of the garrison – and hence the highest authority – in most of the principal centers of Byzantine Italy, is not securely attested at Rome until the beginning of the eighth century, though it is often assumed that *duces* were installed there, too, rather earlier.[8] In any case, the conduct of municipal affairs was the mandate of agents designated by the provincial government in Ravenna, though these functionaries tended in practice to share in the exercise of power with representatives of the Church of Rome, which with the final

---

[3] The single best treatment of the social and political structures of Byzantine Italy is Brown 1984, to which should be added the many contributions of A. Guillou. The military and political developments of the period 554–751 are conveniently summarized in Zanini 1998, 33–104, and Guillou 1988. All of these works are indebted to the fundamental studies of Diehl 1888, Hartmann 1889 and Bertolini 1941.

[4] Brown 1984, 48–53 and 150–5.

[5] On the Byzantine prefecture of Italy, see Brown 1984, 10–12. The *praefectus urbi* is last mentioned in 599 (*GR* 9, 116 and 117). For an example of the Praetorian Prefect's jurisdiction at Rome (in 602), see below n. 12.

[6] The final reference of 639 is to the "glorious seat of the most eminent prefect": see *P. Ital.* 22, 52. On the increasing predominance of the army and the rise of a militarized ruling class in the seventh century, see Brown 1984; cf. Noble 1984, 2–9; Wickham 1981, 74ff.

[7] *LP* I, 328; *ibid.* 331; *ibid.* 369.

[8] Brown 1984, 53–8; Bavant 1979, esp. 62ff. Delogu (2000a, 93) continues to maintain that the position of duke was instituted at approximately the time of its initial appearance in the sources. Whatever the case, I agree that the first unambiguous attestation of a *dux Romae* occurs only in reference to events of 711 (*LP* I, 392), after which mention of the office becomes increasingly common (e.g. *LP* I, 403).

demise of the old Roman senate became the lone locally constituted authority of any significance.[9]

But for all that the eminence of the popes was great and growing, their role in secular affairs prior to the eighth century should not be overstated. The pontificate of Gregory I is usually seen as a watershed moment in Rome's transition to papal rule, a notion that stems principally from the fact that an anomalously massive quantity of papal correspondence survives from Gregory's reign, which furnishes frequent glimpses of the pope acting as *de facto* leader of his city during the chaotic years after 592 when it was repeatedly threatened by Lombard armies and cut off from the rest of Byzantine Italy. It has hence been claimed that from this time on, the bishops of Rome took the lead in provisioning the city, maintaining its buildings, and generally arrogating to themselves the erstwhile prerogatives of the civic administration.[10] The important fact too often overlooked is that Gregory did rule in exceptional times, when Rome's isolation from the provincial authorities in Ravenna and the preoccupation of its Byzantine garrison and commanders with the defense of strategic centers elsewhere in central Italy combined to create a void on the "home front" that the pope was best situated to fill. It by no means follows that the temporal mandate of the papacy was dramatically and permanently expanded; and there is in fact better reason to think that any extraordinary powers assumed by Gregory reverted to the purview of secular administrators for at least a century following the return of somewhat more stable conditions after 598.[11]

Turning specifically to the issue of urban infrastructure, there is good evidence that Gregory himself, near the end of his reign, still expected the responsibility for maintenance to devolve on imperial officials. In 602, he asked a subdeacon in Ravenna to entreat the Praetorian Prefect to dispatch an official with all possible haste to take charge of the Roman aqueducts, which were rapidly falling into a ruinous state.[12] Clearly, Gregory was not

---

[9] While a role in government may initially have been envisioned for the senate, it seems never to have recovered from the shock of the Gothic Wars, and instead teetered toward extinction over the second half of the sixth century, disappearing finally after 603; see Brown 1984, 21–37; Arnaldi 1982.

[10] See e.g. Llewellyn 1993, 141; Durliat 1990, 148ff.; Noble 1984, 9–12; Arnaldi 1982, 6ff.

[11] Cf. Delogu 2001, 10ff.; 2000a, 93ff.; Marazzi 2001b, 43ff. See now also Humphries 2007.

[12] GR 12, 6: *Praeterea ante aliquantum temporis experientiae tuae praeceperamus, ut apud eminentissimum filium nostrum praefectum ageret, quatenus cura formarum committi Augusto viro clarissimo debuisset, pro eo quod omnino sollicitus atque strenuus vir est; et ita hactenus distulisti, ut nobis nec, quid egeris, indicaris; et ideo apud eundem eminentissimum filium nostrum vel modo omni agere intentione festina, ut formae praedicto clarissimo viro per omnia committantur, quatenus sollicitudine sua aliquid in eas valeat reparare.*

supposed to concern himself directly with the aqueducts, nor could he appoint an agent of his own choosing to do so. Rather than as an independent authority, the pope appears here as an accomplice of the civil bureaucratic apparatus, inspired by a pastoral concern for living conditions in his city that led him to advise and admonish more than to command.

Much the same can be said for the rest of the seventh century, for which period there is only a garbled interpolation in the *LP*, to the effect that Pope Honorius I (625–38) occupied himself with the mills on the Janiculum and a concomitant restoration of the Aqua Traiana, to set against a number of indicators of continued secular control over public buildings.[13] When Boniface IV (608–15) set out to transform the Pantheon into a church, he had first to seek the permission of the emperor Phocas.[14] Honorius likewise needed a special dispensation from Heraclius to strip the temple of Venus and Rome of its bronze roof-tiles, which went to the repair of St. Peter's.[15] When the emperor Constans II visited Rome in 663, he had his agents strip the city of all the bronze they could get their hands on, which was promptly embarked on ships bound for Constantinople.[16] Not even the roof-tiles of the Pantheon, which his predecessor had granted to Boniface for consecration as a church, were spared. It should finally be recalled that the imperial palace, where Constans II likely stayed during his twelve days in Rome, continued to be presided over by a civic official called the *curator palatii Urbis Romae*.[17] The logical conclusion is that the monumental patrimony of Rome remained in the seventh century the titular possession of the emperor, who was represented locally by officials attached to the Byzantine civil service, among which a *curator aquarum* and a *curator palatii* are securely attested.[18] While the influence of the popes is not to be discounted, in the few documented instances where they looked to intervene directly in the profane landscape of the city, it was more often than not with the purpose of enriching the holdings of the Church.

---

[13] *LP* I, 324: *Et ibi constituit mola in murum in loco Traiani, iuxta murum civitatis, et formam qui deducit aqua in lacum Sabbatinum et sub se formam qui conducit aqua Tiberis.* I would be cautious of assuming on the basis of this rather suspect passage that Honorius was in overall charge of the water supply of the city, as Brown has it; his further claim that the popes henceforth also "assumed responsibility for the city's walls" is not minimally supported by the text (Brown 1984, 12).

[14] *LP* I, 317.   [15] *LP* I, 323.   [16] Paul the Deacon, *Hist. Lang.* 5, 11; *LP* I, 343.

[17] The office belonged to Plato, father of John VII, who died in 687; see Chapter 1, n. 107; cf. Delogu 2000a, 94.

[18] Above nn. 12 and 17.

As for the Aurelian Wall, it is conspicuously absent from the documentary records of the period. On the analogy of the palace and the aqueducts, it too was likely under the care of a *curator*, though it is not impossible that the commanders of the garrison were responsible for co-ordinating the upkeep of the Wall they defended. The almost complete lack of pertinent information is perhaps the most useful available indicator. With all due caveats about arguments from silence, the reticence of the sources is nonetheless likely to reflect a reality that saw a minimum of work accomplished around the defensive perimeter. With the city and its buildings controlled by representatives of a distant authority that was itself stretched economically and militarily to the breaking point, it is logical to postulate that interventions on the Wall were limited to the most essential, localized repairs of damage that threatened to compromise its defensive integrity, for all that the inherent bias in favor of Church-sponsored projects in the predominantly ecclesiastical sources for the period (the *LP* above all) may have further reduced the apparent extent of "Byzantine" civic building initiatives.[19] The popes, meanwhile, themselves possessed of limited resources for use even in ecclesiastical building projects, are still more unlikely to have occupied themselves with nineteen kilometers' worth of financial liability for which they were not technically responsible. As neither administrators nor popes could assert autonomous control over the Wall and its various legacies, in other words, there was little incentive for either to do anything worth publicizing.

From the end of the seventh century, however, the balance of power in Rome would begin to change fundamentally, and with it the relationship between the city and its enceinte. In step with a growing current of Italian opposition to eastern intervention in the affairs of the peninsula, above all in matters of religious policy, the Roman pontiffs came increasingly to assert their independence from Constantinople, and to take a more active role in local government and administration.[20] Silver coinage bearing papal monograms appeared to herald the nascent temporal sovereignty of the popes, progressing from tentative beginnings under Sergius (687–701) and Constantine (708–15) to more regular issues from the time of Gregory III (731–41) onward.[21] More tellingly still, the popes began to

---

[19] The difficulties of identifying such hypothetical seventh-century repairs in the standing fabric of the Wall (none have been convincingly individuated) have been discussed above in Chapter 1; on the pervasive downplaying of Byzantine projects in the *LP*, see Coates-Stephens 2006.

[20] Delogu 2000a, 100–2; Noble 1984, 16ff.; Bertolini 1968 [1958], 265–308.

[21] See Morrison and Barrandon 1988, esp. 158ff.; cf. Delogu 1989, 97–105.

profit from the support of the military contingents stationed in Italy, which since the mid seventh century had been composed mainly of local levies, essentially militias with roots in the territories they defended, as opposed to the mobile detachments of the standing Byzantine army that had previously been in place.[22] Hence, the Roman garrison came to identify itself progressively more with local interests, which were increasingly represented by the person of the pope.

In 653, the exarch had still been able to deport Pope Martin to Constantinople – allegedly over the wailing protests of the clergy and laity – with the apparent complicity of the troops at Rome.[23] Yet forty years later, when the *protospatharius* Zachary was sent to Rome to do the same with Pope Sergius, the imperial official famously had to hide under the pope's bed to escape the outraged fury of the Roman army and people.[24] In *c.* 725, the supreme Byzantine official in the city, the recently arrived *dux Romae* Marinus, was reduced to conspiring with disaffected members of the Roman clergy in a failed attempt to assassinate Gregory II, in whose removal he evidently expected no support from the army.[25] When the exarch Paul was ordered by Emperor Leo III to apprehend the pope shortly thereafter, he was unable even to approach the city, instead finding his passage blocked at the Salarian Bridge by an armed multitude.[26] By the 720s, if not earlier, the force of Roman arms was effectively an instrument of papal policy.

The abortive attempts to depose Gregory II came during the initial phases of a series of events that has justly been seen as the prelude to the establishment of *de facto* papal autonomy.[27] A first crisis was provoked by the pope's refusal to pay additional taxes levied on Church lands by Emperor Leo III, as a result of which Church patrimonies in southern Italy and Sicily were subtracted from Roman jurisdiction when it proved impossible to install a more pliant figure on the throne of Saint Peter. The rupture between Rome and Constantinople was further exacerbated with the promulgation of iconoclasm by the eastern emperor in 726–7, a policy

---

[22] Toubert 2001, 81–7; Brown 1984, 82ff.; Noble 1984, 234–6.

[23] There is at any rate no indication that the Roman garrison made any attempt to prevent the deportation of the pope: see *LP* I, 338, with Llewellyn 1993, 152ff.; Bertolini 1968 [1958], 285–8.

[24] *LP* I, 373–4; Llewellyn 1993, 160–61.   [25] *LP* I, 403.

[26] *LP* I, 404; cf. Paul the Deacon, *Hist. Lang.* 6, 49.

[27] See Marazzi 1993; 1991; Noble 1984, 28–60; Ullmann 1970, 44–52; *contra* Llewellyn 1986, who defends the older view that nothing approaching autonomous papal government existed prior to the 750s.

which the pope led Italy and the rest of the Christian West in firmly repudiating. Relations between the imperial and papal courts were irreparably damaged; and Rome and its immediate hinterland – an area roughly corresponding to modern Lazio – dropped out of the networks of trade and communications that had previously linked the region with the rest of the Byzantine Mediterranean.[28] From the time of Gregory III (731–41) on, the popes began to act more and more like independent sovereigns, treating with foreign heads of state and seeking new alliances with (amongst others) the Franks to ensure the survival of their incipient regional polity, and defending the possessions of the Church and its servants against the inroads of Lombards and Byzantines (soon to become *nefandissimi Graeci*) alike.[29]

The establishment of temporal hegemony on the part of the popes proceeded in lock step with their assumption of responsibility for the defenses of the city. After Sisinnius punctuated the twenty days of his reign in 708 by commissioning the preparation of mortar for the circuit, which his immediate successor Constantine is not recorded as having used, it was left to Gregory II to launch the first recorded campaign of restoration conducted under papal auspices. When the "various tumults" of his pontificate prevented him from finishing the project, Gregory III carried the initiative of his predecessor through to conclusion.[30] As they were laying the political and ideological foundations for the "Republic of Saint Peter," that is, the two Gregories were also rehabilitating the urban enceinte, and in the process placing it unequivocally and ostentatiously under their personal tutelage. The "imperial" Wall guarded by "imperial"

---

[28] The thesis that the years around 730 constituted a crucial turning point in relations between Rome and the East is now increasingly backed by archaeological data. Of special note is the exactly contemporary collapse of the Byzantine trimetallic monetary system, which had remained relatively robust throughout the seventh century and the opening decades of the eighth: see Rovelli 2001 and 2000. While the precipitous decline in imported ceramics from Africa and the East at Rome from the beginning of the eighth century must in part reflect the widely attested, systemic breakdown of Mediterranean-wide trade networks that occurred at the time (see above Chapter 4, n. 128), the local situation will have been compounded by the break with Byzantium. The ceramics from the eighth-century deposit at the Crypta Balbi in particular have led to propositions – in anticipation of necessary further study – that the loss of Church patrimonies in Sicily and the far South prompted still greater reliance on Campanian and domestic produce: see Romei 2004, esp. 278–85; Arthur 1993.

[29] Cf. Patlagean 2002, 24–6; Noble 1984, 44ff.; Arnaldi 1981, esp. 393–9. Gregory III was entreating the Franks for their support already in 739 (*CC* 1–2), though the call was not heeded until the 750s. On *nefandissimi Graeci*, see *CC* 30 (*c.* 761–6), p. 536; cf. *CC* 11, p. 506 (the *pestifera malitia* of the Greeks in 757); and *CC* 32, p. 539: *impia hereticorum Grecorum malitia*.

[30] For the relevant passages in the *LP*, see above Chapter 1, nn. 109–111.

contingents of the seventh century gave way to a papal bastion, serviced by the Church and manned by troops whose loyalties lay in practice (whatever their nominal allegiance) more with the popes than with the emperors in Constantinople and their agents. The Wall thus appears as a finely calibrated barometer of a changing political climate, and an important component in the assertion of pontifical control over the city of Rome, as it would remain for the next century and a half.

The middle decades of the eighth century saw the steady consolidation of the rule of the popes, a process punctuated by Steven II's conclusion of a formal alliance with the Franks in 754, which markedly enhanced the stability and prestige of the papal *res publica Romanorum*, and paved the way for the more programmatic conceptualization of the temporal sovereignty of the Church most famously embodied in the "Donation of Constantine," produced (probably) under Paul I (757–67).[31] The dominion of St. Peter and the worldly authority of its regents jointly reached their pinnacle under Hadrian I (772–95), who worked tirelessly during his long reign to restore to Rome a physical presence befitting the resurgent capital of what was no longer a strictly spiritual empire.[32] Among his many projects for the embellishment of the city and the restoration of its infrastructure, Hadrian included two separate campaigns of repair on the Wall,[33] the first recorded since Gregory III, which between them likely comprised the most extensive of all the early medieval restorations.

The first phase of work dates to 776, two years after the defeat of the Lombards and the establishment of relative peace under Frankish rule. As it cannot then have been directly connected with the final Lombard incursions into Roman territory in 773–4, the initiative is best envisioned as a general overhaul aimed at rectifying the worst of the damage sustained amidst the tumults of the preceding decades, most serious among them

---

[31] *Constitutum Constantini*, H. Fuhrmann, *MGH Fontes iuris germanici antiqui*, 10. There is now a solid consensus that the document dates to the second half of the eighth century (the salient points of a massive bibliography are reviewed in Noble 1984, 134–7); though the more precise attribution to Paul I is not assured, the arguments in its favor are strong; see e.g. Arnaldi 1987, 141–7; Fuhrmann 1973. On the alliance with the Franks and its repercussions in Rome, see Patlagean 2002, 29ff.; Arnaldi 1987; Noble 1984; Bertolini 1968 [1948]; 1941, 547–698.

[32] Cf. Delogu 2000b, 217. On Hadrian's building activities, in addition to Geertman's seminal work (Geertman 1975, esp. 7–36), see Bauer 2003, 189–203; Noble 2000c; Pani Ermini 1992; Krautheimer 1980, 109ff.

[33] Duchesne's suggestion that the second passage describing work on the Wall merely repeats the first has been convincingly refuted by Geertman, whose proposed chronology for the two distinct phases I have followed below; see Duchesne, *LP* I, ccxxxvi; *contra* Geertman 1975, 29.

perhaps the siege of 756, when several aqueducts clearly did suffer serious harm that was left for Hadrian to fix "after the space of twenty years had already passed," at the same time he was attending to the Wall.[34] The considerable sum of 100 pounds of gold was spent on the repair, a figure (equivalent to 7,200 *solidi*) that must have represented a sizeable chunk, if not the entirety, of the annual construction budget of the Roman Church.[35]

Hadrian's decision to commence a second phase of repairs fourteen years later in 790 is more noteworthy still.[36] In the first place, Rome was arguably safer in *c.* 790, after sixteen years of a stabilizing Carolingian presence in the Italian peninsula, than it had been at any time in the preceding two centuries. Indeed, the restoration of the aqueducts at the time of the first renovation of the Wall indicates that, already in 776, the city was considered sufficiently secure to justify the rebuilding of these fragile and exposed structures. Moreover, and *a fortiori* still more surprising, the later restoration very possibly surpassed the scope of the first effort, if the fact that no additional projects are attested for the period – as there had been in plenty when the Wall was initially refurbished in 776 – is any indication.[37] The extensive maintenance performed on the circuit in 790 was thus an expensive undertaking of manifestly high priority that strictly practical considerations of tactical military utility seem inadequate to explain. It will hence be well to inquire in more detail into why Hadrian did what he did: the answers should reveal much about the new

[34] The *forma Sabbatina* and *forma Iovia* were both restored *per evoluta viginti annorum spatia*, almost certainly in the same year as the Wall (*LP* I, 503–4); scholars since Duchesne have (I think correctly) assumed that much of the damage was done in 756, and counted forward twenty years to obtain a date for the refurbishing of both Wall and aqueducts: see Duchesne, *LP* I, ccxxxiv; Geertman 1975, 22–4. On Hadrian's reconstruction of the aqueducts, see Coates-Stephens 2003a; 2003b; 1999; 1998. The only improvements to the Wall undertaken by Hadrian in anticipation of the Lombard attacks, according to the *LP*, involved work on some of the gates: see *LP* I, 493; cf. Pani Ermini 1992, 496–7.

[35] One-fourth of the annual revenues of the Church was earmarked for construction projects; see *Liber Diurnus* (Foerster), p. 81. Based on the reported yearly return from the Sicilian patrimonies in the early eighth century, which amounted to 25,000 *solidi*, Durliat estimated the total yearly budget of the Roman Church at this period at a maximum of 50,000 *solidi* (Durliat 1990, 556–7), an amount that must subsequently have declined dramatically following the loss of Sicily and the other southern Italian patrimonies in 732–3. If Durliat's numbers are anywhere near the mark, the total annual take of the Church in the later eighth century is unlikely to have been much greater than 28,800 *solidi* (the figure that results from multiplying Hadrian's expenditure of 7,200 *solidi* on the Wall by four).

[36] *LP* I, 513; see below n. 41. The passage occurs in the narrative covering the fourteenth indiction (the year 790), according to Geertman's chronological schema; see Geertman 1975, 29 and 32.

[37] Cf. Geertman 1975, 29.

prominence of the Wall, and the crucial role it came to play in molding physical and mental topographies in the "Republic of St. Peter."

6.2   The Aurelian Wall and Pope Hadrian's Rome: the home front

In his dual capacities as ruler of a local polity and rector of western Christendom, Hadrian was playing simultaneously to a domestic and an international audience in the performance of his office. The stature of the Aurelian Wall was such that it came to inform papal policy with regard to both "audiences," as we shall see in what follows, beginning closer to home and proceeding to the far fringes of Europe.

It has been frequently observed that the construction boom that began with Gregory II and peaked under Hadrian I and Leo III was part and parcel of the papal takeover of Rome;[38] and certainly it is safe to say generally that Hadrian's successive restorations of the Wall were an architectonic assertion of his status as the leading patron and protector of what had become more than ever a "city of the church."[39] There are several further observations to be made, however, which may between them permit a more nuanced explanation for the decision to "re-refurbish" already serviceable defenses in a time of unparalleled peace and growing prosperity.[40]

To begin with, it bears repeating that the scale and logistical complexity of the enterprise were remarkable for their time, so much so that the extraordinary mobilization of resources and the massive projection of papal control over lay craftsmen and workers required to complete the task were plausibly envisioned as desirable ends in themselves.

What was needed above all was manual labor; and the two *LP* passages on the Hadrianic restorations do, in fact, place particular stress on the provenience of the workforce and the expenditures made for its upkeep:

So indeed the God-protected prelate, seeing that the walls of the city of Rome were through the ravages of time consigned to ruin, with many towers in various places destroyed all the way to the ground, collecting with most skillful diligence all the

---

[38]   See the sources cited above at n. 32.   [39]   The phrase is Marazzi's (2000, 35).

[40]   That the Wall was defensively viable before the restoration of 790 seems much the likeliest conclusion, given that it remained unbreached throughout the Lombard siege of 756, was repaired in 776, and thereafter suffered neither attacks nor reported natural disasters in the years leading up to 790 (the most severe event of Hadrian's pontificate was the flood of December 791, which occurred a year after the final restoration).

cities of both Tuscia and Campania [northern and southern Lazio, respectively], together with the people of Rome and its suburbs and also all the ecclesiastical patrimonies, and apportioning sections to all, with Church rations and wages, he renewed and adorned the whole city by restoring the circuit.[41]

From the sound of it, Hadrian conscripted laborers from the far corners of the papal "state," drawing them from the resident population of Rome, its surrounding countryside and the towns of Lazio, and from Church estates, which by his time must have meant primarily *domuscultae* operating under the direct supervision of the ecclesiastical administration at the Lateran. This picture is broadly confirmed by the description of the building of Leo IV's wall around the Vatican in the following century, where the biographer again stressed the contribution of both lay and ecclesiastical contingents. In this case, two extant inscriptions confirm the participation of "militias" from two *domuscultae*, each of which was tasked with erecting a length of wall and one or two towers.[42]

Beyond what can be gleaned from these few brief descriptions of the major mural projects in Rome, the sparse surviving evidence for the early-medieval building industry in Rome and Italy permits a few additional general observations about the organization and composition of the personnel assembled by Hadrian.[43] The projects of 776 and 790 will have

---

[41] *LP* I, 513 (*anno* 790): *Ipse vero Deo protectus praesul conspiciens muros huius civitatis Romanae per olitana tempora in ruinis positos et per loca plures turres usque ad terram eversas, per suum sollertissimum studium totas civitates tam Tusciae quamque Campaniae congregans, una cum popolo Romano eiusque suburbanis necnon et tota ecclesiastica patrimonia omnibus per pedicas dividens cum sumptis dapibusque apostolicis, totam urbem in circuitu restaurans renovavit ac decoravit; on the earlier campaign, see LP* I, 501: *ubi et multa stipendia tribuit, tam in mercedes eorum qui ipsum murum fabricaverunt, quamque in ipsorum alimentis, simulque et in calce atque diversis utilitatibus usque ad centum auri libras expendit.*

[42] *LP* II, 123: *Cepit autem ex tunc de praedicto negotio valde esse sollicitus. Convocansque cunctos sanctae Dei fideles ecclesiae, petens ab eis ore suo consilium qualiter tantam murorum cito valuisset fabricam consummari, tunc omnibus ita visum est, ut de singulis civitatibus massisque universis publicis ac monasteriis, per vices suas generaliter advenire fecisset, sicut et factum est.* The inscriptions read: TEMPORIB(US) DOM(INI) LEONIS Q(UARTI) P(A)P(AE) HANC PAGINE ET DUAS TURRES SALTISINE MILITIA CONSTRUXIT; and HANC TURREM ET PAGINE UNA FACTA A MILITIAE CAPRACORUM TEM(PORE) DOM(INI) LEONIS QUAR(TI) P(A)P(AE) EGO AGATHO E. . .; they are shown in Pani Ermini 1992, figs. 16–17; see also Ward-Perkins and Gibson 1979, 32–3. The *domusculta* of Capracorum is well-known; the *domusculta*(?) of Saltisina is otherwise unattested. cf. generally Marazzi 1998, 258–61; Christie 1991, 8–9.

[43] On the mechanics of Hadrian's building projects, cf. Noble 2000c, esp. 58–73; Pani Ermini 1992, 503ff. On technical standards at Rome and their bearing on the composition of the workforce, see Santangeli Valenzani 2007; 2003b; 2002; more generally on the building industry in early-medieval Italy, see Galetti 2006 and 1994; Fiorani 1996; Parenti 1994; also Ward-Perkins 1984, 179–99, on maintenance of essential infrastructure ("Streets, Bridges and City Walls").

unfolded under the aegis of the *prior vestiarii* (or *vestiarius/vesterarius*), the prominent official whose department at the Lateran was charged with, amongst other things, the management of Church finances, including building expenditures, and the redaction of the *Liber Pontificalis*.[44] While Hadrian twice dispatched his "most faithful *vestiarius* Januarius" to oversee in person important restorations at St. Peter's and St. Paul's,[45] it is not certain that all *vestiarii* were similarly "hands-on" in their approach, and other experts may have been recruited in a supervisory capacity, as Bishop Wilcharius of Sens famously was for the re-roofing of St. Peter's.[46] Whoever they were, the directors will have had at their disposal a cadre of skilled building professionals, a rarified group in early-medieval Italy employed only by those few – mostly bishops and the popes themselves – able to commission monumental buildings in brick and stone. These *magistri murarum*, like the *magistri de ligno et lapide* hired to build walls for the monastery of Bobbio in the 830s, were thus a precious commodity whose very presence betokened elevated patronage.[47] With Hadrian's building boom in full swing, such experts must already have been present in Rome in unusual numbers that presumably grew further with the influx of workers summoned from Tuscia and Campania, some few of whom surely had specialized skills. The majority of those conscripted for the restoration of the Wall, however, were in all probability unskilled laborers, as neither the bulk of the Roman citizenry nor the agrarian population of rural Lazio can have been proficient in the erection of bonded masonry structures. The large-scale participation of novices in the restoration of urban defenses was, of course, a venerable tradition with roots stretching back to late antiquity, and at Rome to Valentian III's proclamation of 440.[48] We might envision work-gangs made up mostly of inexperienced workers, assisted or supervised by one or more relatively able craftsmen, operating at various points around the circuit.

Turning to the physical evidence, it has to be said that the technical standard of the eighth- and ninth-century repairs to the Wall, some of which must belong to the age of Hadrian, makes it difficult to say whether or not they were executed by people who in some sense built for a living.

---

[44] See Geertman 1975, 34–5.   [45] *LP* I, 505–6.

[46] *CC* 65 (*anno* 779–80); cf. Noble 2000c, 65–6; Pani Ermini 1992, 498–505; Krautheimer 1980, 112. Interestingly, the *vestiarius* at the time of the overhaul of the Wall in 790 was the future Pope Leo III (see *LP* II, 1, with Geertman 1975, 34–5), who continued in the post until his election to the pontificate, when he showed his keen interest in the potential of circuit walls by beginning one around the Vatican (*LP* II, 123).

[47] Galetti 1994, 475–6.   [48] See Chapter 1, n. 71.

The early-medieval segments are decidedly irregular and indeed rather amateurish in appearance – particularly in comparison to the ancient brickwork around them – but then so, too, is the masonry of the many churches built or repaired at approximately the same time,[49] the sheer number of which implies the existence of a corps of reasonably experienced professionals engaged in their construction. In the case of the Leonine Wall around the Vatican, where extensive tracts of the original fabric are preserved, the standard of work varies widely from section to section,[50] which proves that some of the work-gangs employed were better at laying regular courses of bricks than others, but little more. If any conclusion is permitted, we might say that in 790, everyone who was anyone in the central Italian building industry, and many others besides, were mobilized, provided for, and set to work by Hadrian's command, thus becoming in a sense his "personal" employees and the agents of his grand designs.

In addition to human resources, the restoration of the Wall required the provision of building materials in quantity. In an age when raw materials were most often recycled from earlier structures, the one commodity that always had to be produced from scratch was mortar. Though its preparation can never have ceased entirely at Rome,[51] the initial repairs to the Wall in the first half of the eighth century had evidently required an exceptional surge in production, judging by the emphasis of the *LP*, where the one non-generic detail in the four-line Life of Sisinnius is his order for the preparation of mortar to be used on the circuit.[52] Gregory II is likewise said to have stockpiled mortar "from the beginning of his pontificate" in anticipation of the planned restoration of the Wall, while the personal funds devoted by Gregory III to the completion of the project went very specifically to "payments to the craftsmen and the expense of buying mortar."[53] Mortar is also the lone material expense listed in relation to Hadrian's repairs, though it appears rather in passing in 776 and not at all in 790: we might assume that the recent flurry of building projects in Rome had engendered a flourishing production apparatus capable of supplying mortar for the Wall without occasioning much comment.

---

[49] Cf. Ward-Perkins and Gibson 1979, 55.   [50] *Ibid.* 56.

[51] As can be deduced from the continuous activity in the sphere of monumental building documented in e.g. Coates-Stephens 1997. The primary ingredients of mortar will, of course, have remained readily available at Rome: the ancient monuments of the city furnished limitless limestone and marble for lime, and *pozzolana* abounded in the papal patrimonies in Lazio; on the mortar-industry at Rome in late antiquity, see above Chapter 2.

[52] *LP* I, 388.   [53] *LP* I, 396 and 420, respectively.

Nonetheless, Hadrian's two restorations must have required prodigious quantities of mortar, which was furnished by a local industry itself subsidized by sizeable papal expenditures.[54]

As for the tufa blocks employed in the Wall, they are all unquestionably recycled from earlier Roman buildings. All the same, a co-ordinated effort was necessary for the labor-intensive process of their recuperation. Though detailed evidence is lacking, such salvage operations must have been performed by dedicated crews authorized to dismantle the remains of older buildings, and to carry off the raw materials to new construction sites.[55] The appropriation and reuse of these blocks thus betokens effective control over, even ownership of, Rome's physical patrimony. In this context, it bears recalling that construction in recycled tufa blocks became really common only beginning with Hadrian. In sending crews amidst the ruins of Rome and ostentatiously displaying the materials they carted off in his monumental architectural commissions, such as the colonnade from the Wall to St. Peter's that was restored with over 12,000 tufa blocks recovered from the banks of the Tiber,[56] Hadrian palpably demonstrated his "ownership" of old Rome in the rising walls of his new city, just as he did by transferring famous surviving Roman sculptures to the Lateran.[57] Whoever – and Hadrian is the best candidate, along with Leo IV – chose to use tufa blocks to restore the enceinte did the same, possessing the old city and leaving the mark of this possession on the face of the new.

Finally, Hadrian's construction gangs will have needed supplies of bricks. It is generally agreed that the large majority of the bricks used in early-medieval Rome were recycled, though bricks and especially roof tiles

[54] There is explicit notice to this effect in 776, when mortar production consumed a chunk worth mentioning of Hadrian's 100 pounds of gold (*LP* I, 501): ...*et in calce atque diversis utilitatibus usque ad centum auri libras expendit.* The mortar used in the Leonine Wall and the early-medieval sections of the Aurelian Wall is generally quite tenacious, though in some cases markedly poorer stuff was employed, for examples of which see Coates-Stephens and Parisi 1999, 89; Ward-Perkins and Gibson 1979, 38.

[55] As occurred during the construction of Santa Maria in Cosmedin in 781–2, in the course of which an existing monument in *Tubertinos tufos* (the *ara maxima* of Hercules?) was razed; some of the blocks thus obtained must be the ones used in the foundations of the church: see *LP* I, 507; cf. Pani Ermini 1992, 490ff.

[56] *LP* I, 507.

[57] Broadly on the conceptual and ideological ramifications of the use of *spolia* in the early Middle Ages, see the recent Spoletan *settimana* on the subject (*Settimane del CISAM* 46, Spoleto, 1999). The most comprehensive evaluation of *spolia* in early-Christian Rome is Hansen 2003; see also the various contributions in Borghini, Callegari and Nista 2004; and cf. the perceptive comments in Spera 1999, 464. On the transfer of statues to the Lateran and more generally on Hadrian's use of *spolia* to appropriate the Roman past, see Hansen 2003, 144–51, esp. 148; Herklotz 1985, 34–42.

did continue to be produced in Rome and elsewhere in Italy throughout the early Middle Ages, albeit on a sporadic and dramatically reduced basis.[58] Old bricks are assumed to have been used for the Wall, too, and the material recovered from a recent collapse of an early-medieval curtain near the Porta Maggiore indeed looks all to have been reused.[59] Yet it is worth pointing out that roof tiles were demonstrably made under Hadrian, as the discovery of a number of specimens stamped with his name proves. Setting aside the two stamped tiles probably attributable to John VII (705–7), he is in fact the one early-medieval pope to leave any evidence of the fabrication of structural ceramics.[60] Barring future finds of stamps belonging to others, we are left with one of two conclusions: either Hadrian was the only pope of his age to make tiles, or he was the only one ostentatiously to publicize the fact.[61] In either case, his was a novel initiative that directly and perhaps not coincidentally recalled the example of the emperors who monopolized brick production in late antiquity.

Did Hadrian's repairs to the circuit themselves prompt the resuscitation of a system of *figlinae*, as the construction of Aurelian's Wall seems to have done? Probably not, especially since all the Hadrianic stamps known to me are on roof tiles, which are *a priori* more likely to have been needed in quantity than more easily recycled bricks.[62] Nonetheless, I would be cautious of blandly assuming that no new bricks were ordered for the circuit, and I find it suggestive that the most zealous restorer of the Wall was the same pope responsible for putting *figlinae* back on the (archaeological) map.

Whatever the reality of such particulars, the key point to be made is that the two campaigns of mural repairs launched by Hadrian placed him firmly, and I think very consciously, in the mold of his late-Roman imperial predecessors. The connection is particularly clear with regard to the provision of labor: for the first time at Rome since late antiquity, massive levies of civilian workers were conscripted to accomplish a program of public works initiated by a strong central authority. In noting this

---

[58] See Galetti 2006, 68–71; 1994, 472–4; Parenti 1994, 487–9; Arthur and Whitehouse 1983.

[59] Coates-Stephens and Parisi 1999.

[60] On the stamps of both John and Hadrian, see Steinby 2001, 143.

[61] Cf. Bauer 2003, 192.

[62] While fragmentary bricks work reasonably well for facing walls, it is considerably harder to build a functional roof with anything other than relatively pristine tiles, as Arthur and Whitehouse point out (1983, 527). The many churches in particular built new or re-roofed under Hadrian would have required large amounts of whole tiles that cannot all have been left over from antiquity.

similarity with late-antique precedent, others have claimed Hadrian's initiative as proof of continuous civilian involvement in the maintenance of essential infrastructure from the fifth century through the eighth.[63] In so doing, they may have underestimated the revolutionary character of Hadrian's policies. There is no evidence of civilian participation *en masse* in public works at Rome during the period of Byzantine hegemony,[64] and the best comparative evidence from elsewhere in Italy demonstrates that, at Verona, it was only with the establishment of Carolingian overlordship that civilians were again employed to repair their wall.[65] More than simply acting like a Roman emperor, Hadrian was resurrecting an elaborate and ramified system of institutional control over a dependent civilian populace; and it was the Wall, and to a lesser extent the aqueducts, that gave him the pretext for doing so.[66] Though the importance of the Wall stands out less sharply in the matter of building materials, here too it can be seen as a component part of a broader assertion of papal control over the mechanisms of supply and production. The repairs of 776 and 790 contributed to the greatest demand for mortar seen at Rome since the sixth century at the latest, when its provision had still been a compulsory *munus* exacted by the state. As for the materials with which the Wall was faced, those that were recycled visibly advertised Hadrian's absolute control over the old imperial capital, while any new ceramic products commissioned for

---

[63] Ward-Perkins 1984, 195–6; Ward-Perkins and Gibson 1979, 32; cf. Noble 2000c, 67. Krautheimer (1980, 111) and Pani Ermini (1992, 503) justly acknowledge the lack of evidence for such continuity between the sixth and eighth centuries.

[64] As noted above with regard to the Wall itself; cf. also Krautheimer and Pani Ermini in the preceding note. Indeed, it is more likely that the coming of the Byzantines to Rome under Belisarius if anything marked the end of mass conscriptions of civilian laborers: Belisarius himself only rather reluctantly used Roman citizens to help defend the Wall (Procopius, *BG* 1, 25, 11ff.), and is never said to have conscripted them wholesale to repair the defenses, apparently preferring to use his own troops instead.

[65] *Codice Diplomatico Veronese* (2 vols., V. Fainelli ed., Venice, 1940–63) I, 147, cited in Ward-Perkins 1984, 196. Ward-Perkins oddly uses this text to support his view that civilian maintenance of urban defenses was a constant between late antiquity and the early Middle Ages, when it actually seems to show that the citizens of Verona had not been responsible for repairing their enceinte under Lombard rule!

[66] Hadrian "assembled a multitude of people" (*aggregans multitudinem populi*; *LP* I, 503) to fix the Aqua Sabbatina, and "assembled a multitude of people from the region of Campania" (*aggregans multitudinem populi partibus Campanie*; *LP* I, 504) for the Claudia, but neither instance conjures up anything like the image of universal participation on the part of the citizenry of Rome and all its surrounding regions conveyed by the passage on the wall-repair of 790 (*LP* I, 513).

the task would have proclaimed him the direct heir of the emperors as a producer as well, as certainly did the new roof tiles that bore his name.

While there can be no doubt that Hadrian's interventions on the Wall provoked a substantial mobilization of human and financial resources that was structurally similar to its late-imperial precedents, it remains to be stressed that the resemblance was neither casual nor purely structural. Hadrian was the leading avatar of a new formulation of the temporal sovereignty of the papacy, and a highly self-aware renovator of the ideal Christian capital that late-antique Rome was perceived to have been.[67] The ensemble of his building enterprises, among which the Wall took pride of place, enabled Hadrian to refashion himself in the image of an "imperial" Christian sovereign by taking direct control of the means necessary to effect his ambitious reconstruction of the city of Rome.

Of course, the desire to preside over monumental construction projects does not fully explain why Hadrian repeatedly fixed the Wall, the repair and revalorization of which was for many reasons a desirable complement to the papal takeover of Rome. Several motives for the rehabilitation of the enceinte have already been suggested in the previous chapter, among them its capacity to reify the physical and liturgical compass of the urban Church, and to frame a new geography of the saints, to which I would here add a political and administrative dimension. By the later eighth century, the growing prestige of St. Peter's and the concomitant urban expansion of its surroundings had engendered a bipolar cityscape divided between the twin axes of the Lateran and the Vatican, two complementary but distinct halves of papal Rome between which the Wall was admirably placed to mediate.

The papal alliance with the Franks and the generally more settled conditions that ensued upon the end of Lombard domination in northern Italy combined to facilitate communications between Rome and the lands beyond the Alps, where the reach of St. Peter's church was great and growing, and thus to swell the crowds of northern visitors thronging the *limina S. Petri*. These pilgrims fuelled the growth of a new urban agglomeration around the church and tomb of the saint, known by the end of the eighth century as the *burgus*, from the Anglo-Saxon word for a town.[68] In addition to the swarm of monasteries, *xenodochia*, *diaconiae*, and so on

---

[67] This was well seen by Krautheimer (1980, 113–14), for all that he tended to exaggerate the relative "darkness" of the period prior to Hadrian; see also e.g. Bauer 2003.

[68] On the origins and development of the Borgo, see Pani Ermini 2001, 317–23, with extensive prior bibliography; Giuntella 1985; Krautheimer 1980, 161–9; Reekmans 1968, 200ff.

instituted by the Church to serve the devout and the needy, the national associations (*scholae*) of the Anglo-Saxons, Lombards, Frisians, and Franks all rose in the vicinity of St. Peter's (they first appear, seemingly fully formed, in 799), as did the Carolingian royal residence built for Charlemagne and thereafter inhabited by his successors during their Roman sojourns.[69] The result was a sort of international suburb geared to meeting the needs of the foreign community, whose devotion to the cult of St. Peter was ultimately what permitted the transalpine spiritual empire of the Roman Church to flourish.

Meanwhile, the Lateran complex was extensively remodeled beginning under Hadrian, who furnished the palace with, amongst other things, a second tower to complement the one erected in the 740s by Zachary I, the last pope to build extensively at the Lateran.[70] If Zachary's tower with its bronze doors was meant to recall the famous Chalke gate of the palace at Constantinople, and thus to proclaim the nascent regal pretensions of the popes, the addition of Hadrian's tower went a step further in imbuing the seat of papal government with a more imposing, even militaristic profile.[71] It is perhaps too much to imagine that the new tower at the Lateran bore an intentional resemblance to those of the Aurelian Wall, but it does seem that Hadrian was acting to endow his official residence with a turreted silhouette wholly in keeping with the profile of the refurbished defenses that surrounded it, which projected a conspicuous air of papal authority. More generally speaking, the efforts of Hadrian and Leo III to restore and embellish the Lateran made of it an official residence and center of government befitting the rising aspirations and the expanded temporal mandate of the papacy.[72]

The Aurelian Wall was quite inevitably – *faute de mieux* – the dividing line between these two "spheres" of Rome; and it was indeed Hadrian's

---

[69] On the *scholae*, see *LP* II, 6, with e.g. M. Perraymond, "Le *scholae peregrinorum* nel borgo di San Pietro," *Romanobarbarica* 4 (1979), 183–200. On the palace, see esp. Brühl 1954; cf. R. Schieffer, "Charlemagne and Rome," in Smith 2000, 285–6.

[70] See *LP* I, 503, with Pani Ermini 2001, 290–1; 1992, 486ff.; Ward-Perkins 1984, 174–6; Krautheimer 1980, 120–2. On the tower built by Zachary I, see *LP* I, 432. The archaeological evidence for the configuration of the Lateran in the early Middle Ages remains extremely threadbare at present, and the textual references are vague and confused: on the current state of the question, see the various contributions to the colloquium *Giornata di studio tematica dedicata al Patriarchio lateranense* (*MEFRA* 2004, 9–178); see also Liverani 1999b.

[71] Cf. Bauer 2003, 198–9; Pani Ermini 1992, 487.

[72] The growing scope, complexity, and influence of the Lateran administration in the eighth and ninth centuries, and the rising prominence of the palace as the nerve-center of the new papal Rome are addressed in e.g. Toubert 2001 and Noble 1984, 212–41.

biographer who first pointed to the Wall as the instrument of their separation, with an ostentatious reference to Charlemagne's request "that he be granted permission to enter the city" to pray in its various churches.[73] The largely irrelevant question of whether Charlemagne asked any such thing aside, the intent of the story was evidently to vaunt the pope as the gatekeeper of the inner citadel of Christian Rome, a place, of course, circumscribed by "Hadrian's" Wall.[74] The regent of the gatekeeper of heaven, that is, was ostentatiously proclaimed to hold sway over the ramparts surrounding the earthly incarnation of the heavenly kingdom.[75] Three generations later, the liminal potential of the papal enceinte would assume more concrete significance with the army of Charlemagne's great-grandson Louis II encamped outside the city, eating the local citizenry out of house and home while the emperor performed his devotions at the Vatican. When Pope Sergius (844–7) heard that Louis' men were seeking to bivouac "inside this most famous city," the pope flatly refused and had the gates of the Wall barred and garrisoned against the Frankish rank and file.[76] In ways both practical and symbolic, the Wall was made to underpin the increasingly articulated distinction drawn between a Vatican region that served as a center of pilgrimage open to all comers, and an intramural polity focused on the Lateran, the administrative seat of an ecclesiastical preserve where even the greatest secular potentates entered only with papal assent. As the prime mover in this new topographical scheme, Hadrian will have had the more reason to put the defensive circuit that was literally its centerpiece in the best possible shape.

---

[73] *LP* I, 497: *obnixe deprecatus isdem Francorum rex antedictum almificum pontificem illi licentiam tribui Romam ingrediendi sua orationum vota per diversas Dei ecclesias persolvenda*; cf. Schieffer 2002, 111–15; Llewellyn 1993, 192–3; Noble 1984, 287–9.

[74] The comments of R. Schieffer (2000, 286) are prescient enough to be quoted in full: "The fact that, from his very first personal appearance in 774, the Frankish protector of the papacy settled on the Vatican hill near St Peter's, and visited the other side of the Tiber only for some hours, is surely to be attributed to Pope Hadrian and his successors' reluctance to allow a new secular power-centre to be established *intra muros*. They were upholding the doctrine of the Donation of Constantine, according to which justice required that the earthly emperor (*imperator terrenus*) should have no authority where the highest priesthood and the head of the Christian religion had been established by the Lord of Heaven." See also *Constitutum Constantini*, lines 261ff., esp. 274–6.

[75] The latter is conceivable as a generic "Heaven" or as Celestial Jerusalem (or both); the allegorical charge of the Aurelian Wall is in either case powerful, and particularly apropos given the contemporary fascination in Francia and Britain with the image of Peter as the gatekeeper of heaven, on which see Zwölfer 1929.

[76] *...ipse a Deo protectus praedictus pontifex a quibusdam audierat quod in hanc famosissimam urbem hospitalitatis causa introire voluissent; sed munitis clausisque portis, ut fieret minime concessit*; see *LP* II, 88–9.

The Wall, in sum, was an instrument ready-made for the projection of temporal control over Rome and its environs. After the more tentative beginnings made by the popes in the first half of the eighth century, it was left for Hadrian to realize the full potential of the fortifications he inherited from Aurelian and Honorius by reasserting in his own name the legacy of absolute authority they exuded. Yet the dynamics of power in early-medieval Rome had changed greatly since the days of the emperors, and the new flood of northern pilgrims was a telling sign of a fundamental new reality faced by its leaders: the international "empire" and even the urban center over which the popes presided were now sustained by the active and willing consent of the peoples who placed themselves beneath the aegis of St. Peter and his Church. The "provincials" thus loomed large in the capital and, as we shall see, their expectations had perhaps as much to do with Hadrian's interventions on the Wall as anything else.

6.3   The Aurelian Wall and the international public of Pope Hadrian's Rome

I would go so far as to suggest that the reincarnation of the Aurelian Wall as a cornerstone of papal Rome cannot adequately be explained without acknowledging the basic reality that the "Republic of St. Peter" was enriched, defended, and empowered primarily by foreigners. Rome was the leading city in western Christendom because people everywhere, great and humble, believed and wanted it to be so.[77] The popes thus had a vested interest in making of their capital a place to inspire awe and reverence amongst the constituent nations of their spiritual empire; and I would suggest that a perimeter wall was manifestly the urban feature best able to excite the awe and reverence of an early-medieval audience. In short, what Rome's international public expected above all from the *caput mundi* and *sedes Petri* was an extraordinarily prepossessing enceinte, which Hadrian took care to give them.

England makes for an especially revealing case-study, both for the strength of its links with Rome and the abiding interest in urban fortifications demonstrated by its native authors. In contrast to the neighboring churches of Gaul and Ireland, with their storied histories and strong local traditions, the Church of England was "officially" created *ex nihilo*

---

[77]   Cf. Smith 2005, 253–92; Tellenbach 1972; Schramm 1929, esp. 28–38; Graf 1882–83, vol. 1, 1–39; vol. 2, 423ff.

beginning in 597 with the arrival at Canterbury of the Roman mission sent by Gregory I, an historical particularity that probably explains to some extent the remarkably fervent attachment subsequently shown by the English to their mother church in Rome.[78] The newly converted Anglo-Saxons embraced the Roman model with precisely the zeal of the convert, shaping their liturgy, their roll of favored saints and martyrs, and their ecclesiastical architecture on Roman exemplars, to the near exclusion of competing local and regional influences.[79] Moreover, they began to demonstrate an unrivalled passion for pilgrimage to Rome, where they soon formed a prominent and influential community, and whence many returned home with books, relics, and firsthand experience of the papal capital that further reinforced ties between their insular Christian community and its continental hub.[80] The Anglo-Saxons were thus both keen observers of, and valuable participants in, the spectacle of papal Rome; and as it turns out, they were also strongly inclined to view a powerful enceinte as the defining topographical feature of a "Roman" city, and of a capital city above all.

An initial indication comes from the description of Constantinople included in the *De locis sanctis*, an account of holy sites in the eastern Mediterranean written *c.* 687 for a Northumbrian audience by the Irish abbot Adomnan.[81] After first stating in no uncertain terms that Constantinople was "beyond doubt the metropolis of the Roman Empire,"[82] Adomnan launched into a brief topographical excursus

---

[78] The importance of pre-existing Christian communities of Irish or native Briton extraction, and their role in the conversion of the Anglo-Saxons, was consistently downplayed by Bede (in e.g. the *Chronica maiora* as well as the *Historia ecclesiastica*) and many of his near-contemporaries, the better to present the English Church as a Roman foundation. Gregory I himself was soon singled out for special veneration as the "apostle of the English," a dignity that unambiguously proclaimed the Roman "paternity" of insular Christianity: see Thacker 1998; cf. Wood 1994, esp. 15–16; Bullough 1981, esp. 340–2.

[79] In addition to W. Levison's still fundamental overview (Levison 1946, esp. 15–44), see e.g. Smith 2005, esp. 286ff.; Howe 2005 and 2004; Brooks 2000; Thacker 2000.

[80] See Levison 1946, 36–44; and Llewellyn 1993, esp. 178–81, who calls his ancient countrymen "the most eager of all for the Roman pilgrimage"; cf. also Perraymond 1979, 189–91; Tellenbach 1972, 700ff. Bede epitomized this ardor in his account of King Caedwalla's decision to abdicate and finish his life in Rome, an initiative that *his temporibus plures de gente Anglorum, nobiles, ignobiles, laici, clerici, viri ac feminae certatim facere consuerunt* (*Historia Ecclesiastica* 5, 7).

[81] *CCSL* 175, 175–234. Adomnan based his descriptions on the eyewitness account of the Gallic bishop Arculf, shipwrecked in England during his return from the east (see Bede, *Historia Ecclesiastica* 5, 15). For recent thoughts on the composition of the *De locis sanctis*, see Limor 2004.

[82] *De locis sanctis* 3, 1, 2: *Quae proculdubio Romani est metropolis imperii...*

that ended up as little more than a portrait of the city walls, the only structure singled out for mention:

This imperatorial city is surrounded for twelve miles by a circuit of walls that is hardly small. It has its corners on the sea, turning as at Alexandria or Carthage to follow the seashore, and lofty curtains reinforced by closely spaced towers in the likeness of Tyre. Inside the walls of the city are numerous houses, of which the majority, stone-built and of amazing size, rise up in the likeness of the dwellings of Rome.[83]

When attempting to furnish his readers with a mental picture of Constantinople, to epitomize the "imperatorial city" that was for him the living essence of an imperial capital, Adomnan seized immediately on the image of its enceinte. More than all the other buildings in the city combined, the walls were the thing worth talking about.

A century later, similar motifs would surface in more elaborate form in Alcuin's long poem on the bishops, kings, and saints of York (*Versus de patribus regibus et sanctis Euboricensis ecclesiae*),[84] where an enceinte again became the featured token of civic dignity and *romanitas*. The mural emphasis is the more noteworthy for its appearance in a work of self-consciously Romanizing sympathies, in which Alcuin was concerned to root the conversion of Northumbria firmly in the Roman mission to England; to understate programmatically the prominent role played by Irish clerics in the development of the Northumbrian church; and to tout York as an urban center in the Roman mold.[85] Indeed, it was the surviving monumental fabric of the city, the urban legacy of its Roman founders become the cultural heritage of their self-proclaimed successors, that was to proclaim it the worthy secular capital and metropolitan see of Northumbria.[86] It is hence especially telling that Alcuin chose to headline his opening encomium of York with an allusion to its Roman wall, which in addition to being the first monument portrayed was further very explicitly lauded as the *sine qua non* for the security and glory of the city and thus also of all the territory under its sway:

---

[83] *Ibid.* 3, 1, 4: *Haec itaque imperatoria civitas non parvo murorum ambitu per duodecim milia passum circumcincta angulos iuxta situm maris habens per maritimam, ut Alexandria sive Kartago, constructos oram et ad Tiri similitudinem crebris insuper turribus commonitos muros, domus intra civitatis moenia numerosas, ex quibus plurimae mirae magnitudinis lapideae instar Romae habitaculorum fabricatae consurgunt.*

[84] See Godman 1982. In its final form, the work likely dates between 781–2 and 792–3 (xxxix–xlvii).

[85] Coates 1996; Godman 1982, xlvii–lxxv; Bullough 1981.

[86] In addition to the articles cited in the preceding note, cf. La Rocca 2003, 410–11.

Roman might first founded this (city) lofty with its walls and towers, calling into service the native British peoples as associates and contributors to the works...that it would be a common emporium of land and sea, and become for its leaders the secure power of the kingdom and glory of the empire and a terror for opposing arms.[87]

For Alcuin, in other words, it was the Roman wall of York that had given the city the potential for greatness.

It was a potential that was first fully realized – albeit temporarily – with the baptism of King Edwin and the elevation of his capital to the status of a metropolitan see in 634, a crowning moment in the history of the city, in the telling of which the enceinte twice reappears.[88] After the king "decided to receive baptism with his people beneath the lofty walls of the city of York,"[89] he moved to exalt the status of the local church, paving the way for York to become the metropolis of its own ecclesiastical province, and thus by definition to enter into a highly select grouping of the most prestigious cities in Christendom:

When the festive day of the blessed occasion dawned, (Edwin) along with his children and leaders, and with the people following, was given to Christ in the eleventh year of his reign in the life-giving font within the walls of the aforementioned city, whose summit he thenceforth raised more sublimely on high, and decreed that it would be the metropolis of his realm.[90]

For all that "the walls" (*moenia*) was undoubtedly a convenient synecdoche for "the city," the unparalleled repetition of the word in the space of ten lines is remarkable, particularly coming as it does in reference to the watershed events that first brought York to a position of undisputed ecclesiastical and temporal pre-eminence in northern England, a subject

---

[87] *Versus*, 19–26: *Hanc Romana manus muris et turribus altam fundavit primo, comites sociosque laborum indigenas tantum gentes adhibendo Britannas ... ut foret emporium terrae commune marisque et fieret ducibus secura potentia regni et decus imperii terrorque hostilibus armis.*

[88] Edwin converted on Easter eve, 627, and Pope Honorius moved to recognize York as the second archbishopric of England (alongside Canterbury) seven years later in 634, when he sent *pallia* for the bishops of both metropolitan sees, that the one might consecrate the successor of the other; see Stenton 1971, 113–15, with Bede, *Historia Ecclesiastica* 2, 17–18. The grimmer reality was that Edwin had already been killed in 633 at the battle of Heathfield, a decisive defeat that resulted in the overthrow of his Christian kingdom and the postponement of the final triumph of Christianity in Northumbria for decades (Bede, *Historia Ecclesiastica* 2, 20; cf. Stenton, 116); a full century would pass before York regained its archiepiscopal stature in 735.

[89] *Ibid.* 194–6: *Affluit interea tempus paschale per orbem, quo rex cum populo statuit baptisma subire Euboricae celsis etiam sub moenibus urbis...*

[90] *Ibid.* 199–204: *Dum festiva dies inluxit temporis almi, cum gnatis ducibusque simul, cum plebe sequenti, undecimo regni Christo sacratus in anno est fonte salutifero praefatae in moenibus urbis, cuius abhinc culmen sublimius extulit ille, metropolimque sui statuit consistere regni.*

dear to Alcuin's heart and crucial to the theme of the poem as a whole.[91] "The lofty walls of the city of York" thus seem carefully chosen to embody an urban center that itself took on loftier stature ("whose summit he thenceforth raised more sublimely on high") with the conferral of archiepiscopal rank, a promotion that bound the city and its church more tightly to Rome, the great "citadel" (*Romana arce*) whose popes would henceforth personally endow the archbishops of York – as Gregory I, the revered "apostle" of England had originally planned – with the *pallium*, the symbol of their special authority.[92] Hence, especially given Alcuin's personal acquaintance with Pope Hadrian and his firsthand experience of Rome,[93] it is possible that he was thinking of the Aurelian Wall when he crafted his descriptions of York, or at any rate relating its enceinte to an urban paradigm largely conditioned by the example of Rome. It is quite certain that he viewed the Roman wall of York as the primary physical marker of its greatness, the sign that demonstrated the appurtenance of the city to a Christian cultural and spiritual universe that continued to gravitate around its ideal center at Rome.

Also from England comes the oldest extant vernacular description of a Roman ruin, a brief poem of the tenth century written in Old English and included in the so-called Exeter Book.[94] "The Ruin" elegizes the faded glory of a quintessentially Roman city and the grander way of life that seemed to have passed with it; and yet again, the feature chosen to introduce the place was its perimeter wall, which occupies the first line of the poem and sets the scene for all of what follows:

Wondrous is the wall of stone, broken by fate; the castles have decayed; the work of giants is crumbling. Roofs are fallen, ruinous are the towers, despoiled are the

---

[91] The advocacy of a harmonious union of ecclesiastical and temporal power at York, conspicuously lacking in his own time, was one of Alcuin's principal preoccupations in the "York Poem" (cf. Bullough 1981, 351–2), whence the brief (very brief – see above n. 88) flowering of York under Elbert became a crucial paradigm for the lost concord he lamented: this incarnation of the city thus represented Alcuin's ideal vision of York, an ideal in which the Roman enceinte featured with obvious prominence.

[92] *Ibid.* 205–09: *Sic quoque Gregorius praesul decreverat olim, semina dum vitae Romana misit ab arce gentibus Anglorum: confestim praecipit urbem hanc caput ecclesiis et culmen honoris haberi, pallia pontificesque in ea vestire sacratos.* On the events of the period, see above n. 88; cf. also Levison 1946, 33–6. For the English use of Gregory as "a universal, apostolic saint, who could authenticate the credentials of a British patriarchate or of the Northumbrian church and royal house," see Thacker 1998, 80–3.

[93] Cf. Llewellyn 1993, 245–9.

[94] See *Exeter Book, The*, Krapp and Van Kirk Dobbie 1936. On the composition and textual history of the manuscript, see esp. ix–xvi; the text of "The Ruin" is at pp. 227–9, with brief commentary at lxiv–lxv.

towers with their gates; frost is on their cement, broken are the roofs, cut away, fallen, undermined by age. The grasp of the earth, stout grip of the ground, holds its mighty builders, who have perished and gone; till now a hundred generations of men have died. *Often this wall, grey with lichen and stained with red, unmoved under storms, has survived kingdom after kingdom; its lofty gate has fallen [...] the bold in spirit bound the foundation of the wall wondrously together with wires...* Stone courts stood here; the stream with its great gush sprang forth hotly; *the wall enclosed all within its bright bosom;* there the baths were hot in its centre; that was spacious... (italics mine).[95]

The terminology is sufficiently generic to leave the identification of the ruin (Bath? Rome? A Roman Anyplace?) problematic,[96] which is perhaps the most important point. It was a Roman city because it had all the characteristic or even stereotypical features expected of such a place:[97] stone-built buildings, baths, palaces, and first and foremost a city wall, which not only opens the poem but is subsequently twice more singled out for mention. It was a "regal" and Roman urban center, which in the mind of the tenth-century poet was largely made by its perimeter wall.

But if England provides an especially vivid sense of "provincial" fascination with Roman enceintes, it is by no means the only one. As an exhaustive study is the work of another book, two further examples will serve in its stead.

Certainly the Carolingians and their Ottonian and Salian imperial successors, whose connections with Rome bear no further repeating, were similarly taken with the image of perimeter walls, and specifically with that of the Aurelian Wall. The unified vision of Rome and its Wall that prevailed at the court of Charlemagne comes through best in the two extant epitaphs composed in Francia for Pope Hadrian upon his death at the end of 795. One is the famous text very probably composed by Alcuin, and inscribed on the slab of black marble which Charlemagne sent to St. Peter's in honor of his longtime friend and collaborator.[98] The second

---

[95] The translation, slightly adapted, is that of R. K. Gordon, *Anglo-Saxon Poetry* (London, 1929), 84.

[96] On the debate over the location, see e.g. Settis 2001, 1004; Krapp and Van Kirk Dobbie 1936, lxiv–lxv.

[97] Cf. Howe 2005, esp. 32–4; Settis 2001, 1004.

[98] The text of the inscription is reproduced at *PL* 98, col. 1,350–1, as well as in Wallach 1959, 178–97, where the author makes a strong case for Alcuin's authorship. On the technical characteristics – workmanship, materials, provenance, etc. – of the epitaph, see Story *et al.* 2005.

was written by Alcuin's close acquaintance Theodulf, bishop of Orléans; it too was evidently intended to serve as Charlemagne's "official" eulogy for Hadrian, and to appear "over the tomb of Pope Hadrian," presumably in the place occupied in the event by Alcuin's verses.[99]

Both epitaphs devote exactly one couplet to the relationship between the pope and the city of Rome. Alcuin for his part returned to the image of the "Roman citadel" (*Romana arce*) which he had previously employed in the York Poem. As Edwin had at York, so too Hadrian "lifted up" or "exalted" his city with his patronage:

With doctrines and riches and walls (*muris*) he lifted up your fastnesses (*arces*), renowned Rome, honor and head-city of the world.[100]

Surely the Aurelian Wall was meant to feature prominently amongst the "walls" which Hadrian built for the greater glory of the Roman *arces*, if it was not indeed the primary subject of the reference. Meanwhile, Theodulf took a different approach to a like theme by turning Hadrian into the Wall of Rome incarnate:

You, Rome, remember always this lord,
Who was the guardian of your riches, [who was] your arms and your wall.[101]

The pope was thus made to personify the product of his single most drastic topographical intervention on the Roman cityscape. He was the bulwark of his city, a towering personality who for Theodulf found his architectural analogue in the enceinte he so laboriously restored.

In short, when both authors sought to demonstrate in the space of two lines that Hadrian was a great patron of the greatest Christian city, they turned to mural imagery in their effort to capture succinctly the grandeur of the man and the place alike. In the eyes of these two leading literary

---

[99] Preserved in various manuscript redactions of Theodulf's metrical works under the heading *super sepulcrum Hadriani papae*, the epitaph presents itself, like Alcuin's, as Charlemagne's "personal" lament for the deceased pope (*MGH Poetae* I, 489–90): *Aurea funereum complectit littera Carmen,/Verba tonat fulvus et lacrimosa color./Promere quae Carolum compellit amorque dolorque/me tuus, Hadriane praesul amate nimis,/Pontificum specimen, lux plebis, norma salutis,/Vir pie, vir sapiens, vir venerande satis*; cf. lines 16–17 of the inscription at St. Peter's: *Post patrem lacrimans Karolus haec carmina scribsi,/Tu mihi dulcis amor, te modo plango, pater.*

[100] Lines 13–14: *Doctrinis, opibus, muris erexerat arces,/Urbs caput orbis honor, inclyta Roma, tuas.* This passage might well be added to the list of parallels between the epitaph and Alcuin's other writings adduced by Wallach in his argument for Alcuin's authorship of the inscription, given its linguistic and conceptual similarity to the lines in the York Poem reproduced above (see nn. 89–90).

[101] *MGH Poetae* I, 490, lines 22–3: *Praesulis istius semper, tu Roma, memento,/qui tibi tutor opum, murus et arma fuit.*

Figure 6.1 *Kaiserbulle* of Charlemagne with gates of Rome. (After Schramm 1983 [1928], figs. 5c–5h.)

lights of Charlemagne's kingdom, the Wall, the city, and Hadrian were effectively inseparable.

The continental conception of Rome is further attested on coins and medallions, beginning with a series of medals (*Kaiserbulle*) coined under Charlemagne himself.[102] On these pieces, Rome is represented by a gateway with a single arch and rounded flanking towers bearing a resemblance to the gates in the Wall that seems more than coincidental, to the point that the travertine blocks of the façades were differentiated from the brick of the towers (Figure 6.1). Hence, these should perhaps be seen less as generic fortifications[103] than as condensed bits of the Aurelian Wall, itself chosen as the condensed essence of all that was "Rome."

Similar mural imagery would recur for centuries on the reverses of imperial issues, and though the use of circuit walls as a representational trope was hardly limited to depictions of Rome, no other city in the

---

[102] See e.g. Schramm 1983 {1928}, p. 38 with figs. 5c–h.

[103] *Contra* Tellenbach 1972, 685–6, who emphasizes the generic nature of Carolingian representations of Rome and their lack of identifiable features, thus passing over the one identifiable feature whose very uniqueness makes it all the more remarkable. Surely there is no *a priori* reason not to expect "portraits" of urban landmarks on medieval coins: it is hardly doubtful, for example, that the church featured on coins minted at Speyer under Henry IV (1056–1106) is in fact the famous cathedral of that city (see Schramm 1983, fig. 171.80).

208 a

208 b

209 a

209 b

Figure 6.2 *Kaiserbulle* of Frederic I Barbarossa. (After Schramm 1983 [1928], figs. 208a–b and 209a–b.)

realm was so dominated in the numismatic canon by the profile of its enceinte.[104] A particularly arresting vision of Rome occurs on a type issued under Frederick Barbarossa in the twelfth century, where the symbolic heart of his Holy Roman Empire was distilled into an image of the Coliseum encircled by the Wall (Figure 6.2). The traditional symbol of Roman eternity was thus juxtaposed with another iconic monument of – at least in this instance – apparently comparable magnitude, as if to append a coda to the famous lines, *quamdiu stat colyseus, stat et Roma...*, popularly attributed to Bede. *Quamdiu stant muri...*

Yet the legend of Rome's walls captured imaginations even beyond the frontiers of Christendom. In the numerous accounts produced by Arab geographical writers from the ninth century on, the vaunted fortifications of the Christian capital are among the few constants in a dizzyingly varied congeries of chimerical marvels and wild assertions.[105] Rome is nearly

---

[104] For examples produced under the Ottonian and Salian emperors, see Schramm 1983, figs. 118b; 138b; 153b; 194b.

[105] See e.g. Scarcia 2002; Miquel 1975; Nallino 1966.

always said to be surrounded by a double circuit of walls, a tradition perhaps inspired by the separation of the Wall into two sections by the Tiber, or more probably by the binary pairing of the Leonine and Aurelianic circuits, or even just possibly by a lingering memory of the Servian Wall.[106] The most likely explanation of all may be simple confusion with Constantinople, where the older Constantinian ramparts were long preserved within the land walls of Theodosius II; certainly in other particulars Arab geographers repeatedly confounded or conflated the old Rome with the new.[107] For present purposes, it makes little difference whether the double-wall trope was derived from Rome, or Constantinople, or both. As in the case of the anonymous Roman city described in "The Ruin," the ambiguousness of the setting itself proclaims the more important underlying reality: "Rome" the Christian capital, whatever and wherever this was construed to be, was unthinkable for these distant commentators without ramparts of mythical proportions that exceeded even the reality of the awesome circuits in existence at both places.

The point of all of this is very simply to say that the peoples whose belief in Rome made it the enduring heart and soul of Christian Europe wanted and needed their spiritual capital to be mightily fortified. A Roman city was inconceivable without a wall, a Roman capital all the more so, and *a fortiori* Rome itself most of all. Hadrian's restoration of the Aurelian Wall thus served to gratify the Christian masses – and theoretically also to impress potential enemies – with the vision of Rome they already expected and cherished, and to place the mural dreams of future generations on a firm foundation in material reality.

The Wall thus fits neatly into the conceptual matrix recently proposed by Salvatore Settis in a fascinating article on "Rome outside of Rome" in the early Middle Ages, where the author focuses on a dialectical vision of the relationship between the center and its "peripheries of memory."[108] For Settis, views of Rome throughout the Christian world

---

[106] Cf. Miquel 1975, 287; Nallino 1966, 880–1.

[107] The geographers of Muslim Spain, however, were generally better-informed on the "old" Rome than their more numerous eastern counterparts, and included features in their descriptions clearly derived from Rome as opposed to Constantinople; see Miquel 1975, 289–91, and esp. Scarcia 2002. As they, too, spoke of a double wall at Rome, I am inclined to think that the idea has some basis in Roman topographical reality, though it is perhaps most likely that the topography of both cities fostered the legend of the double enceinte, another of the many "real" similarities between Rome and Constantinople that contributed to the frequent confusion – not always unintentional on the part of Christian writers – between the two.

[108] Settis 2001.

and beyond were constantly inspired by the transmission of ideological and iconographical echoes from the center; yet at the same time, Romans had nothing like a monopoly on the legacy and the popular image of their city. While paradigms of Rome on the one hand radiated outward like concentric ripples on the surface of a pond, the image is not complete without imagining these same ripples then reflecting back off the banks of the pond, variously changed by the moment of contact, and again converging to impact on their point of origin: "The fame of Rome 'traveled' in two directions: from the city itself it was diffused to the most remote lands, but it also 'returned' from these places towards Rome, and perhaps helped to save it from the constant danger of forgetting itself."[109] Precisely: the Aurelian Wall gave the world a mental picture of Rome befitting its identity as the *caput mundi*, but it was left to "the world" to come forward to impress upon Romans the importance of making their city live up to its (all-important) reputation by keeping the Wall in the most impressive shape possible.

In imposing a vision of the city on Hadrian which he found himself almost constrained to realize, the Aurelian Wall in a sense shaped the pope as much as he shaped it, whence the story of what he did to the circuit can fairly take its place in the history of the Wall as agent. If the Wall had once been an instrument of the imperial will that brought it into existence, it had by the eighth century taken on a life of its own as a mastodontic holdover from an earlier age, an inescapable presence imbued with the collective weight of centuries and redolent of the legacy of imperial Rome. Hadrian inherited a monument that was at once the unmistakable proof of the majestic dimensions the city had once reached – a sort of urban high-water mark – the container of the urban church, and the public persona of the city. It was therefore a thing to be treated with extreme delicacy. To leave it in ruins was to leave the city with a ruined appearance hardly suitable for the center of the Christian universe. To wall off a part of the circuit in the interest of creating a smaller, more easily defended, and maintained citadel around, say, the Lateran was to place the remainder of the city with its hallowed churches and relics and storied monuments on less privileged ground, to amputate parts of an ancient whole, and consequently visibly to proclaim the extent to which Rome was reduced from the days of its glory. If Rome was to be the place the popes and their followers everywhere wanted it to be, the enceinte had to be ripristinated in its entirety. Thus it was that the Wall and its various local and

---

[109] *Ibid.* 994.

international audiences had their own particular logic to impress upon
Hadrian, as he sought both to make Rome his own and to etch the
contours of his rejuvenated capital into the far-flung "peripheries" of
Roman memory.

6.4   Old walls don't die, they just fade away...

Hadrian's two mural restorations were the product of the unique historical
moment that made them possible and indeed desirable, a time of
expanding horizons when the circuit afforded a pope endowed with
unprecedented local authority an opportunity to build on a scale com-
mensurate with his grand vision of what Rome and the papacy were to
mean to the Christian world. It was a combination of circumstances that
was not to be repeated for centuries.

Amongst Hadrian's successors, only Leo IV would be credited with a
restoration of the Aurelian Wall, this undertaken in the considerably less
auspicious climate that ensued upon the devastating Saracen raid of 846,
when the pillaging of St. Peter's and the extramural periphery sent pulses
of shock and outrage throughout the lands in the spiritual orbit of the
Roman Church.[110] In addition to his repairs to the existing circuit, the
pope launched an ambitious project beginning in 848 to fortify St. Peter's
and the surrounding Borgo.[111] The result was the most ambitious construction program undertaken in ninth-century Rome, a four-year effort
to erect a narrow rectangle of fortifications with a perimeter of *c.* 3km
stretching from the Castel Sant'Angelo on the Tiber to the high ground
behind St. Peter's. Hardly a replacement for the Aurelian Wall, which was,
of course, undergoing concurrent restorations, the Leonine Wall functioned as an extension of the older circuit, built to bring the Vatican
within the compass of the existing urban defenses as a whole, which the
new wall was, in fact, made to resemble as closely as possible, albeit on a
considerably reduced scale.[112] While Leo's wall was in part a response to
the growing importance of the previously undefended Vatican region in

[110] See *LP* 2, 115, with Chapter 1, above.
[111] The lengthy contemporary account of Leo's project is at *LP* 2, 123–5; *cf.* n. 42, above. On the
Leonine Wall, in addition to the fundamental Ward-Perkins and Gibson 1979 and 1983, see
also Meneghini and Santangeli Valenzani 2004, 63–5; Pani Ermini 1992, 514–18; Giuntella
1985; Bella Barsali 1976, 201–14.
[112] On the conscious emulation of the architectural features of the Aurelian Wall by the builders
of the Leonine Wall, see e.g. Meneghini and Santangeli-Valenzani 2004, 64–5.

the life of the city as a whole, it also worked actively to impart a new aura of urban grandeur to the neighborhood it surrounded. As was so often the case, the wall made the city, in a sense: the dedication of the circuit in 852 was the occasion for the pope's rechristening of the area, modestly enough, as the *civitas Leoniana*.

But whereas Hadrian's mural repairs are best seen as an elaborate form of political theater, the timing and circumstances of Leo's additions to Rome's defenses cast them in the light of relatively practical expedients designed to give real protection in the face of an ongoing threat which local and Carolingian arms had proven themselves signally incapable of combating, as well as to reassure friends and admonish foes that the city would never again fall such easy prey.[113] These latest fortification projects thus seem primarily topical responses to a topical problem, a factor that may help to explain the disinclination of subsequent generations without direct experience of the sack of 846 to maintain the same level of interest in their walls. For while the pontificate of Leo IV in a way represents a peak in the history of Rome's urban defenses, when the linear extent of its functioning fortifications was greater than ever before, it was immediately followed by an unusually lengthy period of apparent neglect.

After Leo's death in 855, there is no unequivocal testimony of further repairs to the Wall until 1157, when the senate of the nascent *comune* refurbished it and publicized the act with dedicatory inscriptions.[114] The Wall took on a much lower profile in the historical record for three centuries, in other words, shortly after reaching its apogee as a cornerstone in the assertion of papal sovereignty at home and abroad. The obvious question is why. It is an issue that should be tackled not merely to explain my chosen chronological terminus, but above all because the apparent decline in "official" interest in the Wall leads directly back to the central query of how and why it was important in the first place, for its fall from prominence is intimately connected to the disaggregation of the early-medieval incarnation of papal Rome which it had been so instrumental in forming.

Let it first be stressed that the Wall itself hardly disappeared, nor did it cease to be useful; on the contrary, Rome was constantly menaced in the later ninth and tenth centuries by an unending succession of Christian

---

[113] If the awed descriptions of Rome's walls given by Arab geographers from the later ninth century on are any indication, Leo may deserve some credit for the apparent fulfillment of the latter objective; cf. Scarcia 2002, 158–9.

[114] See e.g. Mancini 2001, 59–68.

secular potentates and Arab and Hungarian raiders, all of whom were quite consistently kept at bay by the ramparts.[115] But while it is possible and even likely that essential maintenance was still performed, as the defenses continued to function effectively a century and more after the time of Leo IV,[116] there is no sign that any major projects worth boasting – or writing – about occurred: in addition to the silence of the sources, there is the further important fact that no convincing examples of period repairs have been identified in the standing fabric of the Wall, this in marked contrast to the extensive and numerous eighth–ninth and twelfth–thirteenth century interventions identified on the basis of reasonably solid typological parallels. The best conclusion is that the leaders of Rome concerned themselves little with the circuit in the intervening centuries, for all that it was if anything more needed than ever at the time.

The motives for the eclipse of the enceinte lie, I think, amongst the series of historical conjunctures that changed the Roman landscape drastically beginning in the late-ninth century, in the process rendering the very concept of its all-encompassing defenses temporarily obsolete. My necessarily condensed summary of these events and processes will I hope not do excessive violence to the scholarship on which my conclusions are based.

For all that the chaos and institutional discontinuity of the "long tenth century" may have been exaggerated by earlier generations of scholars, it is difficult to avoid the impression that a turning point was reached with the death in 877 of Charles the Bald, the last of the Carolingian line to exercise a semblance of real authority over Rome, and the murder of the charismatic Pope John VIII in 882.[117] Thereafter, *de facto* control over the city devolved upon leading members of the nobility, who turned the papal

---

[115] Among them the Saracen raiders based semi-permanently on the river Garigliano who became a constant presence in the Roman countryside at least until their decisive defeat in 915; the Hungarians who seem rarely if ever to have left Italy for a generation following their arrival in 924 (after a first incursion in 899), and plundered up to the gates of the city in the early 940s; King Ugo of Provence, who twice tried unsuccessfully to take the city in 933 and 936; and the recently crowned emperor Otto I, who besieged the city for a month in 964 before finally starving the defenders into submission; all of these events are discussed in e.g. Brezzi 1947, 105–34.

[116] As in the case of the siege of Otto II in 964, cited in the preceding note.

[117] Certainly the anonymous (and partisan) tenth-century author of the *De imperia potestate in urbe Roma libellus* already saw an epochal shift in the years around 880; see esp. pp. 208–10 (Zucchetti ed.). The best historical overview of the period in question remains that of Brezzi 1947, though it is now in some respects dated. Among more recent studies, I have found the following particularly useful: Marazzi 2001b, 57–69; Wickham 2000a; Llewellyn 1993, 256–315; Arnaldi 1991; Toubert 1973, 960ff.

dignity to their own usually conflicting ends, installing a series of compli-
ant figures – fifteen between 882 and 914 alone – on the throne of Peter
and thoroughly subverting the autonomous authority of the office in the
process.[118] Though the popes had been drawn almost exclusively from the
local nobility since the 750s, the extension of effective Carolingian influence over Rome in the first part of the ninth century had served to curb
the worst outbreaks of internecine strife and to preserve the papacy from
the grip of purely local, partisan interests.[119] With the end of this stabilizing presence, the papacy lost much of its independence as an institution,
along with all but nominal hegemony over the city, which was henceforth
riven by internal power struggles between opposing aristocratic factions
and their supporters.

Internal chaos was in turn compounded by external factors, chief
among them the recurring presence of hostile forces in the Roman countryside. Successive waves of invaders serially depredated the patrimonies
of the Church and other rural holdings, and created further a climate of
chronic instability throughout the peninsula that impeded the arrival
of pilgrims, along with the pious offerings they brought, in their former
multitudes.[120] This combination of factors can only have diminished the
productive surplus and the disposable income available to Rome's leaders,
and depleted in particular the church coffers that in centuries past had
underwritten the upkeep of the city.[121]

The squabbling noble clans that controlled the papacy and ran the city
from the end of the ninth century were hence in no position to mobilize
anything like the quantities of human and material resources for the

[118] After 914, under the more stable government of Theophylact and his heirs, the papacy became
if anything more subject to secular authority, as Benedict of Soracte (amongst others) was
quick to note: *erat (Albericus) enim terribilis nimis, et aggrabatum est iugum super Romanos et
in sancte Sedis apostolice. eiectus Marinus papa non audebat adtingere aliquis extro iussio
Alberici principi* (*Chronicon*, p. 166–7). Generally on contemporary expressions of disgust at
the conduct of the popes and the state of the papacy, see e.g. Llewellyn 1993, 298–300; Arnaldi
1991, 43ff.; Schramm 1929, 64–7.

[119] See Noble 2000a, 568–74; 1984, esp. 188–205.

[120] Cf. Llewellyn 1993, 297; Toubert 1973, 970–1. On the various hostile incursions into Roman
territory, see above n. 115. The episode often chosen to illustrate the dire state of Italian
road-communications dates to the pontificate of John IX (898–900), who was unable even to
provide for safe transport of the beams needed for the repair of the Lateran basilica, ruined
shortly before under Steven VI (see Llewellyn 1993, 294; Brezzi 1947, 96); it was finally
restored years later under Sergius III (904–11); see *LP* II, 236.

[121] On the sources of funding available to the builder-popes of the eighth and ninth centuries,
see the interesting speculations in Noble 2000c, 79–83, in addition to the essential Delogu
1988a and 1988b.

embellishment of urban infrastructure that Hadrian I and Leo IV had once commanded. Moreover, there is cause to expect that what resources there were remained concentrated in private hands, as Rome no longer had leaders with sufficient authority to transcend conflicting local interests and marshal the consensus necessary for the realization of burdensome public works. Even Alberic, the closest thing to a supreme overlord seen in tenth-century Rome, lacked both the institutional prestige and the brute strength to convince his independent-minded noble peers to "volunteer" any substantial portion of their limited wealth for an enormous commission like the Wall that none would have been able to claim for their own.[122]

Further, Alberic achieved his twenty-plus years (932–54) of relative peace and tranquility only through a policy of determined isolationism, discouraging foreign potentates from meddling in Roman affairs, claiming authority only over a restricted circle of territory in central Italy, and in short running Rome more as a run-of-the-mill city-state on the southern Italian model than the capital of western Christendom.[123] The isolation of the city was increased by the perils of the roads leading to it, which as noted previously must have discouraged many prospective pilgrims and other foreign visitors from attempting the journey. Rome thus lost much of the international audience which the popes had once hoped to awe, and with it a primary motive for projecting the conspicuous (and costly) air of physical grandeur formerly underpinned by the Wall.

Dependent on a fractious and self-serving nobility, supported by the revenues from an impoverished countryside, and with relatively few foreign visitors distinguished or otherwise to impress, Alberic was in no position to consider patronizing a wall so vastly out of scale with the social, economic, and political realities of his day.

Even the relative concord that prevailed during Alberic's life dissipated upon his death. Factional strife between leading families again became a constant fact of Roman life, and the physical face of the city changed accordingly over the course of the tenth and eleventh centuries, the period in which Rome took on the rough outline of the form it would retain

---

[122] On the tenuous and ultimately ephemeral nature of Alberic's primacy (the position he constructed for himself as *princeps Romanorum* died with him), see Llewellyn 1993, 306–7, with the more nuanced view in Wickham 2000a, 158–62. By Alberic's time, the local nobility was in fact busily building strongholds in the countryside around Rome, thereby if anything increasing their effective autonomy and their ability to resist the unwelcome imposition of any sort of centralizing authority: see Toubert 1973, 303–68; cf. also Brown 1984, 218–19.

[123] Cf. Marazzi 2001b, 66; Brezzi 1947, 116 and 124.

through the high Middle Ages and beyond. In the tenth century, central public spaces maintained quite continuously since the days of the empire were suddenly swamped by private dwellings, as the recent excavations in the fora of Trajan and Caesar have demonstrated with particular clarity.[124] Both areas suddenly filled up with small houses and became discrete neighborhoods, each perhaps under the patronage of a powerful family that sought to group the clients it relied on for public standing and raw power in its own urban quarter.[125] The leading nobles themselves lived in increasingly elaborate compounds called *curtes*, isolated and self-contained urban islands furnished with residences, churches, stables, gardens, and so on.[126] Put simply, the breakdown of centralized authority in Rome led in short order to the takeover of formerly public spaces by competing private individuals, and the division of the city into spheres of influence punctuated by the nucleated settlements of leading nobles. This process culminated with the onset of urban *incastellamento* proper, when aristocratic residences began to metamorphose into real fortified compounds, outfitted with the menacing towers mentioned with increasing frequency in the property documents beginning in the eleventh century.[127]

Hence, a contentious climate within the city, external chaos and straitened economic conditions, and the eclipse of the papacy as a transcendent force in local and international politics probably all had their part in turning Rome from a city of one great Wall into one of many smaller ones. What had previously been an urban unity – a community – fragmented politically and topographically together with the enceinte that had once made of it a cohesive ensemble. Nor was this close correlation between the state of the defenses and the waning fortunes of Rome lost on contemporaries, if Benedict of Soracte is any indication. When he closed the historical chronicle (*Chronicon*) he wrote in the last quarter of the tenth century by lamenting the depths to which the city had fallen in the preceding century, he concluded with a lapidary epitaph for all that it had once been:

Alas, Rome!… You were too lovely. Your whole wall with its towers and battlements looked like this: you had three-hundred-eighty-one towers, forty-six

---

[124] See Meneghini and Santangeli Valenzani 2004, 175–88; Santangeli Valenzani 2001a; Meneghini 2000b.

[125] Cf. Meneghini and Santangeli Valenzani 2004, 48.

[126] See Manacorda 2006; Santangeli Valenzani 2004, 47–51 and 57–9; Meneghini and Santangeli Valenzani 2004, 47–51; cf. Santangeli Valenzani 2000, 108–9.

[127] Hubert 1990, esp. 185–9.

castellated towers, six-thousand, eight-hundred battlements, your gates fifteen. Alas, Leonine city! Once you were captured, and then left for the king of the Saxons... [Fin].[128]

The sad legacy of generations of civil strife was all to be read in the Wall, which had once *had* features worthy of all that Rome once *was*, but was no more.

For Benedict, then, the condition of the Wall was inextricably bound up in the condition of the city as a whole. Ultimately, I hope if anything to have given some sense of how Benedict's impression came to be possible, and of why indeed it was so prescient.

I hope, that is, to have shown that after the initial cataclysm of the Wall's construction, its profile as a spatial terminator and a point of topographical and symbolic reference grew ever greater, as the monumental fabric of the city not coincidentally tended toward a more lacunose – one might even say amorphous – state. Where there was once a Wall of the city in the late empire, there came, in the early Middle Ages, to be a city of the Wall. It was the enduring and physically most ubiquitous symbol of Rome's past glory and its greatest remaining claim to fame, the monument that more than any other proclaimed the continuing vitality of the city and its institutions, among which the Church was paramount. Into the ninth century, it was the most fundamental guarantor of urban community and continuity in ways both practical and intangible, protecting the city at the same time it represented and embodied and structured it. Only when Rome disintegrated in a way it never had between the third century and the ninth was the Wall allowed to crumble, too.

In the end, however, the Wall was too deeply etched into the Roman cityscape to be forgotten, or perhaps it is better to say that the Roman cityscape had been too fundamentally conditioned by the Wall to allow for its disappearance. The fact that the *abitato* of the city occupied a small fraction of the circuit when it was again conspicuously overhauled in 1157, as it continued to do until after the unification of Italy in 1870, was almost irrelevant: the Wall was Rome, and Rome was the Wall, and that was essentially that. When Pope Nicholas V rebuilt sizeable chunks of the circuit in *c.* 1450, he followed squarely in the footsteps of his early-medieval forebears, re-girding the again staunchly papal city with a mural

---

[128] *ve Roma!... nimium speciose fuistis. omnes tua moenia cum turres et pugnaculi sicut modo repperitur: turres tuarum tricenti octoginta una habuistis, turres castellis quadraginta sex, pugnaculi tui sex milia octo centies, portes tue quindecim. ve civitas Leoniana! dudum capta fuistis, modo vero a Saxonicum rege relicta...*

crown that dwarfed its real extent and thus worked again as so often before to proclaim the Christian capital greater than the sum of its parts, and more pointedly to renew the ancient association between Rome and Celestial Jerusalem.[129] So, too, when cartographers from the Renaissance on mapped vast tracts of intramural nothingness in the interest of framing their views of Rome with the silhouette of the Aurelian Wall, they reprised on paper the same "mural-centric" topography that Nicholas had rendered anew in stone. In their various ways, these later generations remained subject to an urban legacy forged and tempered, as we have seen, in the six centuries between the emperor Aurelian and Pope Leo IV.

[129] On Nicholas V's efforts to reinvigorate the traditional links between Rome and Celestial Jerusalem, and generally to strengthen the power and autonomy of the papacy – both projects that demanded the restoration of the Wall – see Fagiolo and Madonna 1972, 389.

∾ | Conclusion

So what, after all, is in a Wall? I hope the preceding thoughts about the Aurelian Wall, prime specimen that it is, between them indicate productive avenues of inquiry into what walls do and why we often care so much about them. As a case-study, the example of Rome has much to reveal, beginning (but only beginning) with the assorted mural phenomena that I have tried to outline over the course of this study. Together, these observations make a start at exploring a neglected structural constant in Roman history, by illustrating to some extent how the Aurelian Wall came to dominate physical and mental landscapes of the Eternal City like no other manmade feature, ever. I hope in the end to have laid plausible foundations for the following conclusions about the special relationship that arose between Rome and its enceinte, which might then become a useful point of departure for those interested in the wider implications of the Roman particulars.

Tactical efficacy – defense, in a word – was a necessary pretext for a structure as enormous and costly as the Aurelian Wall, an unobjectionable sanction for an initiative that would have otherwise been more galling in its grandiose uselessness than Nero's Golden House, for example. The Wall inevitably and inescapably had a pragmatic mandate, and for over fifteen centuries it remained a legitimate means of protecting and controlling the area it enclosed. If I have shown anything, however, I hope it is that "defense" is not the final word in the history of the Aurelian Wall, but rather the beginning, the shared and palatable premise that justified a project with an almost infinite range of further uses and implications both practical and symbolic.

Already in its infancy under Aurelian, the enceinte was an integral component in an administrative restructuring of the urban collective, which involved a reform of the *annona* and the infrastructure that supported it, as well as a seemingly novel and lasting redefinition of the role of the *collegia* – which in a way is to say of the individual or the private citizen – in the service of the state. The Wall need not have been the motivating factor for the various reforms outlined in Chapter 2 to have been envisioned nonetheless as a valuable complement to, and component of, Aurelian's scheme to recast the topographical and institutional framework of public services at Rome. The Wall was, further, a testament to the supreme authority of the emperor who willed it into being, a concrete sign of his control over human and material resources and a monument to his dominance at Rome.

Even at the moment of its construction, then, the Wall was not planned, presented, and perceived solely as an unfortunate necessity, a shameful token of the fact that the empire was no longer able to defend itself along its frontiers. As I have suggested in Chapter 3, the place of a Wall around the capital of the empire was in the 270s AD likely a vexed and ambivalent concept; surely disquieting on some level, the appearance of the Aurelian Wall nonetheless need not have been taken solely as a sign of impending apocalypse looming behind the silhouettes of Germanic riders. Surely the Wall was no such thing by the beginning of the fifth century, when it was ostentatiously heightened under Honorius, embellished with Christian symbols, and subsequently used to add verisimilitude to the programmatic representation of Christian Rome as the earthly prototype of the Celestial Jerusalem. The urban ideal changed drastically throughout the Roman world between the third century and the fifth, as enceintes became first ubiquitous and respectable, and later, in various stages beginning on the periphery and proceeding toward the Mediterranean heart of the empire, laudable. While the influence of Rome and its Wall on the conceptual rehabilitation of urban defenses is impossible to gauge in all its particulars, the impact of the *caput mundi* and *sedes Petri* on its many imitators – Trier, Milan, Ravenna, Constantinople, for example – was somewhere between significant and profound.

But if the Wall was on the one hand an instrument of policy and a tool in the hands of the late-imperial administration that created it, it was also, increasingly, an independent presence on the Roman scene, an integral part of the cityscape that became for subsequent generations a precondition of life in and around the city, no more avoidable than Rome's seven hills, say, or the Tiber. From the beginning, it redefined the character of individual neighborhoods, reconditioned patterns of road and river traffic in various parts of the city, and indelibly altered the relationship between a city center and its surroundings that would never again blend fluidly one into the other, as documented in the first part of Chapter 4. The enceinte then grew to condition the parameters of life throughout the city and its immediate hinterland in new and if anything more fundamental ways with the passage of centuries, as patterns of settlement and communications adapted to what was in effect a changed geographical reality. As the city center was connected to the outside world only via the roads that passed through the functioning gates in the Wall, the map of city and suburbs alike was increasingly contoured along these privileged axes – approximately one for every mile of curtain by the sixth century – where people and goods tended to concentrate, often leaving, in the straitened conditions of the early Middle Ages, precious little in the interstices.

In Chapter 5, we see that the Wall also brought about a whole new way of conceptualizing urban space and delimiting the boundaries thereof. Already made the incarnation of the *pomerium* before its completion, Aurelian's Wall thereafter became an ever-more important point of reference in the definition of the city proper. Phrases like *in urbe* came from the fifth century on to mean quite unequivocally *intra muros*, both in secular law and administration and in the histories and administrative protocols of the ecclesiastical hierarchy, which early on embraced the Wall as the physical container – and also the monumental face – of the Church of Rome *stricto sensu*. So fundamental had the Wall become to the essence of Christian Rome that it played a leading role in both the religious and the secular initiatives of the popes who became, from the mid eighth century on, the undisputed sovereigns of the city and its surrounding territories in central Italy. The relics that by then constituted the most precious possessions of the Roman Church were transferred wholesale within the contours of the Wall, an expedient designed not only to protect a finite and dwindling resource, but further to make of the entire walled area of Rome a Christian citadel, a vast enclosure stuffed with the holiest panoply of saintly remains in all of Christendom, whose immensely potent spiritual cache was to complement and even overshadow the corporeal might and presence of the Wall itself, like the saints who loom over the enceinte in the apse mosaic at S. Prassede.

Yet the popes who achieved full temporal sovereignty over Rome in the eighth and ninth centuries had additional reasons, outlined in Chapter 6, for devoting enormous resources to the upkeep of an enceinte that dwarfed the reduced material and demographic profile of the early-medieval city. Their well-publicized restorations of the circuit allowed these popes to present themselves as rulers and patrons of the entire urban collective, and publicly to usurp the role of the Roman emperors and their Byzantine successors who had owned and overseen the physical fabric of the city. The Wall was a tangible link to a glorified past, a dramatic vestige of the ideal Christian capital that late-imperial Rome had become in the eyes of early medieval pontiffs like Hadrian I. It was also the surviving monument that best matched the scale of papal ambitions, a fitting frame for the earthly seat of the successors of Peter, the self-proclaimed regents of a universal Church centered on Rome. In its peerless monumentality, moreover, it was admirably suited to impress the foreign potentates and pilgrims who protected the Roman Church and filled its coffers with pious offerings: as I have argued, these mostly transalpine visitors were conditioned to view an enceinte as the hallmark of a Christian, Roman city. The claims to pre-eminence of the papal capital thus stood only to be enhanced by the presence of the most impressive circuit wall imaginable.

Little could anyone in Aurelian's day have imagined what lay in store for the new defensive circuit then rising around the city. Still less will it have occurred to anyone that they were witnessing the birth of what would become very nearly a surrogate Rome, a thing as transcendent and enduring as the city itself, susceptible of being endlessly reinvented without ever being totally effaced. While the city itself dwindled in the centuries after Aurelian, the Wall literally grew, and with it its reputation and its visual and cognitive presence, to the point where much of the essence of "Rome," its imperial legacy and its evolving present as capital and citadel of Christendom, came to be transposed upon the enceinte. It was a great weight to place upon a wall; but as past and present examples from around the globe suggest, walls in one way or another have a way of bearing loads, particularly of the social, cultural, and symbolic sort, that often far exceed the expectations of their creators.

Appendix A: Numerical data

The following figures result from measurements conducted on the various sectors of the Wall. Sector N (southern Trastevere) has been omitted for lack of statistically significant remains. Three types of measurements were made: the module of the brick facing, inside and out (with a preference for the external facings); the dimensions of the projecting faces of the towers; and the thickness of the curtains. I attempted to make measurements only where I thought the extant remains an accurate reflection of the dimensions of the structure in its original phase. In the case of modules, limited measurements were also made on the sections heightened under Honorius. The level of coverage in various parts of the circuit is not uniform, nor do I make any claims about the statistical exhaustiveness of the data, but rather present them, for whatever they are worth, in the hope that they represent a step beyond the vague and sometimes conflicting generalities traditionally advanced regarding the measurements of the Wall. With this disclaimer, they are best left to speak for themselves.

All figures are in centimeters and meters. For the modules, (int.) indicates a measurement taken on the inside of the Wall, and (Hon.) work I think executed during the campaign of 401–3. The data are arranged by category, and further subdivided by sector, identified by the letter that precedes each measurement. In exceptional cases, more specific locations are given.

Dimensions of projecting towers (in meters)

B: 7.59 × 3.48; 7.60 × 3.55; 7.76 × 3.63; 7.57 × 3.51
C: 7.21 × 3.48
E: 7.67 × 3.67; 7.72 × 3.56
F: 7.85 × 3.58; 7.76 × 3.67; 7.72 × 3.56
G: 7.68 × 3.57
H: 7.63 × 3.58
J: 7.60 × 3.50; 7.68 × 4.03; 7.65 × 3.54
L: 7.50 × 3.47; 7.73 × 3.64; 7.65 × 3.49
P: 7.72 × 3.57

Thickness of curtains (in meters)

B: 3.62; 3.68; 3.61
C: 3.60
F: 3.66; 3.67
G: 3.67
H: 3.50
L: 3.66; 3.50

Modules (in centimeters)

A: 29; 30.5; 27 (int.)
B: 29; 27; 25 (int.)
C: 28; 27; 27
D: 26; 27; 28; 31
E: 27; 30; 31
F: 27; 25; 28
G: 28; 27; 27 (int.); 32 (Hon., int.)
H: 32 (int.); 31 (int.); 29 (int.); 34[1]
J: 34 (? First curtain past Porta Metronia, below Honorian module of 30);
28; 26; 25
K: 29; 30
L: 29; 27; 27; 27; 28 (int.); 29 (int.); the following all (Hon.): 34.5 (int.);
30 (int.); 35 (int.)
M: 27; 29; 29 (int.); the following all (Hon.): 34; 29; 32; 27
O: 29; 31
P: 29; 30

River wall, south of Testaccio

Dimensions of one standing tower: 4.3 × 1.16 (internal); 4.47 × 1.13/1.11
(external).
Modules: (tower) 32; 32.5; 34; (curtains): 30; 32.

---

[1] These measurements are all taken from the galleried curtains at an unusually low elevation
that I believe replaced Aurelianic originals (beween tower H6 and the Porta Metronia):
see Chapter 1.

Appendix B: The fourth century revisited: the problem of Maxentius

While the rudiments of a comfortable reconciliation between archaeology and written sources have at last been established for the primary stages of the Wall's construction, problematic issues remain, some of which have hardly been raised to date, much less resolved. The majority of the difficulties relate to the sections of the Wall that do not belong to the two principal building campaigns of Aurelian and Honorius, the most ancient of which, executed in *opus vittatum*, have come generically to be attributed to Maxentius, for the motives discussed above in Chapter 1. The identification, however, is neither as certain nor as straightforward as has been suggested.

A first problem is that many of the *vittatum* interventions in the Wall now often confidently ascribed to Maxentius diverge markedly in their technical characteristics. Some of them, indeed, resemble securely dated high- and late-medieval work far more than other tracts of *vittatum* in the Wall or, for that matter, in the buildings of Maxentius' villa. A second question, raised before but never, to my mind, satisfactorily resolved, relates to the sheer extent of many of the putatively Maxentian repairs, particularly in the northern sectors of the Wall, and above all to the towers, several of which have been refaced almost from the ground up in *vittatum*.[1] Even given the concerns voiced about the occasionally deficient bonds between the Aurelianic brick facings and the concrete core behind, this seems a remarkable amount of decay to have occurred in the three decades between the completion of the Wall and the reign of Maxentius, particularly as the upper sections of several of these towers were rebuilt for their entire thickness, and not simply on their exterior surfaces.[2] In the third place, the identification of many ostensibly

---

[1] Cf. Mancini 2001, 26.

[2] Cf. Cozza 1987, 25–6; several such towers in the northern part of the circuit, between the Portae Pinciana and Salaria, are analyzed in more depth in Cozza 1993; see 97, 101, etc.; though as Mancini justly says, Cozza rather understates the case in calling the lacunae in this part of the Aurelian circuit "piccoli danni" (26). One noteworthy example of the scope of the repairs required is tower B18, which was reconstructed in *vittatum* literally from the ground up; cf. Mancini 2001, 26; and Cozza 1993, 118. Mancini implausibly cites poor bonds between the Aurelianic facing and core as the

Figure B.1 Curtain L4–5. Archers' slits in heightened *vittatum* curtain (the second from left is a later addition). The Honorian brickwork begins at the top, well above the Aurelian rampart-walk.

Maxentian tracts as such requires, on close examination, the acceptance of one of two postulates, neither currently much in vogue. Either Maxentius (1) did in fact build sections of the Wall well above their original elevation, or (2) the *vittatum* in these areas is not his. The best example occurs in the sector between the Portae Appia and Ardeatina, where several curtains preserve extensive tracts of *vittatum* that rise several meters above the level of the Aurelianic rampart walk, from which they begin, to the springing of the Honorian masonry above (Figure B.1).[3] Fourth, there is Colini's crucial observation of the curtain near the Porta Maggiore, which bears

cause of what, on the "Maxentian hypothesis," amounted to the collapse of the whole structure within thirty years of its building. The occasional failure of the original brick curtains to adhere to their backing, a phenomenon which certainly did occur in places, was first described by Procopius (*BG* 1, 23, 15), and rather later by Richmond (1930, 61).

[3] The extent of the work here hardly accords with Cozza's contention that Maxentius performed only essential maintenance on dilapidated sectors of the Wall (1987, 26); Brienza and Delfino have recently called attention to the signs of heightened curtains in *vittatum* which they – following the *communis opinio* – attribute to Maxentius; they unwisely follow Todd 1978 in claiming that some of these heightened curtains reached 15–20m in elevation (!), which Todd was only able to claim because he thought the really substantial elevation of Honorius the work of Maxentius; see Brienza and Delfino 2006, esp. n. 5.

clear traces of two discrete interventions between the Aurelian brickwork below and that of Honorius above.[4] Finally, Maxentius is no more explicitly said to have laid a single brick in the Wall than anyone else who reigned between the death of Probus and the accession of Honorius, a factor that perhaps merits more serious consideration in light of the previous caveats than it has yet received. For all of these reasons, neither the attribution to Maxentius, nor broader questions of what went on with the Wall from *c.* 280 to 400, should be regarded as definitively resolved. A brief reevaluation is called for.

It is undeniable that most of the earliest *vittatum* interventions in the Wall occur between strata clearly belonging to Aurelian and Honorius, and should therefore date somewhere in the intervening 120 years, despite the fact that much of the work is more closely paralleled in structures dating variously between the fifth century and the later Middle Ages.[5] It is also true that much of the rest, realized in files of small, rectangular blocks of tufa regularly interspersed with one or two courses of brick, bears a close resemblance to the technique employed in a number of buildings dated securely within or near the reign of Maxentius.[6] The contrast in styles is at times dramatic, even from one tower to the next. Tower B8 (Figure B.2) has regular files of rather homogeneous bricks, separated by small, quadrangular *tufelli*, and hence looks characteristically Maxentian. In tower B9 (Figure B.3), meanwhile, the pieces of tufa are larger and far less regular, with single courses of more fragmentary brick undulating among their contours. Yet on stratigraphical grounds, both sections should date between Aurelian and Honorius, as should other similarly diverse repairs, particularly between the Portae Pinciana and Salaria.[7] Given further that

[4] Above Chapter 1, n. 63.

[5] The best examples of surviving sixth-century *vittatum*, which indeed closely recall much of what is found in the Wall, come from the churches of S. Giovanni in Porta Latina, built between 500 and 550, and S. Lorenzo *fuori le mura*, constructed under Pelagius II (579–90). For S. Giovanni in Porta Latina, Krautheimer (1980, 68) suggested a date around 550, with which Heres concurred (1982, 145–6); at *CBCR* 1, 515–17, a date closer to 500 is proposed; on S. Lorenzo, see *LP* 1, 309; cf. *CBCR* 2, 1–144. The catalog and detailed plates included in Cecchelli (ed.) 2001 are a convenient source of ready reference for these and other contemporary constructions at Rome.

[6] Such *vittatum* occurs between the Portae Appia and Ardeatina; in the north wall of the Castra Praetoria (cf. Cozza 1998, 33ff.); and in many other localized segments elsewhere in the circuit. It compares closely with the structures of the Villa of Maxentius on the Via Appia; with the ambulatory of S. Sebastiano, located just across the road and dating probably no later than the reign of Constantine; and with parts of the Basilica of Maxentius in the forum.

[7] Towers B16 and B18 likewise look remarkably dissimilar: in B16, a higher percentage of tufa is used relative to brick, and the blocks are less regular in size and shape than in B18, where single courses of bricks and *tufelli* alternate at more regular intervals.

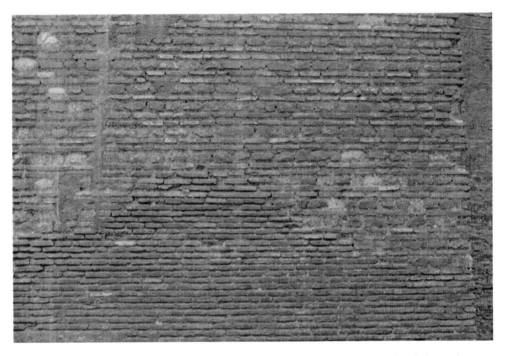

Figure B.2 Tower B8, faced in regular *opus vittatum* with Aurelianic brick immediately beneath.

Figure B.3 Tower B9, side view. *Vittatum* springing from Aurelianic brick. The later repair at right is of the twelfth or thirteenth centuries.

a millennium's worth of subsequent work on the Wall often closely approximates the standard of the rougher sort of ancient *vittatum*, and that the more regular type continued to be used in Rome at least through the seventh century, it is best acknowledged that attempts to date these *opus vittatum* repairs on typological grounds alone are largely futile.[8]

Still, in light of the remarkable diversity of raw materials and styles found in such close proximity, it would be truly remarkable had the work all been accomplished in the six years of Maxentius' reign. This scenario would require imagining that masons operating literally side by side held themselves to strikingly dissimilar technical standards and, moreover, that some worked exclusively with freshly cut, homogeneous blocks of tufa, while their neighbors were left to cobble together a hodgepodge of rough and variegated fragments of recycled tufa, peperino, and marble. More improbably still, it would mean that at least one curtain near the Porta Maggiore was raised twice, and furnished each time with a new parapet and merlons, in the same six-year period.[9] Surely these phenomena are more plausibly explained within a more extensive chronological arc, perhaps embracing the better part of the fourth century. This extended timeframe also accounts better for the extent of the pre-Honorian repairs, which a century and more of wear would more convincingly have occasioned than the passage of thirty years.

And indeed, a glance at the historical record provides ample fodder for alternate, albeit purely hypothetical, attributions. Maxentius was only the first in a series of fourth-century imperial claimants or pretenders, all of whom sought to consolidate and legitimize their authority in the ancient capital of the empire.[10] None of them, naturally, was treated very kindly in subsequent histories written under the auspices of the victors; and Constantine's appropriation of the impressive architectural

---

[8] *Vittatum* walls that look remarkably like the less regular pre-Honorian repairs on the Aurelian Wall were still being built in Rome in the high Middle Ages, as the narthex of San Clemente and the rear wall of the chapel of S. Andrea on the Caelian, both from the twelfth century, clearly demonstrate. Meanwhile, the basilica by St. Agnese, dated between 337 and 350, and S. Paolo *fuori le mura*, rebuilt in the 380s, are both executed in the neat files of brick and *tufelli* that also characterize the buildings of Maxentius. Even the seventh-century church of S. Agnese features regular *vittatum* that could easily pass for Maxentian.

[9] See above, Chapter 1, n. 63, with Figure 1.19.

[10] The political circumstances of Maxentius' reign, and the legal foundation of his claim to the throne, are well summarized in Barnes 1981; the colorful, entertaining and partisan account of Lactantius (*DMP*, 27) is accurate in its main contours, its unremitting hostility notwithstanding. The exhaustive account *par excellence* for the period remains that of Seeck 1910, esp. 77ff.

accomplishments of his predecessor's six-year reign has traditionally been used by way of explanation for the lack of references to Maxentius' alleged interest in the Wall.[11]

Yet the same logic applies equally well, if not better, to the historical legacy of two subsequent usurpers. From 350 to 352, Rome and the western provinces were under the *de facto* control of the renegade general Magnentius. While it is not clear how much time, if any, he spent at Rome, the senate had thrown in its lot with the usurper, and his prefects governed the city in his name. Magnentius suffered a defeat at Mursa in 351, in the wake of which he fell back on Italy, which remained in a state of armed readiness for a full year leading up to the final invasion of Constantius in the fall of 352.[12] Four decades later, another imperial claimant, Eugenius, is known for the close personal interest he took in the affairs of the city, where his authority and prestige rested largely on the support of the senate, whose favor he assiduously courted, and whose leaders were bound closely to his cause.[13] He is known certainly to have been in Rome for some months before his defeat at the battle of the river Frigidus in September of 394.[14]

To sum up: both Magnentius and Eugenius were in effective control at Rome for many months; both had good reason to look to its security and to make preparations against imminent attack; and both, moreover, ruled in periods when the Wall had had considerably more time to deteriorate than it had under Maxentius. *A priori*, the only reasons to privilege Maxentius are, first, that he was in power a bit longer, and is known to have built extensively elsewhere in and around Rome; and second, that he is said to have begun a ditch around the Wall in the *Chronograph* of 354. Yet on closer examination, these factors may if anything strengthen the case in favor of the others. First, it is noteworthy that the one source willing to credit Maxentius with improvements to the fortifications of the city very specifically refers only to the digging of an unfinished ditch, and not to any rebuilding or repair of the Wall. Further, considering the length of Maxentius' reign, it would be strange that he accomplished so little, were he the one to have undertaken that preliminary heightening of the

---

[11] On Maxentius' building program, see Curran 2000, 56–63; and *ibid.* 76ff. on Constantine's largely successful attempt to obliterate Maxentius' topographical legacy in the city. Cf. Cullhed 1994, esp. 50ff.; Richmond 1930, 251–6.

[12] See Hunt 1998, 14–22.

[13] Eugenius' tumultuous two-year reign, and his close relationship with the Roman senatorial aristocracy, are discussed in two classic articles by H. Bloch (Bloch 1963 and 1945); cf. more generally Matthews 1975, 238–50.

[14] Matthews 1975, 242.

Wall that apparently was attempted at some point prior to Honorius. Honorius doubled the height of the whole circuit in something like two years, and Maxentius himself had time to realize other projects of surpassing grandeur, and considerably less practical value, given the perilousness of his position. Surely he could have done more than elevate slightly a few scattered curtains, had he applied himself to upgrading the enceinte. To my mind, the exiguous interventions on the raised curtains near the Porta Maggiore and the Porta Appia, for example, look rather more like what parvenu usurpers (or their agents) might be expected to accomplish in the course of a few tumultuous months preceding an impending encounter with the reigning emperor.

From all of this speculation, two more concrete points emerge. First and foremost, it is apparent that more than one campaign of repair and reconstruction occurred in the 120 years between Probus and Honorius. Therefore, any blanket attribution to Maxentius, or to any single figure or historical circumstance, is already an oversimplification that will inevitably fall short of the whole truth. Second, there is no overwhelming compulsion to assume that Maxentius was even one among the several involved parties, though he may well have been. Magnentius, Eugenius, and perhaps also any of Rome's "legitimate" emperors, from Diocletian to Theodosius I, might just as well, more or less, have added some or all of the various pieces of the puzzle in *opus vittatum*.[15]

---

[15] In the case of localized repairs, moreover, there is no need to imagine even that the initiative came from the emperors themselves: the city prefects were charged with the maintenance of public buildings, a mandate that certainly included essential maintenance on the Wall; see Chapter 2.

Appendix C: The post-Honorian additions to the Porta Appia and other fifth- and sixth-century construction

While a precise chronology for the post-Honorian additions to the Porta Appia is difficult, a few remarks may be hazarded.

As others have said, the foundations of the Honorian towers subsided rather dramatically at an early date, destabilizing them dangerously and opening large fissures in their exteriors, some of which were extensively repaired in the 1920s.[1] It has thus been suggested that the additions to the towers were meant to buttress them, tempting some to connect their construction with damage sustained in the earthquake of 443.[2] This hypothesis is not without its problems, however. To begin with, its proponents assert that the new top chambers were added after the "buttresses"; yet if the towers were unstable enough already to require buttressing, it is hardly probable that they would subsequently have been singled out, as very few towers anywhere along the Wall were, for further heightening.[3] More importantly, similar square shells were added around Honorian towers at three other gates, the Portae Flaminia, Tiburtina, and Praenestina-Labicana, none of which seems to have been affected by serious problems with subsidence, earthquake-related or otherwise.

The fact remains that both the square casings and the top chambers do appear to have been added after the gate had suffered significant damage, consonant with what an earthquake might be expected to provoke.[4] The year 443 thus remains a possible *terminus post quem*;

---

[1] See Richmond 1930, 125–6.   [2] See e.g. Cambedda and Ceccherelli 1990, 48.

[3] Yet this is precisely what Richmond suggested (1930, 142), all the more implausibly as he further postulated an intermediate phase between the buttressing of the towers and the addition of the tops, in which the cement vaults of the Honorian tower were replaced by wooden floors for the express purpose of lightening the unstable towers! His relative chronology remains the standard to this day, as a visit to the *Museo delle Mura* in the gate itself demonstrates; cf. also Cambedda and Ceccherelli 1990, 48–52, where the same (buttressing – emergency removal of vaults – new addition) sequence is maintained.

[4] The upper portion of the north tower, for example, springs from a jagged break in the Honorian masonry below; the contrast is most clearly visible on the interior facing. Perhaps during the same reconstruction campaign, massive buttresses in *opus vittatum* were built inside both towers. In addition to stabilizing the existing structures, they permitted their further

but as it seems unlikely that reconstruction on such a grandiose scale was undertaken during the turbulent years between the sack of Rome in 410 and the end of the fifth century, I am inclined to move the *terminus post* to the period of Theoderic, the first ruler after Honorius to whom significant work on the Wall can be credited, during whose reign another powerful earthquake shook the city, in 502.[5] A number of circumstantial indications from elsewhere in the circuit broadly support this hypothesis, and may permit its further refinement, by assigning the upper chambers in brick to Theoderic, and the marble facings to a still later period, perhaps best associated with the rule of Narses.

The stamped brick of Theoderic from the Porta Flaminia is of particular interest for its potential relevance to the Porta Appia, which the Porta Flaminia resembled more closely than any other gate. Studies made before and during its demolition show that it, too, had square marble bases built around the outside of pre-existing Honorian towers, and a single arch in a marble curtain built at the same time as the casings.[6] That the marble facings were ancient and not, as a later tradition had it, of the fifteenth century is evident from, among other things, the fact that they were sunk more than 4.5 m below ground in 1706, and thus significantly deeper even than the final ancient level of the Via Flaminia.[7] For the sequencing of the building phases of the Porta Flaminia, which came most clearly to light when it was dismantled, Visconti's contemporary description of the facing of the towers underneath the marble coating is of exceptional importance. He noted that the brickwork of the east tower was executed in regular masonry composed of reddish and yellow recycled bricks absolutely characteristic of Honorius, while the surface of the west tower had subsequently been partially refaced in "bad brickwork" (*cattiva opera*

---

heightening, and supported the vaults of the new top chambers, with which they are closely integrated.

[5] Chapter 1, n. 70.

[6] Audebert's careful description recalls the original appearance of the gate before the restorations of Pius IV in 1561–2: "Ceste porte estoit n'y a pas longtemps en forme d'Arc Triomphal, sur lequel elle avoit esté bastye se servant de l'archade qui se trouva en ce lieu; qui fut, selon la commune opinion, du temps de Bélisaire que nous pouvons remarquer par ce qu'avons veu cy-devant, avoir esté fort curieux de rebastir les portes de la ville de Rome: Joinct aussy que les murs des deux costéz de ceste porte touchant à icelle, ont esté par lui bastyz, tels qu'on les veoit encores aujourd'huy fort entiers" (Müntz 1886, 124).

[7] Lanciani (*FUR*, 1) has the paving of the Via Flaminia at 3.29 m below ground level. The full case for the antiquity of the towers is effectively made by Richmond (1930, 193–4).

laterizia), which he thought later than the fifth century.[8] This gives a sequence that corresponds closely with the one proposed for the Porta Appia, with a post-Honorian construction phase in brick, followed by the addition of the marble facings.

Moreover, at the Porta Flaminia, there is good reason to suspect that construction did occur in Theoderic's time, thanks to the discovery of the stamped brick. Although there is sadly no record of where exactly the surviving exemplar was found, the facings of the Honorian towers are by far the likeliest place, as these were evidently the only parts of the structure still containing ancient brickwork when it was demolished.[9] This leaves the repair in the west tower, in the "bad brick" that Visconti thought characteristic of the sixth century or later, as the obvious location of choice, though this can never be proven beyond doubt. Still, the sum of the evidence is suggestive. First, the marble facings of the Porta Flaminia were added on top of a repair, apparently executed after the Honorian towers were built, and which very plausibly contained Theoderic's bricks; and second, they were demonstrably ancient, but on the same arguments adduced previously in connection with the Porta Appia, probably not the work of Belisarius himself. If Theoderic and Belisarius are eliminated, Narses remains as the logical candidate for the final construction phase. There is thus substantial temptation to assign to the Porta Flaminia a building sequence similar to the one

---

[8] Visconti in *BullCom* (1877), 210: "…l'altra torre quivi scoperta (the western one), simile alla compagna quanto alla forma ed alla altezza, è comparsa edificata con opera molto più regolare, e rivestita di mattoni gialli e rossi quali furono quelli adoperati esternamente da Honorio nelle sue riparazioni del recinto aurelianèo." Richmond argued strenuously against Visconti's attribution of the brick towers to Honorius, but only because he thought their second phase (the elevation and refacing) the work of Maxentius (1930, 191–3). Cozza follows Richmond in proposing that the marble facings were added directly to the Aurelianic towers by Honorius, thereby failing in the same way his predecessor did to account properly for the crucial intermediate periods (1992, 100ff.; cf. 1987, 49). In so doing, Richmond and Cozza both give Visconti less than his due: he was unequivocal that the masonry of the west tower was irregular and decidedly "late" (he thought it certainly after the fifth century); and while typologies of late antique *opus latericium* have been considerably refined since his day, it is still hardly likely that he would have mistakenly labeled Honorian work, with which he was in fact precociously familiar, as "medieval" (*ibid.*, 192). Even on the most critical reading of Visconti, his report still proves that the marble casings at least were added after Honorius: as there is no evidence anywhere in the Wall for repairs in brick executed between Aurelian and Honorius, the brick reconstruction of the east tower cannot be thought earlier than 401–3, whence the superimposed square shell must date still later. Sadly, no detailed visual record of the later masonry of the east tower is extant, which might otherwise make for a compelling comparison with the work at the top of the Porta Appia.

[9] This is immediately evident in a drawing made at the time of the demolition, reproduced in Cozza 1992, 98.

Figure C.1 Porta Appia, keystone on interior of gateway.

proposed for the Porta Appia, with an intermediate restoration of Theoderic followed by a final intervention under Narses.

Turning back to the Porta Appia, a final chip of circumstantial evidence may be added to the pile of indications that favor attributing the marble façade to Narses. On the keystone of the interior archway, there is an incised cross with a Greek inscription to Saints George and Conon (Figure C.1). While there will never be irrefutable proof that this unique inscription does not date before the Gothic Wars, it makes better *a priori* sense to assign a dedication in Greek to two eastern soldier-saints to a period after the coming of a Byzantine garrison to the city. As I think it most plausible that the keystone was carved at approximately the time when the arch and its surrounding curtain were erected, a sixth-century date again seems best for the structure as a whole.

My reasons are these: while the cross is often included in discussions of other inscribed crosses on the keystones of Honorian gates, it is in fact rather less similar to the others than has been suggested (Figures C.2–C.3).[10] First, there are concentric chords within each of

---

[10] By Cozza, for example, whose plates of the various inscribed keystones if anything emphasize just how unique the one at the Porta Appia is, in style and content alike (Cozza 1987, figs. 12–14); cf. Richmond 1930, 107, whose simplified illustration lends to the Appia keystone a spurious air of conformity. Interestingly, the *communis opinio* before Richmond held that all the crosses on the gates belonged to the period of the Gothic Wars, an idea popularized by Nibby and subsequently often repeated; see Nibby 1820, 319 (Pinciana); 367 (Latina); 370–1 (Appia), etc. While Richmond was right to argue that the majority find

Figure C.2 Porta Pinciana, keystone on exterior of gateway.

Figure C.3 Porta Pinciana, keystone on interior of gateway.

the four arms of the cross that appear nowhere else on the Wall. Further, the incisions are much deeper, and the chisel marks more evident and meandering, than in any of the others. The inscription (another unique feature) shares these general characteristics, and indeed looks very much

closer parallels in the fifth century, he failed to account for the very exception to the rule at the Porta Appia which his predecessors had perhaps heeded too much; in both cases, the assumption that all the inscribed keystones were contemporary and typologically linked led to generalizations and, I think, error.

like the work of the same hand. That the keystone was a unified composition is implied also by the three horizontal bands that traverse its face. These separate the cross and the inscription below into separate registers, and look very much like guidelines scored into the blank stone immediately prior to its working. Had the cross been incised before anything else, the uppermost of the bands could surely have been moved a bit higher to allow more space for the words ΘEOY XAPIC, which in the event had to be sandwiched rather awkwardly between it and the arc of the circumscribed cross below. Of course, as has been previously said, the keystone could have been carved at any point after the arch was built.[11] I think not, however. Given that the Honorian gates likely featured their decorated keystones from the beginning, it would seem strange had the keystone of the Porta Appia, one of the very most important gates of the city, been left blank for any length of time, much less a century and a half.[12] Hence, we have a keystone unique both for its inscription and its technical characteristics, probably sculpted when the arch in which it rests was built. On the acceptance of the simple proposition that the Porta Appia was refaced after Honorius' time, such speculations will perhaps seem less gratuitous, and even logical: the Greek inscription may very simply belong to a "Byzantine" gate; and to one better attributed to Narses in the years following the Gothic Wars than to Belisarius during the midst of the conflict.[13]

Elsewhere around the circuit, there is still less evidence for the dating of post-Honorian work. Ideally, however, other remains of the fifth and

---

[11] E.g. by Richmond (1930, 108 and 136).

[12] It is at least certain that the (Honorian) crosses over the rear arch of the Porta Pinciana and the front of the Porta Asinaria were original features of the keystones, as they are in relief.

[13] Modern commentators on the Wall have a way of citing Nibby where his opinions coincide with theirs, while ignoring his many now obvious misconceptions and errors. I will do the same here, as I am convinced that in the case of the Porta Appia, Nibby had it right; he at any rate proceeded from the solid assumption that the marble facings of the gateway and towers were later than Honorius, which Richmond and others failed to appreciate: "La sua construzione, e l'altezza delle torri, la rendono una delle più magnifica di Roma, quantunque l'arco della porta stessa sia di forma poco regolare, e disgustosa [!] all'aspetto: questo e le cattive modinature delle torri ci fanno inclinare a riputarla opera posteriore alla Guerra Gotica ed a meglio appoggiare questa congettura si presta la croce greca, che nella chiave dell'arco nell'interno della porta stessa si vede grafito dietro un disco, sul quale in lettere di forma semibarbara del VI., o VII. secolo leggesi..." He concludes that the inscription "accresce certamente peso alla conghiettura, che i Greci Bizantini rifabbricassero questa porta forse dalla Guerra Gotica malmenata" (1820, 370–1).

sixth centuries should be recognizable in places where they are directly attached to Honorian brickwork, and themselves topped by characteristic interventions of the eighth and ninth centuries, which can now often be identified with some confidence. Signs of earthquake damage to the Honorian walls merit special attention, as any major effects from the quakes of 443 and 502 would almost certainly have been repaired by 536/7 at the latest. Lucos Cozza has recently called attention to one possible example in the north wall of the Castra Praetoria, where subsidence possibly caused by an earthquake was mended with reused bricks set in wide mortar beds not uncharacteristic of Theoderic's epoch.[14] A repair in curtain A24–5 is a second likely candidate. Here, an extensively rebuilt section of the curtain springs directly from the jagged edge of the Aurelianic brickwork at its base. It features two string courses, the lower of which is composed of small, projecting triangular fragments of brick that occur nowhere else in the Wall. It is further distinguished from the adjacent Honorian curtains by the noticeably different color and texture of the mortar, and still more by a row of putlog holes considerably less regular, in shape and spacing, than their neighbors. Moreover, a projecting triangular buttress of a type seen nowhere else in the circuit forms an integral component of the fabric of the repair (Figures C.4–C.5).

Indicators for dating are circumstantial but suggestive. The side of the adjacent tower A24, rebuilt completely in *opus vittatum* that should not postdate the medieval period, lies over the brick refacing, thereby

---

[14] See Cozza 1998, 36; cf. Coates-Stephens 1998, 171 and n. 15. A number of other sections of the Wall have been placed in the sixth century in recent years, some more plausibly than others, but none with much certainty: Cozza agreed with Nibby that the first tower west of the Porta Flaminia (A26) was extensively repaired at this time, with no further comment. Heres attributed a stretch between the Porta Ostiensis and the Tiber, built mostly in heterogeneous brick with intermittent tufa courses, to Theoderic, again without further explanation (1982, 143, with plate 43, 1–2). G. Ortolani seeks to attribute the pentagonal towers added to the Castra Praetoria to Theoderic, without any convincing reason for doing so (Ortolani 1990, 237ff., esp. 244–6). My examination of the towers, which are bonded directly with Aurelianic brickwork in the adjoining curtains, convinces me that Richmond and Cozza are on much firmer ground in calling them Aurelianic: see Cozza 1998, 32; Richmond 1927b, 12–22. Several other recent articles assert the probability of repairs under Theoderic, without offering new suggestions for their individuation: see Pizzi 1998, esp. 53–6; Pani Ermini 1995, 222. In addition to following Ortolani's suggestion about the towers of the Castra Praetoria, however, Pani Ermini questionably assumes that the attested restoration of Rome's *moenia* under Theoderic relates exclusively to the city walls (*contra*, see above Chapter 1, n. 72), which inclines her to overestimate the probable extent of Theoderic's repairs.

Figure C.4 Curtain A24–5: possible restoration of Theoderic with projecting spur.

Figure C.5 Curtain A24–5, detail; note string course at top and Aurelianic masonry at bottom left.

providing a rough *terminus ante quem.* Since there is no evidence of Honorian masonry, the repair may reasonably be assumed to have replaced it, and therefore to date after 403. As the regularity of the masonry and the (relative) homogeneity of the bricks are unparalleled in any work on the Wall datable between the eighth century and the later Middle Ages, the fifth and sixth centuries present themselves as much the most likely period. Finally, the extent of the damage is consonant with what one might expect an earthquake to provoke; and indeed, the unique projecting spur is perhaps best explained as an attempt to buttress the Wall, here backed nearly to its full height by a mass of earth that a seismic event might well have destabilized. A date in the years immediately following the earthquakes of 443 or 502 thus seems to account best for the ensemble of these various factors.

A greater degree of certainty in dating these and other localized repairs will be difficult to achieve. While enough masonry survives in Rome to give some idea of the standards that prevailed at various times, such indicators hardly permit precise attributions, especially when the sample to be dated consists of a few square meters of heterogeneous material used to plug a gap in the Wall's facing. Typological comparisons are no more helpful in dealing with the one larger sample that potentially belongs to the period in question: the *opus vittatum* repairs, concentrated in the northern sector of the Wall, but present elsewhere as well, which are often quite indiscriminately referred to Maxentius. The narrative of Procopius certainly makes it tempting to imagine that some work between the Portae Flaminia and Salaria in particular is of the sixth century, as Nibby, Richmond and Heres all have done.[15] During the siege of Rome in 537–8, the Gothic camps and the vast majority of their attacks on the Wall, many conducted with siege equipment, occurred in exactly this vicinity.[16] Without doubt, these events make for a more compelling explanation of the near-total destruction of multiple towers and curtains than the passing of the three relatively tranquil decades between their construction and the reign of Maxentius. There are, further, plenty of "late" examples of sloppy *vittatum* elsewhere in Rome to cite as parallels, which indeed appear

---

[15] Nibby 1820, 317ff.; Richmond 1930, 266; Heres 1982, 143–4.

[16] The Goths built seven fortified camps in total, one on the right bank of the Tiber in the "plain of Mars," and the other six between the Portae Flaminia and Praenestina-Labicana (*BG* 1, 19, 2). On Gothic siege engines, *ibid.* 1, 21, 3ff.; for attacks on the Wall, see esp. *ibid.* 1, 22, 1ff.; 1, 23, 1; 1, 23, 13ff.; etc.

Figure C.6 Tower B16, side view.

very different from the standard conception of what early-fourth-century work should look like.[17]

The problem, very simply, is that the appearance and technical attributes of *opus vittatum* are highly questionable dating criteria;[18] and a dizzying assortment of *vittatum* recurs between Aurelianic and Honorian strata. Yet there are localized *vittatum* repairs that manifestly postdate Honorius. The previously mentioned tower A24, rebuilt entirely in *vittatum*, is obviously later than the Honorian curtain to the west, and that of Theoderic (?) to the east, as the joins on both sides of the tower demonstrate. On the east side of tower B16, two different types of *vittatum* are separated by a prominent fissure: here at least is evidence for repairs at different dates; and the technique of the presumably later work on the "outer" side of the fissure would not be out of place in the sixth century or later (Figure C.6). It is certainly distinct from, and less regular than, the adjacent section, which does in turn fit well in the fourth century. Elsewhere in the circuit, there are many other *vittatum* repairs, above all to towers, whose relationship to their flanking

---

[17] See Appendix B.   [18] *Ibid.*

Figure C.7 Tower A21, in medieval *opus vittatum.*

Figure C.8 Tower L6 (right), in medieval *vittatum*, with pre-Honorian *vittatum* at left in curtain L6–7.

curtains places them definitively later than the Honorian heightening. They may date anywhere from 403 through the Middle Ages, but they were emphatically not built by Maxentius or any of his near contemporaries (Figures C.7–C.8).[19]

---

[19] A partial listing should be sufficient to caution against generic Maxentian, or even pre-Honorian, attributions. Tower A21 (Figure C.7) is almost wholly realized in a very neat *vittatum* with courses of the hard black *selci* characteristic of the high Middle Ages (which distinguishes the work here from that at the nearby tower A23, which has tufa blocks more typical of, though not exclusive to, late-antique *vittatum*). In the Appia-Ardeatina sector, where there are fourth-century repairs to the curtains, the towers are refaced in an entirely different sort of *vittatum*, again bonded to the Honorian curtains, which they must postdate (e.g. L6 [Figure C.8] and L10). There are similar examples between the Portae Latina and Appia (towers K11 and K12). Farther south, tower L23, also built up against Honorian curtains, is reconstructed from the ground up, inside and out, in *vittatum* that, again, could be sixth-century as well as anything else. The top of tower L40, on the other hand, has been refaced in *vittatum* which, as it springs directly from work of the twelfth or thirteenth centuries, must be still later.

Appendix D: The Aurelian Wall and the refashioning of the western tip of the Campus Martius

The building of the river wall and the destruction of the Pons Neronianus provide an interpretive key for the subsequent history of the western tip of the Campus Martius, from late antiquity to the present. The presence of the Wall clarifies and often reconciles many apparently diverse arguments made about the disputed topography of the region, and permits the reconstruction of a sequence of events that explains much about the dramatic topographical transformation of the area between the high empire and the early Middle Ages. I begin with a sequence of premises that seems to me to account best for the surviving topographical indicators and the often opposing positions taken by past scholars on a variety of points.

The river crossing at the site of the future Pons Neronianus, and the two primary axes of communication that converged on the riverbank in this spot, the "Via Recta" running east to west, and the Via Tecta from the south-east to north-west, all date well before the imperial period (Figure 4.1). A ferry at the *vada Tarenti* likely existed by the fourth century BC (Coarelli 1977, 842; 1997a, 77 and 130; cf. La Rocca 1984, 65–6). All previous arguments made to the effect that one or both roads did not reach the Pons Neronianus have them ending at the north–south road leading to the Pons Aelius, which led nowhere before the building of the bridge to the mausoleum, if it even existed. There is no question that both the "Via Recta" and the Via Tecta are older than any river crossing on the site of the Pons Aelius, and that the known remains of both are aligned more or less perfectly with the Pons Neronianus.

The "Via Recta" was always acknowledged to have passed beyond the road to the mausoleum, leaving little doubt that it reached the Pons Neronianus. Then S. Quilici Gigli tried to prove that the "Via Recta" never extended to the bridgehead of the Pons Neronianus, but ended always at the (much later) street leading to the (much later) Pons Aelius, because she wanted the Tarentum literally blocking the Pons Neronianus (the one place of all those suggested where it is least likely to be), claiming that the paving stones documented by Lanciani (see *FUR* tav. 14) on the river side of the street to the mausoleum in fact belonged to a paved plaza (a "slargo"; see Quilici Gigli 1983, 51–4). E. La Rocca likewise doubted that this road went all the way to the bridge (1984, 65ff.; he thought the Tarentum blocked it as well as the "Via Recta"), leading him to adopt the position that neither of the two main roads through the Campus Martius actually reached the bridge on which they converged! Yet there is no reason to think that Lanciani was mistaken in his identification of the basalt ashlars of a roadbed; in addition to the points made by Coarelli (1997a, 77–8) in his rebuttal, I add only the following note regarding several structures that according to Quilici Gigli blocked the path of the "Via Recta" to the bridge (1983, 51–2). These poorly documented remains located near the modern Corso Vittorio Emanuele probably did just that: as their foundations were laid more than a meter above the early imperial ground level, they will have been built only after this part of the street was rendered useless by the destruction of the Pons Neronianus (more on this later).

As for the Via Tecta, not a stone has been found past the point where it was detoured north to the Pons Aelius (at the modern intersection between the Via dei Banchi Vecchi and the Via del Pavone). Yet as Coarelli has stressed repeatedly, the ancient trunk of the road must have crossed the river at the Pons Neronianus; and the far-western sector of the Campus Martius is, in fact, principally oriented along the direct axis between the Circus Flaminius and the bridge traced by the surviving sections of the road. In 1977, Coarelli made the further important point that the north–south extension of the road toward the Pons Aelius could only date from Hadrian's time or later (Coarelli 1977, 819–21, with fig. 1).[1] Yet remarkably, he has recently contradicted himself and expressed doubts about the existence of the hypothetical final tract of the republican Via Tecta, all the while stressing the crucial importance and great antiquity of the route (probably the Via Triumphalis itself) between the Circus Flaminius and the Pons Neronianus; and at the same time restoring the Tarentum and the Trigarium immediately adjacent to, and on the same alignment with, the hypothetical axis of the street![2]

---

[1] Coarelli 1977 821, n. 34: "Questo ramo (to the Pons Aelius) è certamente più tardo dell'altro, e non si può concepire prima della costruzione del ponte e del Mausoleo di Adriano."

[2] Perhaps following the doubts expressed in La Rocca 1984, 66–7, who proposed not only that the ancient street always turned suddenly north on the road to the mausoleum, but further that there was no connection at all with the Pons Neronianus, as one could not even have subsequently turned left onto the "Via Recta," which La Rocca thought also ended suddenly at the road to the mausoleum. Coarelli's change of heart seems all the stranger, not only for his map with the reconstructed locations of the *Trigarium* and *Terentum* (*sic*, 1997a, 86), but also

In the end, the only powerful objection to extending both streets directly to the Pons Neronianus is the lack of remains. None of the further arguments predicated upon this fact succeed in explaining why the streets should have ended abruptly, or in locating obstructions in the vicinity of the bridgehead (least of all the Tarentum, as Coarelli shows [1997a, 74ff.]). On the other hand, I think the building of the river wall, the destruction of the Pons Neronianus, and the subsequent aggrandizing of the street to the Pons Aelius together provide a good explanation for the total disappearance of the old course of the Via Tecta, and the near-disappearance of the "Via Recta." Even if the columns of the former and the paving of both were not simply transposed to the new termination of the triumphal way, becoming part of the new *porticus maximae* that culminated in the arch of Gratian, Valentinian, and Theodosius (as I think likely happened), there were plenty of other places where the fine components of what had recently become two blind alleys might have ended up.

Hence, it seems to me that the "whole work of the porticus maximae," which the triumphal arch of Gratian, Valentinian, and Theodosius "concluded," is best construed in relation to a new colonnade built along the new final section of the Triumphal Way leading to the Pons Aelius. In building the new colonnade, and perhaps also restoring the existing trunk of the road farther south, these emperors would have restored the architectural integrity of the whole route, from its beginning to the urban periphery at the river, an intervention that could very plausibly have led to its rechristening as the *porticus maximae*, a term that suggestively appears for the first time in the dedication of the arch.

For the subsequent history of the area once traversed by the two streets, a remarkably consistent topographical picture emerges, which is framed admirably by the observations of two eminent Roman archaeologists who disagree fundamentally over the entire character of the region, which for present purposes will be limited to the tip of the "handle" of the Campus Martius (in modern terms a rough rectangle formed by the Tiber on the west and north, the Via San Filippo Neri on the south, and the Via dei Banchi Vecchi – Via del Banco Santo Spirito on the east). For Coarelli,

for his accompanying remarks on the via Triumphalis (*ibid.* esp. 127–35), all of which point to the existence of an ancient and direct connection between the Circus Flaminius, and more specifically the Porta Carmentalis in the Servian Wall, and the crossing on the site of the Pons Neronianus; see e.g. 130: "...partendo dalla *porta Carmentalis*, esso (the via Triumphalis) si dirigeva in linea retta verso il passaggio del Tevere, corrispondente al successivo Ponte Neroniano. L'antichità di questi *vada Tarenti* ci è assicurata – come abbiamo visto – dalla connessione con il santuario arcaico del *Terentum*..."

concerned primarily with the republican topography of the Campus Martius, it was practically rural space, an extra-pomerial periphery occupied by the horse-training grounds of the Trigarium, the important connected shrine of the Tarentum, and a few workshops along the river (Coarelli 1977; Coarelli 1997a, esp. 77–8). For Lorenzo Quilici, attempting to reconstruct the Roman topography of the area that he thought preserved in its medieval remains, it was the diametrical opposite: a densely populated residential neighborhood.[3]

It is a study in overlooking late antiquity from opposite ends. Coarelli says that the area retained its rural character "for the whole period of the empire," while Quilici wants towers and *palazzi* of the high Middle Ages to preserve the outlines of a robust Roman urban quarter.[4] Coarelli is entirely correct in saying that there are almost no republican and early imperial remains, as is Quilici in noting the many structures of the twelfth and thirteenth centuries with roots plausibly reaching back centuries earlier. In projecting these opposing realities beyond their just chronological limits, however, both overlook the crucial moment of transition, when the neighborhood stopped being what Coarelli describes, and became what Quilici does. In the process, however, both furnished tantalizing clues about the lost transitional period, which I propose was characterized by the following progression.

Before Aurelian, the area was sparsely populated and extra-pomerial, occupied largely by the Tarentum and the extensive grounds of the Trigarium, and crossed by the two main roads in the Campus Martius on their path to the one ancient river crossing. Then, the Wall was built, and the Pons Neronianus immediately or soon thereafter disabled. In addition to rendering the final tracts of the "Via Recta" and Via Tecta useless, the appearance of the Wall almost immediately resulted in one additional development of locally great importance, by bringing the western periphery of the Campus Martius within the *pomerium* for the first time.[5] As the existence and functions of the Tarentum-Trigarium complex were strictly linked to its extra-pomerial location (Coarelli 1977, 820–2;

---

[3] Quilici 1983.

[4] Coarelli 1997a, 131; Quilici 1983. While Coarelli's use of the phrase "per tutto il corso del impero" occurs in relation to the *pomerium*, which I suspect he means to discuss in its pre-Aurelianic contours, his phrasing necessarily implicates the fourth and fifth centuries as well, and leaves the impression that he thought the ancient layout of the area remained generally static through the end of the empire.

[5] The *pomerium* was made coextensive with the Wall upon Aurelian's return from Palmyra in 274 (see *HA Aur.* 21, 9, with Chapter 5.1, above).

1997a, 82–3 and *passim*; E. La Rocca 1984, esp. 68), both will in all probability have gone immediately out of use, leaving the ground available for other uses (as it otherwise must have been following the prohibition of public pagan ritual in the fourth century).

With the end of the cult sites and the major roads, this exposed section of the Tiber floodplain will no longer have been kept clear of alluvial deposits. The ground level, today some 9 m above the early imperial quota, was likely rising already after three devastating floods in the second half of the fourth century, which left well over a meter of sediment in warehouses by Testaccio (Meneghini in *BullCom* 1986, 593–95; cf. Le Gall 1953, 29). At the same time, this open space along the river south of the Pons Aelius had become prime real estate, the closest intramural area to the complex at St. Peter's, at a time when settlement was already tending to concentrate within the circuit in e.g. Trastevere and the Esquiline. At a later date, the cutting of the aqueducts during the Gothic sieges in the sixth century will have made a location on the Tiber all the more desirable.

The foundations and paving stones uncovered near the Corso Vittorio Emanuele at 1.10 m above the early imperial elevation of the Via Recta did not block the road: they rose above it on a wholly new orientation, distinct from the ancient roads and shrines truncated or rendered irrelevant by the Wall, and subsequently buried.[6] The main streets that henceforth led to the river were those corresponding with the *posterulae* in the river wall.[7] More houses were built, more sediment accumulated, and the area was well on its way to becoming what Quilici saw in its medieval remains: a warren of houses and narrow lanes built on top of, and with no appreciable connection to, the carefully tended open spaces and highways of republican origin that Coarelli saw.

The limited archaeological explorations that have occurred in this densely packed medieval neighborhood permit little to be said about the dating and origins of the post-classical levels. The structures found by the Corso Vittorio Emanuele were not published (nor perhaps excavated) in a way that allows firm conclusions to be drawn, save that they were built a bit more than a meter above a road that I believe to have been in service

---

[6] The original report of the finds is in *Notizie* 1931, 313ff.; cf. Quilici Gigli 1983, esp. 52.

[7] Again, the contrast between Quilici and Coarelli is informative: Quilici (1983, esp. 70ff.) convincingly demonstrates the connection of several medieval cross-streets leading to the Tiber with *posterulae* in the river wall, streets which Coarelli (1997a, 78ff.) is quick to point out actually show, in the majority of cases, no signs whatsoever of belonging to the republican and early imperial road network. Here is a hint that the Wall may have been one of the primary determinants in the creation of the new topography of the region, as well as in the end of the old.

not far past the 270s.[8] A meter and more of alluvial deposits could easily have accumulated in the following century, as I suspect will have occurred. The examples of Trastevere and the Esquiline, coupled with the proximity of the area to the Vatican, incline me further to imagine that new settlement in the vicinity of the Tarentum and Trigarium was beginning already in the fourth century, when the population of the city as a whole remained high. I have little doubt that the process was under way after the Gothic wars of the sixth century, when the whole "handle" of the Campus Martius was on the road to becoming the nucleus of Rome's medieval *abitato*. I am certain of one thing: the "medieval" development of the region into a residential neighborhood did not, and could not, begin before the building of the Aurelian Wall. By definitively cutting existing topographical networks in the case of the roads, and invalidating them in the case of the shrines, the fortification of the riverbank laid the groundwork for the subsequent "re-zoning" of the western tip of the Campus Martius. The event may further have provided an initial, more or less immediate impetus to settlement. Unfortunately, the vague and relative chronology permitted by the existing archaeological data is insufficient to make an ironclad case.

---

[8] They must indeed belong to a "sistemazione successiva," as Quilici Gigli suggested (1983, 52), which there is no cause to think (as the author does) respected earlier arrangements, among them the orientation of the "Via Recta."

Appendix E: The Pons Agrippae and the Pons Aureli: a tale of two bridges

The piers 140 meters upstream of the modern Ponte Sisto came to light in 1887, when work on the banks of the Tiber and the exceptionally low level of the river at the time combined to reveal a series of pilings spanning the river at this point. The results were published by L. Borsari, first in preliminary form in the *Notizie degli Scavi* (1887, 322–7), and then in the *Bullettino Comunale* of the following year (1888, 92–8). Borsari had no doubt that these were the foundations of a bridge, which he associated with the Pons Agrippae, the existence of which was demonstrated for the first time in an inscription coincidentally discovered not far upstream in the same year, recording restorations to the Tiber banks under Claudius that extended *a Tr[ig]ar[io] ad pontem Agrippae* (*CIL* 6, 31545). Since no remains of the superstructure turned up on the riverbed, he conjectured that the original Pons Agrippae was spoliated to build the Pons Aureli/ Antonini just downriver, remnants of which had been found ten years earlier.[1] As the twin names of the latter inevitably recalled the person of Marcus Aurelius Severus Antoninus Bassianus Caracalla, and as the Severan emperors occupied themselves with the banks of the Tiber, and had property in Trastevere, Borsari speculated that the newer bridge was built in the Severan period (*BullCom* 1888, 95–7).

This interpretation left one glaring difficulty: why would the Severan emperors have built a new bridge just downstream from the old one, instead of repairing (if even necessary) the latter? Unable to resolve this question to his satisfaction, G. Gatti decided that Borsari's new piers could not have belonged to a bridge, whence he proposed that they were pieces

---

[1] The riverbed below the old Pons Agrippae was investigated in 1887, when the level of the Tiber was unusually low; absolutely nothing was found: see the report of L. Borsari in *BullCom* 16 (1888), 92–8, esp. 96 on the results of the search, described as "assolutamente negativo." Meanwhile, study of the riverbed by the Pons Aureli turned up most of the bridge, including an entire section of the central arch, lying largely intact where it had pivoted on its axis and fallen in what must have been a particularly bad flood; that of December 791 is usually suggested. Generally on the finds, see Lanciani in *BullCom* 1878, 241–8, with the summary in Le Gall 1953, 295–301 (the identification with the Pons Agrippae aside); on the later history of the bridge and the flood of 791, cf. also Hubert 1990, 109–10.

of an immense "Augustan era" building that had fallen into, or rather across, the river (*Notizie* 1887, 306–13). With the final publication of the plan of the remains in the following year, it became still more difficult to take this hypothesis very seriously. The problem of the two neighboring bridges, however, remained.[2]

Then in 1939, G. Calza published a fragment of an inscribed calendar (*fasti*) from Ostia (*Notizie* 1939, 361–5), which included, for the year 147, the following entry: [–] *K. Febr. imp. Antoninus Aug(ustus) pontem Agrippae dedic(avit)*. This made the problem still more acute: Borsari's distinction between the Pons Agrippae and the Pons Aureli (which Calza also accepted) now implied that the old bridge had undergone major repairs only a half-century before it was ostensibly dismantled, and the new one built.

J. Le Gall immediately seized on this new information to resuscitate Gatti's contention that only one of the two bridges was in fact a bridge (Le Gall 1953, 210–11 and 305–11). He decided that, since the Pons Aureli was also called the Pons Antonini in late antiquity and the early Middle Ages, it must have been one and the same with the Pons Agrippae rededicated by Antoninus Pius as the Pons Antonini, though he was at a loss to explain how the name Aurelius came about, since it did not appear in the official titulature of Pius; he thought this last problem "assez curieux," and left it at that (210). As the bridge downstream at the site of the Ponte Sisto is without question the one later called both the Pons Aureli and the Pons Antonini, this had to be also the Pons Agrippae. The suspiciously bridge-like piers upstream were explained as a defensive barrier built along with the Wall, which would have been used to anchor chains in times of war to impede the passage of boats from upstream (an expedient devised by Belisarius, according to Procopius, *BG* 1, 19, 24ff.). In support of his argument, Le Gall adduced an important passage in Procopius, where the latter says that when the walls in Trastevere were built, they were connected with the rest of the circuit with a new bridge (*BG* 1, 19, 10):

ζεύξαντες οὖν ταύτῃ τὸν ποταμὸν γεφύρᾳ, ξυνάπτειν τε τὸ τεῖχος ἔδοξαν καὶ οἰκίας συχνὰς ἐν χωρίῳ τῷ ἀντιπέρας δειμάμενοι μέσον τῆς πόλεως τὸ τοῦ Τιβέριδος πεποίηνται ῥεῦμα ("It seemed good, spanning the river in this place with a bridge, to join the wall together; and building dense houses in the land on the far side, they [the 'ancient Romans'] put the stream of the Tiber in the middle of the city.")

---

[2] Borsari's views were accepted by G. Calza (*Notizie* 1939, 364), and more recently by R. B. Lloyd (1979, 200–1), and Galliazzo (1995, vol. 2, 7–10), none of whom, however, were able to explain satisfactorily why, with a perfectly good bridge recently restored under Antoninus Pius, there would have been reason to build another just downstream.

Le Gall took the "bridge" that Procopius describes to mean the pilings of his defensive barrier, which would thus have extended the line of the land wall in Trastevere across the Tiber to join the river wall on the far side. Though this explanation of the upstream piers has not swayed all from the two-bridge scheme, Le Gall's arguments have continued to attract exponents, particularly in Italy. Variations on the theme, with various minor modifications and additions, some cited previously and others not, include: F. Coarelli in *LTUR* 4, see under *pons Agrippae; pons Aurelius, pons Valentiniani;* 1977, 824–6; 1997a, 81; 124–5, etc.; D'Onofrio 1982, 203ff.; Quilici 1983, 66–7; La Rocca 1984 (see especially the fold-out map[3]); Cozza 1986, 104–7; Hertz 1991, 303–5.

Le Gall's reading of Procopius has been taken up by Cozza (1986, 104) and Coarelli (e.g. 1997a, 81, with n. 36) as especially powerful testimony to the effect that the structure upstream was built along with the Wall. If anything, the passage proves just the opposite. First, Procopius makes it clear that the structure connecting the fortifications on both sides of the Tiber was a bridge, built to allow communication across the river, and presumably also access to the dense housing he describes. This would clearly have entailed the construction of a solid superstructure over the pilings (a construction in wood can be ruled out), of which not a stone remained on the riverbed by the pilings upstream. Second and more importantly, Procopius' description of the new bridge actually fits the

[3] The author hypothesizes an ancient street leading straight to the pillars upstream, which nonetheless are not said to belong to a bridge. In the previous year, L. Quilici (1983, 66–7) did precisely the same thing in an article ironically devoted to the survival of Roman streets in the Middle Ages, arguing that the modern Vicolo del Polverone follows an ancient street leading straight to what he follows Le Gall in describing as a barrier across the river. Yet he equivocates, and ends up calling the structure a bridge and describing it as such, because it obviously was; he even cites several watercolors of the late nineteenth century that show the massive bridgehead in fine *opus quadratum* of marble or limestone (described also by Borsari in his initial report), complete with an arch that he compares with those of the Pons Aelius (67, with notes 70 and 71; the structure goes from being called a "sbarramento fluviale," to the "ponte delle mura," to a "ponte," all in the space of a single paragraph). Quilici concludes by imagining a massive bridge over the river, with a narrow central aperture, "proprio per obbligare sotto questa il traffico ed il controllo del fiume". But if the structure was a simple barrier as Le Gall suggested, there will have been no need to incorporate all the architectural refinements of a grand public bridge, including a wide bridgehead supported by a monumental arch (which further happens to intersect perfectly with an ancient street); yet if it was a bridge, as e.g. Quilici seems to imply (and Procopius says outright), in addition to the problem of its superstructure disappearing without a trace, we are required to make the mirror image of precisely the argument that led Le Gall *et al.* to reject the first Pons Agrippae, by claiming that Aurelian built a second bridge just upstream of an older and perfectly functional bridge, and in a far more exposed location to boot!

location of the structure downstream on the site of the Ponte Sisto far better. This is exactly where the river walls on both sides of the river terminated, several sections of which were in fact documented by Lanciani on the right bank between the old Pons Agrippae and the Ponte Sisto (a crucial piece of evidence too frequently overlooked).[4] The bridge downstream thus literally joined the ends of the two sections of the Wall separated by the river to form a continuous circuit (Figure 4.2).[5] With this one crossing in place, and Procopius is clear that there was only one, there was every reason not to leave (or build) another in a more exposed position just upstream, breaching the river wall at a point where it could have been reached easily by attackers on the right bank of the river. Therefore, since the piers upstream cannot have provided a second functioning river crossing, they cannot possibly be related to the structure that Procopius says was built along with the Wall, which was unquestionably intended to permit movement and communications across the river.

This leaves only the fragment of the *fasti*, with its notice that the Pons Agrippae was restored by Antoninus Pius. Yet the interpretation that made this evidence for attaching the toponyms Agrippae, Antonini, and Aureli to the same structure stemmed purely from the *a priori* conviction that the construction of a second bridge made no sense; and it failed completely to explain why the Pons Agrippae/Antonini came also to be called the Pons Aureli.[6] It took only the observation that the earlier bridge upstream was disabled upon the building of the Wall to restore ample sense to the presence of a second bridge not far away, and consequently to obviate any need to explain away remains that looked so much like a bridge as something else (see Taylor 1995, 82–90). This observation also accounts fully for the origin of the name Pons Aureli, the transfer of the name Pons

[4] See *Notizie* 1884, 237, for a section of river wall 60 meters above the Pons Aureli/Ponte Sisto (and *c.* 80 meters below the Pons Agrippae); and *ibid.* 1885, 342, for another section 130 meters upstream from the Pons Aureli, and thus quite possibly on the very spot where it bisected the bridgehead of the Pons Agrippae. Cozza did notice Lanciani's reports of the river wall below the Pons Agrippae, but chose to discount them, suggesting for no apparent reason that Lanciani's identification be re-examined to see if he hadn't simply mistaken a "reinforcement of the river bank" with the river wall (1986, 107 with n. 8).

[5] The same situation is described in a papal document of 1018, where the Pons Aureli is called the Pons Fractus: *incipiente primo termine a fracto ponte, ubi unda dividitur per murum...*; see Hubert 1990, 110, n. 45.

[6] I wonder if Le Gall's hypothesis was not further inspired by a conviction that "La décadence" (the heading of the final section of his book) of the later third century was such that nothing of note could possibly have been built, besides of course the Wall itself, which for him was "le signe de la décadence" *par excellence* (Le Gall 1953, 294). This same sensibility perhaps underlay his attempt to make the Pons Probi a simple restoration of the Pons Neronianus.

Antonini, and the lack of remains under the old bridge upstream. And of course, the standing remnants of the old Pons Agrippae were more than adequate as whatever sort of defensive barrier one might wish to envision, leaving the effort of building equally massive pilings *ex novo* to be more plausibly connected with the erection of the functioning bridge downstream. Strategic concerns may well explain why the old pilings were left in place, and why the land wall in Trastevere was made to reach the riverbank just above them, positioning them admirably as a first line of defense, but extremely poorly as a connector with the other side of the river.

In sum, I think it beyond reasonable doubt that the Pons Agrippae, restored by Antoninus Pius in 147, was demolished when the Wall was built, and replaced by a new bridge erected *ex novo* 140 m downstream, at the point where the walls on both sides of the river were made to end.

Bibliography

Editions

Alcuin. *Versus de patribus regibus et sanctis Euboricensis ecclesiae*, ed. and trans. P. Godman, *The Bishops, Kings and Saints of York*, Oxford, 1982.

Ammianus Marcellinus. *Ammiani Marcellini rerum gestarum libri qui supersunt* (2 vols.), ed. W. Seyfarth, Leipzig (Teubner), 1968.

Annales regni Francorum, ed. F. Kurtze, *MGH SRG*, Hanover, 1895.

Anonymous. *De imperia potestate in urbe Roma libellus*, ed. G. Zucchetti, *Fonti per la Storia d'Italia* 55, Rome, 1920, 187–210.

Anonymous. *De rebus bellicis*, ed. and trans. A. Giardina, *Le cose della guerra*. Milan, 1989.

Anonymous. *S. Fulgentii Episcopi Ruspensis Vita. PL* 65, cols. 117–50.

Anonymous Valesianus, ed. T. Mommsen, *MGH AA* 9, 1, Berlin, 1892, 249ff.

Augustine. *De Civitate Dei* (2 vols.), eds. B. Dombart and A. Kalb, Stuttgart (Teubner), 1993.

Aulus Gellius. *Noctes Atticae*, ed. C. Hosius, Leipzig (Teubner), 1903.

Aurelius Victor. *Liber de Caesaribus, praecedunt Origo gentis Romanae et Liber de viris illustribus urbis Romae, subsequitur Epitome de Caesaribus*, ed. F. Pichlmayr, Leipzig (Teubner), 1961.

Ausonius. *Decimi Magni Ausonii Burdigalensis Opuscula*, ed. S. Prete, Leipzig (Teubner), 1978.

Bede. *Historia ecclesiastica gentis anglorum*, ed. and trans. J. E. King, London (Loeb), 1930.

Bedae opera. CCSL 118–123, Turnholt, 1955–.

Benedict of Soracte. *Chronicon*, ed. G. Zucchetti, *Fonti per la Storia d'Italia* 55, Rome, 1920.

Cassiodorus Senator. *Magni Aurelii Cassiodori Senatoris opera. CCSL* 96–8, Turnholt, 1958–73.

Chronica, ed. T. Mommsen, *MGH AA* 11, 2, Berlin, 1894, 109ff.

"*Chronographus Anni CCCLIIII*", ed. T. Mommsen, *MGH AA* 9, 1, Berlin, 1892, 13ff.

Cicero. *De oratore*, ed. K. Kumaniecki, Leipzig–Stuttgart (Teubner), 1969.

Claudian. *Claudii Claudiani Carmina*, ed. J. B. Hall, Leipzig (Teubner), 1985.

Codex Carolinus, ed. W. Gundlach, *MGH EP* 3, Berlin, 1892, 469–657.

Codex Theodosianus. Theodosiani Libri XVI cum Constitutionibus Sirmondianis et Leges Novellae ad Theodosianum Pertinentes. 2 vols., eds. T. Mommsen and P. M. Meyer, Berlin, 1905.

Codice Topografico della città di Roma. 4 vols., eds. R. Valentini and G. Zucchetti, Rome, 1940–53.

Collectio Avellana, ed. O. Günther, *CSEL* 35, Vienna, 1895.

Constitutum Constantini, ed. H. Fuhrmann, *MGH Fontes iuris Germanici antiqui* 10, Hannover, 1968.

Corpus Inscriptionum Latinarum. Berlin, 1862–.

Corpus juris civilis. 3 vols., eds. T. Mommsen *et al.*; revised edn. ed. W. Kunkel, Heidelberg, 1954.

Curiosum Urbis Romae; Notitia Urbis Romae. VZ 1, 63–192.

Damasus. *Epigrammata Damasiana*, ed. A Ferrua, Rome, 1942.

Die nichtliterarischen lateinischen Papyri Italiens aus der Zeit 445–700 (2 vols., Acta Instituti Romani Regini Sueciae, Series in 4°, XIX:1–2.), ed. O. Tjäder, Lund and Stockholm, 1955–82.

Dio Cassius. *Historia Romana*, 5 vols., ed. L. Dindorf, Leipzig (Teubner), 1863–5.

Diokletians Preisedikt, ed. S. Lauffer, Berlin, 1971.

Einhard. *Translatio et miracula sanctorum Marcellini et Petri auctore Einhardo*, ed. G. Waitz, *MGH Scriptores* 15, 1, Hannover, 1888, 238–64.

Eugippius. *Vita Severini*, ed. T. Mommsen, *MGH SRG* 26, Berlin, 1898.

Eutropius. *Eutropi Breviarium ab urbe condita*, ed. F. Ruehl, Leipzig (Teubner), 1887.

Exeter Book, The, eds. G. P. Krapp and E. Van Kirk Dobbie, *The Exeter Book.* New York and London, 1936.

Fontes ad topographiam veteris urbis Romae pertinentes, vol. I, ed. G. Lugli, Rome, 1962.

Frontinus. *De aquaeductu urbis Romae*, ed. C. Kunderewicz, Stuttgart and Leipzig (Teubner), 1998.

Gregory I. *Dialogues*, ed. and trans. A. de Vogüé and P. Antin, *Sources Chrétiennes* 251, 260, 265, Paris, 1978–80.

 Homeliae XL in evangelia, ed. J.-P. Migne, PL 76, Paris, 1848.

 Registrum, eds. P. Ewald and L. Hartmann, *MGH EP* 1–2, Berlin, 1891–9.

Gregory of Tours. *Historia Francorum*, ed. B. Krusch, *MGH SRM* 1, 1, Hanover, 1884.

Herodian. *Ab excessu divi Marci libri octo*, ed. K. Stavenhagen, Leipzig (Teubner), 1967.

Inscriptiones Christianae Urbis Romae. 3 vols., ed. G. B. De Rossi, Rome, 1861–8.

Inscriptiones Christianae Urbis Romae, nova series. 6 vols., eds. A. Ferrua and A. Silvagni, Rome and Vatican City, 1922–75.

Inscriptiones Graecae ad Res Romanas Pertinentes. 4 vols., eds. R. Cagnat and G. Lafaye, Paris, 1911–27.

Inscriptiones Latinae Christianae Veteres. 3 vols., ed. E. Diehl, Berlin, 1924–31.

Inscriptiones Latinae Selectae, ed. H. Dessau, Berlin, 1892–1916.

Isidore of Seville. *Etymologiae.* 2 vols., ed. W. M. Lindsay, Oxford, 1911.
    Historia Gothorum Wandalorum Sueborum, ed. T. Mommsen, *MGH AA*
        11, 2, 241ff.
Jerome. *Eusebii Pamphili chronici canones latine vertit, adauxit, ad sua*
        tempora produxit S. Eusebius Hieronymus (*Chronicon*), ed. J. Fotheringham,
        London, 1923.
    Epistulae (8 vols.), ed. and trans. J. Labourt, Paris (Budé), 1949–63.
Jordanes. *Getica* and *Romana,* ed. T. Mommsen, *MGH AA* 5, 1, Berlin, 1882.
Julian (emperor). *Convivium,* ed. F. Hertlein, *Iuliani imperatoris quae*
        supersunt praeter reliquias apud Cyrillum omnia, vol. 1, Leipzig (Teubner),
        1875, 393–432.
Lactantius. *De mortibus persecutorum,* ed. and trans. J. L. Creed, Oxford, 1984.
Leges Langobardorum, eds. F. Bluhme and A. Boretius, Hannover, 1868.
Le iscrizioni dei sec. VI-VII-VIII esistenti in Italia. 2 vols., ed. P. Rugo,
        Cittadella, 1974.
Leo I. *Sermones,* ed. A. Chavasse, *CCSL* 138–138a, Turnholt, 1973.
Libanius. *Opera Omnia.* 12 vols., ed. R. Foerster, Leipzig (Teubner), 1903–.
Liber Diurnus Romanorum pontificum, ed. H. Foerster, Bern, 1958.
Liber Pontificalis, ed. L. Duchesne, with additions by C. Vogel, *Le Liber Pontificalis.*
        Texte, introduction et commentaire. 3 vols., Paris, 1955–7.
    trans. Davis, R., *The Book of Pontiffs* (*Liber Pontificalis*). *The ancient*
        biographies of the first ninety Roman bishops to AD 715, 2nd edn.,
        Liverpool, 2000.
Livy. *Ab urbe condita,* eds. R. S. Conway, C. F. Walters, S. K. Johnson and
        A. H. MacDonald, 5 vols., Oxford, 1914–65.
Malalas, John. *Ioannis Malalae Chronographia,* ed. J. Thurn, *Corpus Fontium*
        Historiae Byzantinae 35, Berlin and New York, 2000; ed. L. Dindorf,
        Bonn, 1831.
Marcellinus Comes. *Chronicon* and *Auctarium,* ed. T. Mommsen, *MGH AA* 11,
        2, Berlin, 1894, 37ff.
Maurice. *Strategicon,* ed. and trans. G. T. Dennis and E. Gamillscheg, *Das*
        Strategikon des Maurikios (*Corpus Fontium Historiae Byzantinae* 17),
        Vienna, 1981.
Notitia Dignitatum, ed. C. Neira Faleiro, *La* Notitia Dignitatum. *Nueva edición*
        crítica y comentario histórico, Madrid, 2006.
Notitia Dignitatum, ed. O. Seeck, Berlin, 1876.
Orosius. *Historiarum adversus paganos,* Libri VII ed. A. Lippold and trans.
        A. Bartalucci, *Le storie contro i pagani* (2 vols.), Milan, 2001.
Paul the Deacon. *Historia Langobardorum,* ed. and trans. L. Capo, *Storia dei*
        Longobardi, Milan, 1992.
Paulinus of Nola. *Epistulae; Carmina,* ed. G. de Hartel, *CSEL* 29–30, Vienna, 1894.
Paulinus of Pella. *Carmina,* ed. C. M. Lucarin, Munich and Leipzig
        (Teubner), 2006.

Pliny the Elder. *C. Plini Secundi Naturalis historiae libri XXXVII.* 6 vols., eds.
    L. von Jan and K. Mayhoff, Leipzig (Teubner), 1875–1906.
Priscus. *Fragmenta*, ed. and trans. R. C. Blockley, *The Fragmentary Classicising
    Historians of the Later Roman Empire*, vol. 2, Liverpool, 1983, 221ff.
Procopius. *Opera Omnia.* 4 vols., ed. J. Haury, Leipzig (Teubner), 1962–4.
Prosper of Aquitaine. *Epitoma Chronicon*, ed. T. Mommsen, *MGH AA* 9.1, 341–485.
Prudentius. *Aurelii Prudentii Clementis Carmina*, ed. M. P. Cunningham, *CCSL*
    126, Turnholt, 1966.
Ruin, The. Anglo-Saxon poetry, trans. R.K. Gordon, London, 1929, 84.
Rutilius Namatianus. *De reditu suo*, ed. and trans. J. Vessereau and F. Préchac,
    Paris (Budé), 1933.
Scriptores historiae Augustae. 2 vols., ed. E. Pohl, Leipzig (Teubner), 1965.
Sidonius Apollinaris. *Epistulae.* 2 vols., ed. and trans. A. Loyen, Paris (Budé), 1970.
Socrates of Constantinople. *Historia Ecclesiae*, ed. G. Hansen, *Sokrates
    Kirchengeschichte*, Berlin, 1995.
Sozomen. *Historia Ecclesiae*, ed. J. Bidez, *Sozomenus Kirchengeschichte*, Berlin, 1960.
Symmachus, Q. Aurelius. *Relationes, Orationes, Epistulae*, ed. O. Seeck, *MGH AA*
    6, 1, Berlin, 1883.
Tacitus. *Annales*, ed. C. D. Fisher, Oxford, 1906.
    Historiae, ed. C. D. Fisher, Oxford, 1911.
Varro. *De lingua Latina*, eds. G. Goetz and F. Schoell, Leipzig (Teubner), 1910.
Vegetius. *De re militari*, ed. A. Önnerfors, Stuttgart (Teubner), 1995.
Versus de Verona. Versum de Mediolano civitate, ed. G. B. Pighi, Bologna, 1960.
Vitruvius. *De architectura*, eds. H. Müller-Strübing and V. Rose, Leipzig
    (Teubner), 1867.
Vulgata Latina. Nova vulgata bibliorum sacrorum editio, 2nd edn., Rome, 1986.
Zosimus. *Zosimi comitis et exadvocati fisci Historia nova*, ed. L. Mendelssohn,
    Leipzig (Teubner), 1887.

Secondary literature

Adam, J.-P. (1984). *La construction romaine. Materiaux et techniques*, Paris.
Aguilera Martín, A. (2002). *El Monte Testaccio e la llanura subaventina. Topografia
    extra portam Trigeminam*, Rome.
Ahunbay, M. and Ahunbay, Z. (2000). "Recent work on the land walls of Istanbul:
    Tower 2 to Tower 5," *Dumbarton Oaks Papers* 54: 227–39.
Alcorta Irastorza, E. (2007). "Muros, torres y escaleras. Aproximación al modelo
    constructivo de la muralla romana de *Lucus Augusti* (Lugo)," in Rodríguez
    Colmenero and Rodá de Llanza (eds.), pp. 285–311.
Aldrete, G. S. and Mattingly, D. J. (2000). "The feeding of Imperial Rome:
    the mechanics of the food supply system," in Coulston and Dodge (eds.),
    pp. 142–65.

Allen, J. R. A. and Fulford, M. G. (1999). "Fort building and military supply along Britain's eastern channel and north sea coasts: the later second and third centuries," *Britannia* 30: 163–84.

Amadei, E. (1965). "Le porte di Roma," *Capitolium* 40: 553–62.

Amory, P. (1997). *People and identity in ostrogothic Italy, 489–554*, Cambridge.

Anderson, J. (1997). *Roman architecture and society*, Baltimore and London.

Andreussi, M. (1988). "Roma: il pomerio," *Scienze dell'Antichità* 2: 219–34.

Appadurai, A. (ed.) (1986). *The social life of things. Commodities in cultural perspective*, Cambridge.

Arena, M.S., Delogu, P., Paroli, L., Ricci, M., Sagui, L. and Venditelli, L. (eds.) (2000). *Roma dall'antichità al medioevo. Archeologia e storia nel Museo Nazionale Romano Crypta Balbi*, Rome.

Ariès, P. (1977). *L'homme devant la mort*, Paris.
  and Duby, G. (eds.) (1987). *A history of private life*, vol. 1: *From pagan Rome to Byzantium*, Cambridge, MA.

Armstrong, H., Pfeiffer, G., and van Buren, A. (1905). "Stamps on bricks and tiles from the Aurelian Wall at Rome," *Supplementary Papers of the American School of Classical Studies in Rome* I: 1–86.

Arnaldi, G. (1981). "Il papato e l'ideologia del potere imperiale," *Settimane del CISAM* 27: 341–407.
  (1982). "Rinascita, fine, reincarnazione e successive metamorfosi del Senato romano (secoli V–XII)," *ASRSP* 105: 5–56.
  (1987). *Le origini dello stato della chiesa*, Turin.
  (1991). "Mito e realtà del secolo X romano e papale," *Settimane del CISAM* 38: 27–53.

Arthur, P. (1989). "Some observations on the economy of Bruttium under the later Roman Empire," *JRA* 2: 133–42.
  (1993). "Early medieval amphorae, the Duchy of Naples and the food supply of Rome," *PBSR* 61: 231–44.
  (2002). *Naples: From Roman town to city-state*. Archaeological Monographs of the British School at Rome 12, London.
  and Whitehouse, D. (1983). "Appunti sulla produzione laterizia nell'Italia centro-meridionale tra il VI e XII secolo," *Archeologia Medievale* 10: 525–37.

Ashby, T. (1902–10). *The classical topography of the Roman campagna*, 4 vols., London and Rome.
  (1927). *The Roman campagna in classical times*, London.

Asso, F. (1953). "Sull'origine dell'altura detta prima 'Monte di Giovanni Roncione', poi 'Monte Giordano'," *Quaderni dell'Istituto di Storia dell'Architettura*: 1: 12–15.

Astutay-Effenberger, N. (2007). *Die Landmauer von Konstantinopel-Istanbul. Historischtopographische und baugeschichtliche Untersuchungen*, Berlin.

Augenti, A. (1996). *Il palatino nel medioevo. Archeologia e topografia (secoli VI–XIII)*, Rome.

(ed.) (2006). *Le città italiane tra la tarda Antichità e l'alto Medioevo. Atti del convegno (Ravenna, 26–28 febbraio 2004)*, Florence.

Azzena, G. (1996). "Trastevere," in *EAA*, Suppl. 2, vol. 4, see under *Roma*, pp. 952–5.

Baatz, D. (1978). "Das Torsiongeschütz von Hatra," *Antike Welt* 9: 50–7.

(1983). "Town walls and defensive weapons," in Hobley and Maloney (eds.), pp. 136–40.

Bachrach, B. S. (1972). *Merovingian military organization 481–751*, Minneapolis.

(1994). "Medieval siege warfare: a reconaissance," *Journal of Military History* 58: 119–33.

(2000). "Imperial walled cities in the West: an examination of their early medieval *Nachleben*," in Tracy (ed.), pp. 192–218.

(2001). *Early Carolingian warfare: prelude to empire*, Philadelphia.

(2002). "Fifth century Metz: late Roman christian *urbs* or ghost town?" *AnTard* 10: 363–81.

Baker, B. G. (1910). *The walls of Constantinople*, London.

Baldovin, J. F. (1987). *The urban character of Christian worship. The origins, development and meaning of stational liturgy*, Rome.

Baldwin, A. (1921). *Five Roman gold medallions or multiple solidi of the late empire.* Numismatic Notes and Monographs 6, New York.

Balil, A. (1970). "La defensa de Hispania en el bajo impero. Amenanza exterior e inquietud interna," in *Legio VII Gemina*, León, pp. 603–20.

Bardill, J. (1999). "The Golden Gate in Constantinople: a triumphal arch of Theodosius I," *AJA* 103: 671–96.

Barnes, T. D. (1981). *Constantine and Eusebius*, Cambridge, MA.

(1982). *The new empire of Diocletian and Constantine*, Cambridge, MA.

(1996). "Emperors, panegyrics, prefects, provinces and palaces," *JRA* 9: 284–317.

Barnish, S. B. J. (1987). "Pigs, plebians and *potentes*: Rome's economic hinterland c. 350–600 A.D.," *PBSR* 55: 157–85.

(1989). "The transformation of classical cities and the Pirenne debate," *JRA* 2: 385–400.

Bauer, F. A. (1996). *Stadt, Platz und Denkmal in der Spätantike. Untersuchungen zur Ausstattung des öffentlichen Raums in den spätantiken Städten Rom, Konstantinopel und Ephesos*, Mainz.

(1997). "Das Bild der Stadt Rom in karolingischer Zeit: der Anonymus Einsidlensis," *RömQSchr* 92: 190–228.

(2003). "Il rinnovamento di Roma sotto Adriano I alla luce del *Liber Pontificalis*. Immagine e realtà," in Geertman (ed.), pp. 189–203.

Bavant, B. (1979). "Le Duché byzantin de Rome. Origine, durée et extension géographique," *MEFRM* 91: 41–88.

Bell, C. (1997). *Ritual: perspectives and dimensions*, Oxford.

Bell, M. (1993). "Mulini ad acqua sul Gianicolo," *Archeologia Laziale* 11.2: 65–72.

Belli Barsali, I. (1976). "Sulla topografia di Roma in periodo carolingio: la 'Civitas Leoniana' e la Giovannipoli," in *Roma e l'età carolingia. Atti delle giornate di studio 3–8 maggio 1976*, Rome, pp. 201–14.

Bertelli, G. (2001). "Elementi da construzione in tufo a Roma tra IV e VII secolo," in Cecchelli (ed.), pp. 151–7.

and Guiglia, A. (1976). "Le strutture murarie delle chiese di Roma nell'VIII e IX secolo," in *Roma e l'età carolingia. Atti delle giornate di studio 3–8 maggio 1976*, Rome, pp. 331–5.

Guidobaldi, A. Guiglia and Spagnoletti, P. Rovigatti (1976–77). "Strutture murarie degli edifici religiosi di Roma dal VI al IX secolo," *Rivista dell'Istituto Nazionale d'Archeologia e Storia dell'Arte* (n.s.) 23–4, 95–173.

Bertolini, O. (1941). *Roma di fronte a Bisanzio e ai Longobardi*, Bologna.

(1947). "Per la storia delle diaconie romane nel alto medioevo sino alla fine del secolo VIII," *ASRSP* 70: 1–145.

(1968) [1948]. "Il problema delle origini del potere temporale dei papi nei suoi presupposti teoretici iniziali: il concetto di 'restitutio' nelle prime cessioni territoriali alla Chiesa di Roma (756–57)," in Bertolini 1968, vol. I, pp. 487–547.

(1968) [1958]. "Riflessi politici delle controversie religiose con bisanzio nelle vicende del secolo VII in Italia," in Bertolini 1968, Vol. II, pp. 265–308.

(1968). *Scritti scelti di storia medievale*, 2 vols., Livorno.

Bintliff, J. and Hamerow, H. (1995). *Europe between late antiquity and the Middle Ages: recent archaeological and historical research in western and southern Europe*, Oxford.

Bird, J., Claridge, A., Gilkes, O. and Neal, D. (1993). "Porta Pia: excavation and survey in an area of suburban Rome. Part 1," *PBSR* 61: 51–113.

Bisconti, F., Nicolaï, V. Fiocchi and Mazzoleni, D. (eds.) (1998). *Le catacombe cristiane di Roma. Origini, sviluppo, apparati decorativi, documentazione epigrafica*, Regensburg.

Bishop, M. C. and Coulston, J. C. (2006). *Roman military equipment*, 2nd edn., London [1993].

Blázquez, J., Remesal, J. and Rodriguez, E. (1994). *Excavaciones arqueológicas en el Monte Testaccio (Roma). Memoria Campaña 1989*, Madrid.

Bleckmann, B. (2004). "Bemerkungen zum Scheitern des Mehrherrschaftssystems: Reichsteilung und Territorialansprüche," in Demandt *et al.* (eds.), pp. 74–94.

Bloch, H. (1945). "A new document of the last pagan revival in the West," *Harvard Theological Review* 28: 199–244.

(1947). *I bolli laterizi e la storia edilizia romana*, Rome.

(1963). "The pagan revival in the West at the end of the fourth century," in Momigliano (ed.), pp. 193–218.

Blockley, R. C. (1998). "The dynasty of Theodosius," in *CAH* 13: 111–37.

Bognetti, G. P. (1966). *L'età longobarda*, Milan.

Borghini, G., Callegari, P. and Nista, L. (eds.) (2004). *Roma. Il riuso dell'antico. Fotografie tra XIX e XX secolo*, Bologna.

Bosio, L. (1983). *La Tabula Peutingeriana*, Rimini.

Bowden, W. and Hodges, R. (eds.) (1998). *The sixth century: production, distribution, and demand*, Leiden and Boston.

Bradbury, J. (1992). *The medieval siege*, Woodbridge.

Braund, Y. (1973). "La Cité de Carcassonne. Les enceintes fortifiées," *Congrès Archéologiques de France* 131: 486–518.

Breeze, D. J. and Dobson, B. (1976). *Hadrian's Wall*, London.

Brezzi, P. (1947). *Roma e l'impero medioevale (774–1252)*, Bologna.

(1959). "L'idea di Roma nell'alto medioevo," *Studi Romani* 7: 511–23.

Brienza, M. and Delfino, A. (2006). "Il *necessarium* presso Porta Salaria a Roma," *BullCom* 107: 107–14.

Brodka, D. (1998). *Die Romideologie in der römischen Literatur der Spätantike*, Frankfurt.

Brogiolo, G. P. (ed.) (2000). *II Congresso nazionale di archeologia medievale*, Florence.

Gauthier N. and Christie, N. (eds.) (2000). *Towns and their territories between late antiquity and the early Middle Ages*, Leiden and Boston.

and Gelichi, S. (1998). *La città nell'alto medioevo italiano. Archeologia e storia*, Rome and Bari.

and Panazza, G. (eds.) (1988). *Ricerche su Brescia altomedioevale*, Brescia.

and Ward-Perkins, B. (eds.) (1999). *The idea and ideal of the town between late antiquity and the early Middle Ages*, Leiden and Boston.

Brooks, N. (2000). "Canterbury, Rome and the construction of English identity," in Smith (ed.), pp. 221–46.

Brown, P. (1981). *The cult of the saints*, London.

(2000). *Augustine of Hippo*, 2nd edn., London and Berkeley [1967].

(2003). *The rise of Western Christendom*, 2nd edn., Oxford.

Brown, T. S. (1984). *Gentlemen and officers: imperial administration and aristocratic power in Byzantine Italy, AD 554–800*, London.

(1998). "Urban violence in early medieval Italy: the cases of Rome and Ravenna," in Halsell (ed.), *Violence and society in the early medieval West*, Woodbridge, pp. 79–89.

Brühl, C. (1954). "Die Kaiserpfalz bei St. Peter und die Pfalz Ottos III. auf dem Palatin," *Quellen und Forschungen aus italienischen Archiven und Bibliotheken* 34: 1–30.

Brulet, R. (1996). "Les transformations du bas-empire," in M. Reddé (ed.), *L'armée romaine en Gaule*, Paris, pp. 223–65.

Brunt, P. A. (1980). "Free labour and public works at Rome," *JRS* 70: 81–100.

Brusin, G. (1967). "Le difese della romana Aquileia e la loro cronologia," *Archivio Veneto*, 5th series, vol. 81: 33–52.

Bühl, G. (1995). *Constantinopolis und Roma: Stadtpersonifikationen der Spätantike*, Zurich.

Bullough, D. (1966). "Urban change in early medieval Italy: the example of Pavia," *PBSR* 34: 82–130.

(1974). "Social and economic structure and topography in the early medieval city," *Settimane del CISAM* 21: 351–99.

(1981). "Hagiography as patriotism: Alcuin's 'York poem' and the early Northumbrian 'vitae sanctorum'," in *Hagiographie cultures et sociétés IVᵉ–XIIᵉ siècles*, Paris, pp. 339–59.

Bury, J. B. (1923). *History of the later Roman empire from the death of Theodosius I to the death of Justinian (AD 395 to AD 565)*, 2 vols., London.

Butler, R. M. (1959). "Late Roman town walls in Gaul," *Archaeological Journal* 116: 25–50.

Cabié, R. (1973). *La lettre du Pape Innocent Iᵉʳ a Décentius de Gubbio (19 mars 416)*, Bibliothèque de la revue d'histoire ecclésiastique, Fascicule 58, Louvain.

Calci, C. and Mari, Z. (2003). "Via Tiburtina," in Pergola *et al.* (eds.), pp. 175–209.

Callu, J. P. (1969). *La politique monétaire des empereurs romains de 238 à 311*, Paris.

Cambedda, A. and Ceccherelli A. (1990). *Le mura di Aureliano: dalla Porta Appia al Bastione Ardeatino*, Rome.

Cameron, Alan (1970). *Claudian. Poetry and propaganda at the court of Honorius*, Oxford.

Cameron, Averil (1985). *Procopius and the sixth century*, London.

Campanati, R. F. (1999). "Jerusalem and Bethlehem in the iconography of church sanctuary mosaics," in Piccirillo and Alliata (eds.), pp. 173–7.

Cantino Wataghin, G. (1992). "Urbanistica tardoantica e topografia cristiana. Termini di un problema," in *Felix temporis reparatio. Atti del convegno archeologico internazionale Milano capitale dell'Impero Romano, Milano 8–11 marzo 1990*, Milan, pp. 171–92.

(1996). "Quadri urbani nell'Italia settentrionale: tarda antichità e alto medioevo," in Lepelley (ed.), pp. 239–71.

(1999). "The ideology of urban burials," in Brogiolo and Ward Perkins (eds.), pp. 147–180.

(2005). "La città tardoantica: il caso di Aquileia," in G. Cuscito and M. Verzár-Bass (eds.), *Aquileia dalle origini alla costituzione del ducato longobardo*, Trieste, pp. 101–19.

and Lambert, C. (1998). "Sepolture e città. L'Italia settentrionale tra IV e VIII secolo," in G. P. Brogiolo and G. Cantino Wataghin (eds.), *Sepolture tra IV e VIII secolo. 7° seminario sul tardo antico e l'alto medioevo in Italia centro-settentrionale*, Mantua, pp. 89–114.

Caporusso, D. (1991). "La zona di corso di Porta Romana in età romana e medioevale," in Caporusso (ed.), *Scavi MM3: ricerche di archeologia urbana a Milano durante la costruzione della Linea 3 della Metropolitana, 1982–1990*, vol. 1, Milan, pp. 237–61.

Carandini, A. (1985). "Hortensia. Orti e frutteti intorno a Roma," in *Misurare la terra: centuriazione e coloni nel mondo romano. Città, agricoltura, commercio: materiali da Roma e dal suburbio*, Rome, pp. 66–74.

Ruggini, L. Cracco and Giardina, A. (eds.) (1993). *Storia di Roma. 3. L'età tardoantica*, 2 vols., Turin.

Cardilli, L., Coarelli, F., Pisani Sartorio, G. and Pietrangeli, C. (1995). *Mura e porte di Roma antica*, Rome.

Carettoni, G., Colini, A. M., Cozza, L. and Gatti, G. (1960). *La pianta marmorea di Roma antica*, Rome.

Carile, A. (2002). "Roma vista da Constantinopoli," *Settimane del CISAM* 49: 49–99.

Carocci, S. (ed.) (2006). *La nobiltà romana nel medioevo*, Collection de l'EFR 359, Rome.

Caroli, M. (2000). "Bringing saints to cities and monasteries: *translationes* in the making of a sacred geography (ninth–tenth Centuries)," in Brogiolo, Gauthier and Christie (eds.), pp. 259–74.

Caruso, G. and Volpe, R. (1989–90). "Le Mura Aureliane tra Porta Tiburtina e Porta Maggiore," *BullCom* 103: 76–8.

Casartelli Novelli, S. (2000). "La 'nuova Gerusalemme' generata dal Cristo. Il *cantus firmus* dell'immaginario di Roma 'capitale cristiana,'" in Pani Ermini (ed.), pp. 153–71.

Casey, J. (1983). "Imperial campaigns and 4th-century defences in Britain," in Hobley and Maloney (eds.), pp. 121–4.

Caspar, E. (1930–1933). *Geschichte des Papsttums von den Anfangen bis zur Höhe der Weltherrschaft, I–II*, Tübingen.

Cassanelli, L., Delfini, G. and Fonti, D. (1974). *Le mura di Roma. L'architettura militare nella storia urbana*, Rome.

Castagnoli, F. (1947). "Il Campo Marzio nell'antichità," *MemAcLinc* 8, 1: 93–193.
(1980). "Installazioni portuali a Roma," *MAAR* 36: 35–42.
(1992). *Il Vaticano nell'antichità classica*, Vatican City.

Cavaliere Manasse, G. (1993). "Le Mura Teodericiane di Verona," in *Teoderico il Grande e i Goti d'Italia. Atti del 13 Congresso internazionale di studi sull'Alto Medioevo*, Spoleto, pp. 635–44.

and Hudson, P. J. (1999). "Nuovi dati sulle fortificazioni di Verona (III–XI secolo)," in G. P. Brogiolo (ed.), *Le fortificazioni del Garda e i sistemi di difesa dell'Italia settentrionale tra tardo antico e alto medioevo*, Mantua, pp. 71–91.

Cecchelli, M. (ed.) (2001). *Materiali e techniche dell'edilizia paleocristiana a Roma*, Rome.

Ceccherelli, M. and D'Ippolito, M. G. (2006). "Considerazioni su alcune fasi costruttive di Porta Appia," *BullCom* 107: 87–106.

Ceresa Mori, A. (1993). "Milano – le mura massimianee," in *Mura delle città romane in Lombardia*, Como, pp. 13–36.

Chaffin, C. (1993). *Olympiodorus of Thebes and the sack of Rome*, New York.

Champlin, E. (1982). "The suburbium of Rome," *American Journal of Ancient History* 7: 97–117.

Chastagnol, A. (1950). "Un scandale du vin à Rome sous le Bas-Empire: l'affair du préfet Orfitus," *Annales Economies Sociétés Civilisations* 5: 166–83.

 (1960). *La préfecture urbaine a Rome sous le bas-empire*, Paris.

 (1964). "Le problème de l'Histoire Auguste: état de la question," in Historia-Augusta-Colloquium Bonn 1963, *Antiquitas* 4.2: 43–71.

Chavasse, A. (1993). "La liturgie de la ville de Rome du Ve au VIIIe siècle," *Studia Anselmiana 112*, Rome.

Chevallier, R. (1972). *Les Voies Romaines*, Paris.

Chevedden, P. (1995). "Artillery in late antiquity: prelude to the Middle Ages," in I. A. Corfis and M. Wolfe (eds.), *The medieval city under siege*, Bury St Edmunds, pp. 131–73.

Christe, Y. (1979). "Traditions littéraires et iconographiques dans l'interprétation des images apocalyptiques," in *L'apocalypse de Jean. Traditions exégétiques et iconographiques*, Geneva, pp. 109–34.

Christie, N. (1989). "The city walls of Ravenna: the defence of a capital, AD 402–750," *Corso di cultura sull'arte ravennate e bizantina* 36: 113–38.

 (1991). *Three south Etrurian churches, Archaeological Monographs of the British School at Rome 4*, London.

 (1992). "Urban defence in later Roman Italy," in E. Herring, R. Whitehouse, and J. Wilkins (eds.), *The archaeology of power: papers of the fourth conference of Italian archaeology*, London, pp. 185–99.

 (ed.) (1995). *Settlement and economy in Italy, 1500 BC–AD 1500: papers of the fifth conference of Italian archaeology*, Oxford.

 (2000). "Lost glories? Rome at the end of empire," in Coulston and Dodge (eds.), pp. 306–31.

 (2001). "War and order: urban remodeling and defensive strategy in late Roman Italy," in Lavan (ed.), pp. 106–22.

 (2006). *From Constantine to Charlemagne. An archaeology of Italy AD 300–800*, London.

 and Rushworth, A. (1988). "Urban fortification and defensive strategy in fifth and sixth century Italy: the case of Terracina," *JRA* 1: 73–88.

 and Gibson, S. (1988). "The city walls of Ravenna," *PBSR* 56: 156–97.

Christol, M. (1997). *L'empire romain du IIIe siècle. Histoire politique (de 192, morte de Commode, à 325, concile de Nicée)*, Paris.

Ciampoltrini, G., Abela, E., Bianchini, S. and Zecchini, M. (2003). "Lucca tardoantica e altomedievale III: le mura urbiche e il pranzo di Rixsolfo," *Archeologia Medievale* 30: 281–98.

Coarelli, P. (1977). "Il campo Marzio occidentale. Storia e topografia," *MEFRA* 89: 807–46.

 (1986). "L'urbs e il suburbio," in *SRIT* II: 1–58.

(1987). "La situazione edilizia di Roma sotto Severo Alessandro," in *L'urbs. Espace urbain et histoire (Ier siècle av. J.-C.–IIIe siecle ap. J.-C.).* Collection de l'EFR 98, Rome, pp. 429–56.

(1997a). *Il Campo Marzio. Dalle origini alla fine della repubblica*, Rome.

(1997b). "La consistenza della città nel periodo imperiale: *pomerium, vici, insulae*," in *La Rome impérial. Démographie et logistique. Actes de la table ronde (Rome, 25 mars 1994).* Collection de l'EFR 230, Rome, pp. 89–109.

Coates, S. (1996). "The bishop as benefactor and civic patron: Alcuin, York, and episcopal authority in Anglo-Saxon England," *Speculum* 71: 529–58.

Coates-Stephens, R. (1995). "Quattro torri alto-medievali delle Mura Aureliane," *Archeologia Medievale* 22: 501–17.

(1996). "Housing in early medieval Rome A.D. 500–1000," *PBSR* 64: 239–60.

(1997). "Dark age architecture in Rome," *PBSR* 65: 177–232.

(1998). "The walls and aqueducts of Rome in the early middle ages," *JRS* 88: 166–78.

(1999). "Le ricostruzioni altomedievali delle mura aureliane e degli acquedotti," *MEFRM* 111, 1: 209–25.

(2001). "Muri dei bassi secoli in Rome: observations on the re-use of statuary in walls found on the Esquiline and Caelian after 1870," *JRA* 14: 217–38.

(2003a). "The water-supply of early medieval Rome," *Acta Instituti Romani Finlandiae* 31: 81–113.

(2003b). "The water-supply of Rome from late antiquity to the early middle ages," *Acta IRN* 17: 165–86.

(2003c). "Gli acquedotti in epoca tardoantica nel suburbio," in Pergola *et al.* (eds.), pp. 415–36.

(2004). *Porta Maggiore: monument and landscape. Archaeology and topography of the southern Esquiline from the Late Republican period to the present*, BullCom Supplement 12, Rome.

(2006). "La committenza edilizia a Roma dopo la riconquista," in A. Augenti (ed.), pp. 299–316.

and Parisi, A. (1999). "Indagine di un crollo delle Mura Aureliane presso Porta Maggiore," *AnalRom* 26: 85–98.

Colin, M. G. (ed.) (1987). *Les enceintes augustéennes dans l'occident romain*, Bulletin de l'École Antique de Nîmes 18, Nîmes.

Colini, A. (1944). *Storia e topografia del Celio nell'antichità. RendPontAc* 7, Rome.

(1948). "Horti Spei Veteris, Palatium Sessorianum," *RendPontAc* 8: 137–77.

Colli, A. (1983). "La tradizione figurativa della Gerusalemme celeste: linee di sviluppo dal sec. III al sec. XIV," in Gatti Perer (ed.), pp. 119–44.

Cooper, C. and Hillner, J. (eds.) (2007). *Religion, dynasty and patronage in early Christian Rome, 300–900*, Cambridge.

Corcoran, S. (1996). *The empire of the tetrarchs. Imperial pronouncements and government AD 284–324*, Oxford.

Corvisieri, C. (1878). "Delle Posterule tiberine tra la Porta Flaminia ed il Ponte Gianicolense," *ASRSP* 1: 79–121; 137–71.

Cosme, P. (1998). *L'État romain entre éclatement et continuité. L'Empire romain de 192 à 325*, Paris.

Cotterill, J. (1993). "Saxon raiding and the role of the late Roman coastal forts of Britain," *Britannia* 24: 227–39.

Coulston, J. (2000). "'Armed and belted men': the soldiery in imperial Rome," in Coulston and Dodge (eds.), pp. 76–118.

  and Dodge, H. (eds.) (2000). *Ancient Rome: the archaeology of the Eternal City*, Oxford University School of Archaeology Monograph 54, Oxford.

Courcelle, P. (1964). *Histoire littéraire des grandes invasions germaniques*, 3rd edn., Paris.

Cozza, L. (ed.) (1952). "Muri portaeque Aureliani," in G. Lugli (ed.), *Fontes ad Topographiam Veteris Urbis Romae Pertinentes* I, pp. 201–34.

  (1986). "Mura Aureliane, 1. Trastevere, il braccio settentrionale: dal Tevere a porta Aurelia-S. Pancrazio," *BullCom* 91: 103–30.

  (1987). "Osservazioni sulle Mura Aureliane a Roma," *AnalRom* 16: 25–52.

  (1987–8). "Mura Aureliane, 2. Trastevere, il braccio meridionale: dal Tevere a Porta Aurelia-S. Pancrazio," *BullCom* 92: 137–74.

  (1989). "Le Mura Aureliane dalla Porta Flaminia al Tevere," *PBSR* 57: 1–5.

  (1992). "Mura di Roma dalla Porta Flaminia alla Pinciana," *AnalRom* 20: 93–138.

  (1993). "Mura di Roma dalla Porta Pinciana alla Salaria," *AnalRom* 21: 81–139.

  (1994). "Mura di Roma dalla Porta Salaria alla Porta Nomentana," *AnalRom* 22: 61–95.

  (1998). "Mura di Roma dalla Porta Nomentana alla Tiburtina," *AnalRom* 25: 7–114.

  (2008). "Mura di Roma dalla Porta Latina all'Appia," *PBSR* 76: 99–154.

Cozzi, L. (1968). *Le porte di Roma*, Rome.

Crow, J. (2001). "Fortifications and urbanism in late antiquity: Thessaloniki and other eastern cities," in Lavan (ed.), pp. 89–105.

Crow, J. (2007). "The infrastructure of a great city: earth, walls and water in late antique Constantinople," in Lavan, Zanini and Sarantis (eds.), pp. 251–85.

Cubelli, V. (1992). *Aureliano imperatore: la rivolta dei monetieri e la cosidetta riforma monetaria*, Florence.

Cullhed, M. (1994). *Conservator urbis suae. Studies in the politics and propaganda of the emperor Maxentius*, Stockholm.

Cüppers, H. (1973). "Die Stadtmauer des römischen Trier und das Gräberfeld an der Porta Nigra," *Trierer Zeitschrift für Geschichte und Kunst des Trierer Landes und seiner Nachbargebiete* 36: 133–222.

Curran, J. (2000). *Pagan city and Christian capital. Rome in the fourth century*, Oxford.

Dagron, G. (1974). *Naissance d'une capitale. Constantinople et ses institutions de 330 à 451*, Paris.

De Blaauw, S. (1994). *Cultus et Decor. Liturgia e architettura nella Roma tardoantica e medievale*, 2 vols., Vatican City.

De Caprariis, F. (1999). "I porti della città nel IV e V secolo d.C.," in Harris (ed.), pp. 217–34.

De Carlo, L. and Quattrini, P. (1995). *Le mura di Roma tra realtà e immagine*, Rome.

De Conno, A. (1991). "L'insediamento longobardo a Lucca," in G. Garzella (ed.), *Pisa e la Toscana occidentale nel Medioevo*, Pisa, pp. 59–127.

De Francesco, D. (2003). "Chiesa romana e proprietà fondiaria nel suburbio tra il IV secolo e l'età gregoriana: riflessioni e problemi," in Pergola *et al.* (eds.), pp. 515–43.

de Jong, M. and Theuws, F. (eds.) (2001). *Topographies of power in the early Middle Ages*, Leiden and Boston.

de la Croix, H. (1972). *Military considerations in city planning: fortifications*, New York.

DeLaine, J. (1995). "The supply of building materials to the city of Rome," in Christie (ed.), pp. 555–62.

  (1997). *The Baths of Caracalla. A study in the design, construction and economics of large-scale building projects in imperial Rome, JRA* Supplement 25, Portsmouth, RI.

  (2000). "Building the Eternal City: the construction industry in imperial Rome," in Coulston and Dodge (eds.), pp. 119–41.

Della Valle, G. (1959). "*Moenia.*" *Rendiconti dell'Accademia di Archeologia Lettere e Belle Arti di Napoli*, n.s. 33: 167–76.

Del Lungo, S. (2004). *Roma in età carolingia e gli scritti dell'anonimo augiense*, Rome.

Delogu, P. (1988a). "Oro e argento in Roma tra il VII ed il IX secolo," in *Cultura e società nell'Italia medievale: Studi per Paolo Brezzi*, Rome, pp. 273–93.

  (1988b). "The rebirth of Rome in the eighth and ninth centuries," in Hobley and Hodges (eds.), *The rebirth of towns in the West AD 700–1050*, London, pp. 33–42.

  (1989). "La *Crypta Balbi*. Una nota sui materiali dell'esedra," in *La moneta nei contesti archeologici. Esempi dagli scavi di Roma*, Rome, pp. 97–105.

  (1993). "La storia di Roma nell'alto medioevo. Introduzione al seminario," in Delogu and Paroli (eds.), pp. 11–29.

  (ed.) (1998). *Roma medievale. Aggiornamenti*, Rome.

  (2000a). "*Solium imperii – urbs ecclesiae*. Roma fra la tarda antichità e l'alto medioevo," in Gurt and Ripoll (eds.), pp. 83–108.

  (2000b). "The papacy, Rome and the wider world in the seventh and eighth centuries," in Smith (ed.), pp. 197–220.

  (2001). "Il passaggio dall'antichità al Medioevo," in Vauchez (ed.), pp. 3–40.

and Paroli, L. (eds.) (1993). *La Storia economica di Roma nell'alto medioevo alla luce dei recenti scavi archeologici. Atti del Seminario Roma 2–3 aprile 1992,* Florence.

and Bellardini, D. (2003). "*Liber Pontificalis* e altre fonti: la topografia di Roma nell'VIII secolo," in Geertman (ed.), pp. 205–23.

Demandt, A., Golz, A. and Schlange-Schöningen, H. (eds.) (2004). *Diokletian und die Tetrarchie: Aspekte einer Zeitenwende,* Berlin and New York.

Deniaux, É. (ed.) (2000). *Rome Antique. Pouvoir des images, images du pouvoir,* Caen.

De Robertis, F. M. (1955). *Il fenomeno associativo nel mondo romano,* Bari.

(1963). *Lavoro e lavoratori nel mondo romano,* Bari.

De Rossi, G. and Granelli, A. (2003). "Tor Marancia e la Via Ardeatina. Ricognizione e lettura del territorio tra 'campagna urbana' ed espansione edilizia," in Pergola *et al.* (eds.), pp. 331–59.

De Rossi, G. B. (1879). *Piante iconografiche e prospettiche di Roma,* Rome.

(1874). "Dei collari dei servi fuggitivi," *Bullettino di Archeologia Cristiana* 5: 41–67.

De Seta, C. (1989). "Le mura simbolo della citta," in De Seta and Le Goff (eds.), pp. 11–57.

and Le Goff, J. (eds.) (1989). *La città e le mura,* Rome and Bari.

Dessau, H. (1889). "Über Zeit und Persönlichkeit der *Scriptores Historiae Augustae,*" *Hermes* 24: 337–92.

Dewar, M. (1996). *Claudian: Panegyricus de sexto consulatu Honorii augusti,* Oxford.

Dey, H. (2004). "Building worlds apart. Walls and the construction of communal monasticism from Augustine through Benedict," *AnTard* 12: 357–71.

Diehl, C. (1888). *Études sur l'administration byzantine dans l'exarchat de Ravenne (568–751),* Paris.

di Gennaro, F. and dell'Era, F. (2003). "Dati archeologici di età tardoantica dal territorio dell' *insula inter duo flumina,*" in Pergola *et al.* (eds.), pp. 97–121.

Dixon, K. and Southern, P. (1996). *The late Roman army,* London.

Dmitriev, S. (2004). "Traditions and innovations in the reign of Aurelian," *The Classical Quarterly* 54.2: 568–78.

D'Onofrio, C. (1971). *Castel Sant'Angelo,* Rome.

(1978). *Castel S. Angelo e Borgo tra Roma e papato,* Rome.

(1982). *Castel Sant'Angelo nella storia di Roma e del papato,* Rome.

Downey, G. (1961). *A history of Antioch in Syria: from Seleucus to the Arab conquest,* Princeton.

Duncan-Jones, R. (1982). *The economy of the Roman Empire: quantitative studies,* Revised edn., Cambridge.

Durliat, J. (1990). *De la ville antique à la ville Byzantine: le problème des subsistances,* Collection de l'EFR 136, Rome.

Duval, Y. M. (1976). "Aquilée sur la route des invasions," *Antichità Altoadriatiche* 9: 237–98.

Edwards, C. (1996). *Writing Rome: textual approaches to the city*, Cambridge.

and Woolf, G. (eds.) (2003). *Rome the Cosmopolis*, Cambridge.

Elton, H. (1996). *Warfare in Roman Europe AD 350–425*, Oxford.

Ensslin, W. (1953). *Die Religionspolitik des Kaisers Theodosius d. Gr.*, Munich.

Esch, A. (2001). "Le vie di comunicazione di Roma nell'alto medioevo," *Settimane del CISAM* 48: 421–53.

(2003). "La viabilità nei dintorni di Roma fra tarda Antichità e primo Medioevo," in Pergola *et al.* (eds.), pp. 1–24.

Esmonde Cleary, S. (2003). "Civil defences in the West under the High Empire," in Wilson (ed.), pp. 73–85.

(2007). "Fortificación urbana en la 'Britannia' romana: ¿defensa militar o monumento cívico?," in Rodríguez Colmenero and de Rodá de Llanza (eds.), pp. 21–46.

Esmonde Cleary, S. and Wood, J. (2006). "Le rempart antique de Saint-Bertrand-de-Comminges," *Gallia* 63: 81–4.

Esposito, A. (2003). *L'organizzazione della difesa di Roma nel Medioevo*, Rome.

Esposito, D. (1997). *Techniche costruttive murarie medievali. Murature "a tufelli" in area romana*, Rome.

Fagiolo, M. and Madonna, M. (1972). "La Roma di Pio IV: la 'Civitas Pia,' la 'Salus Medica,' la 'Custodia Angelica,'" *Arte Illustrata* V, 51: 383–402.

Fasoli, G. (1974). "Città e storia delle città," *Settimane del CISAM* 21: 15–38.

Fentress, E. (ed.) (2000). *Romanization and the city. Creation, transformations, and failures*, JRA Supplement 38, Portsmouth, RI.

Fernández-Ochoa, C. and Morillo, Á. (2005). "Walls in the urban landscape of late Roman Spain: defense and imperial strategy," in K. Bowes and M. Kulikowski (eds.), *Hispania in late antiquity. Current perspectives*, Leiden and Boston, pp. 299–340.

Ferrua, A. (1957–58). "Il catalogo dei martiri di S. Prassede," *RendPontAc* 30–1: 129–40.

Feugère, M. (1993). *Les armes des Romains*, Paris.

Février, P.-A. (1974). "Permanence et héritages de l'antiquité dans la topographie des villes de l'occident durant le haut moyen âge," *Settimane del CISAM* 21: 41–138.

Fiocchi Nicolai, V. (2000a). "Gli spazi delle sepolture cristiane tra il III e il V secolo: genesi e dinamica di una scelta insediativa," in Pani Ermini and Siniscalco (eds.), pp. 341–62.

(2000b). "Sacra martyrum loca circuire: percorsi di visita dei pellegrini nei santuari martiriali del suburbio romano," in Pani Ermini (ed.), I: 221–30.

(2001). *Strutture funerarie ed edifici di culto paleocristiani di Roma dal IV al VI secolo*, Vatican City.

(2003). "Elementi di trasformazione dello spazio funerario tra tarda antichità ed alto medioevo," *Settimane del CISAM* 50: 921–69.

Del Moro, M. P., Nuzzo, D. and Spera, L. (1995–6). "La nuova basilica circiforme della via Ardeatina," *RendPontAc* 68: 69–233.

Grazia Granino Cecere, M., Mari, Z. (eds.) (2001–). *Lexicon Topographicum Urbis Romae, Suburbium*, Rome.

Fiorani, D. (1996). *Techniche costruttive murarie medievali. Il Lazio meridionale*, Rome.

Fogolari, G. (1965). "Verona. Ritrovamenti archeologici nell'ultimo decennio," *Notizie*, Suppl. 19: 35–53.

Foss, C. and Winfield, D. (1986). *Byzantine Fortifications. An Introduction*, Pretoria.

Fourdrin, J.-P. (2002). "Vestiges d'un parapet antique près de la tour du Sacraire Saint-Sernin à Carcassonne," *JRA* 15: 311–16.

Francovich, R. and Noyé, G. (eds.) (1994). *La storia dell'alto medioevo italiano (VI–X secolo) alla luce dell'archeologia*, Florence.

Frantz, A. (1988). *The Athenian agora*, vol. 24: *late antiquity: AD 267–700*, Athens and Princeton.

Frézouls, E. (1987). "Rome ville ouverte. Réflexions sur les problèmes de l'expansion urbaine d'Auguste à Aurélien," in *L'urbs. Espace urbain et histoire (Ier siècle av. J.-C. – IIIe siecle ap. J.-C.)*. Collection de l'EFR 98, Rome, pp. 373–92.

Frutaz, A. P. (1962). *Le Piante di Roma*, 3 vols., Rome.

Fuhrmann, H. (1973). "Das frühmittelalterliche Papsttum und die konstantinische Schenkung," *Settimane del CISAM* 20 (1973): 257–92.

Fulford, M. and Tyres, I. (1995). "The date of Pevensey and the defence of an '*Imperium Brittaniarum*,'" *Antiquity* 69: 1,009–14.

Gabriel, A. (1940). *Voyages Archéologiques dans la Turquie Orientale*, Paris.

Galasso, G. (1965). *Mezzogiorno medioevale e moderno*, Turin.

Galetti, P. (1994). "Le techniche costruttive fra VI e X secolo," in Francovich and Noyé (eds.), pp. 467–77.

(2006). "Tecniche e materiali da costruzione dell'edilizia residenziale," in Augenti (ed.), pp. 67–79.

Galliazzo, G. (1995). *I ponti romani*, 2 vols., Rome.

Garmy, P. and Maurin, L. (eds.) (1996). *Enceintes romaines d'Aquitaine. Bordeaux, Dax, Périgueux, Bazas*, Paris.

Gatti, G. (1936). "L'arginatura del Tevere a Marmorata," *BullCom* 64: 55–82.

Gatti Perer, M. (ed.) (1983). "*La dimora di Dio con gli uomini*": *Immagini della Gerusalemme celeste dal III al XIV secolo*, Milan, 1983.

Gatto, L. (1998). "Riflettendo sulla consistenza demografica della Roma altomedievale," in Delogu (ed.), pp. 143–57.

Gauthier, N. (1999). "La topographie Chrétienne entre idéologie et pragmatisme," in Brogiolo and Ward-Perkins (eds.), pp. 195–209.

Gawlikowski, M. (1994). "Fortress Hatra. New evidence on ramparts and their history," *Mesopotamia* 29: 147–84.

Geary, P. (1990). *Furta sacra. Thefts of relics in the central Middle Ages*, 2nd edn., Princeton.

Geertman, H. (1975). *More veterum. Il 'Liber Pontificalis' e gli edifici ecclesiastici di Roma nella tarda antichità e nell'alto medioevo*, Groningen.

(ed.) (2003). *Il Liber Pontificalis e la storia materiale*, Papers of the Netherlands Insititute in Rome, 60–1, Rome.

Gelichi, S. (ed.) (1997). *I Congresso nazionale di archeologia medievale*, Florence.

(2000). "Ravenna, ascesa e declino di una capitale," in Gurt and Ripoll (eds.), pp. 109–34.

(2002). "The cities," in La Rocca (ed.), pp. 168–88.

(2005). "Le mura di Ravenna," in *Ravenna da capitale imperiale a capitale esarcale. Atti del XVII Congresso internazionale di studio sull'alto medioevo, Ravenna, 6–12 Giugno 2004*, Spoleto, pp. 821–40.

Gell, A. (1998). *Art and agency: an anthropological theory.* Oxford.

Ghilardi, M., Goddard, C. and Porena, P. (eds.) (2006). *Les cités de l'Italie tardo-antique (IVe-VIe siècle). Institutions, économie, société, culture et religion*, Collection de l'EFR 369, Rome.

Giardina, A. (ed.) (1986). *Società Romana e Impero Tardoantico*, 4 vols., Rome. and Vauchez, A. (2000). *Il mito di Roma. Da Carlo Magno a Mussolini*, Bari.

Giartosio, T. (2003). "Murate Vive," *Capitolium*, n.s. I, 1: 6–13.

Gilkes, O., Passigli, S. and Schinke, R. (1994). "Porta Pia: excavation and survey in an area of suburban Rome. Part 2," *PBSR* 62: 101–37.

Gillett, A. (2001). "Rome, Ravenna and the emperors," *PBSR* 69: 131–67.

Giovannini, F. (2001). *Natalità, mortalità e demografia dell'Italia Medievale sulla base dei dati archeologici*, Oxford.

Giovenale, G. B. (1929). "Simboli tutelari su porte del recinto urbano ed altri monumenti dell'antichità," *BullCom* 57: 183–268.

(1931). "Le porte del recinto di Aureliano e di Probo," *BullCom* 59: 9–122.

Giuntella, A. M. (1985). "'Spazio cristiano' e città altomedievale: l'esempio della civitas leoniana," in *Atti del VI Congresso Nazionale di Archeologia Cristiana (Pesaro – Ancona 19–23 settembre 1983)*, pp. 309–25.

(2001). "Gli spazi dell'assistenza e della meditazione," *Settimane del CISAM* 48: 639–91.

Gobbi, G. and Sica, P. (1982). *Rimini*, Rome and Bari.

Goodman, P. J. (2007). *The Roman city and its periphery: from Rome to Gaul*, London and New York.

Gosden, C. (2005). "What do objects want," *Journal of Archaeological Method and Theory* 12: 193–211.

Goudineau, C. (1980). "Les villes de la paix romaine," in G. Duby (ed.) *Histoire de la France urbaine*, vol. 1, pp. 233–391.

Grabar, A. (1946). *Martyrium. Recherches sur le culte des reliques et l'art chrétien antique*, 2 vols., Paris.

Graf, A. (1882–3). *Roma nella memoria e nelle immaginazioni del medio evo*, 2 vols., Turin.

Greene, K. (1986). *The archaeology of the Roman economy*, London.

Gregorovius, F. (1973). *Storia della città di Roma nel medioevo*, 3 vols., trans. A. Casalegno, Turin [1859–72].

Groag, E. (1903). "Domitianus (36) Aurelianus," in *RE* V: 1,347–1,419.

Gros, P. (1992). "*Moenia*: aspects défensifs et aspects représentatifs des fortifications", in S. Van de Maele and J. M. Fossey (eds.), *Fortificationes antiquae*, Amsterdam, pp. 211–25.

Guidi, P. (1923). "L'antico documento cimiteriale cristiano noto sotto il nome di *Catalogo dei cimiteri di Roma*," *RendPontAc* 1: 185–214.

Guidobaldi, F. (1986). "L'edilizia abitativa unifamiliare nella Roma tardoantica," in *SRIT* II: 165–237.

(1999). "Le domus tardoantiche di Roma come 'sensori' delle trasformazioni culturali e sociali," in Harris (ed.), pp. 53–68.

(2000). "L'organizzazione dei *tituli* nello spazio urbano," in Pani Ermini (ed.), I: 123–9.

Guidoboni, E. and Molin, D. (1989). "Effetto fonti effetto monumenti a Roma: i terremoti dall'antichità a oggi," in E. Guidoboni (ed.), *I terremoti prima del Mille in Italia e nell'area mediterranea*, Bologna, pp. 194–223.

Guidoni, E. (1972). "Il significato urbanistico di Roma tra antichità e medioevo," *Palladio* (n.s.) 22: 3–32.

Guilleux, J. (2000). *L'enceinte romaine du Mans*, Saint-Jean-d'Angély.

Guillou, A. (1988). "L'Italia bizantina dall'invasione longobarda alla caduta di Ravenna," in A. Guillou and F. Burgarella (eds.), *L'Italia bizantina. Dall'esarcato di Ravenna al tema di Sicilia*, Turin, pp. 3–122.

Gurt, J. M. and Ripoll, G. (eds.) (2000). *Sedes regiae (ann. 400–800)*, Barcelona.

Gutteridge, A., Hoti, A. and Hurst, H. (2001). "The walled town of Dyrrachium (Durres): settlement and dynamics," *JRA* 14: 390–410.

Halsell, G. (2003). *Warfare and society in the barbarian West, 450–900*, London and New York.

Hanel, N. (2002). "Recent research on the fortifications of the headquarters of the classis Germanica: Cologne-Marienburg (Alteburg)," in *Limes XVIII. Proceedings of the XVIIIth International Congress of Roman Frontier Studies held in Amman, Jordan (September 2000)*, 2 vols., BAR International Series 1084, Oxford, pp. 912–20.

Hansen, I. L. and Wickham, C. (eds.) (2000). *The long eighth century*, (Transformation of the Roman world 11), Leiden, Boston and Cologne.

Hansen, M. F. (2003). *The eloquence of appropriation. Prolegomena to an understanding of spolia in early Christian Rome*, AnalRom Supplement 33, Rome.

Harris, W. V. (ed.) (1999). *The transformations of* Urbs Roma *in late antiquity*, JRA Supplement 33, Portsmouth, RI.

Hartmann, L.-M. (1889). *Untersuchungen zur Geschichte der byzantinischen Verwaltung in Italien (540–750)*, Leipzig.

Haselberger, L. (1997). "Architectural likenesses: models and plans of architecture in classical antiquity," *JRA* 10: 77–94.

Heather, P. (1991). *Goths and Romans 332–489*, Oxford.

Heers, J. (ed.) (1985). *Fortifications, portes des villes et places publiques dans le monde méditerranéen*, Paris.

Heijmans, M. (1999). "La topographie de la ville d'Arles durant l'antiquité tardive," *JRA* 12: 142–67.

(2004). *Arles durant l'antiquité tardive. De la duplex arelas à l'urbs genesii*, Collection de l'EFR 324, Rome.

(2006). "La mise en defense de la Gaule méridionale aux IVe–VIe s.," *Gallia* 63: 59–74.

Heinen, H. (1985). *Trier und das Treverland in römischer Zeit*, Trier.

Heitz, C. (1979). "Retentissement de l'Apocalypse dans l'art de l'époque carolingienne," in Christe (ed.), *L'apocalypse de Jean. Traditions exégétiques et iconographiques*, Geneva, pp. 217–43.

Helen, T. (1975). *Organization of Roman brick production in the first and second Centuries AD*, Acta Instituti Romani Finlandiae IX, 1, Helsinki.

Hellemo, G. (1989). *Adventus Domini. Eschatological thought in 4th-century apses and catacheses*, Leiden.

Henning, J. (ed.) (2007). *Post-Roman towns, trade and settlement in Europe and Byzantium*, 2 vols., Berlin and New York.

Heres, T. L. (1982). *Paries. A proposal for a dating system of late-antique masonry structures in Rome and Ostia*, Amsterdam.

Herklotz, I. (1985). "Der Campus Lateranensis im Mittelalter," *Römisches Jahrbuch für Kunstgeschichte* 22: 1–43.

Hertz, L. E. (1991). "Roma. Aspetti della fortificazione fluviale," *Acta Hyperborea* 3: 297–310.

Hobley, B. and Maloney, J. (eds.) (1983). *Roman urban defences in the West*, London.

and Hodges, R. (eds.) (1988). *The rebirth of towns in the West AD 700–1050*, London.

Homo, L. (1899). "Le domaine imperial à Rome. Ses origines et son développement du Ier au IVe siècle." *MEFR* 19: 101–29.

(1904). *Essai sur le règne de l'empereur Aurélien (270–275)*, Paris.

Howe, N. (2004). "Rome: capital of Anglo-Saxon England," *Journal of Medieval and Early Modern Studies* 34: 1, 47–172.

(2005). "Anglo-Saxon England and the postcolonial void," in A. J. Kabir and D. Williams (eds.), *Postcolonial approaches to the European Middle Ages*, Cambridge, pp. 25–47.

Hubert, É. (1990). *Espace urbain et habitat à Rome du X siècle à la fin du XIII siècle*, Collection de l'EFR 135, Rome.

(2001). "L'organizzazione territoriale e l'urbanizzazione," in Vauchez (ed.), pp. 159–86.

Hubert, J. (1959). "Evolution de la topographie et de l'aspect des villes de la Gaule du IVe au Xe siècle," *Settimane del CISAM* 6: 529–58.

Hughes, Q. (1974). *Military architecture*, London.

Hülson, C. (1894). "La porta Ardeatina," *Röm Mitth.* 9: 320–33.

(1895). "Il tempio del sole nella regione VII di Roma," *BullCom* 23: 39–59.

(1897). "Der Umfang der Stadt Rom," *Röm. Mitth.* 12: 148–60.

Humphries, M. (2000). "Italy 425–605," in *CAH* 14: 525–51.

(2003). "Roman senators and absent emperors in late antiquity," *Acta IRN* 17: 27–46.

(2007). "From emperor to pope? Ceremonial, space and authority at Rome from Constantine to Gregory the Great," in Cooper and Hillner (eds.), pp. 21–58.

Hunt, D. (1998). "The successors of Constantine," in *CAH* 13: 1–43.

Iglesias Gil, J. M. and Ruiz Gutiérrez, A. (2007). "La muralla tardoantiqua de Monte Cildá (Aguilar de Campoo, Palencia)," in Rodríguez Colmenero and Rodá de Llanza (eds.), pp. 451–65.

Jackson, M. and Marra, F. (2006). "Roman stone masonry: volcanic foundations of the ancient city," *AJA* 110: 403–36.

James, S. (2004). *The excavations at Dura-Europos conducted by Yale University and the French Academy of Inscriptions and Letters 1928 to 1937. Final report VII: the arms and armour and other military equipment*, London.

(2005). "The deposition of military equipment during the final siege at Dura-Europos, with particular regard to the Tower 19 countermine," *Carnuntum Jahrbuch* 2005, pp. 189–206.

Janvier, Y. (1969). *La legislation du Bas-Empire romain sur les édifices publics*, Aix-en-Provence.

Johnson, F. (1948). "Who built the walls of Rome?" *Classical Philology* 43: 261–5.

Johnson, S. (1976). *The Roman forts of the Saxon shore*, London.

(1983a). *Late Roman fortifications*, Totowa, NJ.

(1983b). "Late Roman urban defences in Europe," in Hobley and Maloney (eds.), pp. 69–76.

Jones, A. H. M. (1964). *The later Roman empire 284–602. A social, economic and administrative survey*, 3 vols., Oxford.

Martindale, J. R. and Morris, J. (1971). *The prosopography of the later Roman empire*, 2 vols., Cambridge.

Jordan, H. (1878–1907). *Topografie der Stadt Rom in Altherthum*, 3 vols., Berlin.

Karnapp, W. and Schneider, A. M. (1938). *Die stadtmauer von Iznik (Nicaea)*, Berlin.

Keay, S. (1984). *Late Roman amphorae in the Western Mediterranean. A typology and economic study: the Catalan evidence*, BAR International Series 196, Oxford.

Keegan, J. (1993). *A history of warfare*, London.

Kennedy, H. (1985). "From Polis to Madina: urban change in late antique and early Islamic Syria," *Past and Present* 106: 3–27.

Kopytoff, I. (1986). "The cultural biography of things: commoditization as process," in Appadurai (ed.), pp. 64–91.

Kotula, T. (1997). *Aurélien et Zénobie. L'unité ou la division de l'Empire?*, Acta Universitatis Wratislaviensis 1966, Wroklaw.

Kraeling, C. H. (1979). *The synagogue. Dura Reports 8, part 1*, New Haven, CT.

Krause, J.-U. and Witschel, C. (eds.) (2006). *Die Stadt in der Spätantike – Niedergang oder Wandel? Akten des internationalen Kolloquiums in München am 30 und 31 mai 2003*, Stuttgart.

Krautheimer, R. (1980). *Rome, profile of a city, 312–1308*, Princeton.

  (1983). *Three Christian capitals: topography and politics*, Berkeley.

Krautheimer, R., Corbett, S. and Frankl, W. (1937–77). *Corpus Basilicarum Christianarum Romae*, 5 vols., Rome.

Kuhnel, B. (1987). *From the earthly to the heavenly Jerusalem: Representations of the holy city in Christian art of the first millennium*, Rome.

Kulikowski, M. (2004). *Late Roman Spain and its cities*, Baltimore and London.

  (2006). "The late Roman city in Spain," in Krause and Witschel (eds.), pp. 129–49.

Labrousse, M. (1937). "Le 'pomerium' de la Rome impériale," *MEFR* 54: 165–99.

Lambert, C. (1997). "Le sepolture *in urbe* nella norma e nella prassi (tarda antichità – alto medioevo)," in Paroli (ed.), pp. 285–93.

Lamboglia, N. (1957). *Albenga romana e medievale*, Albenga.

  (1970). "La topografia e stratigrafia di *Albingaunum* dopo gli scavi 1955–56," *Rivista di Studi Liguri* 36: 23–62.

Lanciani, R. (1883/1891). "L'itinerario di Einsiedeln e l'ordine de Benedetto Canonico," *Monumenti antichi* 1, 3 (Accademia dei Lincei, Rome, 1891), cols. 5–120 (reprint of *ibid.* 1883, cols. 437–552).

  (1890). "Ricerche sulle XIV Regioni Urbane," *BullCom* 18: 115–37.

  (1892). "Le mura di Aureliano e Probo," *BullCom* 20: 87–111.

  (1897a). *The ruins and excavations of ancient Rome*, Boston and New York.

  (1897b). *Ancient Rome in the light of recent discoveries*, London.

  (1918). "Delle scoperte di antichità avvenute nelle fondazioni degli edificii per le Ferrovie di Stato nella già Villa Patrizi in Via Nomentana," *Rivista tecnica delle Ferrovie Italiane* 14: 3–36.

  (1988). *Forma Urbis Romae*, Rome [1893–1901].

  (1989–2002). *Storia degli scavi di Roma*, 7 vols., Rome.

  (1997). *Appunti di topografia romana nei codici Lanciani della Biblioteca Apostolica Vaticana*, 5 vols., Rome.

Landels, J. G. (2000). *Engineering in the ancient world*, rev. edn., London [1978].

Landers, J. (2003). *The field and the forge. Population, production and power in the pre-industrial West*, Oxford.

La Rocca, C. (1986). "'Dark Ages' a Verona. Edilizia privata, aree aperte e strutture pubbliche in una città dell'Italia settentrionale," *Archeologia Medievale* 13: 31–78.

(1992). "Public buildings and urban change in northern Italy in the early medieval period," in Rich (ed.), pp. 161–80.

(1993). "Una prudente maschera 'antiqua.' La politica edilizia di Teoderico," in *Teoderico il Grande e i Goti d'Italia. Atti del 13 Congresso internazionale di studi sull'Alto Medioevo, Spoleto*, pp. 451–515.

(ed.) (2002). *Italy in the early Middle Ages: 476–1000*, Oxford.

(2003). "Lo spazio urbano tra VI e VIII secolo," *Settimane del CISAM* 50: 397–436.

La Rocca, E. (1984). *La riva a mezzaluna: culti, agoni, monumenti funerari presso il Tevere nel Campo Marzio occidentale*, Rome.

(2000). "L'affresco con veduto di città dal colle Oppio," in Fentress (ed.) pp. 57–71.

Laurence, R. (1999). *The roads of Roman Italy*, London and New York.

(1994). *Roman Pompeii. Space and society*, London and New York.

Lavan, L. (ed.) (2001). *Recent research in late-antique urbanism*, *JRA* Supplement 42, Portsmouth, RI.

(ed.) (2003). *Theory and practice in late antique archaeology*, Leiden and Boston.

Zanini, E. and Sarantis, A. (eds.) (2007). *Technology in transition AD 300–650*, Leiden and Boston.

Lawrence, A. (1964). "Early medieval fortifications near Rome," *PBSR* 32: 89–122.

(1983). "A skeletal history of Byzantine fortification," *Annual of the British School at Athens* 78: 171–227.

Lawrence, M. (1927). "City-Gate Sarcophagi," *Art Bulletin* 10: 1–45.

Lebek, W. D. (1995). "Die Landmauer von Konstantinopel und ein neues Bauepigramm," *EpigAnat* 25: 107–54.

Lefebvre, H. (1968–72). *Le Droit à la ville*, 2 vols., Paris.

(1991). *The production of space*, Oxford.

Le Gall, J. (1953). *Le Tibre, fleuve de Rome, dans l'antiquité*, Paris.

Lenski, N. (2008). "Evoking the pagan past: *Instinctu divinitatis* and Constantine's Capture of Rome," *Journal of Late Antiquity* 1.2: 204–57.

Léon-Dufour, X. (1987). "La presenza nel mondo della città ideale secondo la Bibbia," in Uglione (ed.), pp. 157–72.

Lepelley, C. (ed.) (1996). *La fin de la cité antique et le début de la cité médiévale. De la fin du IIIe siècle à l'avènement de Charlemagne. Actes du colloque tenu à Paris X-Nanterre les 1, 2, et 3 avril 1993*, Bari.

Levison, W. (1946). *England and the Continent in the eighth century*, Oxford.

Liebeschuetz, J. H. W. G. (1992). "The end of the ancient city," in Rich (ed.), pp. 1–49.

(2001). *The decline and fall of the Roman city*, Oxford.

(2006). "Transformation and decline: are the two really incompatible?," in Krause and Witschel (eds.), pp. 463–83.

Limor, O. (2004). "Pilgrims and authors: Adomnán's De locis sanctis and Hugeburc's Hodoeporicon sancti Willibaldi," *Revue Bénédictine* 114: 253–75.

Liverani, P. (1998). "Introduzione topografica," in P. Liverani (ed.), *Laterano 1. Scavi sotto la Basilica di S. Giovanni – I materiali*, Vatican City, pp. 6–16.

(1999a). *La topografia antica del Vaticano*, Vatican City.

(1999b). "Dalle *aedes laterani* al patriarchio lateranense," *RAC* 75: 521–49.

(2003). "L'agro vaticano," in Pergola *et al.* (eds.), pp. 399–413.

(2004). "Arco di Onorio. Arco di Portogallo," *BullCom* 105: 351–70.

Llewellyn, P. (1986). "The popes and the constitution in the eighth century," *The English Historical Review* 101: 42–67.

(1993). *Rome in the Dark Ages*, 2nd edn., New York [1971].

Lloyd, R. B. (1979). "The *Aqua Virgo, Euripus* and *Pons Agrippae*," *AJA* 83: 193–204.

Lo Cascio, E. (1993). "Dinamiche economiche e politiche fiscali fra i Severi e Aureliano," in *Storia di Roma III*, 1: 247–82.

(1997). "Le procedure di *recensus* dalla tarda reppublica al tardo antico e il calcolo della popolazione di Roma," in *La Rome impérial. Démographie et logistique. Actes de la table ronde (Rome, 25 mars 1994)*. Collection de l'EFR 230, Rome, pp. 3–76.

(1999). "*Canon frumentarius, suarius, vinarius*: stato e privati nell'approvvigionamento dell'*Urbs*," in Harris (ed.), pp. 163–82.

Loseby, S. T. (ed.) (1996). *Towns in transition: urban evolution in late antiquity and the early Middle Ages*, Brookfield, VT.

(1998). "Gregory's cities: urban functions in sixth-century Gaul," in I. Wood (ed.), *Franks and Alamanni in the Merovingian Period. An Ethnographic perspective*, Woodbridge, pp. 239–70.

(2006). "Decline and change in the cities of late antique Gaul," in Krause and Witschel (eds.), pp. 67–104.

Lugli, G. (1930–8). *I monumenti antichi di Roma e Suburbio, I – III*, Rome.

(1957). *La tecnica edilizia romana*, Rome.

(1970). *Itinerario di Roma antica*, Milan.

Lynn, J. (ed.) (1993). *Feeding Mars: logistics in western warfare from the Middle Ages to the present*, Boulder.

MacCormack, S. (1981). *Art and ceremony in late antiquity*, Berkeley and Los Angeles.

MacGeorge, P. (2002). *Late Roman warlords*, Oxford.

MacMullen, R. (1988). *Corruption and the decline of Rome*, New Haven.

(1997). *Christianity and paganism in the fourth to eighth centuries*, New Haven.

Manacorda, D. (1990). *Archeologia urbana a Roma: il progetto della Crypta Balbi*, Florence.

(2001). *Crypta Balbi: archeologia e storia di un paesaggio urbano*, Milan.

(2006). "*Castra* e *burgi* a Roma nell'alto medioevo," in Carocci (ed.), pp. 97–135.

Marazzi, F. and Zanini, E. (1994). "Sul Paesaggio urbano di Roma nell'Alto Medioevo," in Francovich and Noyé (eds.), pp. 635–57.

and L. Saguì (1995). "L'esedra della Crypta Balbi e il monastero di S. Lorenzo in
Pallacinis," *Archeologia Laziale* 12: 1, 121–34.

Mancini, R. (2001). *Le mura aureliane di Roma. Atalante di un palinsesto murario*, Rome.

Mango, C. (1985). *Le développement urbain de Constantinople (IVe – VIIe siècles)*, Paris.

(2000). "The Triumphal Way of Constantinople and the Golden Gate,"
Dumbarton Oaks Papers 54: 173–88.

Marazzi, F. (1988). "L'insediamento nel suburbio di Roma fra IV e VIII secolo,"
Bollettino dell'Istituto Storico Italiano per il Medioevo 93: 251–313.

(1991). "Il conflitto fra Leone III Isaurico e il papato fra il 725 e il 733, e il
'definitivo' inizio del medioevo a Roma: un'ipotesi in discussione," *PBSR*
59: 231–57.

(1993). "Roma, il Lazio, il Mediterraneo: relazioni fra economia e politica dal
VII al IX secolo," in Delogu and Paroli (eds.), pp. 267–85.

(1998). *I "Patrimonia Sanctae Romanae Ecclesiae" nel Lazio (secoli IV–X).
Struttura amministrativa e prassi gestionale*, Rome.

(2000). "Rome in transition: economic and political change in the fourth and
fifth centuries," in Smith (ed.), pp. 21–41.

(2001a). "Da suburbium a territorium: il rapporto tra Roma e il suo
hinterland nel passaggio dall'antichità al medioevo," *Settimane del CISAM* 48:
713–52.

(2001b). "Aristocrazia e società (secoli VI–XI)," in Vauchez (ed.), pp. 41–69.

(2006). "Cadavera urbium, nuove capitali e Roma aeterna: l'identità urbana in
Italia fra crisi, rinascita e propaganda (secoli III–V)," in Krause and Witschel
(eds.), pp. 33–65.

and Barnish, S. B. J. (eds.) (2007). *The Ostrogoths from the migration period to
the sixth century: an ethnographic perspective*, Woodbridge.

Markus, R. A. (1997). *Gregory the Great and his world*, Cambridge.

Marrou, H.-I. (1940). "L'origine orientale des diaconies romaines," *MEFR*
57: 95–142.

Marsden, E. W. (1969). *Greek and Roman artillery. Historical development*, Oxford.

(1971). *Greek and Roman artillery. Technical treatises*, Oxford.

Mattern, S. (1999). *Rome and the enemy. Imperial strategy in the principate*,
Berkeley and Los Angeles.

Matthews, J. F. (1975). *Western aristocracies and imperial court AD 364–425*,
Oxford.

Matthiae, G. (1947). "Le porte di Roma in un codice di Carlo Rainaldi,"
Capitolium 22: 68–72.

Mattingly, D. (1988). "Oil for export? A comparison of Libyan, Spanish and
Tunisian olive oil production in the Roman empire," *JRA* 1: 33–56.

Mauck, M. (1987). "The mosaic of the Triumphal Arch of S. Prassede: a liturgical
interpretation," *Speculum* 62: 813–28.

Maurin, L. (1992). "Remparts et cités dans les trois provinces du Sud-Ouest de la Gaule au Bas-Empire (dernier quart du IIIe siècle–début du Ve siècle)," in *Villes et agglomérations urbaines antiques du Sud-Ouest de la Gaule: histoire et archéologie*, Bordeaux, pp. 365–89.

Mazzuco, C. (1983). "La Gerusalemme celeste dell''Apocalisse' nei Padri," in Gatti Perer (ed.), pp. 45–75.

McClendon, C. B. (2005). *The origins of medieval architecture: building in Europe, AD 600–900*, New Haven.

McCormick, M. (1986). *Eternal victory. Triumphal rulership in late antiquity, Byzantium, and the early medieval West*, Cambridge.

(2001). *Origins of the European economy: communications and commerce AD 300–900*, Cambridge.

McLynn, N. (1994). *Ambrose of Milan*, Berkeley and Los Angeles.

Meneghini, R. (1985). "Siti archeologici 1–2," *Bollettino di Numismatica* 5: 15–46.

(1995). "Sepolture intramuranee a Roma tra V e VII secolo d.C. – aggiornamenti e considerazioni," *Archeologia Medievale* 22: 283–90.

(1996). "Episodi di trasformazione del paesaggio urbano nella Roma altomedievale attraverso l'analisi di due contesti; un isolato in Piazza dei cinquecento e l'area dei Fori Imperiali," *Archeologia Medievale* 23: 53–100.

(1999). "Edilizia pubblica e privata nella Roma altomedievale. Due episodi di riuso," *MEFRM* 111, 1: 171–82.

(2000a). "Roma – Strutture altomedievali e assetto urbano tra le regioni VII e VIII," *Archeologia Medievale* 27: 303–10.

(2000b). "L'origine di un quartiere altomedievale romano attraverso i recenti scavi del foro di Traiano," in Brogiolo (ed.), pp. 55–9.

(2001). "La trasformazione del tessuto urbano tra V e IX secolo," in Arena *et al.* (eds.), pp. 20–33.

and Santangeli Valenzani, R. (1993). "Sepolture intramuranee e paesaggio urbano a Roma tra V e VII secolo," in Delogu and Paroli (eds.), pp. 89–111.

(2004). *Roma nell'altomedioevo. Topografia e urbanistica della città dal V al X secolo*, Rome.

(2007). *I Fori Imperiali. Gli scavi del Comune di Roma (1991–2007)*, Rome.

Messineo, G. (2003). "Via Flaminia tra V e VI miglio," in Pergola *et al.* (eds.), pp. 25–46.

Millar, F. (1977). *The emperor in the Roman world*, London.

Miquel, A. (1975). "Rome chez les géographes arabes," *Académie des Inscriptions et Belles-Lettres, Comptes rendus des séances de l'année 1975*, pp. 281–91.

Moccheggiani Carpano, C. (1975–6). "Rapporto preliminare sulle indagini nel tratto urbano del Tevere," *RendPontAc* 48: 239–62.

(1985). "Siti Archeologici 3–7," *Bollettino di Numismatica* 5: 47–64.

Momigliano, A. (ed.) (1963). *The conflict between paganism and Christianity in the fourth century*, Oxford.

Moneti, A. (1990). "Posizione e aspetti del 'tempio' del sole di Aureliano a Roma." *Palladio* 6: 9–24.

Moorehead, J. (1983). "Italian loyalties during Justinian's Gothic war," *Byzantion* 53: 575–96.

Morrison, C. and Barrandon, J.-N. (1988). "La trouvaille de monnaies d'argent byzantines de Rome (VIIe–VIIIe siècles): analyses et chronologie," *Revue Numismatique*, 6th Series, vol. 30: 149–65.

Müller, W. (1961). *Die heilige Stadt. Roma quadrata, himmlisches Jerusalem und die Mythe vom Weltnabel*, Stuttgart.

Müller-Wiener, W. (1977). *Bildlexikon zur Topographie Istanbuls*, Tübingen.

Müntz, E. (1886). *Antiquités de la ville de Rome aux XIVe, XVe, et XVIe siècles*, Paris.

Nallino, M. (1966). "'Mirabilia' di Roma negli antichi geografi arabi," in *Studi in onore di Italo Siciliano*, Florence, pp. 875–93.

Napoli, J. (1997). *Recherches sur les fortifications linéaires romaines*, Rome.

Napoli, M. (1969). "La cinta urbana," in *Storia di Napoli* vol. 2, 2, Naples, pp. 740–52.

Nash, E. (1961). *Pictorial dictionary of ancient Rome*, 2 vols., New York.

Nibby, A. (1820). *Le mura di Roma*, Rome.

(1848–9). *Analisi storico-topografico-antiquaria della carta de' dintorni di Roma*, 3 vols., Rome.

Nichols, F. M. (1889). *The marvels of Rome or a picture of the golden city*, London.

Nieddu, A. M. (2003). "L'utilizzazione funeraria del suburbio nei secoli V e VI," in Pergola *et al.* (eds.), pp. 545–606.

Nixon, C. and Rodgers, B. (1994). *In praise of later Roman emperors. The Panegyrici Latini*, Berkeley and Los Angeles.

Noble, T. F. X. (1984). *The Republic of St. Peter: the birth of the papal state, 680–825*, Philadelphia.

(2000a). "The papacy in the eighth and ninth centuries," in *The New Cambridge Medieval History*, vol. 2, Cambridge, pp. 563–86.

(2000b). "The early medieval papacy," *Catholic Historical Review* 81: 505–40.

(2000c). "Paradoxes and possibilities in the sources for Roman society in the early Middle Ages," in Smith (ed.), pp. 55–83.

Ortisi, S. (2001). *Die Stadtmauer der raetischen Provinzhauptstadt Aelia Augusta-Augsburg*, Augsburg.

Ortolani, G. (1988). "Osservazioni sulle mura di Terracina," *Palladio* 2: 69–84.

(1990). "Le torri pentagonali del Castro Pretorio," *AnalRom* 19: 239–53.

Osborne, J. (1985). "The Roman catacombs in the Middle Ages," *PBSR* 53: 278–328.

Ousterhout, R. (1999). *Master builders of Byzantium*, Princeton.

Palmer, R. E. A. (1980). "Customs on market goods imported into the city of Rome," *MAAR* 36: 217–33.

(1981). "The topography and social history of Rome's Trastevere (southern sector)," *Proceedings of the American Philosophical Society* 125.5: 368–97.

(1990). "Studies in the Northern Campus Martius in Ancient Rome," *Transactions of the American Philosophical Society* 80.2: 1–64.

Panciera, S. (1999). "Dove finisce la città," in *La forma della città e del territorio. Esperienze metodologiche e risultati a confronto. Atti dell'Incontro di studio – S. Maria Capua Vetere 27–28 novembre 1998*, Rome, pp. 9–15.

Panella, C. (1993). "Merci e scambi nel Mediterraneo tardoantico," in *Storia di Roma* III/2: 613–97.

(1999). "Rifornimenti urbani e cultura materiale tra Aureliano e Alarico," in Harris (ed.), pp. 183–215.

and Saguì, L. (2001). "Consumo e produzione a Roma tra tardoantico e altomedioevo: le merci, i contesti," *Settimane del CISAM* 48: 757–818.

Pani Ermini, L. (1989). "Santuario e città fra tarda antichità e altomedioevo," *Settimane del CISAM* 36: 837–77.

(1992). "*Renovatio murorum*: tra programma urbanistico e restauro conservativo: Roma e il ducato romano," *Settimane del CISAM* 39: 485–530.

(1993–4). "Città fortificate e fortificazione delle città fra V e VI secolo," *Rivista di Studi Liguri* 59–60: 193–206.

(1995). "*Forma urbis* e *renovatio murorum* in età teodoriciana," in A. Carile (ed.), *Teoderico e i Goti tra Oriente e Occidente*, Ravenna, pp. 171–225.

(1999). "Roma da Alarico a Teodorico," in Harris (ed.), pp. 35–52.

(ed.) (2000). *Christiana loca. Lo spazio cristiano a Roma del primo millennio*, 2 vols., Rome.

(2000). "Lo 'spazio cristiano' nella Roma del primo millennio," in Pani Ermini (ed.), pp. 15–37.

(2001). "*Forma Urbis*: Lo spazio urbano tra VI e IX secolo," *Settimane del CISAM* 48: 255–323.

and Siniscalco, P. (eds.) (2000). *La comunità cristiana di Roma*, Vatican City.

Parenti, R. (1994). "Le techniche costruttive fra VI e X secolo: le evidenze materiali," in Francovich and Noyé (eds.), pp. 479–96.

Parker, J. (1874). *The archaeology of Rome*, Oxford.

(1879). *Historical photographs. A catalogue of three thousand three hundred photographs of antiquities in Rome and Italy*, London.

Paroli, L. (ed.) (1997). *L'Italia centro-settentrionale in età longobarda. Atti del Convegno Ascoli Piceno, 6–7 ottobre 1995*, Florence.

(2004). "Roma dal V al IX secolo: uno sguardo attraverso le stratigrafie archeologiche," in Paroli and Vendittelli (eds.), pp. 11–40.

and Vendittelli, L. (eds.) (2004). *Roma dall'antichità al medioevo II. Contesti tardoantichi e altomedievali*, Rome.

Paschoud, F. (1967). *Roma Aeterna. Études sur le patriotisme romain dans l'occident latin a l'époque des grandes invasions*, Neuchâtel.

   (1979). "La doctrine chrétienne e l'ideologie imperiale romaine," in Christe (ed.), *L'apocalypse de Jean. Traditions exégétiques et iconographiques*, Geneva, pp. 31–72.

Patlagean, E. (2002). "Variations imperiales sur le theme romain," *Settimane del CISAM* 49: 1–47.

Patterson, J. R. (2000). "On the margins of the city of Rome," in V. M. Hope and E. Marshall (eds.), *Death and disease in the ancient city*, London, pp. 85–103.

Pavan, M. (1987). "Aquileia città di frontiera," in *Atti della XVI Settimana di Studi Aquileisi*, Antichità Altoadriatiche 29, Udine, pp. 17–55.

Pavis d'Escurac, H. (1976). *La Préfecture de l'annone service administratif impérial d'Auguste à Constantin*, BEFAR 226, Rome.

Pavolini, C. (1993). "L'area del Celio fra l'antichità e il medioevo alla luce delle recenti indagini archeologiche," in Delogu and Paroli (eds.), pp. 53–70.

   (ed.) (1993). *Caput africae I. Indagini archeologiche a Piazza Caelimontana (1984–1988). La storia, lo scavo, l'ambiente*, Rome.

   (2004). "Aspetti del Celio fra il V e l'VIII–IX secolo," in Paroli and Vendittelli (eds.), pp. 418–34.

   Dinuzzi, S., Cupitò, C., Fosco, U. (2003). "L'area compresa fra il Tevere, l'Aniene e la Via Nomentana," in Pergola *et al.* (eds.), pp. 47–95.

Pearson, A. (2003). *The construction of the Saxon shore forts*, BAR British Series 349, Oxford.

Pelican, J. (1987). *The excellent empire: the fall of Rome and the triumph of the Church*, New York.

Pergola, P. (1993–94). "Albenga à la fin de l'antiquité: le réveil d'une *civitas*," *Rivista di Studi Liguri* 59–60: 297–319.

   Santangeli Valenzani, R. and Volpe, R. (eds.) (2003). Suburbium: *il suburbio di Roma dalla crisi del sistema delle ville a Gregorio Magno*, Collection de l'EFR 311, Rome.

Perraymond, M. (1979). "Le *scholae peregrinorum* nel borgo di San Pietro," *Romanobarbarica* 4: 183–200.

Pharr, C. (1952). *The Theodosian Code*, New York.

Picard, J.-Ch. (1969). "Étude sur l'emplacement des tombes des papes du IIIe au Xe siècle," *MEFR* 81: 725–82.

   (1998). *Évêques, saints et cités en Italie et en Gaule. Études d'archéologie et d'histoire*, Collection de l'EFR 242, Rome.

Piccirillo, M. and Alliata, E. (eds.) (1999). *The Madaba Map centenary, 1897–1997*, Jerusalem.

Pietri, C. (1976). *Roma christiana: recherches sur l'Église de Rome, son organisation, sa politique, son idéologie de Miltiade à Sixte III (311–440)*, BEFAR 224, 2 vols., Paris.

   (1997). *Christiana Respublica. Éléments d'une enquête sur le christianisme antique*, Collection de l'EFR 234, 2 vols., Rome.

Piganiol, A. (1947). *L'empire chrétien (325–395)*, Paris.

Pizzi, A. (1998). "L'organizzazione della difesa di Roma tra V e VI secolo," in Delogu (ed.), pp. 51–62.

Platner, S. B. and Ashby, T. (1929). *A topographical dictionary of ancient Rome*, Oxford.

Potter, D. S. (1990). *Prophecy and history in the crisis of the Roman empire. A historical commentary on the thirteenth Sibylline Oracle*, Oxford.

(1999). *Literary texts and the Roman historian*, London and New York.

(2004). *The Roman empire at bay AD 180–395*, London and New York.

Potter, T. W. (1995). *Towns in late antiquity*, Oxford.

Price, M. J. and Trell, B. (1977). *Coins and their cities*, London.

Pullan, W. (1999). "The representation of the late antique city in the Madaba Map. The meaning of the Cardo in the Jerusalem Vignette," in Piccirillo and Alliata (eds.), pp. 165–71.

Purcell, N. (1999). "The populace of Rome in late antiquity: problems of description and historical classification," in Harris (ed.), pp. 135–61.

Quacquarelli, A. (1987). "La Chiesa come città celeste nell'iconografia del IV secolo," in Uglione (ed.), pp. 185–202.

Quarenghi, C. (1880). *Le Mura di Roma*, Rome.

Quercioli, M. (1993). *Le mura e le porte di Roma*, 2nd edn., Rome.

Quilici, L. (1974). "La campagna romana come suburbio di Roma antica," *La Parola del Passato* 29: 410–38.

(1983). "Il Campo Marzio occidentale," *AnalRom* Supplement 10: 59–85.

(1987). "La posterula di vigna casali nella pianificazione urbanistica dell'Aventino e sul possibile prospetto del tempio di Diana," in *L'urbs. Espace urbain et histoire (Ier siècle av. J.-C.–IIIe siècle ap. J.-C.)*. Collection de l'EFR 98, Rome, pp. 713–45.

Quilici Gigli, S. (1983). "Estremo Campo Marzio. Alcune osservazioni sulla topografia," *AnalRom* Supplement 10: 47–57.

Rance, P. (2005). "Narses and the battle of Taginae (Busta Gallorum) 552: Procopius and sixth-century warfare," *Historia* 54: 424–72.

Rebuffat, R. (1986). "Les fortifications urbaines du monde romain," in P. Leriche and H. Tréziny (eds.), *La fortification dans l'histoire du monde grec*, Paris, pp. 345–61.

Reekmans, L. (1968). "L'implantation monumentale chrétienne dans la zone suburbaine de Rome du IVe au IXe siècle," *RAC* 44: 173–207.

(1989). "L'implantation monumentale chrétienne dans le paysage urbain de Rome de 300 à 850," in *Actes du XIe Congrès international d'Archéologie Chrétienne, Lyon, Vienne, Grenoble, Genève et Aoste (21–28 septembre 1986)*. Collection de l'EFR 123, Rome, pp. 861–915.

Ricci, M. (1997). "Relazioni culturali e scambi commerciali nell'Italia centrale romano-longobarda alla luce della Crypta Balbi in Roma," in Paroli (ed.), pp. 239–73.

Rich. J. W. (ed.) (1992). *The city in late antiquity*, London.

Richardson, L. (1992). *A new topographical dictionary of ancient Rome*, Baltimore.

Richmond, I. A. (1927a). "Il tipo architettonico delle mura e delle porte di Roma costruite dall'Imperatore Aureliano," *BullCom* 55: 41–67.

(1927b). "The relation of the Praetorian Camp to Aurelian's Wall of Rome," *PBSR* 10: 12–22.

(1930). *The city wall of imperial Rome. An account of its architectural development from Aurelian to Narses*, Oxford.

(1931). "Five town-walls in Hispania Citerior," *JRS* 21: 86–100.

and Holford, W. G. (1935). "Roman Verona: the archaeology of its town-plan," *PBSR* 13: 69–76.

Rickman, G. (1980). *The corn supply of ancient Rome*, Oxford.

Righini, V. (2005). "Opus listatum," in *Ravenna da capitale imperiale a capitale esarcale. Atti del XVII Congresso internazionale di studio sull'alto medioevo, Ravenna, 6–12 giugno 2004*, Spoleto, pp. 841–85.

Rizzo, S. (1993). "Le Mura Aureliane da Porta Pinciana a Porta Salaria," *BullCom* 95: 113–15.

(1993). "Le Mura Aureliane tra via Valenziani e corso d'Italia," *BullCom* 95: 115–16.

Roberts, M. (1993). *Poetry and the cult of the martyrs. The Liber Peristephanon of Prudentius*, Ann Arbor, MI.

(2001). "Rome personified, Rome epitomized: representations of Rome in the poetry of the early fifth century," *American Journal of Philology* 122: 533–65.

Rodriguez-Almeida, E. (1981). *Forma urbis marmorea. Aggiornamento generale 1980*, Rome.

(1984). *Il monte Testaccio: ambiente, storia, materiali*, Rome.

Rodríguez Colmenero, A. and Rodá de Llanza, I. (eds.) (2007). *Murallas de ciudades romanas en el occidente del imperio, Lucus Augusti como paradigma*, Lugo.

Roeck, B. (1989). "Gerusalemme Celeste e spirito geometrico. Sull'iconografia e sulla storia sociale delle mura cittadine: dall'esempio di Augusta," in De Seta and Le Goff (eds.), pp. 291–320.

Romei, D. (2004). "Produzione e circolazione dei manufatti ceramici a Roma nell'alto medioevo," in Paroli and Venditelli (eds.), pp. 278–311.

Romeo, P. (1965–67). "Il restauro delle Mura Aureliane di Roma," *BullCom* 80: 151–81.

Rossi, M. and Rovetta, A. (1983). "Indagini sullo spazio ecclesiale immagine della Gerusalemme celeste," in Gatti Perer (ed.), pp. 77–115.

Rossini, L. (1829). *Le porte antiche e moderne del recinto di Roma*, Rome.

Rostovtzeff, M. I. (1957). *Social and economic history of the Roman empire*, 2nd edn., Oxford.

Rostovtzeff, M. I., Brown, F. E., Welles, C. B. and Bradford, C. (eds.) (1939). *The excavations at Dura-Europos conducted by Yale University and the French Academy of Inscriptions and Letters. Preliminary report of the seventh and eighth seasons of work 1933–1934 and 1934–1935*, New Haven.

Roth, J. P. (1999). *The logistics of the Roman army at war (264 BC – AD 235)*, Leiden, Boston and Cologne.

Rougé, J. (1957). "*Ad ciconias nixas,*" *Revue des Études Anciennes* 59: 320–28.

(1966). *Recherches sur l'organisation du commerce maritime en Méditerranée sous l'empire romain*, Paris.

Rovelli, A. (2000). "Monetary circulation in Byzantine and Carolingian Rome: a reconsideration in the light of recent archaeological data," in Smith (ed.), pp. 85–99.

(2001). "Emissione e uso della moneta: le testimonianze scritte e archeologiche," *Settimane del CISAM* 48: 821–52.

Rykwert, J. (1976). *The idea of a town. The anthropology of urban form in Rome, Italy and the ancient world*, London.

Saghy, M. (2000). "Pope Damasus," *Early Medieval Europe* 9: 273–87.

Saguì, L. (1993). "Crypta Balbi (Roma): conclusione delle indagini archeologiche nell'esedra del monumento romano. Relazione preliminare," *Archeologia Medievale* 20: 409–18.

(ed.) (1998). *Ceramica in Italia: VI-VII secolo. Atti del convegno in onore di John W. Hayes. Roma, 11–13 maggio 1995*, Florence.

(2002). "Roma, i centri privilegiati e la lunga durata della tarda antichità. Dati archeologici dal deposito di VII secolo nell'esedra della Crypta Balbi," *Archeologia Medievale* 29: 7–42.

Salzman, M. R. (1990). *On Roman time: the codex calendar of 354 and the rhythms of urban life in late antiquity*, Berkeley.

Sansoni, A. (1969). *I sarcofagi paleocristiani a porte di città*, Bologna.

Santangeli Valenzani, R. (1996–97). "Pellegrini, senatori e papi. Gli *xenodochia* a Roma tra il V e il IX secolo," *Rivista dell'istituto nazionale d'archeologia e storia dell'arte*, serie III; 19–20: 203–26.

(1997). "Edilizia residenziale e aristocrazia urbana a Roma nell'altomedioevo," in Gelichi (ed.), pp. 64–70.

(1999). "Strade, case e orti nell'alto medioevo del foro di Nerva," *MEFRM* 111, 1: 163–9.

(2000). "Residential building in early medieval Rome," in Smith (ed.), pp. 101–12.

(2001a). "I Fori Imperiali nel Medioevo," *Röm. Mitth.* 108: 269–83.

(2001b). "L'Itinerario di Einsiedeln," in Arena *et al.* (eds.) pp. 154–59.

(2002). "Il cantiere altomedievale. Competenze techniche, organizzazione del lavoro e struttura sociale," *Röm. Mitth.* 109: 419–26.

(2003a). "Vecchie e nuove forme di insediamento nel territorio," in Pergola *et al.* (eds.), pp. 607–18.

(2003b). "Struttura economica e ruoli sociali a Roma nell'altomedioevo: una lettura archeologica," *Acta IRN* 17: 115–26.

(2004). "Abitare a Roma nell'alto medioevo," in Paroli and Vendittelli (eds.), pp. 41–59.

(2007). "Public and private building activity in late antique Rome," in Lavan, Zanini and Sarantis (eds.), pp. 435–49.

Saradi, H. (1995). "The Kallos of the Byzantine City: the development of a rhetorical topos and historical reality," *Gesta* 34: 37–56.

(2006). *The Byzantine city in the sixth century: literary images and historical reality*, Athens.

Savage, S. (1940). "The cults of ancient Trastevere," *MAAR* 17: 26–56.

Saxer, V. (1989). "L'utilisation par la liturgie de l'espace urbain et suburbain: l'exemple de Rome dans l'antiquité et le haut moyen âge," in *Actes du XIe Congrès international d'Archéologie Chrétienne, Lyon, Vienne, Grenoble, Genève et Aoste (21–28 septembre 1986)*. Collection de l'EFR 123, Rome, pp. 917–1033.

(2001). "La chiesa di Roma dal V al X secolo: amministrazione centrale e organizzazione territoriale," *Settimane del CISAM* 48: 493–632.

Scarcia, G. (2002). "Roma vista dagli arabi: Appunti su Abū 'Ubayd al-Bakrī (sec. XI)," *Settimane del CISAM* 49: 129–71.

Scarpa, P. (1953). "Porta Asinaria," *Capitolium* 28: 87–92.

Schieffer, R. (2000). "Charlemagne and Rome," in Smith (ed.), pp. 279–95.

(2002) "Die Karolinger in Rom," *Settimane del CISAM* 49: 101–27.

Schmiedt, G. (1968). "Le fortificazioni altomedievali in Italia viste dall'aerio," *Settimane del CISAM* 15: 859–927.

(1974). "Città scomparse e città di nuova formazione in Italia in relazione al sistema di comunicazione," *Settimane del CISAM* 21: 503–607.

Schramm, P. (1929). *Kaiser, Rom und Renovatio*, 2 vols., Leipzig.

(1983). *Die deutschen Kaiser und Könige in Bildern ihrer Zeit, 751–1190*, revised edn., Munich [1928].

Schwarz, P. A. (2003). "The walls of Augsburg, provincial capital of Raetia," *JRA* 16: 644–7.

Seeck, O. (1910). *Geschichte des Untergangs der antiken Welt*, vol. 1, Berlin.

Serlorenzi, M. (2004). "Santa Lucia *in Selcis*. Lettura del palinsesto murario di un edificio a continuità di vita," in Paroli and Vendittelli (eds.), pp. 350–79.

Settia, A. (1988). "Lo sviluppo di un modello: origine e funzioni delle torri private urbane nell'Italia centrosettentrionale," in *Paesaggi urbani dell'Italia padana nei secoli VIII–XIV*, Bologna.

Settis, S. (2001). "Roma fuori di Roma: periferie della memoria," *Settimane del CISAM* 48: 991–1,013.

Simonelli, A. (2001). "Considerazioni sull'origine, la natura e l'evoluzione del pomerium," *Aevum* 75: 119–62.

Smith, J. (1998). "The translation of the Blessed Marcellinus and Peter," in P. Dutton (ed.), *Charlemagne's courtier: the complete Einhard*, Peterborough, pp. 69–130.

  (2000). "Old saints, new cults: Roman relics in Carolingian Francia," in Smith (ed.), pp. 317–34.

  (ed.) (2000). *Early medieval Rome and the Christian West. Essays in honour of Donald A. Bullough*, Leiden and Boston.

  (2005). *Europe after Rome. A new cultural history 500–1000*, Oxford.

Sommella, P. (2007). "Le mura di Aureliano a Roma (osservazioni generali)," in Rodríguez Colmenero and Rodá de Llanza (eds.), pp. 49–57.

Sommella Beda, G. (1972). *Le mura di Aureliano a Roma. Esposizione documentaria organizzata dal Centro internazionale per lo studio delle cerchia urbane (C. I. S. C. U.), a cura di Giuseppina Sommella Beda, Lucca MCMLXXII*, Lucca.

  (1973). *Roma, le fortificazioni del Trastevere*, Lucca.

Sommer, M. (2005). *Roms orientalische Steppengrenze. Palmyra – Edessa – Dura-Europos – Hatra. Eine Kulturgeschichte von Pompeius bis Diocletian*, Stuttgart.

Southern, P. (2006). *The Roman army: a social and institutional history*, Santa Barbara, CA.

Spagnesi, P. (1995). *Castel Sant'Angelo la fortezza di Roma*, Rome.

Speck, P. (1973). "Der Mauerbau in 60 Tagen," in H.-G. Beck (ed.), *Studien zur Frügeschichte Konstantinopels*, Miscellanea Byzantina Monacensia 14, Munich, pp. 135–78.

Speidel, M. P. (1994). *Riding for Caesar. the Roman emperors' horse guards*, London.

Spera, L. (1999). *Il paesaggio suburbano di Roma dall'antichità al medioevo. Il comprensorio tra le vie latina e ardeatina dalle mura aureliane al III miglio*, Rome.

  (2003). "Il territorio della Via Appia. Forme trasformative del paesaggio nei secoli della tarda antichità," in Pergola *et al.* (eds.), pp. 267–330.

Spiegel, E. M. (2006). "Im Schutz der römischen Stadtmauer. Das Gebiet des Clarenklosters in römischer Zeit," in W. Schafke (ed.), *Am Römerturm. Zwei Jahrtausende eines kölner Stadtviertels*, Cologne, pp. 8–22.

Spieser, J.-M. (1984). *Thessalonique et ses monuments du IV au VI siècle. Contribution à l'étude d'une ville paléochrétienne*, BEFAR 254, Paris.

  (2001). *Urban and religious spaces in late antiquity and early Byzantium*, Burlington, VT.

Squatriti, P. (1998). *Water and society in early medieval Italy, AD 400–1000*. Cambridge.

(2002). "Digging ditches in early medieval Europe," *Past and Present* 176: 11–65.

Staccioli, A. (1969). "L'arco di Druso e la Porta S. Sebastiano," *Capitolium* 44: 143–8.

Stasolla, F. R. (1998). "A proposito delle strutture assistenziali ecclesiastiche: gli xenodochi," *ASRSP* 121: 5–45.

Steinby, E. M. (1974–5). "La cronologia delle figlinae doliari urbane dalla fine dell'età repubblicana fino all'inizio del III sec," *BullCom* 84: 7–132.

(1978). "Ziegelstempel von Rom und Umbegung," in *RE* suppl. XV, Munich, pp. 1,489–1,531.

(1986). "L'industria laterizia di Roma nel tardo impero," in *SRIT* II: 99–164.

(ed.) (1993–8). *Lexicon topographicum urbis Romae*, 6 vols., Rome.

(2001). "La cronologia delle 'figlinae' tardoantiche," in Cecchelli (ed.), pp. 127–50.

Stenton, F. R. (1971). *Anglo-Saxon England*, reprint 2001, 3rd edn., Oxford.

Story, J., Bunbury, J., Felici, A. C., Fronterotta, G., Piacentini, M., Nicolais, C., Scacciatelli, D., Sciuti, S. and Venditelli, M. (2005). "Charlemagne's black marble: the origin of the epitaph of Pope Hadrian I," *PBSR* 73: 157–90.

Strobel, K. (1993). *Das imperium Romanum im "3 Jahrhundert", Modell einer historischen krise?*, Stuttgart.

Stryzgowski, J. (1893). "Das goldene Thor in Konstantinopel," *Jahrbuch des kaiserlich deutschen archäologischen Instituts* 8: 1–39.

Syme, R. (1968). *Ammianus and the Historia Augusta*, Oxford.

(1972). "The composition of the Historia Augusta: recent theories," *JRS* 62: 123–33 (reprint Syme 1983, pp. 12–29).

(1978). "The pomerium in the *Historia Augusta*," in *Bonner Historia Augusta Colloquium 1975/76*, pp. 217–31 (reprint Syme 1983, pp. 131–45).

(1983). *Historia Augusta Papers*, Oxford.

Taylor, R. (1995). "*A citiore ripa aquae*: aqueduct river crossings in the ancient city of Rome," *PBSR* 63: 75–103.

(2003). *Roman builders. A study in architectural process*, Cambridge.

Tellenbach, G. (1972). "La città di Roma dal IX al XII secolo vista dai contemporanei d'oltre frontiera," in *Studi storici in onore di Ottorino Bertolini*, Pisa, pp. 679–734.

Tengström, E. (1974). *Bread for the people (Acta instituti romani regni sueciae 8°, XII)*, Stockholm.

Thacker, A. (1998). "Memorializing Gregory the Great: the origin and transmission of a papal cult in the seventh and early eighth centuries," *Early Medieval Europe* 7: 59–84.

(2000). "In search of saints: the English church and the cult of Roman apostles and martyrs in the seventh and eighth centuries," in Smith (ed.), pp. 247–77.

Thompson, E. A. (1982). *Romans and barbarians, the decline of the Western Empire,* Madison, WI.

Thompson, H. A. (1959). "Athenian twilight: AD 267–600," *JRS* 49: 61–72.

Thunø, E. (2002). *Image and relic. Mediating the sacred in early medieval Rome,* *AnalRom* Supplement 32, Rome.

Todd, M. (1978). *The walls of Rome,* Totowa, NJ.

(1983). "The Aurelianic wall of Rome and its analogues," in Hobley and Maloney (eds.), pp. 58–67.

Tomassetti, G. (1975–80). *La campagna romana antica, medioevale e moderna,* revised edn. L. Chiumenti and F. Bilancia, 7 vols., Rome [1910–26].

Toubert, P. (1973). *Les structures du Latium médiévale.* 2 vols., Rome.

(2001). "Scrinium et Palatium. La formation de la bureacratie romano-pontificale aux VIIIe–IXe siècles," *Settimane del CISAM* 48: 57–117.

Toynbee, J. M. C. (1944). *Roman medallions,* New York.

(1971). *Death and burial in the Roman world,* London.

Tracy, J. (ed.) (2000). *City walls. The urban enceinte in global perspective,* Cambridge.

(2000). *"To wall or not to wall: evidence from medieval Germany,"* in Tracy (ed.), pp. 71–87.

Trout, D. (2005). "Theodelinda's Rome: *Ampullae, Pittacia,* and the image of the city," *MAAR* 50: 131–50.

Tucci, G. (2004). "Eight fragments of the marble plan of Rome shedding new light on the Transtiberim," *PBSR* 72: 185–202.

Tzafrir, Y. (1999). "The holy city of Jerusalem in the Madaba Map," in Piccirillo and Alliata (eds.), pp. 155–63.

Uglione, R. (ed.) (1987). *La città ideale nella tradizione classica e biblico-cristiana,* Turin.

(1987). "La città ideale nel '*De Civitate Dei*.' Dalla storia alla metastoria," in Uglione (ed.), pp. 203–18.

Ullmann, W. (1960). "Leo I and the theme of papal primacy," *Journal of Theological Studies,* n.s. 11: 25–51.

(1970). *The growth of papal government in the Middle Ages: a study in the ideological relation of clerical to lay power,* 3rd edn., London.

Van der Meer, F. (1938). Maiestas domini. *Théophanies de l'apocalypse dans l'art Chrétien,* Studi di Antichità Christiana 13, Paris and Rome.

Van Emden, W. (2000). "Medieval French representations of city and other walls," in Tracy (ed.), pp. 530–72.

Van Milligen, A. (1899). *Byzantine Constantinople: the walls of the city and adjoining historical sites,* London.

Vauchez, A. (ed.) (2001). *Roma medievale. Storia di Roma dall'antichità a oggi,* vol. 2, Rome and Bari.

Verrando, G. N. (1981). "Note di topografia martiriale della via Aurelia," *RAC* 57: 255–82.

Virgili, P. (1985). "Porta San Sebastiano," *BullCom* 90: 309.

Virlouvet, C. (1995). *Tessera frumentaria. Les procédures de la distribution du blé public à Rome à la fin de la république et au début de l'empire*, BEFAR 286, Rome.

Vismara, G. (1999). "La città dei morti nella tradizione del diritto romano," *Studi Medievali*, 3rd series, 40: 499–514.

Volpe, R. (1993). "Lo scavo di un tratto urbano dell'aqua Marcia," *Archaeologia Laziale* 11: 2, 59–64.

(2000). "Il Suburbio," in A. Giardina (ed.), *Storia di Roma dall'antichità a oggi*, vol. 1: *Roma antica*, Rome, pp. 183–210.

von Petrikovitz, H. (1971). "Fortifications in the North-Western Roman Empire from the third to the fifth centuries AD," *JRS* 61: 178–218.

Wacher, J. (1995). *The towns of Roman Britain*, 2nd edn., London.

(1998). "The dating of town walls in Roman Britain," in J. Bird (ed.), *Form and fabric. Studies in Rome's material past in honour of B. R. Hartley*, Oxbow Monograph 50, Oxford, pp. 41–50.

Waldron, A. (1990). *The Great Wall of China: from history to myth*, Cambridge.

Wallach, L. (1959). *Alcuin and Charlemagne: studies in Carolingian history and literature*, Ithaca, NY.

Waltzing, J. P. (1895–1900). *Étude historique sur les corporations professionnelles chez les Romains depuis les origines jusqu'à la chute de l'Empire de l'Occident*, 4 vols., Louvain.

Ward-Perkins, B. (1984). *From classical antiquity to the Middle Ages: urban public building in northern and central Italy AD 350–800*, Oxford.

(1997). "Continuitists, catastrophists and the towns of post-Roman northern Italy," *PBSR* 65: 157–76.

(1998). "The cities," in *CAH* 13: 371–410.

(2000). "Constantinople, imperial capital of the fifth and sixth centuries," in Gurt and Ripoll (eds.), pp. 63–79.

and S. Gibson (1979). "The surviving remains of the Leonine Wall," *PBSR* 47: 30–57.

and S. Gibson (1983). "The surviving remains of the Leonine Wall. Part II: The Passetto," *PBSR* 51: 222–39.

Warland, R. (2003). "The concept of Rome in late antiquity reflected in the mosaics of the Triumphal Arch of S. Maria Maggiore in Rome," *Acta IRN* 17: 127–41.

Watson, A. (1999). *Aurelian and the third century*, London and New York.

Wells, C. M. (1980). "Carthage: the late Roman defences," *Roman Frontier Studies 1979*, 12: 999–1004.

Whittaker, C. (1994). *Frontiers of the Roman Empire. a social and economic study*, Baltimore.

Wickham, C. (1981). *Early medieval Italy: central power and local society 400–1000*, London.

(1999). "Early medieval archeology in Italy: the last twenty years," *Archeologia Medievale* 24: 7–20.

(2000a). "*The Romans according to their malign custom*: Rome and Italy in the late ninth and tenth centuries," in Smith (ed.), pp. 151–67.

(2000b). "Overview: production, distribution and demand, II," in Hansen and Wickham (eds.), pp. 345–77.

(2005). *Framing the early Middle Ages: Europe and the Mediterranean, 400–800,* Oxford.

Wikander, O. (1979). "Water-mills in ancient Rome," *Opuscula Romana* 12 (Swedish Institute at Rome): 13–36.

Williams, S. (1985). *Diocletian and the Roman recovery,* London.

Wilson, A. (2000). "The Water-mills on the Janiculum," *MAAR* 45: 219–46.

Wilson, P. (ed.) (2003). *The archaeology of Roman towns. Studies in honour of John S. Wacher,* Oxford.

Wiseman, F. (1956). *Roman Spain; an introduction to the Roman antiquities of Spain and Portugal,* London.

Witcher, R. (2005). "The extended metropolis: *Urbs, suburbium* and population," *JRA* 18: 120–38.

Witschel, C. (1999). *Krise, Rezession, Stagnation?: der Westen des römischen Reiches im 3. Jahrhundert n.Chr.,* Frankfurt.

(2001). "Rom und die Städte Italiens in Spätantike und Frümittelalter," *Bonner Jahrbücher* 201: 113–62.

(2004). "Re-evaluating the Roman West in the 3rd c. AD," *JRA* 17: 251–81.

Wood, I. (1994). "The mission of Augustine of Canterbury to the English," *Speculum* 69: 1–17.

Wood, J. (2002). "The wall-top of the late-Roman defences at Saint-Bertrand-de-Comminges," *JRA* 15: 297–309.

Zanini, E. (1998). *Le Italie bizantine,* Bari.

(2007). "Technology and ideas: architects and master-builders in the early Byzantine world," in Lavan, Zanini and Sarantis (eds.), pp. 381–405.

Zwölfer, T. (1929). *Sankt Peter: Apostelfürst und Himmelsförtner. Seine Verehrung bei den Angelsachsen und Franken,* Stuttgart.

Index